HUMAN NATURE
AND PUBLIC POLICY

HUMAN NATURE AND PUBLIC POLICY
Scientific Views of Women, Children, and Families

Edited by
Lynette Friedrich-Cofer

PRAEGER

New York
Westport, Connecticut
London

Library of Congress Cataloging-in-Publication Data

Human nature and public policy.

1. Social policy — Congresses. 2. Family policy —
Congresses. 3. Social values — Congresses.
4. Developmental psychology — Congresses.
I. Friedrich-Cofer, Lynette.
HN18.H782   1986   361.6′1   86-18210
ISBN 0-275-92344-4 (alk. paper)

Library of Congress Catalog Card Number: 86-18210
ISBN: 0-275-92344-4

First published in 1986

Praeger Publishers, 521 Fifth Avenue, New York, NY 10175
A division of Greenwood Press, Inc.

Printed in the United States of America

The paper used in this book complies with the Permanent
Paper Standard issued by the National Information Standards
Organization (Z39.48-1984).

10 9 8 7 6 5 4 3 2 1

Contents

Preface

To paraphrase Kierkegaard, we live our professional lives forwards and understand them backwards. The forward thrust of psychology, particularly developmental psychology, has been animated by recent calls to contribute to the formation of sound and rational public policy. At the same time, however, criticisms of a sanguine positivistic science that promised objective truths to a frail and value-ridden humanity have multiplied. The uncomfortable awareness that our scientific choice of problems, theoretical orientations and empirical methods are embedded in social contexts no less than the selection and interpretation of findings used to influence parents, institutions and social policy has intensified. There has been, however, much less attention given to the history of scientific assumptions about human nature and the individual and collective good than to the "conclusions" of scientific experts who advocate specific policies. Moreover, the reality of the gargantuan leap between conceptual formulation and concrete outcomes in the lives of individuals is often well repressed in scientific and political dialogue.

The chapters in this volume are a result of two conferences, funded by the MacArthur Foundation, in which participants brought diverse views to the examination of the history of investigations of women, children, and families. *Some of the participants focused on history and theory while others were invited to reflect on their own efforts to conduct empirical research of potential relevance to serious social problems. Throughout the chapters the issue of how social values determine the content, methods, and applications of our approaches to developmental problems is evident. Historian John Demos and political

*We are grateful for the financial support provided by the John D. and Catherine T. MacArthur Foundation. We should also like to thank Professor Bibb Latane for supportive services provided by the Institute for Research in Social Science, The University of North Carolina at Chapel Hill, and for his kind invitation for the group to meet at the Nags Head Conference Center. Jon and Helen Mullis helped to make our Nags Head stay especially comfortable. We should also like to acknowledge the many contributions of Pat Eichman who deciphered conference tapes, typed many of the manuscripts, and provided editorial assistance.

theorist Jean Elshtain provided broader perspectives on the discipline of psychology and the political process. The initial papers changed strikingly with the exchange of ideas and rendered the discussion tapes obsolete. The chapter by Sheldon White and the concluding chapter by Jean Elshtain attempt to convey the unifying themes that animated the discussion: the research-policy configuration and our understandings of family and gender differences in cultural contexts.

The reader should be forwarned that the chapters reflect the diversity of the participants, and their assigned tasks. The book is not intended to be systematic nor the chapters to be parallel. Part I: Using Science to Build Human Needs and Values into Social Policies and In-stitutions includes three chapters that deal with the scientific-policy alliances constituted in the past. Part II: Adventures in Contemporary Efforts to Do Relevant Research includes three chapters in which authors reflect on their respective research efforts and the complex-ities of translating findings into policy recommendations. Part III: What Kind of Science Can We Expect to Help Us Manage Complicated, Changing Social Arrangements? includes two chapters that suggest ways in which the research-policy alliance needs to be reconstructed. Those who expect ready recommendations for policy makers will be disappointed. Jean Elshtain describes the dilemma of the authors caught in "quick-sand: methodological, normative, political." What results is a series of cautionary tales — not pessimistic, but full of cau-tion.

INTRODUCTION:
On Reading this Text
Jean Bethke Elshtain

We live in the era of discourse. Much of the currently exciting, if occasionally faddish, work in the human sciences and literature revolves around questions of what we are saying and how. Who is reader? Who is author? The intensity of our focus on discourse is understandable, in part, because we find it so difficult to 'discourse' with one another — to talk around the particular languages of our disciplines and to talk seriously to one another. Yet the times demand such talk. We live in a complex age of social change — some might call it disintegration — where neither the center nor much else seems to hold. We need to create new ways of thinking, to be sure, but we also need to rescue old habits threatened by the relentless pressures we call modernity. And we can do that only through language, through speech and discourse. Despite the many difficulties involved, then, we must make interdisciplinary moves. After all, as difficult as it is to figure out what those who do not share our specialized language might be saying we are not in the position of Wittgenstein's lion who, if he could talk, we could not understand.

Psychology, at its inception, was a moral science: that is part of its grand tradition. Psychology involved ideals of what human beings are, ought to be, or might become. In this way psychological discourse shares a common ground with political theory, my own enterprise. Rousseau once said that he who hopes to separate politics from morals will never understand either. Similarly, he who proposes to separate psychology from morals must fail — this despite concerted attempts to turn psychology into a watery "value-free" discipline. Practitioners of psychology as free from the taint of moral values indulge themselves in a discourse that permits infinite back-pedaling; that proffers a license to evade where questions of morality and the political implications of their own enterprise are concerned. But the contributors to this volume, each in his or her diverse way, rescues psychology as an activity that presumes, in Freud's trenchant phrase, to take the soul as its territory and its concern. That is a great responsibility. Freud's masterful discussion is worth quoting at length:

> For it is not so easy to play upon the instrument of the soul. I am reminded at this point of a world-famed neurotic, although certainly

he was never treated by a physician but existed only in a poet's imagination: I mean Hamlet, Prince of Denmark. The King appointed the two courtiers, Rosenkranz and Guildenstern, to follow him, to question him and drag from him the secret of his depression. He wards them off; then flutes are brought on the stage and Hamlet, taking one of them, begs one of his torturers to play upon it, telling him that it is as easy as lying. The courtier excuses himself for he knows no touch of the instrument, and when he cannot be persuaded to try it, Hamlet finally breaks out with these words: "Why, look you now, how unworthy a thing you make of me, you would play upon me. — You would pluck out the heart of my mystery; you would sound me from my lowest note to the top of my compass; and there is much music, excellent voice, in this little organ; yet you cannot make it speak. *'Sblood, do you think I am easier to be played on than a pipe? Call me what instrument you will, though you can fret me you cannot play upon me"* [act 2, sc. 2] (Freud, 1905/1963, pp. 63-69).

As human scientists we recognize that there are in our ranks those who make 'unworthy things' of their subjects, who objectify human beings and reduce them to entities that can be simply dissected. The essayists in this volume are unanimous in rejecting reification of their subjects. They understand that human life is fragile; that we are vulnerable to the decivilizing features, as well as open to the humanizing aspects, of the social contexts in which we live and breathe and have our being: the researcher no less than the subject. But this is the beginning not the end of wisdom. We are still left with the task of "thinking what we are doing," in Hannah Arendt's happy phrase.

Importantly, we are invented to think about our received terms of discourse and how they help us to link up (or prevent our linking up) public ethics and private virtues. To this task the political theorist brings terms of discourse none of us can escape. I am thinking of words like *justice, equality, freedom, power, authority.* We all know these terms and there are ways in which we share an understanding of their meaning and import. But we may also differ in our understandings. The meaning of such high voltage words as 'equality' is "essentially contested." 'Equality' can never be reduced to a single stipulation and we can never hope for final cloture to debates as to its range of meaning and application. This means our visions of what the just, free, or liberated society should look like will also differ — and that is the stuff of political debate. Nor, indeed, *should* we aim for cloture: to do so is the death of politics. Coerced consensus destroys the *res publica*, the public thing. Open debate and discussion helps to keep it alive.

We are, at present, in danger of drifting away from the form of inquiry inaugurated by Plato and Aristotle and, in its civic republican and communitarian aspects, traceable through Aquinas, Rousseau, Montesquieu, de Tocqueville, Jefferson, and such twentieth century, home grown theorists of American democracy as John Dewey, Randolph Bourne, Jane Addams, and George Herbert Mead. To show you how great a distance yawns between ourselves and these bold theorists of commonwealths, think of how much easier it is for us to talk about 'private interests' than a commonweal. Think of how readily we understand those who *use* the public sphere to gain private ends but the trouble we have comprehending selfless action in behalf of a common good.

Similarly, those who trench upon the terrain of social science in its face as public policy are frequently immured in the language of "management of human resources" as the tasks undertaken by professional "social service providers." We do not blanch at the term "client." But pause and reflect, for a moment, at the distance between a client as a passive consumer of expert services and a citizen as a being who participates actively in the process of free government and in helping to determine the terms of his or her own social existence. The language of bureaucratese is neither the language of developmental psychology as a moral science nor that of classical construals of citizenship and politics. It is the language of bureaucratese we in the human sciences must begin to challenge.

If we focus on these respective languages we can, perhaps, begin to take the measure of the present, assessing what we have gained together with what we may have lost. David Rothman in an essay on "The State as Parent," notes the double-edge of social reform: both compassion and control fused in an unholy alliance as we try to intervene with various targeted groups or classes. When such populations, whether retarded, physically handicapped, black, brown, or women at least some of the time, have problems that are identified by experts with solutions similarly shaped by experts, their citizenship fades and their clientage takes center stage — or may. That, at least, is the worry. Rothman asks: "Will we as a society be able to respect rights but not ignore needs? Can we do good to others but on their terms?" (Rothman, 1978, p. 95).

These are the inescapable questions free citizens must put to themselves. As well, Rothman's questions bring us back full circle, back to the ground shared by the developmental psychologists who contribute to this volume and by political theorists. For to speak of the citizen, to note rights as well as needs, is to conjure with first and fundamental things. It is to ponder what makes us good and turns us sour.

It is to vex ourselves with why some move ahead and others fall away. It is to lose sleep over why some are found, or find themselves, and others are lost, or lose themselves. Psychology enters at the ground floor, with the creation of human beings with a civic capacity and passion or, alternatively, beings caught in a tangle of apathy and despair. For we must ask not only: *what* is the citizen but *who*? What institutions and ideas and relations serve as the matrix out of which good persons and decent citizens arise? What forces and dislocations sever the individual from his or her civic capacities as well as his or her 'developmental potential'? We have, in such questions, a recipe guaranteed to produce Exedrin headaches all 'round: no doubt. But a knowing headache is better by far than the false comfort of denial.

In refusing to separate politics from morals, Rousseau posed the following paradox: "In order for an emerging people to appreciate the healthy maxims of politics ... the effect would have to become the cause; the social spirit, which should be the result of the institution, would have to preside over the founding of the institution itself; and men would have to be prior to laws what they ought to become by means of laws" (Rousseau, 1762/1978, p. 169). In otherwords, Rousseau is asking: If our social world is corrupt, what shall serve as the basis for moral action? Where might the redoubts of decency be found? Where does one discover principles to live and act by?

We are drawn back to Aristotle and his vision of citizenship as a form of action geared toward the good of the whole. We find our humanity; we realize our individual human potentiality, in and through action together with others. Participation is one essential feature of the human person, just as such individual participation is a constitutive feature of the human community. Only in this way do human beings discover their civic capacities and they require a surround of a particular kind to make this discovery possible.[1]

There are many ways to enter a text and to interpret its author or, in this instance, authors. But given the convergence of concerns with human identity, purpose, and meaning, and the implications of social policies on the present and the future, 'thinking Aristotle' seems an apt place to begin.

REFERENCES

Freud, S. (1963). On psychotherapy. (J. Bernays, trans.) Reprinted in P. Rieff (ed.), *Therapy and technique* (pp. 63-75). New York: Collier Books. (Originally published, 1905.)

Rothman, D. (1978). The state as parent. In W. Gaylin, I. Glasser, S. Marcus, and D. Rothman (eds.), *Doing good. The limits of benevolence* (pp. 67-97). New York: Pantheon Books.

Rousseau, J. J. (1978). *The Social contract, with Geneva manuscript and Political economy.* (R. D. Masters, ed.). New York: St. Martin's Press. (Originally published, 1762.)

NOTE

1. For a complete discussion of Aristotle—then—and Aristotelianism revisited see Chapters 1 and 7 of my (1981) *Public man, private woman. Women in social and political thought.* Princeton, NJ.: Princeton University Press.

I

Using Science to Build Human Needs and Values into Social Policies and Institutions

1

Building Human Nature into Social Arrangements

Sheldon H. White

The authors in this volume are behavioral and social scientists concerned with what our disciplines have to offer to contemporary American society. The chapters center on developmental psychology and what it has to say about families and children, but we are not all developmental psychologists. Questions about developmental psychology's relevance are taken as symptomatic of three larger questions that concern many behavioral and social scientists nowadays.

- We know now that human activities are far more complex and subtle than the movements of physical objects. How should sciences of people differ from sciences of things?
- We are not going to predict human activities with equations or models to any large extent. Nor are we going to control human behavior with behavioristic technology. What can we expect, practically speaking, from sciences of people?
- What role should the behavioral and social sciences have in recognizing peoples' fundamental needs and values? What are the ethical risks we confront in so doing?

Questions like these reflect emancipation mixed with uncertainty. The "soft sciences" are more and more standing clear of the "hard sciences," uncertain about the programs of scientific development to which we should turn, a little nervous about setting aside old visions of ultimate absoluteness and certitude. Can we expect society to keep on paying for research in the behavioral and social sciences if we surrender the claim that someday such research will deliver absolute, unbiased, impeccably objective formulas?

Developmental psychology has just been through a period in which both the theoretical and practical possibilities of the field took on a new prominence. In the 1960s and early 1970s, there was a renaissance of theory and research. In that same era, developmental psychology and developmental psychologists played a prominent role in the social programs of the War on Poverty. Now there is some retrenchment. Piagetian theory, the largest single intellectual force stimulating and shaping the renaissance, turned out to have some limitations. On the policy side, it became clear that programs addressing the health, education, and welfare of families and children need something more than a theory of cognitive development to guide them.

Bronfenbrenner (1979) has argued that a policy-relevant developmental psychology must be based on the study of families in the social situations in which they live and there is now a movement toward the study of human development in ordinary human situations (Rogoff & Lave, 1984).

Where should the researcher who wants to study child development stand? Does he or she come out of the ivory tower, seize fragments of data like a tiger seizing its prey, and then drag the data back into the ivory tower to be digested into timeless truths? Or should the researcher stand in the everyday world of the child? Where? Should researchers stand in the dozens of situations that a child lives in during a day? Who should the research speak to? An astonishing number and variety of people participate in children's socialization nowadays—mothers, fathers, brothers, sisters, teachers, priests, school counselors, physicians, television producers, employers of the young, school committee members, administrators of government-sponsored projects and programs, lawyers, psychotherapists, dieticians, toy manufacturers, music teachers, boy scout leaders, policemen, judges, social workers, sports trainers, coaches—which of these are the clientele of the developmental psychologist?

SCIENCE AS A SOURCE OF GOALS AND VALUES

In Chapter 2 "Human Nature and Social Policy," Charles Cofer traces the intertwining of psychology and political reasoning over the past four centuries. Social theorists have again and again tried to define the fundamental parameters of the human mind and character in order to design the political arrangements people need. There are groups of such political-psychological theorists, dividing on some big questions. One big question is whether people are inherently good or evil. If you believe that people are inherently evil, as Niccoló Machiavelli tended to, you design for more and tougher government. If you believe people are inherently good, as Jean Jacques Rousseau believed, then you are for less government. A second big question is whether people may be changed by their circumstances, for better or for worse. A third big question, slightly more complex, asks what people's fundamental powers and motives really are; in addressing this third question, one writer after another has put forth a list-making kind of psychological theorizing.

Beginning at the time of the Reformation, Cofer reviews some lists of human essences proposed by one writer after another. The list-making tradition has prevailed for several centuries, though what has gone into the lists has changed. First, there were the medieval faculties, then "powers of the mind" and "springs of action" in the seventeenth century. Then in the eighteenth century faculties once again but incarnated as phrenological bumps, and then in the late nineteenth and twentieth centuries — coming all in a rush, as a discipline of psychology got established — traits, needs, instincts, drives, motives, values, and personality factors.

Psychological-political analysis was much of what "philosophy" was before the twentieth century. John Locke, Thomas Hobbes, Bishop Berkeley, David Hume, David Hartley, James Mill, John Stuart Mill, etc., were all social and political writers who found it necessary to put up some speculative psychology to form a basis for their political visions. Why? Cofer quotes James Madison:

> But what is government itself but the greatest of all reflections on human nature? If men were angels, no government would be necessary. If angels were to govern men, neither external nor internal controls on government would be necessary. In framing a government which is to be administered by men over men, the greatest difficulty lies in this: you must first enable the government to control the governed; and in the next place to control itself (p. 42).

Government practices *are* a theory of human nature. If one seeks to renegotiate what government can or should do, then it seems to be necessary to articulate explicitly some conceptions of people's needs, motives, powers, and goals. The persistence of Cofer's list-making tradition suggests that each generalization wants and uses new categorizations of human powers and motives. Such categorizations were routinely offered in the moral philosophy courses that, in the nineteenth-century small American college, were ancestral to scientific psychology courses (White, 1984b).

Notice that there have been some systematic changes over time in Cofer's genealogy.

Early writers simply declare their lists of basic human characteristics. There are no tests a characteristic has to pass to be judged a characteristic. Little overall organization is proposed. At best, characteristics were loosely grouped. Aquinas, following Aristotle, proposes that humans have three orders of faculties composed under a hierarchical vegetative, sensitive, and rational soul. In the late eighteenth century, Thomas Reid set forth long lists of the animal and intellectual powers of the mind. In the early nineteenth century, Jeremy Bentham set forth lists of human motives and interests.

Somewhat later writers gave their lists a physical focus. Gall and Spurzheim blended together traditional faculty psychology with some neurophysiological rationalizations to produce a grounded conceptualization of the powers of the mind. To some people in the middle of the nineteenth century, phrenology was a scientific approach to the mind. Textbooks used in American colleges taught it. Sophisticated people had their heads read and, apparently, took it seriously.

Near the turn of the century, psychological writers turned to instincts as the fundamental essences of human nature. Now a tradition of list making began that was, to a modest degree, founded on naturalistic observations of animal behavior. Individual instincts were rationalized in evolutionary terms. Instinct-based explanations were widely accepted and used near the turn of this century. Predisciplinary writers such as Romanes wrote about human nature in terms of instincts. So did early psychologists like James, Hall, Freud, Thorndike, and McDougall. In a era of evolutionism, instinctive accounts of human nature were only common sense.

It was too easy to propose fundamental human instincts. Cofer quotes from Bernard's attack on biological determinism in 1924. The critical sociologist was able to compile over 5,000 instinct terms from the books of his time, suggesting that instinct-listing had become an undisciplined and empty game in the early twentieth century, as faculty-listing had been in the nineteenth. Objective tests appear in the twentieth century, based on methodological rules governing standardization, reliability, and validity. As weak as "test theory" has been in the twentieth century, it has imposed some discipline on the modern continuations of the list-making tradition. Contemporary psychological attributions of powers and motives to people tend to be grounded upon the practices and the possibilities of testing.

One or two twentieth-century entities, such as n-achievement, are actively studied, related to other entities and variables. The categorizations and tests of the twentieth century are linked with diagnostic and therapeutic practices.

Cofer is, toward the end of his chapter, skeptical about the list-making tradition he has traced through. He questions whether there has been, in fact, any yield of the tradition. But there is more to the contemporary descent of the list-making tradition than the lists of the present. As the biological and human sciences ripened, they translated the motivologies of the past into new forms of motivology speculatively derived from the new scientific work.

A SCIENCE OF HEALTHY-MINDEDNESS VERSUS A SCIENCE OF SICK SOULS

New, hard thinking about bodies, minds, and morals was rampant in the late nineteenth century. People had to contend with the thesis that men were descended from monkeys. Many people were upset by the proposition, not simply because it forced them to recognize some hairy relatives but because it seemed to detach them from God and because it threw human society and the human soul into a strange light.

Social and political deliberations about human affairs more and more used the perspectives of scientists and scientific thinking. In the twilight of the romantic era, some evolutionary prophets went to extremes. The strong ideologies of the late nineteenth century suggest some of the emotions and fears that animated the "normal science" of the time. To borrow William James's (1902) useful distinction among religionists, not entirely inappropriate here, some espoused a "science of healthy-mindedness" and some sought for a "science of sick souls."

Morality, Justice, and Progress in Nature

Many in the late nineteenth century were enthusiastic about a philosophy of progress which seemed to say that nature steered things toward the good. There was a benign drift in things, and if men had the wit and patience to read the book of nature and submit to what it told them they would pursue the paths of righteousness. In the early nineteenth century, this was the contention of Deism, a pantheistic theology that held that God's purpose was immanent in all the laws and the mechanisms of the natural world. In the late nineteenth century, Thomas Huxley defined the Almighty as "the sum of the customs of matter" and argued repeatedly and vigorously that Nature enforced the Good:

> The more I know intimately the lives of other men (to say nothing of my own), the more obvious it is to me that the wicked does not flourish nor is the righteous punished. . . . The ledger of the Almighty is strictly kept, and every one of us has the balance of his operations paid over to him at the end of every minute of his existence (cited in Hearder, 1966).

> The absolute justice of the system of things is as clear to me as any scientific fact. The gravitation of sin to sorrow is as certain as that of the earth to the sun, and more so — for experimental proof of that fact is within reach of us all — nay, is before us all in our own lives, if we had but the eyes to see it (cited in Irvine, 1955, p. 130).

Add to Huxley's doctrine of the inherent benignity of nature some principles of progress, holding that basic developmental or evolutionary processes make Nature march toward an ever-greater Good and you arrive at a positive, optimistic science of healthy-mindedness that appealed to many in the late nineteenth century. The healthy-minded science favored political conservatism. Interfere with the scheme of things and you may hurt rather than help.

The role of the scientist.

The healthy-minded science gave the scientist a rather central position in the determination of goals, values, and possibilities for social action. The scientist was the reader of the book of nature and the student of the "customs of matter." The scientist could be taken as a species of secular priest deciphering and declaring those paths of righteousness that lead from Is to Ought. Developmental psychology in Herbert Spencer's or James Mark Baldwin's or Heinz Werner's sense, as a general science of evolving systems (White, 1976, 1984b) was central to this kind of priesthood. Late nineteenth-century theories of children's cognitive development were largely built by mixing the social-developmental philosophies of men like Comte and Spencer with evolutionary theory. Such theories were, very literally, efforts to provide a unified account of the growth of bodies, minds, and morals in childhood (White, 1983a).

The rosy, progress-oriented ideologies led straight to a mythic picture of a rosy, progress-oriented child. The child peeks out at us in Lynette Friedrich-Cofer's chapter as Rousseau's Émile — innocent, good, wise in the ancient ways of childhood, a freestanding soul to be fostered but not forced by adults (see Chapter 3, "Body, Mind, and Morals in the Framing of Social Policy"). This mythic child re-emerges in Sandra Scarr's chapter, "Cultural Lenses on Mothers and Children," as "the Good child who could be trusted to grow up largely on his own," an invention of Darwin's time, and then again in the twentieth century as the Gesellian child with an inveterate, inborn tendency toward optimal development.

Sciences of Sick Souls

Not-so-optimistic people in the late nineteenth century worried about human problems of motivation, spirit, vitality, healthfulness, respect for the law, and the willingness or ability to be freestanding in society. Many agreed there were signs of a crisis of the human spirit. There were three schools of thought about the crisis, one which said it was psychological, a second which saw it as a derivative of social problems, and a third which saw it as a manifestation of *degeneracy* loose in society. Each school of thought defined a unique point of entry for corrective action and, in so doing, declared a special role for the scientist in the determination of means and/or ends of action.

Crisis of vitality.

In the late nineteenth century, a growing number of neurologists moved toward a quasi-psychiatric practice to confront disorders of the will called *neurasthenia*, *nervousness*, and *nervous prostration*. The legends of our time say that it was Sigmund Freud who first made the pilgrimage from neurology to psychiatry and begat psychotherapy, but Freud was part of a broad pattern of his time. George Beard (1881, 1898) and Silas Weir Mitchell (1899, 1902) were prominent among the American physicians who gave malaise of the spirit a medical interpretation and so led the way toward what is now called the "medical model" of psychiatric treatment, but there were many others. It seems likely that important aspects of the "mental hygiene" and "mental health" programs that were to come along in the twentieth century grew out of this earlier work. This line of thinking assimilated all social problems to problems of the individual. Lewis Terman remarked in a 1911 paper, "The problem of *vitality* underlies almost every social and political situation confronting us" (Gilbert, 1977, p. 15). The problems of the individual were to be addressed by programs of mental and physical hygiene to which early psychologists such as Terman gave serious attention (cf. Seagoe, 1975, pp. 55-63).

The Social View

Many looked at things just the other way around, attributing the loss of individual vitality to the disarray of social conditions. The individual had lost his or her connection with the community and with meaningful work, and so there was *anomie* or *alienation*. The apparent psychological problems of people were epiphenomenal, shadows cast by faulty social arrangements. E. A. Ross in *Social Control* (1901), said that individualistic, voluntaristic, melioristic solutions to social problems would no longer suffice. Social reforms were called for. The role of the social scientist was to improve the effectiveness of social programs, by developing statistics to provide a picture of social conditions and by studying the consequences of programs and policies in society.

Social scientists were given this role by those, like the Fabians in England, who believed that society might be reformed by evolutionary and noncataclysmic measures. There were some, like the anarchists and communists, who held that effective social change could only take place by revolutionary means. Evolutionary or revolutionary proponents of the centrality of social problems generally gave psychology only a minor place as a potentially relevant science. In the tradition of Auguste Comte and Karl Marx (and of Vygotsky today) the human psyche and its problems are derivatives of social arrangements.

John Dewey never realized a fully viable social psychology near the turn of the century. One of the strengths of Dewey's program for a social psychology and, perhaps, one of the reasons why it still attracts interest today is that Dewey tried to envision the individual and his or her problems in a historical context of ever-changing social conditions.[1]

Crises of Degeneracy

A third "science of sick souls" near the turn of the century confronted what it saw as degeneracy. Statistics seemed to show rising divorce rates, insanity, criminality, immorality, and physical deterioration. Some commentators linked such statistics to physical, moral, and social degeneracy.

Who were the degenerates? Various writers said that degeneration, or degenerate tendencies, were to be found in neurasthenics, hysterics, epileptics, retardates, people with obsessions or phobias, people with "depravities of appetite," neurotics, individuals with a tendency to swoon, people with a tendency to make up jargon or doggerel verse, criminals, the insane, mystics, artists, and geniuses.[2] Some linked vagabonds and tramps to degeneracy, arguing that their wandering ways was an atavistic reversion to the nomadic ways of primitive human societies.

One line of thought linked degeneracy to counterevolutionary trends due to the mingling of races, the immigrations of foreigners, or the overbreeding of the poor. Some scientists favored this view, and they favored research designed to find the sources of retardation, crime, and social dependency in atavisms and constitutional weaknesses among individuals in the population. A number of prominent early American psychologists were eugenicists, and some were active in favor of the restriction of immigration. This has been much written about in recent years as a kind of scandalous fact about early American psychologists, that they dabbled in reactionary politics with arguments that went beyond the warrant of their data. But a fair reading of the lives scientists led in the late nineteenth century will show that many brought their science into the political and moral arena, that they saw nothing much wrong with it—they expected that of themselves as scientists, and others expected it of them—and that very few individuals (then or now) have been blessed with unassailable data offering a solid prescription for social action.

There was another school of thought that linked degeneracy to a harmful softening of American life. People were moving from the country to the city. There was much rural nostalgia, and widespread concern about what might happen to children raised in the unnatural and debilitating environment of the city street. G. Stanley Hall was prominent among those who said that city life, feminine schoolteachers, and a loss of respect for the primitive and rough parts of human nature would weaken the moral fiber and spirit of American youth. Hall devoted a substantial part of his two-volume *Adolescence* (1904) to proposals for social and educational strategies that would fit with natural processes of child development and the special character of the child's mind.[3] People saw such proposals as the role and raison d'être of child study.

CHANGING HUMAN DEVELOPMENT IN A CHANGING WORLD

An early form of developmental psychology came into existence as child study in the late nineteenth century. Child study was not a scientific program for the study of child development, although university members like G. Stanley Hall tried to lead the movement in that direction. Fundamentally, child study was a many-sided political movement reflecting the commitment of a number of adults to a new and serious interest in the nature and possibilities of childhood. Why was there so much new adult interest in children? "Growing up" was undergoing serious changes in the late nineteenth century. It was taking longer. It was becoming more complicated and demanding. It involved an increasing number of adults who had, somehow, to find new goals and standards for their dealings with children and with one another.

It took longer for a child to grow up in the late nineteenth century, longer to become an independent and responsible adult. The path to adulthood passed through education, more and more of it as time went on. Growing up became more complicated. Trails toward adulthood branched and rebranched as a proliferating occupational structure. Children had choices to make and tests to pass as they sought for a viable and favorable place in the occupational niche system.

As growing up lengthened, so did the period during which the family gave some support and took some responsibility for the child. Yet family members were with the child less throughout the day. Farm families had moved to the city. More adult work took place away from the child. Men left the household to do their jobs during the day and then, gradually, so did women.

Families did not and could not provide children with all the training and knowledge they needed to find a place in society. Increasingly, schools shared in the socialization of children. Discussed as educational institutions alone, schools in actuality provided a complex mixture of social functions: some education, some day care, some political socialization, some slotting or tracking toward different sectors of the occupational structure, some "warehousing" of older children, some social control of adolescents, etc.

For children without families, or for families with limited resources for the upbringing of children, or for children with different physical and mental handicaps, community agencies provided support. The support was double-edged. Under legally specified conditions, these supportive people could supervene and take the child from the family.[4] A proliferating occupational structure of "whole child professionals" appeared to stand beside families and teachers as adult figures in the growing child's life.

The documents of the late nineteenth century give rich records of the many-sided politics of childhood of that time (Bremner, 1970-71). Child study was one of the crystallizations of that bargaining process.

THE BARGAINS OF CHILD STUDY

In the late 1890s and early 1900s, G. Stanley Hall tried to understand the basic needs of children and youth through scientific child study, and then he sought ways to build respect for those basic needs in the design of institutions of child care, socialization, and education. What Hall did, other developmental psychologists have done since. Developmental psychology has been a science of design (*one* science of design) for institution building in the designed societies of the twentieth century.

Alexander Siegel and I have tried to trace through the social bargains involved in child study. No political movement is ever single-minded, driven by one set of purposes, of course, by definition. Child study was of some interest to: college presidents, who saw in it a way of building bridges between universities and schools; psychologists, who saw it as a significant arena for basic psychological inquiry; educators, who saw it as a potential foundation for professionalization; social workers, who saw it as providing knowledge that might both support and justify social welfare and rehabilitative efforts; clinical psychologists, who saw child study as a nucleus for training schools for the retarded, psycho-educational programs, and child guidance; and parents, mothers mostly, who were drawn to child study because it seemed to help them with a sudden onrush of new responsibilities and choices they confronted at the turn of the century. Hall dealt with all these audiences and in so doing he confronted the living meaning of the social and behavioral sciences in American society in a broad way that few before or since have attained (Siegel & White, 1982; cf. Hall, 1923; Ross, 1972).

People concerned about children—families, teachers, social workers, physicians, bureaucrats, etc.—worked out a new set of bargains with one another near the turn of the century. The bargains had to do, fundamentally, with the responsibility and authority the several actors would have in the care and socialization of children. If the social writers of the seventeenth and eighteenth centuries had to mix psychological theory with their political theory, it was no less incumbent upon the social activists of the early twentieth century to base their bargains upon conceptions of the fundamental powers and motives of the child. G. Stanley Hall's judgments about the fundamental nature of children and child development, among others, formed part of the basis for those older bargains. We unearth those old judgments periodically, buried in the foundations, when we question some of those older social bargains.

Sandra Scarr's chapter in this volume shows just such an unearthing process (see Chapter 5, "Cultural Lenses on Mothers and Children"). She finds old ideas about womanhood buried as a kind of skeleton behind the dilemmas of career versus family that many women feel today.

> In my view, current dilemmas of motherhood arise from a mismatch between ideas about mothers and children that suited the late nineteenth and early twentieth centuries and the current realities of family life. *The conflict is not between being a mother and having a career; it is between nineteenth century ideas about children and today's women* [emphasis added] (p. 207).

What did G. Stanley Hall and child study have to offer to these bargaining parties? Hall offered ideas about children that were used in the construction of much of the system of roles, responsibilities and authorizations that was negotiated in his time. Probably, he offered ideas about directionality to those who tried to think in a larger way about programs and policies of health, education, and welfare.

After Hall, there were others who put forth influential conceptions of childhood. Scarr considers the mythic child offered by three prominent figures: Gesell, Watson, and Freud. How could three such strongly contrasting conceptions of childhood have been sold at one and the same time to the American public? Maybe there is more than one "public" for the findings of developmental psychologists. Maybe there is a market for differing kinds and levels of philosophies of childhood.

ADVENTURES IN THE POLITICAL PROCESS

Political reasoning and psychological reasoning have been intertwined for centuries. How are both of these kinds of reasoning brought to bear on the working policies, programs, agencies, budgets, laws, and codes of political institutions? Suppose that in the early twentieth century child study went beyond everyday knowledge and everyday reasoning. Systematic observations of children began to partly replace and partly augment them. Groups of people combined their efforts to create *social proof structures*. That is, there began to be communities of people acting in rule-bound ways designed to maximize their collective creation of knowledge about children (White, 1977). How were the data of this new practice of child study translated into the practices of working social institutions?

Lynette Friedrich-Cofer's chapter, "Body, Mind, and Morals in the Framing of Social Policy" traces the complicated and conflicted pathways by which some simple needs of children were partly met, partly not met, in the growth of American educational institutions in the twentieth century.

She begins her story with a wondrous account of a recent French program of academic reform. In the 1950s, it was recognized that French children needed to give more time to physical health and recreation to balance their demanding academic labors in school. So France's Ministry of Education financed a small treatment-control study of a more balanced school program, using nine classrooms. The results of this study seeming positive, larger scale studies of the "one-third time" program were done in the 1960s and, finally, there was a complete adoption of the system nationwide in 1969. Friedrich-Cofer comments, "What is so remarkable about this tale, for an American, is the reasonable and modest way the social policy seemed to evolve."

From the standpoint of our pluralistic society, governments with centralized management can often do remarkable things, of course. But there are some other remarkable features of the tale. First, the needs of American children for physical education and conditioning *had* been recognized since the turn of the century in the United States. Second, the French program of gradual, progressively tested, implementations of a new educational practice follows an R & D model of educational innovation that Americans have admired but have found elusive in their actual management practices in this century.

G. Stanley Hall's child study gave considerable attention to children's physical needs. In 1892, Hall devoted a whole number of his new journal, *Pedagogical Seminary*, to "school hygiene." One of Hall's close associates at Clark, William H. Burnham, contributed to that journal and 10 years later we find him sending out a Clark child study questionnaire on "The Hygienic Conditions of Normal Schools." One of Hall's most eminent students, Lewis M. Terman, did his first substantial work on school hygiene.[5]

Americans born in the country—and this included most Americans at the turn of the century—were worried, no less than the French in the 1950s, about the potentially debilitating effect of school classrooms on the physical condition of American children. G. Stanley Hall's heart was in the virtues of country life. He directed his program of child study questionnaires, and his big volumes on adolescence, toward a vision of a child who was first and early a creature of nature, later and *very* gradually a creature of science and logical reasoning and delicate moral judgments.

Hall unhesitatingly brought his vision into play in making recommendations about what parents and schools and social institutions should do about child rearing. Hall found many in American life eager to cooperate with him in efforts to establish parks, playgrounds, athletic programs, programs of school hygiene, and movements like the Boy Scouts to meet children's physical needs. An American Association of Physical Education was formed in 1895. Physical education became "established" at just about the same time psychology became established (The American Psychological Association was founded in 1892), and Friedrich-Cofer's chapter gives indications of a proliferating organizational structure in 1900s—an American Athletic Union, a National Amateur Athletic Foundation, A National Collegiate Athletic Association. How did all this clear vision and positive political action eventuate in the condition of American schools in 1979, when it was estimated that only a third of children aged 10 to 17 participated in physical education classes?

It is not so simple to build the basic needs of children into the machinery of large-scale institutional structures. No adult feels comfortable all day long in all the rule-governed social situations in which adults live. What Friedrich-Cofer is dealing with in her chapter, I believe, are the vicissitudes of children's needs in the larger *designed* social systems which we have put together for them.

Tyack (1974) has written a classic history of American attempts to create a "one best system" of public education in the early 1900s — education standardized across the country, rational, planned, efficient like the railroads, managed, employing the knowledge and the skills of scholars and scientists. G. Stanley Hall figures in Tyack's history, as do other turn-of-the-century American psychologists. Tyack's title, and his history, are ironic, of course. It isn't possible to create a one best system for people who differ on many important dimensions. Friedrich-Cofer's chapter sketches some of the ways in which mischief accrues as children's needs are brought into the political process.

Children's Needs in the Design of a Social System

What do you have to do to reflect children's needs in the design of a larger social system?

Childhood has to become talkaboutable in some language amenable to design and management decisions. Friedrich-Cofer's history begins amongst the political-psychological ideologies of Cofer's seventeenth-and eighteenth-century social theorists. We get a small sense of the meaning of the list-making tradition. Writers like John Locke and Jean Jacques Rousseau were interested in the rational design of larger human social arrangements. They built schemes of people in words and then, upon those schemes, they built schemes of government. We think of Locke and Rousseau as visionaries who painted with a broad brush, but Friedrich-Cofer shows that they could offer precise, concrete, child-sized political-psychological prescriptions.

John Locke spoke about children's physical needs in his thoughts on education, and then he made recommendations about practices having to do with exercise, diet, and hygiene. Rousseau disagreed with Locke's ideological emphasis to a degree but he gave his mythical child Émile a mythical education centering on physical and sensory experience until age 12. One could catch glimpses of real children and real schools in political-psychological descriptions given in such writings and a next obvious step was to try to visit those realities.

Some kinds of "applied" and "basic" observations of children need to be established to give some grounding and discipline to proliferating ideological discussions. A second step in the reflection of children's needs required some small steps over the line from fantasy to reality. Locke and Rousseau were distinguished representatives of a sea of social theorists and ideologists who, in the rising tide of political liberalism of the 1700s and 1800s, propounded diverse mythical children and diverse mythical schemes of education. The point of it all was to build a new reality in human social arrangements and, in fact, some realities had to be visited if only to adjudicate among the many utopian and apocalyptic myths.

Friedrich-Cofer's chapter indicates the assortment of experimental schools and data-gathering efforts that came to life in the eighteenth and nineteenth centuries. Phrenology was given much scientific credence in the early part of the nineteenth century and it had an important influence on educational reformers such as Horace Mann. Then in the latter part of that century a wider body of scientific studies came into play in the discussions of children's physical needs — social statistics, physiology, anatomy, infant mortality studies, rates of rejection for military service, and many anthropometric studies. G. Stanley Hall, almost uniquely among early American psychologists, remained sensitive throughout his career to the rich, diverse plurality of "data bases" about childhood, or possibly pertinent to judgments about it, that had come into existence in his time.

Not one but a number of extractions of scientific studies of childhood may be made to reflect children's needs in the political process. The several extractions are characteristically "impure" and they are often rivalrous. The thesis that children need exercise, physical care, and fresh air to be healthy and well seems nonproblematic. Yet it was complicated to build exercise and health care into schools. Friedrich-Cofer's history shows how, in one political forum after another, campaigns for these programs had to be mingled with campaigns for common schooling, the kindergarten, public health and sanitation, feminism, and parks and playgrounds. Politics is not a very precise business.

The recognition of children's needs in practical programs may take place not once but several times, and then the several extractions may war against one another. Friedrich-Cofer traces the rivalry between two traditions of physical education for children, one a tradition of investment in exercise for all children, the other a tradition of investment in competitive sports for an athletic elite among schoolchildren.

Early twentieth-century American schools did, indeed, put into place health- and exercise-oriented programs. But then a second political process began. Competition-oriented school athletics programs serving a gifted minority of schoolchildren competed with and, to a considerable extent, drew resources away from the programs designed for everybody. Social arrangements evolve and change over time. One may need to design and redesign toward children's needs to maintain their place in the scheme of a social institution.[6]

SCIENTIFIC MYTH MAKING ABOUT CHILDREN

Sandra Scarr's chapter, "Cultural Lenses on Mothers and Children," is the first of three chapters in this volume presenting recent research work and discussing the contemporary scientific and social meaning of developmental psychology. What has become of the science of child study as it has evolved to become contemporary developmental psychology? What is the role of developmental psychology in contemporary social arrangements for children? Scarr's chapter says that there have been three trends.

1. Developmental psychology is losing its earliest hopes that scientific child study would find Truths and Natural Laws governing child development, and that such truths and laws would tell us how to rear children.
2. Developmental psychology has become a source of conceptions about childhood and human nature in American society — not unitary conceptions, but multiple and at times rivalrous images of the child's essential nature and of the child's potential for change.
3. Developmental psychology has served from time to time as an instrument of power, not always benign.

Sciences of Child Study

We think of psychology as something that was invented all at once — say, in Wundt's Leipzig laboratory in 1879 — but there is respectable evidence that psychology has been a house of several empiricisms from the very beginning, and that these several empiricisms have "matured" at very different rates.[7]

Experimental psychology was the first part of psychology to develop a plausible cooperative research activity, because it began by gathering together established projects, methods, and equipment from physics and biology laboratories in Europe. Later-maturing parts of psychology have had to try to invent methods and methodology while struggling against presumptions imported with those physical and biological projects.

An internal politics of psychology departments began at the beginning and goes on endlessly. Experimental psychologists have hoped that their physicalistic methods would ultimately handle all psychological questions, and they have usually swept aside the skepticism and recalcitrance of their colleagues as symptoms of "fuzzymindedness." On the other side, psychologists of personality and society and motivation and development have dismissed the importunities of their hard-nosed colleagues as territorial invasions based on nothing more than arrogant and simplistic scientism. The "softer" psychologies have tended to proliferate declarations, prospectuses, and demonstrative studies, nervously waiting for that 'great breakthrough' when they will be born again into unquestionable scientific respectability.

Developmental psychology has built up a substantial body of knowledge and methods since G. Stanley Hall's first fumbling questionnaire studies. Are we at last ready to step forward to declare the Truths and Natural Laws governing children's behavior? Scarr, one of the most able and productive researchers of our time, points out that there may be no Truths simply lying around in the world waiting for us. Knowledge is a construction of the human mind. We do not find absolute facts, nor do we prove things to our colleagues with them. "Scientific theories are judged by their persuasive power in the community of scientists." What is worse, there may be optional Truths. Scientific study of children gives us "many sets of facts that arise from different theory-guided perspectives."

Scarr in Chapter 5 "Cultural Lenses on Mothers and Children," gives a vivid image of the psychologist confronting a sea of events and constructing a bounded, dimensionalized, variable-ized ecology within which scientific analysis may proceed:

> The psychological world in which we conduct research is, in my view, a cloud of correlated events, to which we as human observers give meaning. In the swirling cloud of interacting organisms and environments, most events merely co-occur. As investigators, we construct a story (often called a theory) about relationships among events. We select a few elements and put them into a study. By so doing we necessarily eliminate other variables *a priori* from possible analysis, and we preconstrue causal relationships among the events. One cannot avoid either the theoretical preconceptions or the selection of variables to study, but one can avoid exaggerated claims for the causal status of one's variables (p. 221).

In the twentieth century, American developmental psychologists committed themselves to careful observations of children, but they looked at them within frames of observation and they were forever condemned to get the children and the frames mixed up with one another. Looking at a child being raised by its mother in one decade, developmental psychologists oriented themselves to "the problem of father deprivation." (*Children without fathers lack something important. The task of the researcher is to identify the sequelae of the deprivation and to locate remedial or supplemental treatments.*) In the next decade, children without fathers lived in "alternative family lifestyles." (*Children without fathers may or may not have a problem. The task of the researcher is to help society to arrange schools, health care, family support practices, child care, etc., so as to give reasonable support to diverse family forms.*)

Can we use research to predict the consequences of parental activities and to prescribe optimal parenting practices? Scarr argues that the research designs that have been used to study the consequences of parental practices are misleading to begin with and ultimately may simply be inadequate for the task. She reviews some of her own data on mother-infant interaction. She begins with a finding that the observed use of positive parental management techniques — the mother's way of teaching her child, and the mother's use of reason rather than punishment for misbehaviors — is positively correlated with the child's IQ over a period of 18 months. The cause-effect interpretation, that the mother's management is elevating the IQ of the child, is extremely seductive. The interpretation "makes sense" and it provides us with a happy scientific occasion for asserting on evidence what most of us would want to assert anyway, that one should use decency and reason in rearing children.

But the basic finding may be a little more beautiful than true. Scarr enters a number of other variables into the picture: the mother's education and IQ, the child's communication skills, the child's social adjustment, the correlation of the child's behavior at an earlier time with the mother's behavior at a later time, etc. It is not at all clear that the mother is producing major aspects of the baby's cognition and personality. Maybe the baby is producing the mother's behavior. Maybe the direct relationships between mother behaviors and infant behaviors reflect genetic transmissions of cognitive and personality factors.

Scarr concludes, "The system in which parental and child behaviors occur is, in my view, intrinsically confounded. The truth about this world cannot be simulated by the isolation of single variables . . . " (p. 230). She argues that neither correlational nor experimental methods will give us simple truths about parent-child rearing practices, probably because simple truths — that is, simple, monotonic patterns of billiard-ball causation governing two or three variables that determine one another in isolation from all others—do not exist. There is orderliness in human development, but it is a complicated orderliness created by biological, psychological, and social systems in interaction.

Child Study as a Source of Myths

Why do people keep using the data of developmental psychology to set forth simple principles of parenting and teaching children? A glance at the shelves of any bookstore will show that there is a market for principles. Developmental psychologists may slowly perfect their methods. There are many people who must deal with children now and who want whatever first approximations we have.

G. Stanley Hall's child study gave conceptions and values to American society, that is, images and stories attaching meaning, ethicality, directedness, and connectedness to the tasks of the growing child and the adults responsible for care, guidance, and education. A series of terms were given new shadings and senses and nuances of meaning through those images and stories. Words such as 'child', 'man', 'woman', 'mother', 'father', 'family', 'learning', 'optimal child development', 'adjustment', 'normal', 'abnormal', 'advanced', 'retarded', 'gifted', 'intelligent', 'creative', etc., may have only one meaning in a physicalistic or indicative sense, but such words have differing emotional and philosophical nuances as they are used in different situations and styles of discourse.

Scarr reviews the changing images of children and mothers and families in nineteenth- and twentieth-century American society. During the nineteenth century, sweeping social changes in where people lived and how they worked caused obvious changes in family functioning and, with those changes, changes in people's ideas about what families normally do and what they should do.

At the turn of the century, some part of the task of suggesting public images of child development fell to the student of child study. G. Stanley Hall, among others, stepped up to the task willingly. His two-volume *Adolescence* (1904) gave many picturesque images of children at various ages. Hall used his images to rationalize diverse recommendations for rearing children. The recommendations were grounded in part on intuition, in part on limited amounts of data, and in part on a sense of practical problems and possibilities in parenting and schooling. Hall addressed a diversity of issues of "pedagogic matter and method" such as "motor education ... and will-training ... the pedagogy of the English literature and language, history, drawing, normal and high schools, colleges and universities, and philosophy . . . nature and the sciences. . . Menstruation and the education of girls . . . hygiene, crime, and secret vice . . . social and religious training . . . and the education of the heart" (1904, pp. xi-xii). In the beginning, developmental psychologists such as Hall did not try to persuade themselves and others that they pursued a distant, austere, basic, value-free inquiry.

Hall's writings appear to continue the historic political/psychological ideological tradition traced through by Cofer in Chapter 2. But now the tradition is pursued by other means. Hall focuses on a small part of social design—the organization of expectations about children and parents and families and schools and youth clubs into a cooperative system for the care and socialization of children. Hall is not a pure ideologist. He mixes a large amount of diverse data from others into the construction of his ideology; he generates data designed to elaborate and explore his ideology to a limited extent; he communicates regularly with people who are actively engaged in rearing children and to a limited extent he engages in dialogues with such people.

The contemporary child welfare/developmental psychology coalition appears to be a specialized modern descendant of Cofer's political/psychological tradition. In Chapter 5, Scarr points to one of the clearest evidences of that descent. "Two major themes are woven through all discussions of children and child-rearing: Is child nature basically good or bad? And, do children need careful and detailed nurturance, or is their growth basically programmed by nature?" (p. 207). These questions are, precisely, two of the three large questions addressed by the social theorists of Cofer's political/psychological tradition some 300 years before.

The third task faced by Cofer's theorists was the listing of the powers and motives of the human mind. Some developmental psychologists have set forth children's powers and needs in publicly influential ways that rival the public influence of earlier theorists of childhood such as Locke and Rousseau.

Scarr discusses briefly the writings of Arnold Gesell, Sigmund Freud, Erik Erikson, and John B. Watson. These men have played a role as "experts" in mid-twentieth century American society. Though Scarr has all the qualifications of an "expert" on child development herself, the word "expert" is not a nice word as she uses it and she does not use the term approvingly. In the twentieth century, numerous experts about child development have given well-formed, plausible, persuasive, but contradictory advice. They were essentially rivalrous myth makers.

The growth of the social and behavioral sciences in the twentieth century was marked by some strong faith in the inexorable power of science to sweep away superstition, bias, and confusion. Science would lead one to objective, clear, singular truths. Such facts would dictate possible management of physical, human, and social things, harmonizing human actions with physical nature, human nature, and the larger, benign plan of evolutionary biology.

Developmental Psychology as a Source of Instruments of Power

Developmental psychology has become an instrument of power, serving diverse interests in the continuing processes of bracing old social institutions or bringing new ones into American society. At times, developmental psychology has been an instrument of the strong against the weak, at times an instrument of the weak against the strong.

Scarr's chapter is a "hot" chapter. She writes as a distinguished participant in the contemporary scientific history of developmental psychology and she also writes as a woman. She introduces us to G. Stanley Hall as someone who is swindling the mothers and women of his time, (p. 210) and as one of a band of experts who are (see Chapter 5, "Cultural Lenses on Mothers and Children").

One of the nice things about traditional notions of "value-free science" is the idea that political and ethical immunities are built into the scientific processes of the developmental psychologist. The developmental psychologist knows (or deludes himself into thinking that he knows) that there is no political or ethical interest governing his choice of problem and direction of his work. But there is much twentieth-century evidence to testify that value orientations are built into the work of the behavioral and social scientist, and that problems accrue when this is not recognized.

STUDYING AND WORKING WITH ADOLESCENT AGGRESSION

How do you find scientific orderliness in a cloud of variables within which all effects are basically confounded? The complexities of human behavior seem beyond calculation at times but it is an everyday fact that people find regularity in others' behavior. People hold jobs in which they manage children, help children to manage themselves, and educate them. Can we improve their efficacy with empirical studies?

Robert and Beverly Cairns are guardedly optimistic in their chapter, "On Social Values and Social Development: Gender and Aggression" (see Chapter 4). They believe that practices of scientific

·research can be found that have a degree of buffering against bias. Such research can give practically useful guidance if it is conducted in systems-oriented programs designed to build upon the existing knowledge of practitioners.

What practical problems can developmental psychologists address? The Cairns suggest problems of learning and behavior, the effects and prevention of abuse and neglect, the emergence of the child's violence toward others, and the treatment of children's self-abusive habits. This is their 1980s list, to which they add items from John B. Watson's 1913 list — problems of development in infancy, the psychological effects of drugs and other substances, the effects of advertising, and juvenile justice. Here, as in other places in this volume, contemporary developmental psychology is seen as a continuation of a tradition.

The passage from basic inquiry to practical utility is difficult. "Moving from data to application is like taking a stroll down the Grand Canyon, or a saunter up the Matterhorn" (Cairns, Chapter 4, p. 193). To begin with, the orientation to practicality throws one into a dilemma. Personal values and commitments contend against the need to maintain a dispassionate and objective weighting of the empirical evidence. Development psychology has elaborated methodological safeguards: standards of reliability and validity of measurement, conventions for reporting data, techniques of statistical analysis, and other procedures designed to reduce suggestibility and biases. But such protections may now be overprotecting developmental psychology's research:

> More subtly, the conventions that have been adopted for publication in modern psychological journals make it difficult to reject any sane hypothesis. The problem is that most phenomena of social import are determined by multiple factors. With large numbers of subjects, the null hypothesis is a relatively impotent guide to truth. The problem for developmental psychology is not merely to determine whether or not variables have "significant" effects but to determine how these variables are organized and weighted over ontogeny (p. 180).

Gender Differences in Violence

Borrowing from Binet and Simon, the Cairns adopted five canons of procedure designed to resolve the science-social dilemma as it confronted them in the execution of their own research program. Special features of their research on aggressive behavior reflect their adoption of those canons, and seem suggestive about how, generally, research on developmental psychology ought to be brought to bear on everyday problems of children.

Programmatic Research.

The Cairns have mounted a sustained, diversified research program designed to map out the phenomena of children's aggression. They have mixed research strategies, working nomothetically with a larger sample of 660 children between 9 and 17 years of age, and more idiographically with a subset of 80 children, 40 of them "high risk" and 40 control. The research program research is problem-centered, designed to pursue three goals: (1) to describe the development of various forms of aggression; (2) to discover what can and cannot be predicted over time in development; and (3) to look for factors that might be addressed in programs of control and amelioration.

Orientation to a Phenomenon.

The Cairns are studying a phenomenon of children's behavior that has some "standing" in the everyday world. The topic of children's aggression does not depend upon the recent trends in the research literature or a theorist-of-the-moment for its legitimacy as a research problem. It has a robust existence. It will be around, and will be of interest, in the future.

Search for Convergent Evidence.

Are there gender differences in the incidence of violent behavior? Several research reviews disagree. But an examination of other lines of evidence says the differences are large and meaningful after age 10. The gender differences materialize in the preadolescent years, and this is one reason why the research literature is in disagreement. Crime figures show a highly reliable, historically stable, 10:1 gender difference in violent crime. The difference cannot be an artifact of local features of U. S. culture because similar differences have been recorded as far back as thirteenth-century England. Similar gender differences are observed in species other than humans.

Broad Mapping of Causation and Control.

Recognizing that they are dealing with a system of behavior governed by biological, psychological, and social controls the Cairns have explored, on the one hand, the biological rhythms and sequences of development and, on the other, social practices for regulating violence maintained by teachers, peers, and social institutions.

Not all interventionistic psychologists are interested in so wide-ranging an exploration. They prefer to "stay close to behavior" and they contend that all the issues of environmental control over behavior, real or imaginable, should be discernible in the flow of stimuli, responses, and reinforcements in the immediate vicinity of the subject.

The Cairns argue that too much weight has been given to mechanisms of learning in discussions of human behavior in the past. Learning as we know it in the laboratory—that is, mechanisms of classical and operant conditioning—may be fundamentally devices for local adjustments of behavior, and may not be a basis for major and long-term changes in behavior organization. "Indeed, a strong case can be made for the proposition that the primary function of learning—social and otherwise—is to facilitate local, time-bound accommodations that cannot be achieved as effectively by less plastic structural or genetic changes" (p. 190).

Commitment to the Study of Application.

For the Cairns, the application of research begins with the deliberate effort to understand the knowledge of the practitioner and the specific problems faced by the practitioner:

> We suspect that a key to forming a successful bridge between data and application is to begin with the expertise and experience of the practitioners. When this happens, we find that the most pressing needs expressed by professionals cover questions of amelioration and change that lie at the limits of the research available, including our own. In the course of addressing these concerns, we have also found it useful to use the research information at hand to identify, build upon, extend, or modify the strategies that are being employed by professionals (p. 194).

There are reciprocal effects of workshops with practitioners, benefitting the basic substance of the inquiry as well as serving to augment its practicality. Practitioners are by no means singular. The Cairns have worked at the "grassroots" level with children, parents, and teachers and at the policy level with North Carolina State agencies.

THE FAMILY AND PSYCHOPATHOLOGY

A third case study is offered by Alfred Baldwin, Clara Baldwin, and Robert Cole in their chapter on "Differential Stresses of Family

Life on Mothers and Fathers" (see Chapter 6). They report on their studies of family interaction processes as part of the University of Rochester Child and Family Study, a collaborative study of children at risk for schizophrenia involving 146 famililes.

An effort was made to study the family in interaction as a system — its "group mind" — and within that context to look for signs of the child's vulnerability to mental illness and, more broadly, at the social competence of the child. The authors give credit to Roger Barker for pioneering in the study of the effects of behavior settings upon children's behavior and for the discovery of some straightforward effects of social-system variables, for example, big schools versus little schools, availability of community settings, upon individual children's behavior.

One of the novelties of the twentieth century was a new emphasis on parenting, which demanded more time, more skill, and more resources as children took longer to grow up and more and more faced complex choices in schooling and vocational selection. Parenting became much more substantial and more vulnerable as professionals began to play their roles beside parents, supporting them in some ways and placing pressure on them in others. These professionals were to a degree rivalrous with families. Their situation made them so. Presumptive weaknesses of family function could be construed as grounds for their own sovereignty over a problem. Failures in teaching or other services to children could be attributed, argumentatively, to shortcomings at home.

At the time of the poverty programs many assumed that childhood disadvantage reflected parental deficiencies which might be remedied if parents were supplemented, or replaced, by professionals offering early care and preschool education. Many saw this need for professional supplementation as the fundamental justification for Head Start and, slightly later, for "developmental day care." The mother of the disadvantaged child was often pictured as understimulating (or, occasionally, overstimulating) the child.

These attributions to the families of the poor, followed a literature on psychopathology which for some time had made similar assumptions about the familial genesis of mental disorder. One of the unforgettable characters of that literature is the "schizophrenogenic" mother.

The University of Rochester Study

Like the Cairns, these authors built their research upon a clear-cut, existing social problem in some need of amelioration. They studied individuals over periods of time. They worked closely with professionals. Yet there were nonetheless problems in maintaining the exact intended focus of application of the study.

The diagnostic criteria for schizophrenia changed over the life of the study. Sixty of the patient parents in the study had been diagnosed as schizophrenic at the beginning of the study, but later only 18 met the researchers' restrictive criteria for schizophrenia. There was a change in official mental health nomenclature, from DSM II to DSM III, that brought with it a general tightening of psychiatric standards for diagnoses of this disorder.

But not only schizophrenia was changing. Baldwin, Baldwin, and Cole are persuaded that family configurations have been changing in American society over the 15-year life of their study. "But we believe that if we recruited the sample today we would find more families where both parents were working, more families in which the wife established a career before becoming a mother, more families in which fathers carry a real share of the homemaking and child rearing responsibility" (p. 261).

The diagnostic nomenclature for psychopathology is notoriously "soft" and subject to change, but this general kind of problem occurs elsewhere where one seeks to apply developmental psychology. The Cairns' studied adolescent violence and some forms of that violence seem to be stable across centuries of human history. But legal procedures and services for juveniles have changed. Expectations for what mothers and fathers should do change historically.

The developmental psychologist addresses a curiously shifting social reality. The truths he studies are not quite timeless. The development of the child reflects ever so slowly changing epigenetic processes set in contexts of rather rapidly changing human institutions.

What did the authors find in their studies of the interaction patterns of the families? Although there are many speculative theories about the disordered family politics of the mentally ill, the study revealed a surprisingly normal pattern of interaction between children and their patient parents in the family setting. There was a lower level of interaction involving the patient parent, as though the disorder used up energy that might have been used for social exchange. Where there were influences of disorder, their exact effect depended upon where they impinged upon the family as a system of interchange. For example, illness casts a different shadow on the family when the mother and father have it:

> We believe that two very different processes are underway in the
> mother-patient and father-patient families. In mother-patient

families the mother responds directly to her children and her husband. She is a barometer of the family; everyone's functioning improves and declines together. In the father-patient families we speculate that the mothers act to compensate for their husband's illness. Her warmth is a response to his illness and thus negatively related to his later mental health (p. 258).

But the children and the families were active in coping with the problems of parental disorders in individual ways. Some children turned toward the problem, "seemed to develop a real empathy and understanding of the parental illness." Other children distanced themselves. Still other children turned toward a special person, like a grandmother. Some families joined religious groups. The authors emphasize the fact that statistical methods simply would not have recovered large parts of the most important adaptation patterns of many of the families.

DEVELOPMENTAL PSYCHOLOGY AS A HUMAN ENTERPRISE

The chapters in this volume address the history and political traditions of developmental psychology and they are unusual in doing so. Only recently have developmental psychologists begun to actively explore the history of their field—at about the same time that an interest in public policy appeared. Developmental psychologists can well use an understanding of their unique history.

Developmental psychology confronts issues that have historical roots as old as the questions of epistemology which we conventionally think of as the philosophical ancestry of psychology. There were theories of cognitive development in the scientific literature before the coming of child study. Those theories, in turn, were preceded by several centuries of "universal histories" and developmentalisms in the philosophical literature (White, 1983a).

In the twentieth century, developmental psychology has taken shape more slowly than experimental psychology because more had to be invented. It has taken trial and error to find appropriate methods and it has taken time for developmental psychologists and their audiences to come to terms with the possibilities and limitations of those methods.

Developmental psychology will not be explained by a "philosophy of science," new or old. It is more than an exercise in pure logic or communication. It is an extension of the political/psychological tradition traced out by Cofer. Developmental psychology is a human enterprise and it will understand its powers and weaknesses in the general way in which people understand themselves: (1) by reflecting on its own activities; (2) by seeing the consequences of its actions on people and events around it; (3) by efforts to recognize the continuities and discontinuities of its history. Developmental psychology is a part of social history, and it clarifies its conditions and possibilities by a reading of that history.

Family History as the Study of Transformational Experiments

John Demos's chapter, "The Family's Changing Past: Myths, Realities, and Works-in-Progress" is a report of present-day activity in family history (see Chapter 7). Family history is a large part of the ecology in which one finds the child development addressed by child study. Demos says, "Psychology is the study of human beings and human experiences that are themselves in temporal motion. And psychology can ignore this element of motion only to its considerable peril." (p. 269).

Vygotsky has argued that the organization of human activities can only be understood through "transformational experiments"—the person confronted with an adaptive crisis and revealing his or her nature in efforts to change. Historical study reveals to the developmental psychologist that the roles and relationships among actors with which they deal have been changing over time: in Friedrich-Cofer's chapter, "Body, Mind, and Morals in the Framing of Social Policy," changing school practices toward athletics; in Scarr's chapter, "Cultural Lenses on Mothers and Children," different roles of the mother; in the Baldwin, Baldwin, and Cole chapter, "Differential Stresses of Family Life on Mothers and Fathers," shifting criteria for mental illness and shifting constellations of family patterns. Historical examination suggests what is stable and not so stable, critical and not so critical in the terms and objects with which the psychologist deals — 'child', 'mother', 'father', 'child development,' etc.

There are four principal sectors of contemporary family-historical work.

Demography.

Historians have examined quantitative indexes of family function in the past: *mean household size, age of marriage, frequency of remarriage*, etc. Such studies have eroded some myths about trends in family life — that the extended family of times past is giving way to the nuclear family; that people are marrying later than they used to. It seems important that social indicators of the past be read as accurately as possible. Real or imagined time trends are again and again declared to define contemporary social and research issues — the "loss of a sense of community," the "crisis of the family," the "disastrous decline in school achievement scores," etc.

Structural analyses.

Some family historians study power relations and allocations of roles and responsibilities among members of the family. Structural studies delineate the special situation of various social actors vis a vis one another and in so doing give important suggestions about their typical motives and needs. Histories of women's social situation have delineated the needs that have given rise to the feminist movement. Feminist history has given a picture of the gradual disenfranchising and entrapment of women from the colonial era to the present. Women lost a place in public and vocational affairs and they became entrapped in "home-making" and "polite culture."

Studies of the situation of the adolescent are similarly useful in suggesting the private and public motives that underlie the institutions of contemporary youth culture.

> To some extent, modern adolescence expressed an altered balance of social circumstance — the decline of apprenticeship, the growth of mass public education, the development of new living situations for young people exiting from their families of origin. But also there was an innerlife aspect — the growth of "identity diffusion" (in Erik Erikson's terms) in the face of ever-widening life-choices (Demos, Chapter 7, p. 278).

Emotional experience.

A form of historical writing called *psychohistory* has sought to go beyond statistics and situational indexes toward the understanding of meanings and values felt by people in the past. A well-known psychohistorical argument says that adults were normally callous and brutal toward children in the past. Facts of history point to this, it is said — the fact that children were not mentioned much in adult diaries or correspondence, the fact that two children in the same family might be given the same name, the fact that strong physical and psychological punishments were once used, the prevalence of child labor, the prevalence of infanticide, Puritan ideas that one had to break a child's will, etc. But past facts have to be looked at in context no less than present facts, and there are facts about the past that do not fit in easily with the "childhood as nightmare" hypothesis. It remains to be seen whether we can, in fact, read the normative emotional experiences of people in the past.

External relations.

The fourth kind of family history applies structural analysis to the situation of the family within the larger society. How do families relate to other social units? Demos suggests that there have been three developmental stages in the relationship of the family to the larger community in recent American history. In colonial times, the family was a commonwealth or a community, a small world unto itself. In the nineteenth century, as people increasingly left the home to find work and education, the family took its place as a refuge. In the twentieth century, the family serves as an encounter group.

Studies of family history have an important role to play in contemporary studies of childhood. There has been an "unceasing traffic between our past, our present, and our future," Demos argues.

THE PERSON AND THE POLITICAL SITUATION

Rae Carlson's chapter, "Affects, Ideology, and Scripts in Social Policy and Developmental Psychology," addresses an alternative possibility of psychology and its place in American political deliberations (see Chapter 8). Contemporary work in psychology is dominated by a normative, nomothetic approach:

> Pick up any recent directory of graduate programs in psychology, and you will find that the only course work universally required for graduate work in psychology consists of courses in experimental methods and statistical analysis. Mastery of a limited set of research methods is sanctified as the means to *any* intellectual inquiry in our field. Implicitly, we communicate indifference about (because we cannot measure) a candidate's breadth of knowledge, depth of insight, or engagement in substantive problems. Essentially, our academic socialization is that of providing our symbolic children with hammers; we should not be surprised when they go about hammering everything in sight (p. 304).

An alternative psychology has waited in the wings. It took form in the studies of personality in nature, society, and culture undertaken in the 1930s and 1940s by psychologists in the personological tradition of Henry Murray, Gordon Allport, and Kurt Lewin. The tradition can be traced forward in time to the writings of Silvan Tomkins and backward to the psychoanalytic theorizing of Freud and Jung.

What kind of psychology do we need to speak to the political process?

> Any policy-relevant formulation of individual psychology must be prepared to answer three questions: (1) What are the fundamental motivations of individuals? (2) What larger world views govern their lives? (3) How are the particularities of experience organized into some program-for-living? These questions apply equally to those who make policy and those who are served (or not served) by it (p. 289-90).

Silvan Tomkins's personology seems to be a reasonable basis for the contemporary continuation of a political/psychological tradition. Tomkins offers, not lists, but the rudiments of a system or model of human motives and schematizations of themselves. Affects, primitives and givens in human experience organize perception, interest, and cognition. From these arise an "ideo-affective posture," what most people would think of as a personal outlook or a personal set of values. The individual forms a philosophy that is a personal edition of philosophies that we have encountered before in this volume:

> The assumptions underlying humanistic and normative positions are rarely made explicit, yet they pervade our basic feelings about life. Are people basically good, or must their evil propensities be guarded against? Are values that which human beings wish, or do values exist independent of our wishes? Should people maximize satisfaction of their affects and appetites, or should they be governed by norms that in turn modulate appetites and affects? Is human weakness to be tolerated and ameliorated, or forbidden and punished? (Carlson, Chapter 8, p. 291).

The individual internalizes idealized images of society in the form of scenes or scripts and the society in turn incorporates idealized images of what the individual ought to be like. Carlson argues private ideas and social power relations flow back and forth into one another.

Biologically, men and women have a different organization of affects. Male affect is, on the positive side, specialized toward excitement and on the negative side specialized for anger and contempt/disgust. Female affect is, on the positive side, specialized for enjoyment and, on the negative, toward distress, fear, and shame.

A male-dominated conceptualization of the games and roles of society colors the way in which the participation of men and women is read. Male feelings are read as characterological. Female feelings are read as "mere" emotion and symptomatic of weaknesses of personal fiber.

> Taken together, these two phenomena—gender specialization in the socialization of affect and the failure to recognize the ubiquity of affect—have produced effects of enormous consequence in both intellectual and social life. Insofar as the masculine pattern captures qualities "officially" valued by males and females alike, the triad of excitement, anger, and contempt/disgust is fostered throughout society. Insofar as this pattern is not recognized as affective in nature, only the "feminine" affects of joy, distress, fear, and shame are considered truly "emotional" (p. 294-95).

Psychological research should help us to recognize the "ideo-affective" ideologies underlying people's responses to public issues. Developmental psychologists should try to understand the processes and conditions of affect-socialization that govern public opinion. Looking at the diverse situations of contemporary family life, it should seek to de-standardize our "standard family" set of contemporary myths and norms and stereotypes. "Rather than assuming some 'standard' portrait of family life, we need to conceptualize the different scenes and scripts that actually govern people's lives—recognizing that these are no longer contained within the family, but are very much a product of wider social forces" (p. 298). Is there now some growth of a more reasonable contemporary political/psychological tradition using the social and behavioral sciences? Carlson sees some positive trends. There is greater recognition of affect in the research literature. There is a revival of important elements of the personological tradition in contemporary writings. The social and behavioral sciences are shedding the traditional dogmas of a "value-free," physicalistic approach to human behavior. These trends are beautifully exemplified in the chapters of this volume.

REFERENCES

Beard, G. M. (1881). *American nervousness: Its causes and consequences.* New York: J. P. Putnam's & Sons.

———. (1898). *Sexual neurasthenia: Its hygiene, causes, symptoms and treatments* (5th ed.). New York: E. D. Treat.

Bremner, R. H. (Ed.). (1970-71). *Children and youth in America: A documentary history* (3 Vols.). Cambridge, MA: Harvard University Press.

Bronfenbrenner, U. (1974). The origins of alienation. *Scientific American, 231,* 53-61.

_____. (1979). *The ecology of human development: Experiments by nature and by design.* Cambridge, MA: Harvard University Press.

Cox, C. M. (1926). *Genetic studies of genius: II. The early mental traits of three hundred geniuses.* Stanford University, CA: Stanford University Press.

Dewey, J. (1972). My pedagogic creed. In *John Dewey: The early works, 1882-1895* (Vol. 5). Carbondale and Edwardsville, IL: Southern Illinois University Press, 84-95. (Originally published, 1887.)

_____. (1972). Plan of organization of the University Primary School. In *John Dewey: The early works, 1882-1895* (Vol. 5). Carbondale and Edwardsville, IL: Southern Illinois University Press, 223-43. (Originally published, 1895.)

_____. (1972). Ethical principles underlying education. In *John Dewey: The early works, 1882-1895* (Vol. 5). Carbondale and Edwardsville, IL: Southern Illinois University Press, 54-83. (Originally published, 1897.)

Edelstein, W. (1983). Cultural constraints on development and the vicissitudes of progress. In F. S. Kessell & A. W. Siegel (Eds.), *The child and other cultural inventions*, 48-81). New York: Praeger.

Ellis, H. (1926). *A study of British genius.* Boston: Houghton Mifflin.

Galton, F. (1869). *Hereditary genius: An inquiry into its laws and consequences.* London: MacMillan.

Gilbert, J. B. (1977). *Work without salvation: America's intellectuals and industrial alienation, 1880-1910.* Baltimore: The Johns Hopkins University Press.

Hall, G. S. (1904). *Adolescence: Its psychology and its relations to physiology, anthropology, sociology, sex, crime, religion, and education* (2 vols.). New York: Appleton.

_____. (1923). *Life and confessions of a psychologist.* New York: Appleton.

Hearder, H. (1966). *Europe in the nineteenth century: 1830-1880.* London: Longman.

Irvine, W. (1955). *Apes, angels, and Victorians.* New York: McGraw-Hill.

James, W. (1890). *Principles of psychology.* New York: Appleton.

_____. (1895). Degeneration and genius. [Reviews of books by Dallemagne, Lombroso, Nordau, and Hirsch.] *Psychological Review, 2,* 287-95.

_____. (1902). *Varieties of religious experience: A study in human nature.* New York: Modern Library.

Lombroso, C. (1891). Genius: A degenerative epileptoid psychosis. *Alienist and Neurologist, 12,* 356-71.

McDougall, W. (1920). *The group mind: A sketch of the principles of collective psychology with some attempt to apply them to the interpretation of national life and character* (2d ed., rev.). New York: G. P. Putnam's.

Mitchell, S. W. (1899). *Wear and tear.* Philadelphia: J. B. Lippincott.

_____. (1902). *Fat and blood: An essay on the treatment of certain forms of neurasthenia and hysteria* (8th ed.). Philadelphia: J. B. Lippincott.

Nordau, M. (1895). *Degeneration* (2d ed.). New York: Appleton.

Rogoff, B., & Lave, J. (Eds.). (1984). *Everyday cognition: Its development in social context.* Cambridge, MA: Harvard University Press.

Ross, D. G. (1972). *G. Stanley Hall: The psychologist as prophet.* Chicago: University of Chicago Press.

Ross, E. A. (1901). *Social control*. Cleveland: Case Western Reserve University Press.

Seagoe, M. V. (1975). *Terman and the gifted*. Los Altos, CA: William Kaufmann.

Siegel, A. W., & White, S. H. (1982). The child study movement: Early growth and development of the symbolized child. In H. Reese & L. P. Lipsitt (Eds.), *Advances in Child Development and Behavior* (Vol. 17). 233-85. New York: Academic Press.

Taylor, E. (1983). *William James on exceptional mental states: The 1986 Lowell lectures*. New York: Charles Scribner's Sons.

Terman, L. M. (1911). The relation of the manual arts to health. *Popular Science Monthly, 78,* 602-9.

_____ . (1926). *Genetic studies of genius: I. Mental and physical traits of a thousand gifted children*. Stanford University, CA: Stanford University Press.

Tyack, D. B. (1974). *The one best system: A history of American urban education*. Cambridge, MA: Harvard University Press.

White, S. H. (1976). Developmental psychology and Vico's concept of universal history. *Social Research, 43,* 659-71.

_____ . (1977). Social proof structures: The dialectic of method and theory in the work of psychology. In N. Datan & H. W. Reese (Eds.), *Life-span developmental psychology: Dialectical perspectives on experimental research*, 59-92. New York: Academic Press.

_____ . (1983a). The idea of development in developmental psychology. In R. M. Lerner (Ed.), *Developmental psychology: Historical and philosophical perspectives*, 55-77. Hillsdale, NJ: Lawrence Erlbaum Associates.

_____ . (1983b). Psychology as a moral science. In F. S. Kessel & A. W. Siegel (Eds.), *The child and other cultural inventions*, 1-25. New York: Praeger.

_____ . (1984a). Studies of developing mentality. [Retrospective review of Heinz Werner's *Comparative Psychology of Mental Development*] Contemporary Psychology, *29,* 199-202.

_____ . (1984b). G. Stanley Hall and the concept of development. Paper presented at Charles D. Smock Memorial Symposium: "The History of Developmental Psychology." Eighth Southeastern Conference on Human Development, Athens, Georgia.

NOTES

1. Dewey's Laboratory School at the University of Chicago, and his Progressivism, have been widely misinterpreted as another entry in a long tradition of "child-centered" approaches to education. A reading of Dewey's thinking about education, and of his design for his school, shows that he was actively concerned to try to understand what must be done during a child's growth to bring it in harmony with society and social development around it. (*cf.* Dewey, 1887/1972, 1895/1972, 1897/1972).

2. The romantic exaggerations of the late nineteenth century seem nicely illustrated by the contrast between two mythic kinds of "genius" that were

much discussed, the *genius-as-superman* and the *genius-as-degenerate*. We are most familiar with the genius-as-superman myth, because that conception has been translated forward in time to become part of the contemporary folklore of IQ testing. With his publication of *Hereditary Genius* in 1869, Francis Galton began the curious tradition of assimilating any and all kinds of human fame to "genius" and, presumably, genetic superiority. Havelock Ellis (1926) continued Galton's studies of British genius and then Lewis Terman imported the tradition in his *Genetic Studies of Genius* series, now assigning famous people retrospective IQ scores (Cox, 1926). But another tradition in the late nineteenth century said genius was a form of degeneracy and, presumably, a product of genetic decline. Cesare Lombroso (1891) diagnosed genius as a form of "degenerative epileptoid psychosis." William James in 1895 reviewed the works of four prominent advocates of the genius-as-degenerate argument and then, a year or so later, set forth his own compromise position, that genius ought to be regarded as an exceptional mental state (Taylor, 1983). A pallid form of the genius-as-superman myth persists today in the tendency to identify IQ scores with any and all forms of human "merit." A pallid form of the genius-as-degenerate myth persists today in the writings of some psychoanalysts, such as Otto Rank, who see the creative individual as someone standing midway between normalcy and neurosis.

3. Interestingly, Hall's educational program was pretty much Rousseau's program for Emile as Friedrich-Cofer describes it — first, sensory and physical education, then intellectual subjects at 12, then moral education at 15. Hall supports this argument with what seems to be a unique analysis of stages of child development and with much data. It is interesting that both Rousseau and Hall proposed to invest serious educational time in children's intellectual and moral development at ages 12-15, at pretty near the time when both Piaget and Kohlberg have argued that these systems of development are mostly over.

4. Edelstein (1983) has provided an instructive account of the different lives children lead when they grow up in a traditional versus a modern society. He describes traditional versus modern Iceland. One large difference is the fact that in traditional societies adult work is attuned to the rhythms of the year, relatively standard for men and women, obvious in its purpose, and likely to take place near where the child spends his or her days. In modern societies, adult work is varied and specialized. It is often complicated, not to be quickly grasped by the child (or any) onlooker, and it tends to be situated far away from where children are. Bronfenbrenner (1974) has argued that children's physical and psychological separation from the adult life of modern societies places the children in a situation of *alienation*.

5. Lewis M. Terman did much work on issues of school health and hygiene at the beginning of his career. The titles of his first three books were, in 1913, *The Teacher's Health: A Study in the Hygiene of an Occupation*; in 1914 (with E. B. Hoag) *Health Work in the Schools*; and, in 1914 again, *The Hygiene of the School Child* (Seagoe, 1975).

6. The British-American social psychologist, William McDougall, (1920) wrote about the willfullness and intransigence of human societies in these terms:

But it is maintained that a society, when it enjoys a long life and becomes highly organized, acquires a structure and qualities which are largely independent of the qualities of the individuals who enter into its composition and take part for a brief time in its life. It becomes an organized system of forces which has a life of its own, tendencies of its own, a power of moulding all of its component individuals, and a power of perpetuating itself as a self-identical system, subject only to slow and gradual change (p. 13).

7. In John Dewey's 1887 *Psychology*, he listed four methods of scientific psychology: the *method of introspection*; the *experimental method*; the *comparative method* [comparing the consciousness of the average human adult with "the consciousness (1) of animals, (2) of children in various stages, (3) of defective and disordered minds, (4) of mind as it appears in the various conditions of race, nationality, etc."] and the *objective method* [studying the *products* of the human mind—language, science, social and political institutions, art, and religion, as sources for interpretation of the way the mind works (Dewey, 1887/1972, pp. 11-16). Three years later, in Chapter 7 of his *Principles of Psychology*, William James stated that the three principal methods of scientific psychology were the introspective method [by which he meant the analysis of mental states being undertaken by contemporaries such as Myers, Charcot, Binet, Janet, and Freud], the experimental method, and the comparative method (James, 1890, I., pp. 185-93). There were several "laboratories" of scientific psychology at the very beginning and this diversity increased until the 1920s when a good number of "schools" of psychology offering diverse real or imagined scientific platforms could be discerned (White, 1977).

2

Human Nature and Social Policy
Charles N. Cofer

Governments at every level must and do make laws and policies concerning their citizens with respect to such matters as health, welfare, education, police protection, the competence of citizens to participate in governmental procedures, and numerous other aspects of social life. There are many kinds or forms of government, and the choice of a particular form by the populace (or some part of it) reflects assumptions about people and their natures. Once a government is established the laws it makes and the policies that guide it probably reflect the assumptions involved in its original creation. William Ellery Channing (1780-1842), a Congregational minister who was later known as "the Apostle of Unitarianism," put the matter this way: "All our inquiries in morals, religion, and politics must begin with human nature. Certain views of man are involved in all speculations about the objects of life and the proper sphere of human action. On such views all schemes of society and legislation are built" (quoted by Curti, 1953a, p. 354).

This chapter is concerned with major views of human nature that have appeared in western thought beginning with the time of the Renaissance and the Reformation. The Reformation was a period during which forms of government alternative to that provided by the church or those provided by princes and kings closely allied with the church were considered and in some cases adopted. We shall see the proposals made by writers such as Hobbes, Locke, and Milton in the seventeenth century and by Rousseau in the eighteenth. These writers made rather general and sweeping claims about human nature and recommended forms of government in accordance with their conceptions of human nature. An example of how views of human nature are reflected in governmental arrangements is provided first by quotations from the *Federalist Papers*.

The broad conceptions of human nature were rejected in the eighteenth century by Thomas Reid in Scotland and Franz Josef Gall a little later in Austria (Vienna) and France. Reid proposed, as did others, for example, Thomas Aquinas, before him, powers or faculties of the mind, and Gall had also proposed faculties the measurement of which he thought could be accomplished by observations on the shape of the skull. Reid's and Gall's faculties offered a much more detailed view of human nature than did the proposals of the early political philosophers and, in Gall's case, there was a recognition of individual differences in each of the several faculties he postulated. In one form or another, for example, as springs of action (Bentham, 1815/1969), as instincts, drives, motives and needs, values and traits, the componential conception of the human mind initiated by the schoolmen, Reid and Gall, has persisted.

All of these topics will be treated in greater or lesser detail in this chapter. In the context of the conference, the chapter also includes, where it is possible to do so, conceptions of the differences and the similarities of the sexes. As will be seen, human nature in women receives at best relatively little consideration.

HUMAN NATURE

This heading embraces many things that are common to members of the species or to some proportion of the members of the species. Conceptions of human nature do vary in several ways across religions, philosophical and political systems, and perhaps other dimensions as well. In some cases, human nature is seen as intrinsically evil, or, as Jonathan Edwards (Curti, 1980, p. 68) said, as depraved, in contrast to alternative views that opposed Edward's revivalist program and postulated rationality in human nature. Curti (1953a, p. 356) indicates that in the period "from 1750 to 1860, the varying branches of Christendom (and we might also include the scattered Jewish synagogues) emphasized in different degrees man's essential baseness and depravity on the one hand and his reason and capacity for receiving grace on the other."

Sometimes it is viewed as intrinsically social or as intrinsically egoistic. Some conceptions hold that it is given at birth and development is seen as the inexorable unfolding of characteristics potential in the genome; others postulate that the environment, especially its social aspects, is crucial to the human nature that develops. Curti (1980, p. xiv) noted that investigations of human nature have sought the influences on its development and have postulated "astrological, supernatural, biological, environmental, and social-cultural" influences. The social and behavioral sciences of this century, however, have concentrated on the last three influences.

An implication of what has just been said is that conceptions of human nature are relativistic. This is probably true in part, but there is sentiment and some evidence that there are universals of human nature. The typical human being is much like any other in gross anatomy and in the senses and the motor skills each possesses. Stature and weight occur within limited ranges of values, and everyone must eat, drink (and sometimes be merry), sleep, have shelter and clothing of some sort. Procreation is essential across the species, and provisions for care, education, and religious instruction of children, within some kind of family structure, are universal. No society is known that has no religion, and rituals for the burial of the dead are common.

It is customary in discussions of human nature from the standpoint of the behavioral sciences to treat it in terms of the motives and emotions of which, it is believed, it is comprised. Such a treatment ignores other sorts of commonalities, such as the universal development of language, thought, aspects of perception, beliefs in causality, the process of attribution of causality, and naive theories about the world and the social environment; what is meant here is that human beings all over the world and for centuries have developed these categories of commonalities; within the categories many variants may appear, for example in language.

However, it is probably the case, at least in the West, that these variations within common categories and the categories themselves have been seen as less involved in what is essential to political organization and social policy than the motivational characteristics of the human being. To put it in a literary but statistical way, it would be that the motivational side is said to account for much more of the variance than do the nonmotivational variables, some of which themselves may be strongly influenced by motivational factors (for example, social perception).

To make this point clear, it will be worth considering for a moment the collection of papers known as *the Federalist Papers* (Rossiter, 1961). These 85 papers were written by Alexander Hamilton, John Jay, and James Madison in 1787-88 as articles published (for the most part) in newspapers in New York. The purpose was to influence the citizens of that state to accept the proposed Constitution of the United States. Although the authors of the Constitution as well as of the papers were well aware of the intellectual and rational capabilities of the members of the 13 legislatures and of the populace, their development of a governmental system of checks and balances was clearly intended to provide for rational consideration and compromises on various issues rather than to allow control to pass to those seized of passion, bias, prejudice, or special and egoistic interests.

Madison wrote, "As there is a certain degree of depravity in mankind which requires a certain degree of circumspection and distrust, so there are other qualities in human nature which justify a certain portion of esteem and confidence" (Rossiter, 1961, p. 346). He also, referring to efforts to reconcile discordant opinions, comments that these efforts comprise "a history of factions, contentions, and disappointments, and may be classed among the most dark and degrading pictures which display the infirmities and depravities of the human character" (p. 231). Although sometimes instances will present "a brighter aspect," "they serve only as exceptions to admonish us of the general truth. . . ." Hamilton, writing of the president's influence on the Senate by the power of nomination, says "the assumption of universal venality in human nature is little less an error in political reasoning than the supposition of universal rectitude" (p. 458). Yet he indicates that "men, upon too many occasions, do not give their own understanding fair play; but, yielding to some untoward bias, they entangle themselves in words and confound themselves in subtleties" (p. 194). Madison put the issues this way:

> But what is government itself but the greatest of all reflections on human nature? If men were angels, no government would be necessary. If angels were to govern man, neither external nor internal controls on government would be necessary. In framing a government which is to be administered by men over men, the great difficulty lies in this: you must first enable the government to control the governed; and in the next place to control itself (p. 322).

Further, "the reason of man, like man himself, is timid and cautious when left alone and acquires firmness and confidence in proportion to the number with which it is associated" (p. 315).

Speaking of the possibility of frequent referral of constitutional questions to the public, Madison (p. 315) says that this procedure would not be wise as it would often arouse the public passions. Further, he observes, "that all the existing constitutions were formed in the midst of a danger which repressed the passions most unfriendly to order and concord" and that the people were confident of their leaders and desired "new and opposite forms, produced by a universal resentment and indignation against the ancient government. . . ." Future situations may not contain such security.

The Constitution drafted to replace the Articles of Confederation, as we all know, established the legislature, the executive, and the Supreme Court as major components of the government in such a way that no one component could gain sway. It may be remarked that this organization with its checks and balances is similar in structure to the one Freud established for the personality; the reader may wish to speculate as to which governmental components are the counterparts of Freud's Id, Ego, and Super-Ego.

The nature of human nature has interested writers of a number of disciplines, from theology and philosophy through the humanities, the social sciences, and the biological sciences. Theological conceptions were modified or sometimes rejected at the time of the Reformation, mainly by writers of political philosophy. Some relevant names are Machiavelli, Hobbes, Locke, and Rousseau, all of whom postulated a basic human nature and suggested social arrangements for its government. In reaction to the ideas of some of these writers, the Scottish philosophy of the eighteenth century proposed alternatives to sensationalism, associationism, and skepticism in the form of the common sense philosophy and the faculties or powers of the mind.

The notions just mentioned were not the products of empirical, scientific investigation and theory. Empirical science in the form of physiology and biology began to have its influence on questions of human nature in the nineteenth century, first through phrenology and then through the theory of evolution; the concept of instinct and its role in survival of organisms in the environment was soon applied to human nature. Adaptation and survival, as well as growth, have been central to concepts proposed to supplant or to coexist with instinct in the twentieth century. Relevant terms are motives, needs, values, and traits.

CONCEPTIONS OF HUMAN NATURE IN POLITICAL PHILOSOPHY

There have been recorded suggestions as to the nature of human nature for perhaps as long as the species has had writing. In this chapter, however, I shall not, with one exception, go further back than the Reformation. The exception is Thomas Aquinas, the thirteenth-century Dominican, whose philosophical and theological writings provide a synthesis of Medieval thought. Some of his views will be discussed later in the context of the faculty psychology.

Although for 300 years before the Reformation numerous sects appeared in southern France, northern Italy, Bohemia, and England, the Reformation is usually dated from Martin Luther (1483-1546), whose 95 theses were proclaimed in 1517; they dealt primarily with attacks on certain aspects of the church, that is, financial abuses, doctrinal abuses, and religious abuses. Luther's rebellion was from the start essentially a religious one. Henry VIII of England founded the

Anglican church in 1534 with himself as the head, and this was more a political than a religious reformation. The parallel in England to the continental Reformation took place in the seventeenth century, with the appearance of numerous sects.

The impact of the Reformation was profound. As Costello (1958) points out, one of the effects was on the law: " ... civil law had been weakened by the proscription of canon law, while the common law was becoming proportionately strengthened ... " (p. 137). Thus, the way was opened "for the social theorists, from Hobbes through Milton to Locke, to find an acceptable view of society as subject to law." They "formulated their theories concomitantly with events in the political world," Hobbes in 1642, Milton in 1649, and Locke in 1688, after the Glorious Revolution (p. 137). Hobbes (1588-1679) and Locke (1632-1704) employed the notion of the social contract as a basis for government. Later, Rousseau (1712-88) also wrote of the social contract. Montesquieu (1689-1755) developed ideas about the balance among components of the government that found their way into the Constitution of the United States. A few words will now be devoted to these writers, as well as to their predecessors, Machiavelli (1467-1527) and Bodin (1530-96).

Machiavelli's doctrines, according to Russell (1945, p. 493), arose from the "moral and political anarchy of fifteenth-century Italy." Machiavelli held posts in the government of Florence, a city-state (when he was not in forced retirement), and he had much experience in the vagaries of government there as well as in the affairs of France, the Holy Roman Empire, and the papacy which he visited a number of times on diplomatic missions. He also organized, in Florence, a militia as an alternative to the use of imported mercenary soldiers.

Machiavelli, like Francis Bacon (1561-1626) later in England, took an empirical and inductive approach, in Machiavelli's case to government. He was concerned with the conditions of political success and to identify them he collected instances of acts that "have proved beneficial and what kinds detrimental to the (political) actors who performed them" (Wood, 1968, p. 506). He studied history and the events with which he was personally familiar to obtain instances indicating support for "a particular proposition about the conditions of political success, and he then searched for further examples that would appear to negate the same maxim; only after careful scrutiny of the negative cases did he decide whether they were in fact negative ... " (p. 506).

Machiavelli's study of history convinced him that human beings have the same passions all over the world. He conceived the human being as essentially evil, but this fact does not preclude the possiblity of cooperative human endeavor.... Man's basic traits are the following: he is a creature of insatiable desires and limitless ambition, and his primary desire is for self-preservation; he is short-sighted, judging most commonly by the immediacy of reward rather than the remote consequences of his actions; he is imitative, tending to follow the example of authority figures; and he is inflexible, so that behavior patterns established though imitation can be changed only to a limited extent (Wood, 1968, p. 507).

Machiavelli held that the characteristics of desiring self-preservation and of short-sightedness would lead the human being to accept the manipulations of leaders and that under life-threatening conditions, "men's desire for self-preservation moves them to act cooperatively and even virtuously: they prove to be industrious, courageous, and self-denying." After the overcoming of a threat, "social virtues can be maintained by astute leadership and national social organization" (p. 507). Machiavelli held that the goal of politics "is the public utility, the security and well-being of the community rather than the moral goals imputed to politics by previous thinkers."

Some of the ill-repute in which Machiavelli has been held comes from his specification of the procedures that governors may use to control the governed. He saw these procedures as necessary in view of the situation in Italy and of human nature. His preferred form of government was the Roman Republic, and his writings on government and the citizen's militia had wide influence on such people as Bacon, Hobbes, Rousseau, Bodin, Burke, Montesquieu, and certain seventeenth-century English writers (Harrington, Neville, and Sidney) whose work was influential on the framers of the United States Constitution.

Thomas Hobbes (1588-1679), John Locke (1632-1704), and Jean Jacques Rousseau (1712-88) developed the theory of the social contract. Prior to Hobbes's discussion of the sovereign, Jean Bodin (1530-96) wrote on French law at a time when there was a movement (of which he was a part) for a code of law that would be independent of Roman law. For public law, Bodin studied the laws of prior and well-known commonwealths in order to determine the best ones. For him, the central theme in his "doctrine of the state is the need, suggested by the disorders of his time, for complete concentration and centralization of political authority" (Franklin, 1968, p. 111). He showed by examples "that in every important and enduring commonwealth all legislative and executive functions are subordinate to some single center" (p. 111), as in monarchies, or sovereign authorities. "...a sovereign authority is a group or person endowed with an intrinsic and inalienable right to exercise, or supervise the exercise of, all the powers that a government may legitimately claim" (p. 111). However, the right is restrained by natural and moral law (Höffding, 1955, p. 45).

Bodin's views of the Sovereign and Machiavelli's of the Prince identify some of the main concerns of the social contract theorists, Hobbes, Locke, and Rousseau. Hobbes wrote when the events that led to the civil war in England (1642-52) and the establishment of the commonwealth (1649-53) and the protectorate (1653-59) were taking place. For about ten years he wrote on political philosophy.

Thomas Hobbes (1588-1679) believed that people first lived in a state of nature, a state of considerable strife and insecurity. The person is incessantly active in the pursuit of various ends, all of which serve the ultimate goal of self-preservation. The state of nature is one of "endless and oppressive insecurity, a war of all against all, where nothing is anyone's with certainty, in which the notions of just and unjust can have no place, and where each literally has a right to everything" (Zagorin, 1968, p. 483). Hobbes considered that self-preservation arose from natural law and is a natural right. "Thus when reason teaches that to secure themselves men must renounce the liberty of the state of nature, the route from anarchy to the commonwealth and civilization has been pointed out" (p. 483).

From these considerations, Hobbes developed the idea of the contract or compact, in which individuals would give over to the sovereign irrevocably their powers in exchange for life and civility. They were obligated to carry out the covenant so long as the sovereign is able to protect them and so long as they are not asked to commit suicide or are not to be executed; these conditions would violate their goal of self-preservation.

John Locke (1632-1704) published his *The Two Treatises of Government* after the glorious revolution of 1688 in which James II was overthrown and William (III) and Mary (II) were awarded the crown. It had been written earlier and it expressed ideals in government and discussed the separation of powers; it was designed to justify constitutional change. Part of his treatise was directed against the divine right of kings, as held to by Robert Filmer (see Elshtain, 1981, pp. 102-8; Russell, 1945, pp. 617-23).

Locke had a conception of the state of nature, but unlike Hobbes's notions, the natural state was not one of ceaseless warfare. He postulated the natural rights to life, liberty, and property (the third was changed to pursuit of happiness in the Declaration of Independence). His state of nature had people living together by reason, or, as Russell (1945, p. 625) put it, in a "community of virtuous anarchists, who need no police or law-courts because they always obey 'reason'," that is, natural law, a law that has a divine origin. In the state of nature each man is the judge in his own cause, as he must defend his rights himself. Government is necessary to overcome this difficulty and is established by the social contract.

Locke's conception of government is a liberal one, that is, it should provide for the rights but it should not be absolute; there should be a separation of the executive, judicial, and legislative powers. The majority should rule (the majority being composed of propertied males; women and the unpropertied being excluded). It is legitimate for the government (primarily the executive) to be overthrown if, as was the case in the reign of Charles I, the executive branch fails to convene the legislature or to take account of its actions.

Locke's views were widely influential. Both Voltaire (1694-1778) and Montesquieu (1689-1755) supported them in France, and Montesquieu's development of the concept of the separation of powers was essentially written into the U.S. Constitution (cf. Madison, paper no. 51, in Rossiter, 1961).

Jean Jacques Rousseau (1712-78) conceived of a state of nature that differed from the states hypothesized by Hobbes and by Locke. For Rousseau, there were stages in the development from the original state of nature to civilization. The original state of nature, as Elshtain (1981, p. 150) puts it, involved solitary individuals forming "bonds with other solitary hominoids given the promptings of basic natural desires." These "isolated nomads . . . ,come together for brief couplings only to break apart and continue on their respective ways" (p. 152). This state develops into a "savage society" in which families in fixed abodes appear, and in which "tools, speech and clusters of residences are created, and human beings, speaking and laboring, grow more truly human and social even as they retain their ties to the original 'natural' condition" (p. 152). Elshtain emphasizes the role of the passions in this development in contrast to Locke's stress on reason.

Ultimately a compact or contract is made, in terms of which individuals put themselves under the "general will," which for Rousseau is the sovereignty of the people. This general will can not, however, rule on individual cases or issues. It exacts the same sacrifices from and provides the same advantages to all citizens. Rousseau, thus, in the social contract has preserved the individual's liberties, as he preserved the liberties of the growing child raised with things rather than through socialization, which started during adolescence.

Hobbes and Locke wrote of men, and John Milton (1608-74), their contemporary, probably reflected the views of their age (as well as that of the Scholastics) in *Paradise Lost* (Book 10, 888-95) in writing concerning Eve:

> Oh, why did God
> Creator wise, that peopled highest Heaven
> with spirits masculine, create at last
> this novelty on Earth, this fair defect
> Of Nature, and not fill the World at once
> with men as Angels, without feminine;
> Or find some other way to generate
> Mankind?

Elshtain (1981) has provided an evaluation of the treatment of women in the works of Filmer, Bodin, Machiavelli, Hobbes, Locke, and Rousseau. She indicates that both Filmer (pp. 102-8) and Bodin (pp. 101-2, note 1) model their concepts of the sovereign on the patriarchal view of the family, which, of course, devalued women and their roles. Machiavelli essentially eliminates women from consideration, especially given his emphasis on the citizen militia. As we have seen, Hobbes's sovereign becomes a ruler by contract, but rules absolutely (with some restrictions). The child is prepared in and by the family for this subjection to the ruler by either parent, but in all probability usually the father.

Locke denies that women should be subjected to a patriarchal father, but yet in nature the man is found to be abler and stronger so that woman should subject herself to him.

Elshtain (pp. 148-70) treats Rousseau, among the contract theorists, the most favorably, because she finds rough parity between the sexes in the original natural state, and, in the second state, "there is no systematic inequality lodged in social structures, no political domination or unjust privilege. Although women and children are dependent in part on men for provisions, they, too, perform necessary and equal household and agricultural works" (pp. 154-55). Yet (p. 157), in the family, the basis of "government or authority lies, in large measure, in the superior strength of the father who deploys it to protect his children and to command their obedience"; this authority is established by nature.

HUMAN FACULTIES AND POWERS

Personal experience enables people to differentiate among their activities, and they reflect these differentiations in the descriptive terms they employ to describe their experiences. Thus, we may say that we are remembering, thinking, feeling, or willing. The result is often a common sense psychology, such as that espoused by Thomas Reid in the eighteenth century. Before we deal with Reid, however, it will be useful to consider certain predecessors of his in the classification of the mental powers or faculties.

Thomas Aquinas (1225?-74), the synthesizer of Scholastic Philosophy, espoused a three-level hierarchy of the powers or faculties as is shown in Table 2-1. His levels appear to correspond to the souls postulated by Aristotle (384-322 *B.C.*). Coppleston (1950/1957, pp. 389-90) comments on Aquinas's levels as follows: " ... the rational and spiritual soul cannot be affected by a material thing or by the phantasm: there is need, therefore of ... the activity ... of the active intellect which illumines the phantasm and abstracts from it the universal or intelligible species, ... producing in the passive intellect the *species impressa*." Functioning in this hierarchy is thus across a level as well as between levels.

A different sort of classification of mental faculties is seen in Leibnitz (1646-1716), who recognized the great division of the mind into understanding and will. This classification either left affective phenomena out, as Leibnitz tended to do, or assigned them to one of the other categories. Apparently the first to postulate a distinct faculty of feeling (in addition to the other two) was Moses Mendelsohn (1729-86), the tripartite division being advanced also in 1777 by Johann

TABLE 2-1. The Hierarchy of Faculties According to Thomas Aquinas.

Level 1. Rational	*Active Intellect*		*Passive Intellect*	*The Will*	
Level 2. Sensitive	The Exterior Senses	The Interior Senses	Power of Locomotion	Appetite	
	Sight	Sensus Communis (general sense)		Concupiscence	
				Good	*Evil*
	Hearing	Phantasia (imagination)		Love	Hate
				Desire	Aversion
	Smell	Vis Aestimativa		Pleasure	Pain
	Taste	(evaluative)		(joy)	(sorrow)
	Touch	Vis Memoritiva			
				Irascibility	
				Good	*Evil*
				Hope	Fear
				Despair	Courage
					Anger
Level 3. Vegetative	Growth		Reproductive	Nutrition	

Source: Combined from Copplestone (1950/1957, pp. 377-78) and from Gardiner, Metcalf, & Beebe-Center (1937/1970, pp. 107-8).

Tetens (1736-1807) and being fully developed by Immanuel Kant (1724-1804) in the *Critique of Judgment* (1790). The *Critique of Pure Reason* (1781) was devoted to knowing and the *Critique of Practical Reason* (1788) to appetition or conation (will), feeling being discussed in the *Critique of Judgment* (cf. Gardiner, Metcalf, & Beebe-Center, 1937/1970, pp. 256-68).

Contemporaneous with Mendelsohn, Tetens, and Kant and developing a rather different set of faculties was the Scottish philosopher, Thomas Reid (1710-96). Reid's contribution included his defense of "common sense psychology" in his commentaries on Berkeley, Locke, and Hume and his espousal of the "Method" of Newton (Ellos, 1981). A similar faculty psychology was proposed by Franz Joseph Gall (1758-1828) and his student, J. G. Spurzheim (1776-1832), in conjunction with a method for assessing from the contours of the skull various abilities, passions, and characteristics of personality.

Thomas Reid (1710-96)

Murphy (1949) comments as follows:

> The tendency to simplify and mechanize mental processes led to a protest against Hobbes' mechanism, and, in particular, against Hume's indifference to the claims of the soul. The protest took shape in the Scottish universities ... where the philosophy was alert to support the claims of established religion against impending infidelity. Skepticism might be all very well as speculation, but it had moral implications, "threatening religion as the state," still closely allied.... Public opinion could not brook an attack upon the core of its [popular education in parochial schools] ethical and religious structure (p. 34).

Scottish Presbyterianism "undertook to create a new philosophy to combat skepticism" (p. 34).

Thomas Reid (for a biography, see Fraser, 1898) was born about 20 miles from Aberdeen and after some schooling at home went for two years to the neighboring parish school. Then he was sent to Aberdeen to the Grammar school, but shortly thereafter (1722) he shifted to Marischal College from which he graduated in 1726. He studied natural and moral philosophy, Greek, and mathematics. The philosophy was largely the idealism of George Berkeley (1685-1753). Following his work at the college, Reid took religious training and later worked at the library in the college, after which he was ordained as a minister of the Presbyterian church and served a parish in the vicinity of

Aberdeen for 14 years. Thereafter, in 1751 he was made a Regent Master at King's College at Aberdeen, where he spent 13 years before moving in 1764 to a professorship in moral philosophy at Glasgow, where he remained for the rest of his life.

A significant event in Reid's life, as it was also in Immanuel Kant's, was reading David Hume (1711-76) early in his pastorate. Reid read Hume's *Treatise of Human Nature* (1729) (Kant responded to Hume's later *Inquiry into Human Understanding*). The conclusions to which Hume came upset Reid's views, and he comments much later "... that in early life he believed the whole of Berkeley's system—till Hume opened his eyes to consequences that follow from the philosophy of Descartes and his successors, which gave me more uneasiness than the want of a material world" (Fraser, 1898, p. 41).

As indicated earlier, Reid's philosophy was that of common sense. Murphy (1949, p. 34) points out that Reid showed "... that we know perfectly well that we have minds, the capacity to perceive real things, to think and act rationally. Reid appealed to the practical reliability of our senses,[1] pointing for example to Newton's studies in optics as showing the right way to approach the problem of our ability to make contact with the external world." Reid likewise opposed the association psychology and insisted on our ability, even as children, to know right from wrong and our freedom to choose between them. Reid, then, built "a new system based on confidence in our intellectual powers: a system based upon common observation as against the subtlety ... of empiricists" (Murphy, 1949, p. 35).

Reid (1785/1969) conceived the mind as active: " ... the mind is from its very nature a living and active being. ... And the reason why all its modes of thinking are called its operations, is, that in all, or in most of them, it is not merely passive, as body is, but is really and properly active" (p. 6).

Reid argues that if there are operations of the mind, there must be powers to operate. As he says, the fact that one is sitting does not mean that there is no power that will enable one to walk. "Every operation therefore implies power; but the power does not imply the operation" (p. 7).

Reid observed that the words *powers* and *faculties* are often used as synonyms. However, he does distinguish faculties from some other powers by saying "that the word *faculty* is most properly applied to those powers of the mind which are original and natural." He continues, "There are other powers which are acquired by use, exercise or study, which are not called faculties but *habits*" (p. 7), for the formation of which the mind has a capacity (cf. Brooks, 1976, pp. 66-71, for a discussion of Reid's use of the word faculty).

Reid divided the actual faculties into two classes—the cognitive and the active, the latter including both will and affect; the tripartite division was not yet acknowledged (Spoerl, 1935, p. 223). However, Reid did not list the faculties he postulated systematically, and authors who have attempted to do so (cf. Brooks, 1976, Spoerl, 1935) do not come out with identical lists. In addition, there were, according to Reid, other characteristics of the mind (see the quote above). Brooks (1976, p. 74, Table 1) lists as mechanical powers instincts (breathing, balance, credulity of children, imitation, belief in causality, sucking, swallowing, and veracity) and habits (articulate language, praying, and pronunciation). He shows additional powers under the headings of Animal Powers (differentiated into appetites, desires, and benevolent and malevolent affections), Rational Powers, and Unclassified Powers. Brooks's Table 3 (p. 76) combines intellectual and active (animal) powers which are shown in separate sets in Table 2-2. Spoerl's (1935, p. 22) list for Reid shows 36 faculties, divided between the Active and Intellectual Powers. There are some differences between his and Brooks's lists, probably because Reid's own characterization of faculties is not always clear.

Reid's influence.

Reid's writings had substantial influence in France, on such people as Roger Collard and Victor Cousin in the nineteenth century (Fraser, 1898, pp. 148-54), and his importance in Scotland remained high through Dugald Stewart and Sir William Hamilton. Reid also had importance in the United States, where the Calvinistic tradition was strong and where Reid's works were employed by certain professors of moral philosophy who were either themselves native Scots or were descendents of such natives.[2] Faculties also appeared in the writings of certain Presbyterian preachers.[3]

Albrecht (1970, p. 30) has observed that "As Wolff, Kant and Herbart prepared the way for experimental psychology in Germany, Reid and the Scottish school prepared the way for it in the United States." The influence of the German philosophy increased in the late nineteenth century, but one can argue that the Scottish influence remained strong.[4] The common sense psychology may have appealed to the American temperament in its practical, no nonsense realistic aspects.

Curti (1953a) discusses the importance of the books of Thomas C. Upham (1789-1872). Upham's texts, Curti says, were widely used, beginning with *A Philosophical and Practical Treatise on the Will* (1834) and continuing with his *Elements of Moral Philosophy*. They

TABLE 2-2. Thomas Reid's Listings of the Animal or Active and Intellectual Faculties.

Intellectual Powers	Animal Powers*
Abstraction	Activity
Apprehension	Affection (confiliate)
Compounding	Attention
Consciousness	Deliberation
Feeling (touch)	Emulation
Generalizing	Esteem (desire of)
Hearing	Esteem (of wise and good)
Invention	Friendship
Judgment	Good for us (on the whole)
Memory	Gratitude
Musical ear	Hunger
Perception	Knowledge, desire for
Reasoning	Love (between sexes)
Reflection	Lust
Seeing	Moral faculty
Smelling	Pity and compassion
Suggestion	Power, desire of
Taste, sense of	Public spirit
Taste, good	Resentment, animal
	Resentment, rational
	Resolution
	Rest
	Thirst

Source: Based on Tables 5, 1, 2, and 3 in "The Faculty Psychology of Thomas Reid" by G. P. Brooks in *Journal of the History of the Behavioral Sciences, 12.* Copyright © 1976 by Clinical Psychology Publishing Co., Inc., Brand, VT. Reprinted by permission.

*Three appetites (liquor, opiates, tobacco) and four desires (equipage, estate, money, and title) appear among the animal powers in Brooks's Table 1 (p. 74) but do not appear in his Table 3.

influenced college students almost to 1890, when James's *Principles of Psychology* was published. Upham's conception of human nature was optimistic, though a highly rational one (Curti, 1953a, p. 168). However, Upham did not

> discuss the inborn traits of women or their mental capacities or the strength of their will. He did not include the women's rights crusade in the wide scope of his humanitarian interests. He may well have shared the dominant view about women's capacities. This view ascribed to them the innate capacity for morality possessed by all human beings but denied, save in exceptional cases, a natural capacity equal to that of man (p. 370).

Upham was a follower of Reid and Locke.

Phrenology

Another use of faculty psychology was made by Franz Joseph Gall (1758-1828), in conjunction with the hypothesis of the localization of the faculties in parts of the brain and with the further hypothesis that the conformations of the skull could be used to detect the strength of the faculties localized in brain regions beneath it. Gall was soon joined by Johann Gaspar Spurzheim (1776-1832), at first Gall's pupil, then collaborator and publicist.

According to several writers (for example, Krech, 1962, pp. 31-32), as a student Gall made observations in his family and his fellow students of the following sort: "Each of these individuals possessed something peculiar, a talent, an inclination, a faculty which distinguished him from others" such as "the beauty of their hand writing, their facility in arithmetic . . . " (quoted by Krech, 1962, p. 31) or their enjoyment of boisterous games. These individual differences vexed Gall, because he could not learn his lessons by heart as easily as some of his schoolmates. Observing these schoolmates later, even in medical school, Gall "discovered their secret: 'I noticed then that they all had large and protruding eyes' . . . " (quoted by Krech, 1962, p. 62). This was his recognition that bodily structure was related to capacities of the mind.

Gall's training was as an anatomist, and he and Spurzheim made contributions to this subject (Krech, 1962, p. 32). However, they were also interested in the brain's functions and, in phrenology, they postulated that various faculties in terms of which people differ reflect the functions of the several regions of the brain; further "there was a correlation between the shape of the skull and the conformations of the brain" (Krech, 1962, p. 33). Thus, by measuring the conformation of the skull one could infer which faculties of the mind were over- or underdeveloped.

Gall developed a list of faculties; they are shown in Table 2-3.[5] He called them determinate faculties. Spoerl (1935, p. 220) says that Gall "turned for assistance to the psychologists, to Condillac, Malebranche, de Tracy, Bonnet, Wolff, and others who were well known in Germany and France. . . . He found numerous faculties that were believed to be the basic powers of the mind." However, the faculties he found, like understanding, will, desire, reason, etc., were, he thought, "worthless for his purposes because they were too abstract, too generalized and not distinctive of character. . . . They were not determinate" (Spoerl, 1935, p. 220). Spoerl quotes Gall as saying that "we need faculties the

TABLE 2-3.　Gall's List of the Determinate Faculties.

1. Instinct of generation	15. Memory for languages
2. Love of offspring	16. Sense of colors
3. Friendship, Attachment	17. Music
4. Courage, Self-defense	18. Mathematics
5. Wish to destroy	19. Mechanical aptitude
6. Cunning	20. Comparative sagacity
7. Sentiment of property	21. Metaphysical depth
8. Pride, Self-esteem	22. Wit
9. Vanity, Ambition	23. Poetry
10. Cautiousness	24. Good nature
11. Educability	25. Mimicry, Imitation
12. Local memory	26. Theosophy, Religion
13. Memory for persons	27. Firmness of character
14. Verbal memory	

Note: There are a number of correspondences between this list and Reid's list (see Table 2-1). However, the 35 faculties listed in other places (for example, Boring, 1950, p. 55, Fig. 1) differ in a number of respects. This list of 35 was taken from Spurzheim. It is the list most often reproduced in textbooks that discuss phrenology.

Source: Rearranged from "Faculties *versus* Traits: Gall's solution" by H. D. Spoerl, 1935-36, *Character and Personality, 4,* 222.

different distribution of which shall determine the different species of animals, and their different proportions of which explain the difference in individuals" (p. 220).

He admitted the existence of other nondeterminate faculties, but "gave them the systematic role of *several attributes* of the true fundamental faculties" (p. 220). The classes (faculties, attributes) did not belong to the categories of knowing, feeling, and willing uniquely; rather every one belonged to all three (p. 221).

Phrenology became a major movement in England, France (where Gall lived for a good part of his life), and in the United States. Spurzheim took the United States virtually by storm in 1832 when he gave a series of lectures on phrenology, just before his death. Bakan (1966, p. 206) has distinguished two kinds of phrenologists as they developed in this country. One he calls the ortho-phrenologists, the other the vulgar phrenologists. The orthophrenologists he considers to be "genuinely scientific," the vulgar phrenologists being those "who exploited phrenology for their own profit." Early on, phrenology appealed to educated persons; later the appeal of vulgar phrenology was to a wide assortment of people. Curti (1943) discusses this phenomenon as follows:

> The vogue for phrenological "readings" among the common people can be in part explained by the prevailing social atmosphere. In a

period when the common man began to feel within him the stir of power and amibition, phrenology had much to offer him. It was not merely that he could have, from a wandering "phrenologist" or at the "parlors" of Fowler and Wells on Broadway, a reading which would set him right regarding the kind of mate that he, with his propensities, should choose; nor was it even that he might be told the vocation or business for which he was best adapted. . . . But as one of the critics of phrenology remarked, the common man seeks for something which will solve all his difficulties, something which will reveal nature's secrets and savor of a mystery or miracle. What the more esoteric mental philosophies were supposed to do for the college-bred man, phrenology claimed to do for any man (pp. 342-43).

Further,

phrenology inspired hope and courage in those depressed by the consciousness of some inability ... phrenology could tell one in which of the desirable propensities he was weak, in which of the undesirable he was overendowed; and by the deliberate cultivation of the one and the inhibition of the other he might in fact alter his endowments (p. 342).

Or as Fowler put it, "self-made or never made" (pp. 342-43).

Whatever its deficiencies, phrenology involved a major commitment to the existence and the assessment of individual differences and to the correction through training of deficiencies in certain desired characteristics and the suppression of undesired ones. Further, it made a strong link of mind to brain and it required that there be at least some localization of function within the brain. Bakan (1966) suggested that phrenology had connections to the later functional psychology (pp. 214-19) that grew up in the United States in the late nineteenth and early twentieth centuries; Spoerl (1935, pp. 225-31) links faculties, factors, and traits of personality.

In the rest of this chapter, the discussion turns to concepts in terms of which human nature can be discussed that are more recent than those treated so far and that are associated with the development of the social and behavioral sciences (and not so much with theology and philosophy) in the period since the development of the theory of evolution. A direct descendent of this theory is the concept of instinct to which attention now turns. Then, related notions that will be described are Utility, Drive, Motive and Need, Value and Trait.

INSTINCT

The reader will have noticed that the accounts of faculties, whether by Aquinas, Reid, or Gall and Spurzheim, provide taxonomies of certain human characteristics. Classification is often seen as propadeutic to the further understanding of a domain of phenomena, and the di- and trichotomous classifications of the phenomena of the mind may be seen in this light. That the two and three-way classifications yielded to the multichotomous schemes of Reid and the phrenologists indicates that finer distinctions were deemed necessary. The concept of instinct continues the differentiation of mental characteristics but in a way that brings human functions into a closer conjunction with those of the nonhuman animal and with biology than did past classifications. For further discussions of the impact of science on views of human nature, see Curti (1953b).

The word *instinct* entered the language in the period of late Middle English and was taken from the Latin *instinctus*, or instigation, impulse.[6] Until the time of Charles Darwin's *Origin of Species* (1859/1936), it and terms of similar meaning (for example, Aristotle's vegetative and sensitive souls; Aquinas's sensitive soul) were used to refer to animal behavior, as indicated by Wilm (1925, p. 40) who attributes the invention of the term instinct to the Stoics: " ... the natural promptings called instincts are purposive activities implanted in the animal by nature or by the world reason or creator for the guidance of the creature in the attainment of ends useful to it, in its own preservation or the preservation of the species, and the avoidance of the contrary." The nonhuman animal did not possess reason or rationality in these views, whereas the human being did possess it and was differentiated from the brute by it.

A major consequence of Darwin's evolutionary theory was to eliminate this discontinuity between animal and human, so that it became appropriate to seek evidence of intelligence or reason in the nonhuman animal and to look for evidence of instincts in the human.[7]

Classifying Instincts

In the latter years of the nineteenth century and into the twentieth, philosophers, biologists, sociologists, and psychologists, in writing textbooks and other sorts of publications, gave lists and classifications of instincts. It is impossible in the present space to describe all of them, but a few examples may suffice to our purposes.

George J. Romanes.

This writer, a close friend of Darwin, devoted a great part of his short life to studies of the continuity of human beings with animals. His first book was published shortly after Darwin's death in 1882. His second book included as an appendix a long paper on instinct by Darwin. Although Boring (1950, pp. 473-74) thinks that Romanes's first book, *Animal Intelligence* (1882), was his most important one, Romanes himself thought that two later books, *Mental Evolution in Animals* (1883) and *Mental Evolution in Man* (1888), were more important. Boring says that these two books suffer "because Romanes lacked a satisfactory classification of human faculties with which to work. He was thrown back upon Locke and the associationists for his terms" (p. 474). In both of the books on mental evolution, Romanes incorporated a large table as a front paper. This table shows rows numbered from 1 through 50 corresponding to 50 levels of development. In the center of this chart is a tree diagram; the trunk shows changes from simple excitability at levels 1-3 through reflex action and volition. On one side of the trunk are branches representing emotion and on the other side, branches representing intellect. Table 2-4 shows a portion of Romanes's chart, giving for levels 16 through 28 the "products" of emotional and of intellectual development, as well as the "psychological" scale defined by animal classes and the ages at which the human reaches each level in development (Romanes promised but did not provide entries to the chart for levels above 28).

William James.

James worked on his *Principles of Psychology* for a good ten years before the two volumes were published in 1890. His chapter on instinct (chapter 24) appeared in popular magazine articles in 1887, so that his thoughts on instinct followed Darwin's book by less than 30 years.

He defined instinct "as the faculty of acting in such a way as to produce certain ends, without foresight of the ends, and without previous education in the performance" (p. 383). James (pp. 404-41) lists a good many instincts and discusses each one at some length.

His list starts with instinctive acts in the young child and includes reflexes like sneezing, snoring, sobbing, vomiting, starting. He goes on to sucking, biting, chewing and grinding the teeth, licking sugar, characteristic grimaces over bitter and sweet tastes, spitting out, clasping, grasping and pointing at objects, carrying objects to the mouth, crying, smiling, holding the head erect, sitting up, standing,

TABLE 2–4. An excerpt from Romanes's Chart of Evolutionary Development.

Level	Emotional Product	Intellectual Product	Psychological Scale	Stages in Man
28	Shame, Remorse, Deceit, Ludicrous	Indefinite morality	Apes, Dogs	15 months
27	Revenge, Rage, Grief, Hate	Use tools	Monkeys, Cats, Elephants, Carnivora, Rodents	12 months
26	Cruelty, Benevolence	Understand mechanisms		10 months
25	Emulation, Pride Resentment, Aesthetic love of ornament, Terror	Recognize pictures, Dream, Recognize words	Birds	8 months
24	Sympathy	Communicate ideas	Hymenoptera	5 months
23		Recognition of persons	Reptiles, Cephalopods	4 months
22	Affection	Reason	Crustacea	14 weeks
21	Jealousy, Anger, Play	Association by similarity	Fish	12 weeks
20	Parental, Social Affect, Sex selection, Pugnacity, Industry, Curiosity	Recognize offspring, Secondary instinct	Insects and Spiders	10 weeks
19	Sexual emotions without selection	Association by contiguity	Mollusca	7 weeks
18	Surprise, Fear	Primary instincts	Larvae of insects	3 weeks
17		Memory	Echinodermata	1 week
16		Pleasure, Pain		Birth

Source: Modified from M. J. Romanes, *Mental Evolution in Man: Origins of Human Faculty,* 1888. Front paper.

locomotion, vocalization, imitation, emulation or rivalry (a very intense instinct). Others are pugnacity, anger and resentment ("... man is the most ferocious of beasts," p. 409), sympathy and hunting (including fighting and chasing). Of women, he says, that they "take offense and get angry, if anything, more easily than men, but their anger is inhibited by fear and other principles of their nature from expressing itself in blows. The hunting-instinct proper seems to be decidedly weaker in them than in men" (p. 415). There are also fear, produced in the child by noises, by strange animals and men advancing toward them, by dark places and by a variety of conditions in adults (including pathological fears), appropria-tion or acquisitiveness, constructiveness, play (differing between the sexes at least in the objects with which playing occurs), curiosity, sociability and shyness, secretiveness, cleanliness, modesty or shame, love (sexual instinct), jealousy, and parental love (stronger in women than in men). Speaking of maternal love, James says "contemning every danger, triumphing over every difficulty, outlasting all fatigue, woman's love is here invincibly superior to anything that man can show" (p. 440).

Further, James says (p. 441), "...no other mammal, not even the monkey, shows so large an array" (italicized in the original).

James was clearly influenced by evolutionary biology, by his own observations, especially of his own children, and by the adaptive significance he could accord to many of the acts he included as being instinctive. He spoke little of individual differences, except for sex differences and differences between children and adults, both for a limited set of the list of instincts. He makes passing references to variations in instinct strength in other cases but to no great systematic effect. James's selection of activities to be called instinctive came, it would seem, from his own interest in matters necessary to survival (of both the individual and the species) and to the adaptation or accommodation to environmental vicissitudes. As a proto-functional psychologist, James influenced a number of people who may be classed in that school, among them Thorndike (who had studied with him) and J. R. Angell (1908). The latter's list of instincts is shorter than James's but includes instincts James proposed, that is, fear, anger, shyness and sociability, curiosity and secretiveness, acquisitiveness, rivalry, jealousy and envy, sexual, parental love (stronger in the mother), play, imitation, and constructiveness.

E. L. Thorndike.

This psychologist wrote a three-volume *Educational Psychology*[8] the first volume of which, published in 1913, was entitled *The Original Nature of Man*. Thorndike required 165 pages to present his ideas of instincts, and in this chapter we can do no more than to give the eight major categories he found it necessary to list, together with a few examples of some of them.

1. Responses of sensitivity, attention, and gross body control.
2. Food getting, protective responses, and anger. This category includes habitation and fear, as well as anger.
3. Responses to the behavior of other humans. This includes mothering, chiefly a tendency in women, although "boys and men share more in the instinctive good will toward children

than traditional opinion would admit, though the tendencies are not so strong, and the responses are different" (p. 82).

Responses to the presence, approval and scorn of men. This category includes gregariousness, attention to other humans, and responses to approval and to scorn. The latter pair (p. 89) is a form of potent social control. Manifestations of approval and disapproval (scorn) are also important. There is the instinct of mastery, more common in the male than in the female, as well as submission to others, given certain conditions. The category includes "other social instincts," such as sex behavior, secretiveness, rivalry, cooperation, suggestability and opposition, envious and jealous behavior, greed, ownership, kindness, teasing, tormenting, and bullying.

4. Responses to the behavior of others: Imitation, general and particular.
5. Original satisfiers and annoyers. From these "grow all desires and aversions" (p. 123). Original satisfiers or instinctive likes are exemplified by the following: "To be with other human beings rather than alone, to be with familiar human beings rather than with strange ones, to move when refreshed, to rest when tired, to be 'not altogether unenclosed' when resting and at night" (p. 123). Original annoyers or instinctive aversions include "Bitter substances in the mouth, being checked in locomotion by an obstacle, being hungry, being looked at with scorn by other men, the sight and smell of 'excrementitious and putrid things, blood, pus, entrails'" (p. 123).
6. Tendencies of minor bodily movements and cerebral connections. This includes vocalization, visual exploration and manipulation, constructiveness, cleanliness, curiosity and mental control (including workmanship and the desire for excellence), play, random movements.
7. Emotions. He seems to accept McDougall's inventory (see below).
8. Tendencies to consciousness, learning, and remembering. These tendencies include the laws of use and of effect.

Thorndike (1913, pp. 205-6) offers Kirkpatrick's (1903) classification of instincts as "one of the best of this type" (p. 205). The major headings are as follows:

1. Individualistic or self-preservative instincts (feeding, fearing, fighting)
2. Parental instincts (for example, sex, courtship, self-exhibition, nest building)

3. Group or social instincts (for example, arrange selves in groups, cooperation, companionship, pride, ambition, rivalry)
4. Adaptive instincts (for example, spontaneous movement, imitation, play, curiosity)
5. Regulative instincts (moral tendency to conform to law, religious tendency to regard a higher power)
6. Miscellaneous (collect and enjoy owning objects, construct or destroy and be a power or cause, express mental states to others and take pleasure in doing so, to adorn oneself, make beautiful things, and have pleasure in contemplating such things)

It must be obvious from the examples given for several of Thorndike's categories that he attributed a great deal of human behaivor to instincts. Such an attribution, of course, has implications for the control or modification of the instinctively given behaviors.

William McDougall

Although Thorndike (1913, pp. 310-11) observed that "there is a warfare of man's ideals with his original tendencies," he also said that "his ideals themselves came at some time from original yearnings in some man." Thorndike did not stress the evil character in human nature, and James did not stress it either. In William McDougall's (1908/1950) *Social Psychology*, however, human nature was seen as an original collection of asocial and amoral instincts, impulses that were so powerful as to make their "moralization" a prime problem for social psychology.

McDougall postulated a number of instincts and with most but not all of them he identified an associated emotion. These instincts are, in his view, the prime movers of conduct as the following quotations from the *Social Psychology* show:[9]

An instinct is an inherited or innate disposition which determines its possessor to perceive, and pay attention to objects of a certain class, to experience an emotional excitement of a particular quality upon perceiving such an object, and to act in regard to it in a particular manner, or, at least, to experience an impulse to such action (p. 25).

Further (p. 38),

directly or indirectly the instincts are the prime movers of all human activity; by the conative or impulsive force of some instinct (or of some habit derived from an instinct), every train of thought, however cold and passionless it may seem, is borne along to its end, and every bodily activity is initiated and sustained. The instinctive impulses determine the ends of all activities and supply the driving power by which all mental activities are sustained; and all the complex intellectual apparatus of the most highly developed mind is but a means toward the ends, is but the instrument by which these impulses seek their satisfactions, while pleasure and pain do but serve to guide them in their choice of the means.

Take away these instinctive dispositions with their powerful impulses, and the organism would become incapable of activity of any kind, it would lie inert and motionless like a wonderful clockwork whose main spring had been removed or a steam-engine whose fires had been drawn. These impulses are the mental forces that maintain and shape all the life of individuals and societies, and in them we are confronted with the central mystery of life and mind and will.

In 1908, McDougall proposed seven instincts, each with an associated emotion, and four instincts without corresponding emotions. The first seven were instinct of flight (fear), instinct of repulsion (disgust), instinct of curiosity (wonder), instinct of pugnacity (anger), instinct of self-abasement or subjection (subjection, or negative self-feeling), instinct of self-assertion or self-display (elation or positive self-feeling), and the parental instinct (the tender emotion), originally primarily maternal but partially transmitted to the male. The instinct of reproduction, the gregarious instinct, that of acquisition, and that of construction complete the list. (There are also minor instincts, such as those that prompt crawling and walking.)

Given this set of impulses as the basis of human nature and conduct, McDougall had to raise the question, "How can we account for the fact that men so moved ever come to act as they ought, morally and reasonably?" (1908/1950, p. 9). McDougall's answer to his own question was an hierarchical organization of sentiments. "A sentiment is an organized system of emotional dispositions centered about the idea of some object" (p. 137). Further, it is through "the systematic organization of the emotional dispositions in sentiments that the volitional control of the immediate promptings of the emotions is made possible" (pp. 137-38). For control, McDougall relied most heavily on the sentiment of self-regard, a sentiment part of whose emotional base includes the emotions of subjection and elation (see above), and control is achieved by the fact that the evaluations of oneself by other people, or by society, can evoke these emotions in conjunction with one's acts, relations to child, wife, etc., and the like. Put another way, the overt expression of some egoistic impulse would run afoul of negative social evaluation (arousing negative self-feeling); expression of care or concern for others, the nation, and the like would elicit social evaluations that might arouse elation or the positive self-feeling. McDougall wished to deny a simple explanation in terms of pleasure and pain, and he evidently thought that positive and negative self-feelings were not simple pleasure and pains.

Freud.

Psychoanalysis has, as Rapaport (1959, p. 137) has commented, been applied to normal and pathological behavior, to anthropology and prehistory, literature, art, mythology, folklore, legend, language, religion, history, and society. Psychoanalysis has not only "... asserted an all-inclusive applicability to the study of man" but it has also "... acted to make this claim good." It has proposed an important view of human nature, one that has underlain its wide applicability and justifies a claim, made by some, to be the most complete theory of human motivation yet proposed.

Freud was trained in neuroanatomy and neurophysiology, under one of the great physiologists of the nineteenth century, Ernst Brücke. The theory of evolution was important to both of them. In addition, Brücke was an adherent of the "Helmholtz school" in physiology which held "that the laws of science were universally applicable and that physical and chemical explanations could be found for physiological events" (Cofer & Appley, 1964, p. 591). The reflex was a central physiological construct, and Freud made use of it, especially in his early work.

Freud was a determinist, and he postulated instincts. He did not trouble himself with a list of instincts but confined himself early on to the sexual instinct but later, after deciding that there are death instincts, including it in the life instincts or Eros, the polar opposite so to speak of the death instincts or Thanatos, as they were sometimes called.

Freud, like McDougall, saw the instinct as a source of energy, in his case a "psychic energy" called libido which somehow arose from bodily processes. The energy was an irritant, producing internal stimuli. "The nervous system is an apparatus having the function of abolishing stimuli which reach it, or of reducing excitation to the lowest possible level, an apparatus which would even, if this were feasible, maintain itself in an altogether unstimulated condition" (Freud, 1915/1949, p. 63). External stimuli can be removed by reflex movements away from them; this cannot be done for internal or instinctual stimuli.

It is important to characterize Freud's concept of an instinct. He thought of an instinct as having as its aim the discharge of tension or energy, a process that gave pleasure, and one may say that in their natural state the instincts obey the pleasure principle. The internal energy was described as arising in one of the (hypothetical) three parts of the personality, the Id, the unconscious reservoir of libidinal energy, "A chaos, a cauldron of seething excitement . . ." (Freud, 1933, p. 104), knowing no morality, no logic, and seeking immediate discharge. In addition to its aim, the instinct had also a source (somewhere in the body), a force or impetus, that is, a degree of intensity related to the strength of the underlying need, and an object, a person or thing, either internal or external, that would enable the aim to be reached.

Source, impetus, and ultimate aim were fairly constant components of the instinct, but object and manner of behavioral expression could vary. Thus, the libido expressed itself in a standard or universal sequence of erotogenic zones or structures—the oral, anal, and phallic zones reflected in such activities as sucking, expulsion or retention of feces, and masturbation.

The Id was conceived as having poor contact with reality and as having little capability for dealing with the environment. This would have been all right so long as there were means of giving the Id its immediate satisfactions. But, as Fenichel (1945, p. 34) observed, without frustration of Id impulses no sense of reality would ever develop. Given that frustration in infancy is inevitable, the individual must deal with reality, and Freud proposed another component of the personality, the Ego, to deal with it. The Ego obeyed the "reality principle" and was charged with arranging for the Id to gain satisfaction directly or indirectly. The Ego had to avoid the censure and punishment that would accompany the direct expression of the narcissistic Id, and also it had to respect the Super-Ego, the third component of the personality, which represents the prohibitions and punishments coming from the parents; it also contains the Ego-Ideal.

The Ego is essentially a mediator among the demands of the Id, the constraints of reality, and the restrictions of the Super-Ego. The Ego, Freud said, is the seat of anxiety arising from the tensions of the Id. The Ego must reduce these tensions and does so through the mechanisms of defense. The mechanisms are designed (by the Ego) to allow some expression of instinctual energy in a form that will disguise the nature of the expression so that reality and the Super-Ego will not know what is going on.

The death or destructive instincts were never so completely specified as were the life instincts, but they were postulated because of the cruelty and destruction of the First World War and evidence that painful memories (for example, traumatic dreams of war veterans) occurred in defiance of Freud's theory of dreams as wish fulfillments. The reliving of painful experiences Freud called the repetition compulsion, a most important factor in his later understanding of neurosis. The aggressive-destructive (death) forces are usually present in all stages of libidinal development (for example, in sadistic and masochistic behaviors).

Male and female children developed through the oral and anal stages in more or less the same way. However, in the phallic phase (between the ages of about four and five), the course of development is different for the sexes. For the boy, Freud saw the Oedipus complex and the castration anxiety as critical. The Oedipus complex means that the little boy develops a sexual-like attraction to his mother. This puts him in competition with the father and brings out a desire to eliminate the father. The girl has opposite tendencies, desiring the father and wishing to displace the mother. The boy, however, realizes that his father is bigger and more powerful than he is. Further, he has perhaps observed (or imagined) the genital differences between him and girls. He assumes that the girl once had a penis but lost it. This, plus any direct threats to the penis made because of his autoerotic manipulation of the organ, arouses the fear of losing it, the castration anxiety. Freud says that the Oedipus complex in the boy is shattered by the castration anxiety; repression of his libidinous impulses and of memory of the infantile experiences occurs, and the boy enters the latency period, a period of relative asexuality, enduring until puberty when infantile sexuality is again aroused and must be worked through before the boy enters the mature genital stage of adulthood.

In the little girl, the events are said to be different in the phallic period. She rejects the mother and desires the father, in part because she believes that she has been deprived of her penis, desires another one (penis envy), holds her mother responsible for her loss, and places her affection on the father because he has the organ she wishes to share. The Oedipus complex is not as thoroughly resolved in the girl as it is in the boy because, not having a penis, she cannot go through castration anxiety. Real life factors prevent her from achieving her desires with the father.

It is clear that Freud's account of the Oedipus complex and of its dissolution was male-oriented, and this was a major point of dispute in the work of some female analysts, especially, early on, Karen Horney (1939).

Freud differs from the other instinct theorists discussed earlier (with perhaps the exception of McDougall). The earlier writers provided a catalog of instincts, of tendencies that may well have derived from considerations of individual or species survival. There is little in them that suggests an hierarchical arrangement or a dynamic organization of the instincts. In Freud, we have only two major instincts (though perhaps a number of sub-instincts could be found in each class), but we have a major dynamic role for these instincts and their derivatives. In Freud, we also have a control organization (the Ego and the Super-Ego, and anxiety and shame) monitoring instinctual impulses and modifying their expression. McDougall also had a dynamic system, organized in the structure of the sentiments, his control apparatus. It would be interesting to speculate as to why Freud, much more than McDougall, had such widespread influence.

The Inherent Moral Sense

In the seventeenth century, as we have seen, Thomas Hobbes emphasized egoistic motives in human nature that would cause conflict and war among the people of a nation, unless they gave over their autonomy to a sovereign who would maintain order and protect them from each other. Freud and McDougall, it will be remembered, erected control procedures in the personality to provide for mobility and to control selfish and aggressive behavior. However, some instinct theorists have provided for an innate moral sense, some of them in criticism of Hobbes.

In this connection one can mention N. Malebranche (1638-1715), who (Drever, 1917, p. 28) classified natural tendencies and emotions into three groups, "the inclination to good in general," including curiosity or the inclination to novelty; "the inclinations toward particular goods," having to do with self-preservation and our welfare; and "inclinations toward particular goods," relative to the welfare of others, that is, "the social tendencies."

Francis Hutcheson (1694-1747) followed and systematized the ideas of Anthony A. C. Shaftesbury (1671-1713). According to Höffding (1894/1900/1955), Hutcheson found in human nature "besides the egoistic instincts, an involuntary desire to help and please others; while, on the other hand, he finds an equally immediate feeling of joy and approval at actions springing from this desire to help and give pleasure" (p. 396). "The moral sense does not come from experience, nor from education, habit, or association of ideas. . . . He believes it to have been originally conveyed by God . . ." (p. 397). Hutcheson also maintained the principle that the best action is the one that "produces the greatest happiness for the greatest number" (p. 397).

These views as to the instinctive basis for the moral sense may anticipate later conceptions of human nature as good, except when it is tainted by the frustrations arising from society's demand for conformity.

The Anti-Instinct Movement

During the second decade of the twentieth century, the postulation of instincts underlying human conduct was rife, and predictable counter-reaction set in, Dunlap's (1919) paper, "Are There Any Instincts?" being perhaps the most forceful statement of the issue. Bernard (1924), a sociologist, brought the anti-instinct reaction to a peak. His effort took two forms. First, he argued that attitudes toward instinct reflect other commitments and that instincts are often very poorly defined. Second, with the help of others, he prepared a 300-page typed list of acts designated as instinctive by one author or another. The large number of behaviors called instinctive without clear justification brought disrepute to the term.

To deal with the first point, Bernard can be quoted to indicate his views (1924, pp. 32-33).

> Often, like their opponents, the biological determinists use the same argument to justify decidedly contradictory policies. For example, one group of instinctivists maintains that the "maternity instinct" and the "instinct of monogamy" demand that woman give up her attempt to get out into the world and sever her ties with the traditional home (Whetham & Whetham, 1912). While another group maintains that the dominant role of the "reproductive instinct" and the "male polygamous instinct" rebels against the restraints upon sex freedom, to which mischievous, artifical modern religion, science and morals have subjected us [Nietzsche, 1968, and Russell, 1917]

Further, Bernard says (p. 33),

> one cannot avoid observing that a conscious ideal or principle or convention has justified the social or individual "necessity" of monogamy, or of freedom of sexual relationships, or of any other "ism" before instinct is invoked in its support, although in some cases ... the principle may be formulated in response to the demand of appetite or of instinctive impulse.

Bernard did not deny the existence of instincts (see p. 84 for his definition); what he objected to was the promiscuous application of the term to almost anything. As he said, if his list of supposed instincts were complete enough it would "show that about every activity, either learned or determined by heredity, which has impressed someone as important has at some time or other been called an instinct" (pp. 174-75).

He attempted to document this point (the second form of his effort) by examining the writings of several hundred contemporary authors in the social and applied sciences, most of whose works were published after 1900. These materials were selected "at random" by the author from his readings and by a number of friends from their readings. In addition, over 300 volumes were searched for instincts by "competent assistants."

Bernard's book lists various classifications of the instincts so recorded. He speaks of general groups of instincts, 2,539 in number, but no specific instincts are included here, and these "instincts" seem to be adjectival modifiers of the word instinct(s), such as morbid, avaricious, altruistic, aggressive, brutish, dangerous, healthy, strong, etc. The second class is composed of 5,684 specific instincts classified into 22 categories. Table 2-5 shows these 22 categories plus a miscellaneous category, each of which is composed of several subclasses, is cited by some number of authors in some number of books, and contains some number of specific instincts (cases).

There are two other categories of instincts. One, numbering 2,238, includes the "indefinite and peculiar instincts" which, like the first category, qualify the word instinct(s) by such terms as inherited, crude, primitive, general, etc. A final class, including 3,585 cases, is that of "instinctive attitudes." This category includes the terms "instinctive" and "instinctively" used to modify some other word or phrase. Although Bernard reports a total for all four of his categories of 14,046 instincts, the looseness of the first, third, and fourth classes probably means that he actually found 5,684 specific instincts. This is still a large number.

Whatever the merits of Bernard's procedures and classifications, the book probably had an important function in showing the bankruptcy of the word. By the end of the decade, the term instinct had almost dropped out of the psychological vocabulary.[10]

Ethology

The term instinct and interest in biological factors in behavior has had a revival since the late 1950s and early 1960s. One source of this revival was the use of instinct in conjunction with animal behavior by the ethologists. Except for the adoption by some of them of an hydraulic model of instinct and except for some dubious extensions to human behavior, the ethologists have defined instinctive acts narrowly and with some precision. However, their extensions to human behavior

TABLE 2-5. Summary of the Classifications of Specific Instincts.

Type	Classes (N)	Authors (N)	Books (N)	Cases (N)
Aesthetic	51	50	51	152
Altruistic	44	49	56	119
Anti-social	100	69	75	185
Disgust or Repulsion	39	21	21	74
Economic	60	69	78	281
Ethical	27	35	36	48
Family	83	82	91	413
Fear and Flight	86	52	55	287
Food	64	59	65	228
Gregarious or Social	149	150	172	697
Intellectual	106	80	86	262
Imitative	16	32	34	91
Migratory and Climatic	31	28	29	64
Play	44	57	61	168
Recessive and Repose	26	19	19	36
Religious	30	34	36	83
Retaliative	41	45	47	96
Self-Abasement	53	47	50	139
Self-Assertive	170	140	161	806
Self-Display	37	33	34	107
Sex	130	126	147	853
Workmanship	63	81	89	266
Miscellaneous	144	66	66	229
Totals	1,594	323	388	5,684

Source: Reproduced from *Instinct: A Study in Social Psychology* (p. 217) by L. L. Bernard, 1924, New York: Holt.

may imply that certain social policies should be followed. Thus, in connection with aggression, Lorenz (1963/1966) has suggested that it would be desirable to provide outlets for aggression such as sports and aggression in TV shows and the like in order to drain off accumulated aggressive energy. He sees this as especially important to the prevention of war which, if fought from a distance (for example, from the air with bombs, long-distance ballistic missiles, etc.), does not provide at first hand gestures of defeat and submission on the part of the vanquished enemy which prevent fatal results in the fights between nonhuman animals.

DRIVE

One consequence of the revolt against instinct was the adoption of the word *drive*, which Woodworth (1918) introduced to the technical vocabulary. Drive, according to Peters (1953, pp. 665-66), was "the objectively testable component of McDougall's more metaphysical concept of 'instinct'. . . ." Drive was clearly a biologically or even physiologically rooted notion, the major examples of which were hunger and thirst (and sex to some extent). Efforts were made to formulate acquired, learned, or secondary drives, based on primary drives like these, but these efforts were not successful. The concept of drive has encountered a number of difficulties and it is no longer appropriate to deal with it further (see Cofer & Appley, 1964, pp. 816-21).[11]

UTILITY

The utilitarians occupy an important place in the history of British philosophy, and they, like their predecessors, held to the doctrine that conduct is and should be devoted to the attainment of pleasure or happiness and the avoidance or termination of pain.

Jeremy Bentham, according to Höffding (1894/1900/1955), questioned the doctrine of the "theory of natural right which assumes an original contract" (as with a sovereign, as Hobbes said); Bentham saw no historical evidence that such a contract was made. Also, he was concerned that

> even if we allow the existence of an original contract, there remains
> the further question as to why men are bound to fulfill contracts or
> promises in general. The only possible answer . . ., in his opinion, is
> as follows: it is to the advantage of society that contracts should be
> observed, hence every individual man must keep his promise; if he
> fail to do so he must be punished, for the suffering which the punish-
> ment will cause him will be outweighted by the good which the
> keeping of promises procures to the society as a whole . . . thus the
> theory of natural right is replaced by the theory of utility (p. 365).

Among other questions, Bentham asked what the motives are which determine the actions of people. Bentham provided an answer to this question in his (1815/1969) table of the springs of action, some of which is shown in Table 2-6.

There are 14 classes of these springs, each with its derivation and its corresponding interest(s) shown, together with the specific motives of the class categorized as neutral, eulogistic, or dyslogistic. Twelve of the classes are called both pleasures and pain, two (12 and 13) are called pains only.

The several categories and their corresponding interests not shown in Table 2-6 are as follows.

TABLE 2-6. Some Examples from Bentham's (1815) *Table of the Springs of Actions*.

		Motives	
	Neutral	Eulogistic	Dyslogistic
1. Of the Taste—the palate—the alimentary canal—of intoxication Interests: of the palate, of the bottle	1. Hunger 2. Need of food 3. Thirst	*Proper:* None *Improper:* Love of pleasure of the social board, of the social bowl	1. Gluttony 2. Voracity 3. Liquorishness 4. Sottishness
2. Of the Sexual Appetite: Sexual interest	1. Sexual desire	None	1. Venery 2. Lust 3. Lechery 8. Salacity 10. Venereal desire
6. Of Curiosity Interest: Of the spying glass	1. Curiosity 3. Love of Novelty 4. Love of experiment	1. Love for knowledge 2. Laudable curiosity	1. Inquisitiveness 2. Pryingness 3. Meddlesomeness
14. Of the Self-Regarding Class The self-regarding interest	1. Personal interest 2. Self-regarding interest	None except for prudence, foresight, circumspection vigilance from Class XIII	1. Self-interest 2. Selfishness

Source: Jeremy Bentham, *A Table of the Springs of Action,* 1815/1969.

3. Of the senses: sensual interest.
4. Of wealth: pleasures of possession-acquisition-affluence-opulence; pains of privation-loss-poverty-indigence. Pecuniary interest, interest of the purse.
5. Of power, influence, authority, dominance, governance, etc.: interest of the sceptre.
7. Of amity, viz., pleasures from the good-will and thence from the free services of this or that individual. Pains derivable from loss of these: interest of the closet.
8. Of moral or popular sanction. Pleasures of good reputation, pain of bad reputation: interest of the trumpet.
9. Of the religious sanction: interest of the altar.
10. Of sympathy: interest of the heart.

It was commented in the section on the political philosophers that they paid little or no attention to women and that Milton's characterization of Eve as "this fair defect of nature" may well have epitomized their views of people of the female gender. Concerning faculties and powers, we found no comments concerning women, though Gall's recognition of individual differences could have been a significant opening for comparisons of the genders. The instinct movement, at least in the lists provided by James, Thorndike, and Freud, recognized differences between the sexes. To James and Thorndike women showed less aggression than men but more parental feeling. Freud traced sex differences to the different familial experiences of boys and girls with respect to the Oedipus and castration complexes; he considered that women manifested "penis envy" and did not achieve as complete a resolution of the Oedipus complex as did the normal boy.

MOTIVES AND NEEDS, VALUES AND TRAITS

Instincts and drives are concepts whose origins lie in biology and physiology. Both concepts survive in studies of animal behavior (sometimes with application to humans) and in studies of the neurochemical processes that underlie such activities as eating, drinking, sexual behavior, the reactions to pain, and, in general, those involved in the survival of the individual or the species.

The taxonomic approach to the characteristics of human nature has continued but in ways different from those of the political philosophers, the faculty psychologists, the instinct theorists, and drive theory. The concepts of motive and need retain some of the impulsive character of instincts and drives, but their biological origins are not specified and the motives or needs postulated are much less general than those offered in political philosophy. Only a few motives have been studied, and the effort has been to examine these motives empirically, even experimentally, in contrast to the essentially introspective and crude observational bases employed by the faculty psychologists and, from about 1890 to about 1920, by the instinct theorists.

Values and traits are notions that are sometimes used entirely descriptively, but sometimes they are given motivational or dynamic significance. This is especially true for values which, in the context of human nature, take on that meaning of the word that Smith (1968, pp. 328-29) says focuses "on the person and his dispositions," rather than on "properties of the objects of choice...." Values may also be predicated on a culture.

The trait concept is employed in an effort to epitomize the consistent patterns of behavior shown by individuals in a culture. In studying traits, investigators have examined all the adjectival and other descriptive terms in the language in order to define the universe of trait descriptive terms. Somewhat similar efforts have occasionally been made in the case of value terms.

Motives and Needs

The words *motive* and *need* have closely similar meanings. However, the word need was used by Henry Murray (1938) because he thought that drive referred more to behavior than did need. Maslow (1954) also used the word need because he conceived that need deprivation would have effects on mental health similar to those of vitamin or protein deficiencies on bodily health. Maslow thought of the needs he listed as instinctoid and as being arranged in a hierarchy. At the top was the supreme need, that of self-actualization. In order below it were esteem, love, belongingness, safety, and physiological needs. Maslow argued that higher needs would not emerge unless lower needs are satisfied. Maslow (1954, Chap. 10) denied that aggression is instinctoid, later (1959) admitting uncertainty on this point.

Murray (1938) and his collaborators proposed 20 needs (listed in Table 2-7) for the study of personality (called personology by Murray). The Thematic Apperception Test (TAT) was developed as one way of measuring needs (Morgan & Murray, 1935). In this procedure, a person is asked to write or tell a story in response to each of 20 pictures that show somewhat ambiguous situations. Murray's list of needs owes much to McDougall and Freud (Murray, 1938, p. 24). Three of the 20 needs he proposed have received extensive experimental attention—achievement, affiliation, and power.

TABLE 2-7.   List of Murray's Proposed Needs.

Need Term	Descriptors
Abasement	Submit, surrender, accept injury, blame, fail, confess
Achievement	Overcome obstacles, attain a high standard
Affiliation	Be near and cooperate with other; loyalty to a friend
Aggression	Fight, revenge, attack, injure, kill; oppose forcefully
Autonomy	Get free, resist coercion, independent, free, unattached
Counteraction	Make up for failure by trying again
Deference	Admire, support, yield to superior, praise, emulate superior
Defendance	Defend against assault, criticism, blame
Dominance	Direct and control others' behavior
Exhibition	Make an impression
Harmavoidance	Avoid pain, escape danger, take precautions; fear of pain
Infavoidance	Avoid humiliation, embarrassment, scorn of others
(Inviolacy)	(A combination of infavoidance, defendance, and counteraction)
Nurturance	Satisfy needs for love, protection, aid in succorant other
Order	Put things in order, arrange, organize; cleanliness, tidiness
Play	Free time in amusement, playful attitude
Rejection	Separate self from other; jilt, snub other
(Seclusion)	(The opposite of Exhibition)
Sentience	Seek and enjoy sensuous impressions
Sex	Form and further an erotic relationship, sexual intercourse
Succorance	Plead for love, protection, aid
(Superiority)	(A composite of Achievement and Recognition)
Understanding	Ask general questions, interest in theory

Note: Each term should be prefaced by the letter N; for example, N Abasement.
Source: Modified from H. A. Murray, *Explorations in Personality*, 1938, pp. 144-45 and 151-226.

Achievement, affiliation, and power.[12]

These three needs proposed by Murray have been studied by David McClelland, John Atkinson, and their associates. They did four things. First, they modified the TAT by selecting pictures that might elicit themes relevant to the needs. Second, the respondent was to tell a story about each picture that answered several questions. Third, they developed a scoring system for each need, analyzing the stories into motivational elements and retaining for the scoring system those elements that changed under conditions designed to arouse a need (see below) but that did not change under nonarousal conditions. Fourth, they have shown differences between groups of individuals scoring high on a need and those scoring low in other experimental and social situations. They have also compared groups within a society and national groups that differ in need scores, especially those for achievement and for power.

The arousal condition for achievement, defined as competition with a standard of excellence, was accomplished by giving male students tests that, the students were told, measure intelligence and leadership ability (McClelland, Atkinson, Clark, & Lowell, 1953). Affiliation was aroused (Shipley & Veroff, 1952) by administering a sociometric procedure in a fraternity. Power was presumably aroused in student candidates for elective office while they were waiting for the election results (Veroff, 1957), and by other procedures (Winter, 1973). In all of these experiments suitable control (nonarousal) groups were used for comparison purposes.

It is not entirely clear why achievement, affiliation, and power were selected for study. Much of the work was initially carried out at Wesleyan University, then an all-male, primarily undergraduate institution, and it is the case that the first experiments on each of the motives were carried out with male subjects even at coeducational universities. It could be argued that at Wesleyan there was no choice, and that males were used when there was a choice to keep the factor of gender constant. Wesleyan students were probably destined, in the majority, for entrepreneurial careers in business; this fact may explain the choice of the achievement motive as the first to be explored with the TAT measure. Affiliation was an outgrowth of some work on insecurity (Shipley & Veroff, 1958, p. 349). Power was highlighted in Adlerian and Sullivanian formulations (Veroff, 1957, p. 2). Other motives were studied, but these three have received the greatest amount of attention.

Research on the relation of need achievement to other behavior in other situations has suggested two things: One is that the original TAT achievement score included fear of failure as well as the motive for success. Later work has "corrected" the achievement score by considering a score on the Test Anxiety Scale (Mandler & Sarason, 1952). This results in a motive for success and one to avoid failure, rather than a single achievement score (Atkinson, 1957; Atkinson and Litwin, 1960). In addition, performance in tasks is determined not only by the algebraic summation of the two motive scores but also by the perceived incentive value of success and of failure (negative), given the subjective estimates of the probabilities of success or failure.

Early experiments (Field, 1951; Veroff, Wilcox, & Atkinson, 1953) were carried out to replicate the findings in women that had been obtained for achievement scores in aroused men and nonaroused men. The arousal and control conditions did not differ in achievement scores; the scores were high. As Maccoby and Jacklin (1974, p. 138) say, these results "certainly do not indicate a generally low level of achievement motivation in girls...." Stewart and Chester (1982) agree. However, Friedrich (1976) developed a women's role achievement scale, and Field (1951) had shown that aroused and nonaroused groups of women differ on the McClelland achievement score when the former group writes stories under the threat of social rejection.

Horner (1974) suggested that college women have a fear of success as indicated by the content of stories they wrote to the cue, "After first term finals Anne (John) finds herself (himself) at the top of her (his) med school class" (p. 101), in contrast to those men wrote (with the male name and pronouns inserted). However, subsequent tests have not replicated Horner's findings (Stewart & Chester, 1982, p. 66). Horner then developed a TAT measure of fear of success (cf. Fleming, 1982), but Zuckerman and Wheeler (1975) registered objections to an early version of this measure.

Sex differences do not appear in the measure of the affiliation motive (Stewart & Chester, 1982, p. 196). As far as the power motive is concerned, men and women respond alike to arousal conditions, but there are sex differences between men and women with high-need power. For example, men more than women express the motive in consumption of alcohol, and there are a number of other differences between men and women with high needs for power.

The long-term stability of TAT achievement scores and characteristics has been reported in several papers. Kagan and Moss (1959) found a modest correlation (a phi of 0.32) between the scores for children at median ages of eight years and nine months and of eleven years and six months. Moss and Kagan (1961) compared TAT achievement scores obtained at age 14 with interview estimates of achievement behavior when the children had reached adulthood. The correlation for females was 0.44; correlations with the adult TAT were 0.52 for females and 0.37 for males.

McClelland (1965a) obtained data on occupational roles of 58 former Wesleyan students tested with the TAT 10 or 14 years earlier. Dichotomizing the TAT scores as above or below the median, he found that 10 of the 12 "business entrepreneurs" were in the high group as compared to only 3 of 14 nonentrepreneurs.

McClelland (1961, 1965b) has studied cross-national differences in economic achievement arising in societies with achievement scores estimated from stories, children's readers, and artistic objects. The correlations are often significant but low.

Much of the work with TAT scores is troubled by evidence of low conventional reliability of the scores and by uncontrolled factors such as story length and IQ (Entwisle, 1972).

Aggression.

Many of the lists of instincts, Bentham's list of the springs of action, and Murray's list of needs include a reference to aggression, presumably an innate factor. Other points of view, however, seem to take aggression as reactive, as a consequence of frustration, pain, attacks on one, exposure to various models, crowding, noise, heat, as a way of gaining goals or other rewards, etc.

We cannot, in this chapter, review all of the work on aggression, and about all that can be said is as follows: Aggression is a virtually ubiquitous feature of human and nonhuman animal behavior, although there are a number of negative instances. There seem to be sex differences in aggression, with boys and men expressing aggression more directly, overtly, and more frequently than do girls and women. Maccoby and Jacklin (1974, pp. 230-33) list 66 studies of sex differences in aggression that appeared in the interval 1966-73. Ninety-four comparisons between the sexes were reported. Fifty-two indicated greater aggressiveness in boys, five in girls, and 37 in neither. Maccoby and Jacklin (1974, pp. 242-43 ff.) think the difference is at least partially biologically determined. Their reasons are:

> (1) Males are more aggressive than females in all human societies for which evidence is available. (2) The sex differences are found early in life, at a time when there is no evidence that differential social pressures have been brought to bear by adults to "shape" aggression differently in the two sexes (see Chap. 8). (3) Similar sex differences are found in man and subhuman primates. (4) Aggression is related to levels of sex hormones, and can be changed by experimental administrations of these hormones.

It is interesting that despite the foregoing, some writers have insisted that there is no necessary characteristic of aggression in human nature. As mentioned earlier, this is a presupposition that is required in a position that places the blame for personal psychological ills on conformity to the standards and values of society.

Fear, anxiety, and emotionality.

One could challenge the classification of the terms in this heading as motivational words, as they can also refer to emotion. However, both Freud and certain other theorists (Miller, the Spences) treated fear and anxiety as motivational factors; it will be remembered that the Ego reacted with anxiety to prompting from the Id and engaged in the defense mechanisms to disguise the promptings, and that fear was seen by drive theorists as the basis for the formation of the secondary drive of anxiety. The motivational status, then, of fear and anxiety probably arises from its role in these theories; in addition, anxiety has played a prominent role in the symptomatology of neurosis.

Emotionality is not a drivelike term but refers essentially to proneness to emotional arousal. It has often been said to be a characteristic of women. Maccoby and Jacklin (1974) review reactions to frustration and comment, "The tendency to show an outburst of negative emotion would appear to be greater in boys after the age of 18 months . . ." (p. 181). This outburst may take the form of behavioral "disorganization" or anger and aggression.

Maccoby and Jacklin (1974, p. 189) say that their review shows that observational studies seldom show sex differences on timidity, but that teacher ratings present girls as more timid and anxious than boys. Girls make higher scores on anxiety scales, but this may be due to the unwillingness of boys to admit to anxiety or fears. They suggest that the claim that girls are more passive than boys does not mean that girls are inactive. Rather, girls may concentrate their attention, whereas the generally high activity of boys leads them to move around a lot in the play room.

Values and Traits

Values.

Values as a property of cultures or of individuals have been studied by anthropologists, sociologists, and psychologists,[13] to name the disciplines most commonly concerned with them. The first two groups have most often studied cultures or subgroups of cultures, the last group the individual's values. Much of the work of anthropologists derived directly or indirectly from psychoanalytic theory, and this work in the 1930s and 1940s tended to stress variations in the child-rearing practices of preliterate societies having different patterns of adult or tribal behaviors, for example, being warlike or peaceable. Psychologists have also looked at child-rearing practices but from a broader theoretical perspective. Questionnaire or interview procedures are the methods typically used in this sort of study and in other cultural studies, although sometimes cultural products (for example, verbal materials) may be analyzed instead. Some relevant reviews and reports of this kind of work may be found in Albert (1956), Dicks (1950), Cantril (1965), Inkeles and Levinson (1954, 1969), Lambert, Hamers, and Frasure-Smith (1979), Minturn and Lambert (1964), and White (1951).

Studies of values other than those involved in child-rearing practices are illustrated by one reported by F. Kluckhohn and Strodtbeck (1961), who described five problem areas in which the value orientations of cultures can be described: (1) The orientation to human nature, that is, is it good, good and evil, neutral, or evil? (2) The human's relation to nature or supernature, that is, is there mastery over nature, subjugation to nature, or harmony with nature? (3) The person's place in the flow of time, that is, past, present, or future. (4) Activity orientation, that is, being, being in becoming, or doing. (5) Relational orientation, that is, lineality, individualism, or collineality. They developed a 22-item interview schedule around these points and administered it to about 100 people, each of whom belonged to one of five more or less separate communities in a region of New Mexico, that is, communities of Navaho, Zuni, Spanish-Americans, Mormons, and homesteaders from Texas and Oklahoma. An example may be summarized from area (5) above to illustrate their interview method. They posed the question of how a well might be drilled, that is, deciding its location and who will do the work. The lineal orientation gave the right of decision to elders or leaders of important families, the decisions of whom would be followed. A collineal relation is illustrated by the case in which after extensive discussion almost everyone agrees as to what is best to do. In individualism, everyone holds to his or her opinion and the decision is made by majority vote. The respondents were asked how such decisions were made in their community. A modified form of this procedure was applied in Japan to 619 respondents by Caudill and Scarr (1962). Table 2-8 shows a summary of the data from these two studies.

Table 2-8 shows that the Spanish-Americans are different from the other New Mexican groups, choosing being over doing and subjugation to nature; along with the Indian groups they choose present time. The Texans and Mormons value individualism, future orientation, dominance over nature, and doing; the Indian groups value collineality, the present, being in harmony with nature, and doing. The Japanese data are not strictly comparable to those of the New Mexico study, but their two most prominent relational patterns are (1) like those of the Texans and Mormons and (2) like the Indian groups. As to time, they again show two patterns, one like the Spanish-Americans, the other like the Texans and Mormons. As to relations to nature, one pattern for the Japanese is like the one for the Texan and Mormon groups; the other, O > S > W, is not the choice of any New Mexico group.

These types of studies can potentially reveal intercultural differences of great importance to intergroup understanding, tolerance, and communication. They highlight some of the ways in which the

TABLE 2-8. Observed Results for the Total Orientation Patterning Analyses.

Culture	Relational	Time	Man-Nature	Activity
Spanish-American	Ind ≥ Coll ≥ Lin	Pres > Fut = Past	Subj > Over > With	Being > Doing
Texan	Ind > Coll > Lin[a]	Fut ≥ Pres > Past	Over > With ≥ Subj	Doing > Being
Mormon	Ind > Coll > Lin[a]	Fut ≥ Past > Pres	Over ≥ With > Subj	Doing > Being
Zuni	Coll > Lin ≥ Ind	Pres ≥ Past > Fut	With > Subj ≥ Over	Doing ≥ Being
Navaho	Coll > Lin ≥ Ind	Pres > Past ≥ Fut	With ≥ Over ≥ Subj	Doing > Being

Japanese culture

Relational[b]	I > C > L	L > I > C	I > L > C	L > C > I	C > L > I	C > I > L
%[c]	32	11	3	5	14	30
Time[b]	Fu > Pr > Pa	Fu > Pa > Pr	Pa > Fu > Pr	Pa > Pr > Fu	Pr > Pa > Fu	Pr > Fu > Pa
%[c]	34	15	2	3	7	31
Man-Nature[b]	O > W > S	O > S > W	S > O > W	S > W > O	W > S > O	W > O > S
%[c]	40	23	8	5	5	15

Notes: [a]Collineal more emphasized in Mormon than in Texas sample.
[b]In the relational category, I refers to individualistic, C to collineal, and L to lineal. In time, Pr refers to present, Pa to past, and Fu to future. In Man-Nature, O refers to mastery over nature, W to being with nature, and S to being subjugated to nature.
[c]These values are average percentages across all items in the category (calculated by writer).

Source: Adapted from Variations in Value Orientations by F. Kluckhohn & F. L. Strodtbeck, 1961, Evanston, IL.: Row, Peterson; and Japanese value orientations and culture change, by W. Caudill & H. A. Scarr, 1962, Ethnology, 1, 52–91.

world differs for different cultural groups. Unfortunately, this kind of investigation has declined in anthropology (Hoebel, 1967) and has not seemed highly influential in psychology.

Measured values.

The effort of many psychologists in the area of values has been devoted primarily to the construction of measures of personal values in terms of which subgroups or cultures can be compared.

The most widely used and investigated procedure for the assessment of values is the Allport & Vernon (1931) *A Study of Values* (see also, Vernon & Allport, 1931), later revised and renamed by Allport, Vernon, and Lindzey (1951). The literature was brought together by Cantril and Allport (1933).

A Study of Values was an attempt to assess personality as a totality, as unique, and in terms of broad functions. It was based on "the most reasonable and convincing *a priori* analysis of the values experienced by men . . .," that of Eduard Spranger (Vernon & Allport, 1931, p. 232). Spranger had proposed six ideal types; Vernon and Allport (1931, pp. 233-36) describe them fully. The values are designated as theoretical, economic, aesthetic, social, political, and religious. Scores on this scale yield a profile for the six values. Norms were established (Cantril & Allport, 1933). Generally, female respondents obtain higher scores than male respondents on aesthetic, social, and religious values, the males scoring higher on the other three. There are many correlates of scores on this scale (Dukes, 1955; Duffy, 1940). Alternative measures have been suggested (cf. Dukes, 1955; Duffy, 1940; Knapp, 1964; Morris, 1942, 1956).

Morris (1956) developed a list of 13 "ways of life" which "differ widely in their content and include values advocated and defended in the several ethical and religious systems of mankind" (p. 1). Morris collected data from many college and university students both in the United States and abroad, including Asian countries. He found rather small cross-national differences. In the U.S. sample, women scored higher than men on three ways of life (sympathetic concern for others; integrate action, enjoyment, and contemplation; and obey the cosmic purpose). They scored lower than men on cultivate independence of persons and things, control the self stoically, and chance adventuresome deeds.

Another procedure for generating a list of values was used by Rokeach (1973) whose value survey is composed of two lists of 18 alphabetically ordered values, one for end-states and one for instrumental values. The respondent is asked to rank order the values in each list separately, with rank 1 being the value of highest importance.

These end-state items were developed by collecting values from a review of the literature, interviews with about 100 adults in a midwestern city, Rokeach's own values and those of 30 graduate students in psychology. Eliminating synonyms, overlapping values, highly specific values reduced the length of the list. The instrumental values were taken from Anderson's (1968) list of personality trait words.

Men and women differ on certain values. The women's rankings have lower median values than those of men for the end-states of a comfortable life, an exciting life, a sense of accomplishment, freedom, pleasure, and social recognition. The men have lower ratings than women for end-states such as a world at peace, happiness, inner harmony, salvation, self-respect, and wisdom. Several of these differences, though significant, are small. There are also differences on instrumental values, women scoring lower than men on ambitious, capable, imaginative, logical. Men score below women on cheerful, clean, forgiving, and loving.

Traits.

The word *trait* has a long history and as used by many writers is essentially a descriptive term (some writers, however, confer a dynamic status on it, cf. Allport, 1937). Allport (1961, p. 347) defined a trait as "a neuropsychic structure having the capacity to render many stimuli functionally equivalent, and to initiate and guide equivalent (meaningfully consistent) forms of adaptive and expressive behavior." A less theoretical definition is given by Pervin (1970, p. 57) as referring "to the consistency of an individual's response to a variety of situations." This kind of definition characterizes much of the work on traits of personality.

Students of personality traits, perhaps more than other investigators who have worked in the areas of this chapter, have attempted to encompass all of the ways in which people's personalities differ from one another. To accomplish this goal, they have examined all the words in dictionaries of English in an effort to find all of the words that designate ways in which people differ from one another. Allport and Odbert (1936) made the first such list, consisting of 17,953 terms. Other investigators have supplemented this list (by consulting an unabridged dictionary) so that the universe of terms numbers about 27,000 (Wiggins, 1979, p. 396). By eliminating synonyms, obscure, archaic, and inappropriate terms, investigators have reduced the number by substantial amounts. Wiggins (1979, p. 396) considers that trait adjectives fall into six classes as follows (with an illustration of each): interpersonal (aggressive), material (miserly), temperamental (lively), social roles (ceremonious), character (dishonest), and mental (analytical).

Studies of the domain of traits employ a reduced number of them and involve testing people by such procedures as ratings or rankings of a person by other people, self-reports of various kinds, and behavioral observations made in situations including experimental ones. The scores made on the measures are then intercorrelated, and the resulting correlations are subjected to a statistical procedure known as factor analysis. This procedure is a means of determining the underlying dimensions of the various measures taken; the goal is to reduce the large number of measures to a much smaller number of fundamental dimensions. By around 1970 (Pervin, 1970, Maddi, 1972), the dominant trait theorists using factor analysis were R. B. Cattell, H. J. Eysenck, and J. P. Guilford. These investigators seemed to take the entire domain of traits as their territory; more recently (cf. Wiggins, 1979, Lanyon, 1984), the emphasis has shifted to a portion of the trait domain, that is, interpersonal traits, the first of the six classes of traits listed by Wiggins (see above). A brief discussion of these approaches follows.

One outcome of Cattell's approach is shown in Table 2-9. This table shows traits common to life-history and questionnaire data (Hall & Lindzey, 1970, p. 390). These are mostly traits of temperament, although B and perhaps M appear to be ability traits. Cattell also speaks of dynamic traits, attitudes, sentiments, and ergs. The following ergs are suggested: "Mating (Sex), Security-Fear, Self-Assertion, Gregariousness, Parental Protection, Exploration (Curiosity), Sensuality, Appeal, and Constructiveness" (Pervin, 1970, p. 405). This list is reminiscent of McDougall's list of instincts.

Not all factor analytic studies of traits agree with Cattell's findings. More recent work has tended to list a smaller number of factors than Cattell has found. Hogan (1983) summarized 11 factor studies published between 1963 and 1980 (not including Cattell's). He finds that the studies agree on six factors: intellectence, adjustment, surgency (somewhat like extraversion), likeability, sociability, and conformity. Hogan (1983) points out that lists of factors "have an atheoretical quality" (p. 66), and he suggests that they might be arranged in a circumplex (a roughly circular form). For personality traits Hogan says that the two major dimensions of the circumplex are conformity (from high to low) and sociability (also from high to low). Various types of personality, including Galen's, would fit into one of the quadrants of the circumplex. Similar traits will be close together and "opposite" traits will be at opposite points on the circumplex. Wiggins (1979, p. 405, Table 2) proposed a circular arrangement with 16 traits each measured by adjectival scales.

TABLE 2-9. Traits Found to be Common in Life and Questionnaire Data by Cattell.

Symbol	Popular Label
A	Outgoing - Reserved
B	More Intelligent - Less Intelligent
C	Stable - Emotional
E	Assertive - Humble
F	Happy-go-lucky - Sober
G	Conscientious - Expedient
H	Venturesome - Shy
I	Tender-minded - Tough-minded
L	Suspicious - Trusting
M	Imaginative - Practical
N	Shrewd - Forthright
O	Apprehensive - Placid

Note: Cattell's techincal names for these traits are not comprehensible in a brief review of his work.

Source: Table reprinted from *Theories of Personality*, 2nd ed. by C. S. Hall and G. W. Lindzey, 1970, New York: Wiley. Copyright © 1970 by John Wiley & Sons, Inc. Reprinted by permission.

COMMENT AND CONCLUSION

The nature of human nature has figured in theological and philosophical writing for several millenia. Conceptions of human nature were usually developed in the context of pressing political and social problems. The Reformation led to concern with the law and with how government should be constituted. From Hobbes, Locke, and Rousseau we have the notion of the social contract. Interestingly, despite the common theme of a compact, these writers differed in their assumptions about human nature, Hobbes seeing it as devoted to self-preservation at all costs through competition and struggle, Locke and Rousseau finding positive features in it. The writings of all three had significant impact on political philosophy and on constitutional provisions of a number of governments, including that of the United States. The work of all three was primarily about men, typically men of property, to the exclusion of much concern for women. With Milton, they might agree in referring to woman as "this fair defect of nature."

The description of human nature in terms of faculties or powers of the mind comes in the common sense psychology of Thomas Reid, whose writings were designed to protect Scottish Presbyterianism from the onslaughts of skepticism, sensationalism, associationism, and hedonism. Reid's work was important to the development of psychology in the

United States as his books and those of his followers were studied in courses on moral philosophy by generations of students in the nineteenth century. Thomas Aquinas had proposed a faculty psychology in the thirteenth century in order (Russell, 1945, p. 453) "to undo the harm done by too close adherence to Arabian doctrines..."; his arguments in *Summa Contra Gentiles* established "the truth of the Christian religion by arguments addressed to a reader supposed to be not already a Christian.... The imaginary reader is usually thought of as a man versed in the philosophy of the Arabs."

The viewpoints mentioned so far are essentially accounts of the mind, although Hobbesian mechanism owed something to physiology. It was not until the nineteenth century that science in the form of anatomy achieved importance in conceptions of human nature. Among the first writers to link mind and brain were the phrenologists, who assigned faculties to locations in the brain, who identified and described individual differences, and whose stress on the conformations of the skull provided a method for assessing a person's characteristics. Further, they offered the hope that one could change various characteristics by exercising those that were desirable but weak and by disuse of those that were strong but undesirable. Phrenology had a great popular appeal in the nineteenth century in the United States. One could be what one wished to be, following the tenets of phrenology.

The widespread postulation of instincts, a little later, came following the theory of evolution and also reflected the importance of biology, especially in "the conception of mind as an instrument which enabled the organism to adjust to its environment or even to transform it..." (Curti, 1943, p. 558). "The biological origin of mind actually in some cases confirmed rather than lessened optimism and faith in man's power to effect progress; after all, had not great headway on the long journey from the world of the lower animals already been made?" (p. 560). The notions of competition for scarce resources and of the survival of the fittest seemed to give, in the United States at least, biological justification for unregulated competition in business and industry.

For some writers after the Reformation there were moral and social instincts. For others, however, human nature, as a consequence of the Fall, was seen as utterly depraved, evil, and egoistic. This latter characterization has dominated many discussions of human nature, especially in the sixteenth and seventeenth centuries. Troland (1928) has observed that a catalogue of motives could be made from the sins described in various religions.

However, in almost all of the lists of proposed instincts we have reviewed, both "good" and "bad" instincts have been included. Thus, most of the classes of specific instincts brought together by Bernard

(Table 2-3) could be seen either as morally neutral or as positive; only 185 cases of antisocial instincts were found and 96 of retaliative instincts, together about 5 percent of the specific instincts. Consultation of the lists given in the text for James, Angell, Thorndike, and Kirkpatrick will support this observation concerning Table 2-3.

The lists of these writers are perhaps more constrained than are many of those to which Bernard objected. The lists consist of acts seen as or deemed to be more or less essential to the survival and well being of individuals and their offspring (and of the species). The criteria for attributing instinctive status to an act, however, were not well defined and were seldom met by careful observation, let alone by experimentation. The role of learning from experiences in the appearance of these behaviors was not usually considered (although Thorndike, in particular, was an exception).

All of the authors cited here are males, and that is very likely true of those discussed by Bernard. We find in the lists some indication of sex differences, mainly in connection with parental functions and with aggression. Differences are attributed to the strengths of instincts in the sexes (and in children, where they are mentioned). Women were endowed with moral purity and thus should rear the young (Curti, 1953a, p. 372). It is probably true that the lists were created by men with men mainly in mind.

Another contrast in conjunction with human nature perhaps first surfaced in the anti-instinct movement of the 1920s; the movement rejected the instinctive basis of many (in some writers, all) behaviors, attributing the behaviors to the effects of experience. There followed the great age of learning theory. The contrast here is between innate nature (for example, instincts) and nurture, that is, learning. Bernard seems to have been partial to the role of nurture. Although Bentham may have thought that there are innate reactions of pleasure and pain, his list of the springs of action implies (at least to this writer) that experience is a significant factor in indicating the affective consequences of various situations and acts.

Lists of instincts were followed by the postulation of drives and later motives, a list of 20 of which was proposed by Murray. Certain of Murray's motives (or needs) have received fairly extensive investigation. Applications of this work have been made to child development (for example, independence training), the development of entrepreneurship in Eastern society, the conception of male alcoholism, risk-taking in children and adults; and the methods developed have been applied to cultural products of antiquity and to modern industrial nations in studies of the correlates of scores on the achievement motive. Sex differences were found in the achievement motive, but current opinion seems to reject their reality.

Psychoanalysis offered a number of ideas that have been reflected in child-rearing practices, not always with success. The role of nature versus nurture figures prominently in discussions of aggression, fear, and anxiety, with psychoanalytic and ethological theories often contrasted with theories arising from learning viewpoints.

There is a good deal of work on values and traits, but there is little agreement or continuity in the studies of values, and it is not at all clear how important traits are to fundamental issues of human nature.

There has been a great deal written about human nature in the last several millenia. There have been numerous proposals and claims, but despite the advent of scientific methods about a hundred years ago, relatively little progress has been made. Recent work has not had the sweep of the proposals by the political philosophers, the faculty psychologists, or the instinct theorists. Perhaps the question of the nature of human nature requires more precision and definition than it has had for advances to be made.

REFERENCES

Albert, E. M. (1956). Classification of values: A method and illustration. *American Anthropologist, 58*, 221-48.

Albrecht, F. M. (1970). A reappraisal of faculty psychology. *Journal of the History of the Behavioral Sciences, 6*, 36-40.

Allport, G. W. (1937). *Personality: A psychological interpretation.* New York: Holt.

———. (1961). *Pattern and growth in personality.* New York: Holt, Rinehart & Winston.

Allport, G. W., & Odbert, H. S. (1936). Trait names: A psycholexical study. *Psychological Monographs, 47* (Whole No. 211).

Allport, G. W., & Vernon, P. E. (1931). *A study of values.* Boston: Houghton Mifflin.

Allport, G. W., Vernon, P. E., & Lindzey, G. (1951). *A study of values* (Rev. ed.). Boston: Houghton Mifflin.

Anderson, N. H. (1968). Likeableness ratings of 555 personality trait/words. *Journal of Personality and Social Psychology, 9*, 272-79.

Angell, J. R. (1908). *Psychology: An introductory study of the structure and function of human consciousness,* 4th ed. New York: Holt.

Atkinson, J. W. (1957). Motivational determinants of risk-taking behavior. *Psychological Review, 64*, 359-72.

Atkinson, J. W., & Litwin, G. H. (1960). Achievement motive and test anxiety conceived as motive to approach success and motive to avoid failure. *Journal of Abnormal and Social Psychology, 60*, 52-63.

Bakan, D. (1966). The influence of phrenology on American psychology. *Journal of the History of the Behavioral Sciences, 2*, 200-20.

Bentham, J. (1815/1969). A table of the springs of action (London: Richard & Arthur Taylor, Shoe Lane). In P. McReynolds (Ed.), *Four early works on motivation* (pp. 477-512 plus fold-out table of springs of action). Gainesville, FL: Scholars' Facsimiles & Reprints. (Originally published, 1815.)

Bernard, L. L. (1924). *Instinct: A study in social psychology.* New York: Holt.

Blight, J. G. (1974). Solomon Stoddard's safety of appearing and the dissolution of the Puritan faculty psychology. *Journal of the History of the Behavioral Sciences, 10,* 238-50.

Boring, E. G. (1950). *A history of experimental psychology* (2nd ed.). New York: Appleton-Century-Crofts.

Brody, B. A. (1969). Introduction. In T. Reid, *Essays on the intellectual powers of man.* Cambridge, MA: MIT Press. (Originally published, 1785.)

Brooks, G. P. (1976). The faculty psychology of Thomas Reid. *Journal of the History of the Behavioral Sciences, 12,* 65-77.

Cantril, H. (1965). *The pattern of human concerns.* New Brunswick, NJ: Rutgers University Press.

Cantril, H., & Allport, G. W. (1933). Recent applications of the study of values. *Journal of Abnormal and Social Psychology, 28,* 259-73.

Caudill, W., & Scarr, H. A. (1962). Japanese value orientations and culture change. *Ethnology, 1,* 53-91.

Cofer, C. N., & Appley, M. H. (1964). *Motivation: Theory and research.* New York: Wiley.

Coppleston, F. (1957). *A history of philosophy: Vol. II. Medieval philosophy Augustine to Scotus.* Westminster, MD: Newman Press. (Originally published, 1950.)

Costello, W. J. (1958). *The scholastic curriculum at early seventeenth-century Cambridge.* Cambridge: Harvard University Press.

Curti, M. (1943). *The growth of American thought.* New York: Harper.

———. (1953a). Human nature in American thought: The age of reason and morality, 1750-1860. *Political Science Quarterly, 68,* 354-75.

———. (1953b). Human nature in American thought: Retreat from reason in the age of science. *Political Science Quarterly, 68,* 492-510.

———. (1980). *Human nature in American thought: A history.* Madison: University of Wisconsin Press.

Diamond, S. (1971). Gestation of the instinct concept. *Journal of the History of the Behavioral Sciences, 7,* 323-36.

Dicks, H. V. (1950). Personality traits and National Socialist ideology: A wartime study of German prisoners of war. *Human Relations, 3,* 111-54.

Drever, J. (1917). *Instinct in man: A contribution to the psychology of education.* Cambridge, UK: University Press.

Duffy, E. (1940). A critical review of investigations employing the Allport-Vernon study of values and other tests of evaluative attitude. *Psychological Bulletin, 37,* 597-612.

Dukes, W. F. (1955). Psychological studies of values. *Psychological Bulletin, 52,* 24-50.

Dunlap, K. (1919). Are there any instincts? *Journal of Abnormal Psychology, 14,* 35-50.

Ellos, W. J. (1981). *Thomas Reid's Newtonian realism.* Washington, DC: University Press of America.

Elshtain, J. B. (1981). *Public man, private woman: Women in social and political thought.* Princeton: Princeton University Press.

Entwisle, D. R. (1972). To dispel fantasies about fantasy-based measures of achievement motivation. *Psychological Bulletin, 77,* 377-91.

Fay, J. W. (1939). *American psychology before William James.* New Brunswick, NJ: Rutgers University Press.

Feibleman, J. K. (1969). *An introduction to the philosophy of Charles S. Pierce.* Cambridge: MIT Press.

Fenichel, O. (1945). The psychoanalytic theory of neurosis. New York: Norton.

Field, W. F. (1951). *The effects on thematic apperception of certain experimentally aroused needs.* Unpublished doctoral dissertation, University of Maryland.

Fleming, J. (1982). Projective and psychometric approaches to measurement: The case of fear of success. In A. J. Stewart (Ed.), *Motivation in society: A volume in honor of David C. McClelland* (pp. 63-96). San Francisco: Jossey-Bass.

Franklin, J. H. (1968). Jean Bodin. In D. L. Sills (Ed.), *International Encyclopedia of the Social Sciences: Vol 2* (pp. 110-13). New York: Crowell Collier & Macmillan.

Fraser, A. C. (1898). *Thomas Reid.* Edinburgh: Olpihant, Anderson & Ferrier.

Freud, S. (1949). Instincts and their vicissitudes. In J. Riviere (Trans.), *Collected papers of Sigmund Freud.* London: Hogarth Press. (Originally published in German, 1915.)

―――――. (1933). *New contemporary lectures on psycho-analysis.* New York: Norton.

Friedrich, L. K. (1976). Achievement motivation in college women revisited: Implications for women, men, and the gathering of coconuts. *Sex Roles, 2,* 47-61.

Fulcher, J. R. (1973). Puritans and the passions: The faculty psychology in American Puritanism. *Journal of the History of the Behavioral Sciences, 9,* 123-39.

Gardiner, H. M., Metcalf, R. C., & Beebe-Center, J. G. (1970). *Feeling and emotion: A history of theories.* Westport, CT: Greenwood Press. (Originally published, 1937.)

Gould, S. J. (1977). *Ontogeny and phylogeny.* Cambridge: Harvard University Press.

Hall, C. S., & Lindzey, G. W. (1970). *Theories of personality* (2nd ed.). New York: Wiley.

Handy, R. (1969). *Value theory and the behavioral sciences.* Springfield, IL: Thomas.

Hoebel, E. A. (1967, March). An anthropological perspective on national character. In D. Martindale (Ed.), National character in the perspective of the social sciences. *Annals of the American Academy of Political and Social Science, 370,* 1-7.

Höffding, H. (1955). *A history of modern philosophy: A sketch of the history of philosophy from the close of the Renaissance to our own day* (Vol. 1). (B. E. Meyer, Trans.). New York: Dover (Originally published, 1894; translated, 1900).

Hogan, R. (1983). A socioanalytic theory of personality. In M. M. Page (Ed.), *Nebraska Symposium on Motivation 1982: Personality—Current theory and research* (pp. 55-89). Lincoln: University of Nebraska Press.

Hollander, B. (1924). McDougall's social psychology; anticipated one hundred years; a contribution to the history of philosophy. *Ethological Journal, 9,* 1-20.

Horner, M. S. (1974). The measurement and behavioral implications of fear of success in women. In J. W. Atkinson & J. O. Raynor (Eds.), *Motivation and achievement* (pp. 91-117). New York: Wiley.

Horney, K. (1939). *New ways in psychoanalysis.* New York: Norton.

Inkeles, A., & Levinson, J. R. (1954). National character: The study of modal personality and sociocultural systems. In G. W. Lindzey (Ed.), *Handbook of social psychology, Vol. 2* (pp. 977-1020). Cambridge, MA: Addison Wesley.

Inkeles, A., & Levison, D. J. (1969). National character: Modal personality and sociocultural systems. In G. Lindzey & E. Aronson (Eds.), *The Handbook of social psychology, Vol. 4* (2nd ed., pp. 418-506). Reading, MA: Addison Wesley.

James, W. (1890). *Principles of psychology, Vol. 2.* New York: Holt.

Kagan, J., & Moss, H. A. (1959). Stability and validity of achievement fantasy. *Journal of Abnormal and Social Psychology, 58,* 357-64.

Kirkpatrick, E. A. (1903). *Fundamentals of child study.* New York: Macmillan.

Kluckhohn, C. (1954). Culture and behavior. In G. W. Lindzey (Ed.), *Handbook of social psychology, Vol. 2* (pp. 921-76). Cambridge, MA: Addison Wesley.

Kluckhohn, F., & Strodtbeck, F. L. (1961). *Variations in value orientations.* Evanston, IL: Row, Peterson.

Knapp, R. H. (1964). An experimental study of a triadic hypothesis concerning the sources of aesthetic imagery. *Journal of Projective Techniques and Personality Assessment, 28,* 49-54.

Krantz, D. L., & Allen, D. (1967). The rise and fall of McDougall's instinct doctrine. *Journal of the History of the Behavioral Sciences, 3,* 326-38.

Krech, D. (1962). Cortical localization of function. In L. Postman (Ed.), *Psychology in the making: Histories of selected research problems* (pp. 31-72). New York: Random House.

Lambert, W. E., Hamers, J. F., & Frasure-Smith, N. (1979). *Child-rearing values: A cross-national study.* New York: Praeger.

Lanyon, R. I. (1984). Personality assessment. *Annual Review of Psychology, 35,* 667-701.

Lorenz, K. (1963/1966). *On aggression.* New York: Bantam. (Originally published, 1963.)

Maddi, S. R. (1972). *Personality theories: A comparative analysis* (rev. ed.). Homewood, IL: Dorsey.

Maccoby, E. E., & Jacklin, C. N. (1974). *The psychology of sex differences.* Stanford, CA: Stanford University Press.

McClelland, D. C. (1961). *The achieving society.* Princeton, NJ: Van Nostrand.

_____. (1965a). N Achievement and entrepreneurship: A longitudinal study. *Journal of Personality and Social Psychology, 1,* 389-92.

_____. (1965b). Toward a theory of motive acquisition. *American Psychologist, 20,* 321-33.

McClelland, D. C., Atkinson, J. W., Clark, R. A., & Lowell, E. L. (1953). *The achievement motive.* New York: Appleton-Century-Crofts.

McDougall, W. (1950). *An introduction to social psychology* (30th ed.). London: Methuen. (Originally published, 1908.)

_____. (1950). *The energies of men: A study of the fundamentals of dynamic psychology.* London; Methuen. (Originally published, 1932.)

Mandler, G., & Sarason, S. B. (1952). A study of anxiety and learning. *Journal of Abnormal and Social Psychology, 47,* 166-73.

Maslow, A. H. (1954). *Motivation and personality.* New York: Harper.

_____. (1959). Psychological data and value theory. In A. H. Maslow (Ed.), *New knowledge in human values.* New York: Harper.

Minturn, L., & Lambert, W. W. (1964). *Mothers of six cultures: Antecedents of child rearing.* New York: Wiley.

Morgan, C. D., & Murray, H. (1935). Method for investigating fantasies: The Thematic Apperception Test. *Archives of Neurology and Psychiatry, 34,* 289-306.

Morris, C. (1942). *Paths of life: Preface to a world religion.* New York: Harper.

_____. (1956). *Varieties of human value.* Chicago: University of Chicago Press.

Moss, H. A., & Kagan, J. (1961). Stability of achievement and recognition seeking behaviors from early childhood through adulthood. *Journal of Abnormal and Social Psychology, 62,* 504-13.

Murphy, G. (1949). *Historical introduction to modern psychology* (rev. ed.). New York: Harcourt, Brace.

Murray, H. A. (1938). *Explorations in personality: A clinical and experimental study of fifty men of college age.* New York: Oxford.

Noel, P. S., & Carlson, E. T. (1973). The faculty psychology of Benjamin Rush. *Journal of the History of the Behavioral Sciences, 9,* 369-77.

Nietzsche, F. W. (1968). *The will to power: A new translation.* W. Kaufmann & R. J. Hillingdale, trans. W. Kaufmann (ed. and commentator). New York: Vintage. (Originally published, 1910-11.)

Pervin, L. A. (1970). *Personality: Theory, assessment, and research.* New York: Wiley.

Peters, R. S. (Ed.). (1953). *Brett's history of psychology.* London: Allen & Unwin.

Rapaport, D. (1959). The structure of psychoanalytic theory: A systematizing attempt. In S. Koch (Ed.), *Psychology: A study of a science, Vol. 3* (pp. 55-183). New York: McGraw-Hill.

Reid, T. (1969). *Essays on the intellectual powers of man.* Cambridge, MA: MIT Press. (Originally published, 1785.)

Roback, A. A. (1952). *History of American psychology*. New York: Library Publishers.

Rokeach, M. (1973). *The nature of human values*. New York: Free Press.

Romanes, G. J. (1883). *Animal intelligence*. New York: Appleton. (Originally published, 1882.)

———. (1891). *Mental evolution in animals*. New York: Appleton. (Originally published, 1883.)

———. (1888). *Mental evolution in man: Origins of human faculty*. London: Kegan Paul, Trench.

Rorty, R. (1979). *Philosophy and the mirror of nature*. Princeton, NJ: Princeton University Press.

Rossiter, C. (Ed.). (1961). *The Federalist Papers*. New York: Mentor (New American Library).

Russell, B. (1917). *Political ideals*. New York: Century.

———. (1945). *A history of Western philosophy*. New York: Simon & Schuster.

Shipley, T. E., Jr., & Veroff, J. (1952). A projective measure of need for affiliation. *Journal of Experimental Psychology, 43*, 349-56.

———. (1958). A projective measure of need for affiliation. In J. W. Atkinson (Ed.), *Motives in fantasy, action, and society* (pp. 83-94). New York: Van Nostrand.

Smith, M. B. (1963). Personal values in the study of lives. In R. W. White (Ed.), *The study of lives: Essays in honor of Henry A. Murray* (pp. 324-47). New York: Atherton.

Spoerl, H. D. (1935-36). Faculties *versus* traits: Gall's solution. *Character and Personality, 4*, 216-31.

Stewart, A. J., & Chester, N. L. (1982). Sex differences in human motives: Achievement, affiliation, and power. In A. J. Stewart (Ed.), *Motivation and society: A volume in honor of David C. McClelland* (pp. 172-218). San Francisco: Jossey-Bass.

Thorndike, E. L. (1913). *Educational psychology, Vol. 1: The original nature of man*. New York: Teachers College.

Troland, L. T. (1928). *The fundamentals of human motivation*. New York: Van Nostrand.

Vernon, P. E., & Allport, G. W. (1931). A test for personal values. *Journal of Abnormal and Social Psychology, 26*, 231-48.

Veroff, J. (1957). Development and validation of a projective measure of power motivation. *Journal of Abnormal and Social Psychology, 54*, 1-8.

Veroff, J., Wilcox, S., & Atkinson, J. W. (1953). The achievement motive in high school and college-age women. *Journal of Abnormal and Social Psychology, 48*, 103-19.

Watson, J. B. (1930). *Behaviorism* (rev. ed.). New York: Norton. (Reprinted after 1957 by University of Chicago Press.)

Whetham, W. C. D., & Whetham, C. D. (1912). *Heredity and society*. (Note: These authors are sometimes known as Dampier and the book may be filed under this name.)

White, R. K. (1951). *Value analysis: The nature and use of the method*. Gardner, NJ: Libertarian Press.

Wiggins, J. S. (1979). A psychological taxonomy of trait-descriptive terms: The interpersonal domain. *Journal of Personality and Social Psychology, 37*, 395-412.

Wilm, E. D. (1925). *The theories of instinct: A study in the history of psychology*. New Haven, CT: Yale University Press.

Winter, D. G. (1973). *The power motive*. New York: Free Press.

Winter, D. G., & Stewart, A. J. (1977). Power motive reliability as a function of retest instructions. *Journal of Consulting and Clinical Psychology, 45*, 436-40.

Wood, N. (1968). Niccolò Machiavelli. In D. L. Sills (Ed.), *International Encyclopedia of the Social Sciences, Vol. 9* (pp. 505-11). New York: Crowell, Collier & Macmillan.

Woodworth, R. S. (1918). *Dynamic psychology*. New York: Columbia University Press.

Zagorin, P. (1968). Thomas Hobbes. In D. L. Sills (Ed.), *International Encyclopedia of the Social Sciences, Vol. 6* (pp. 481-87). New York: Crowell, Collier & Macmillan.

Zuckerman, M., & Wheeler, L. (1975). To dispel fantasies about the fantasy-based measure of fear of success. *Psychological Bulletin, 82*, 932-46.

NOTES

1. As Reid himself put it (1785/1969, p. 49), "Although some writers . . . have disputed the authority of the senses, of memory, and of every human faculty; yet we find, that such persons, in the conduct of life . . . pay the same regard to the authority of their senses, and other faculties, as the rest of mankind." This is acknowledged by Hume. Reid observes further, "For I never heard that any skeptic run his head against a post, or stepped into a kennel, because he did not believe his eyes" (p. 49). Reid here probably employs kennel in the sense of the surface drain of a street, a gutter (*Oxford English Dictionary*).

2. The idea of the faculties is mentioned a number of times in the *Federalist Papers*; Madison (Rossiter, 1961, p. 227) says, however, "The faculties of the mind itself have never yet been distinguished and defined with satisfactory precision by all the efforts of the most acute and metaphysical philosphers," and Hamilton (Rossiter, 1961, p. 474) observes that "the mensuration of the faculties of the mind has, I believe, no place in the catalogue of known arts."

3. For discussions of this influence, see Fulcher (1973), Blight (1974), and Curti (1953a, pp. 365-70).

4. Feibleman (1969, pp. 455-56) has indicated that Charles Sanders Pierce (1839-1914) acknowledged Reid's influence (along with that of Kant) on his philosophy which was an original and important

contribution by an American and which influenced William James. Brody (1969, pp. xxiv-xxv) observed that Reid's ideas were also extremely influential in America. Indeed, before the Civil War Reid's common sense philosophy, which was first brought to America by John Witherspoon and Samuel Stanhope of Princeton, was the only opposition faced by New England's transcendentalism. Moreover, Reid's ideas continued to remain influential in America long after they had lost their influence elsewhere. This was primarily due to the activities of James McCosh (1811-94), a Scottish philosopher who was educated at Glasgow and Edinburgh and who was president of Princeton University from 1868 to 1888.

For further treatments of religious, philosophical, and psychological writings in the history of the United States see Albrecht (1970), Fay (1939), Noel and Carlson (1973), and Roback (1952). Further comments on T. Reid may be found in Rorty (1979, pp. 142 [note 18], 144 [note 22], and 145).

5. Boring (1950, p. 53) says that "Gall had ready for use the faculties of the Scottish School. . . . It was from the lists of Thomas Reid and Dugald Stewart that Gall obtained his analysis of the mind into thirty-seven powers and propensities." He also (p. 59) says that Spoerl (1935) "shows how Gall got his list of faculties from Reid and Stewart of the Scottish School." Krech (1962, p. 34) also indicates that Gall "borrowed liberally from the Scotch and English Psychologists. . . ." Spoerl (1935, pp. 224-25) remarked that while Gall could have used Reid's list, "it seems that Gall had no knowledge of the Scottish faculty psychology. Two of his French critics, Lélut in 1876 and Garnier in 1839, called attention to the nominal similarity. . . . But Lélut held that Gall did not know of the Scottish work, and Garnier, in concurring, added that Gall's intent was to controvert 'the narrow and false psychology of the French philosophers of the 18th century, with which alone he was acquainted.'"

6. Diamond (1971) has provided an extensive account of the history of the words *instinctus* and *instinct* and concludes, among other things, that the concept of instinct did not really emerge until the seventeenth century, although the words, of course, were available earlier. Diamond's interpretation appears to conflict with the one made by Wilm (1925, p. 40), who attributes the invention of the word to the Stoics. Wilm probably had in mind an instinctlike notion of the Stoics which he saw as having the same sense as the word instinct.

7. Another strong biological influence arising out of evolutionary thought was the theory of recapitulation (cf. Gould, 1977). This theory took various forms but can be stated as the view that ontogeny recapitulates the events of phylogeny. Human embryology was one source of

evidence for recapitulation, but interpretations were also advanced holding that intellectual and moral defects, as well as early stages of human development, reflected, on the one hand, "atavistic" remnants of earlier evolutionary stages or, on the other, stages that the child had to pass through on the way to maturity. Applications of this theory (Gould, 1977, Chap. 5) were made involving criminology, racism, child development, primary education, and Freudian psychoanalysis. Gould (1977, p. 168, his emphasis) says that empirical attempts to refute recapitulation theory were unsuccessful but that it fell because "it became *unfashionable in approach* (due to the rise of experimental embryology) and finally *untenable in theory* (when the establishment of Mendelian genetics converted previous exceptions into new expectations)."

8. The three volumes of this work did not appear in chronological order. The third volume was published in 1903 and the other two in 1913.

9. I have relied primarily on the 30th edition of *An Introduction to Social Psychology*. McDougall later substituted the phrase "innate propensity" for instinct and modified the list of instincts (McDougall, 1932/1950). However, there was no real change in his views of original human nature. Bakan (1966, p. 201) cites Hollander (1924) as suggesting a link between phrenology and McDougall's instincts.

10. One reason that the term may have declined in use is Watson's (1930) rejection of it in his popular books and lectures. Another reason may be the Great Depression of the 1930s. It was probably difficult to attribute the massive unemployment of that period to innate factors. Rather, social and economic factors seemed to merit blame. For further discussion, see Krantz and Allen (1967).

11. Although certain "drives" appear to be universal, for example, hunger, thirst, sex, and the like, the objects and the manner of their satisfaction show numerous variations across cultures and subcultures (cf. C. Kluckhohn, 1954, pp. 929-30).

12. The need for power appears to correspond to Murray's Need Dominance (see Table 2-7).

13. The topic of value has been of interest to a number of philosophers. See Handy (1969) for a summary of the views of R. B. Perry, John Dewey, and S. C. Pepper. Handy, himself, holds that value is what satisfies a need (p. 148).

3

Body, Mind, and Morals in the Framing of Social Policy
Lynette K. Friedrich-Cofer

More than 30 years ago in a little school in Vanves, France, an experiment began, financed by the Ministry of Education. Concern had been expressed by French physicians and educators that children's health was being seriously affected by too much academic work and not enough physical exercise and recreation. The nine classrooms of children, ages 6 to 11, were assigned to experimental or control conditions and studied over a ten-year period. Similar small-scale experiments were conducted in other French schools. The experimental plan called for academic work in the morning (with a ten-minute exercise break) and afternoons devoted to physical education and recreation (one to two hours per day), art, music, and supervised study. The children left school at 5:30 and no written homework was assigned for the evenings.

Children were compared on standardized achievement tests, physical examinations, and absentee rates as well as teachers' accounts of disciplinary problems and affective interactions with peers and adults. Despite the four-hour reduction in daily time allotted to academic studies, the academic progress of the experimental children surpassed that of the control children. Their "health, fitness, discipline and enthusiasm" were also superior (Bailey, 1973, p. 427). Parents, teachers, and children were delighted with the innovations.

Gradually more French schools began to adopt the plan and monitor results. By the 1950s, perhaps 1,500 classes were involved. In October 1969, the Ministries of Education and Youth and Sports specified "one-third time" — as the plan came to be known — for elementary schools in the entire country. Subsequently, variations of the French plan have been adopted in many schools throughout Europe, Japan, Australia, and Canada (Bailey, 1979).

What is so remarkable about this tale, for an American, is the reasonable and modest way in which social policy seemed to evolve.[1] Education in the United States has been the barometer of political change. Children have been seen as the means through which social reforms and national priorities are to be achieved. In the shifting tensions between calls for intellectual excellence and universal offerings, moral rigor and naturalism, individualistic self-realization and the common welfare, the child has served a symbolic function. Our views of the child have been focused by the latest definitions of adult deficits, and thus policies are to radiate downward from graduate education to kindergarten, from national to local level. The danger of demands for scientific relevance to social problems in such a climate is that our ways of seeing children are narrowed by shifts in priorities, and our claims of expertise are likely to become inflated as we seek a place in the grand schemes of reform. It is not so surprising, therefore, that the real, embodied child has slipped from our scientific as well as our collective eye.

Mens sana in corpore sano was once a cherished educational tenet in the United States. The health and participation of each child in physical exercise while at school was considered an important responsibility to be assumed by the state. However, by the 1930s the elitist ethos of competitive athletics, with its promise of masculine character building, had come to dominate programs for men and boys. Educators of women and girls, with enormous grass roots support, were able to retain their participatory programs. Federal legislation aimed at ending sex discrimination in and through education in the 1970s demanded sweeping reforms. Men's programs became the measure of the "good," and women should have equal programs. Attention has been riveted to comparisons of opportunities available to male and female athletes for interscholastic and intercollegiate competition. The competitive female athlete has become the symbol of the "new strong woman." That women's programs, and with them their educational philosophy, have vanished has not merited comment. Nor has it been noted that opportunities for physical exercise as a part of school programs have diminished as funds are diverted to competitive athletics. Children in the United States have made a poor showing on a variety of physical fitness tests; only about one-third of children between the ages of 10 and 17 are estimated to participate in daily physical education at school, and the numbers are shrinking (Reiff, Kroll, & Hunsicker, 1978).[2] Young children and poor children, especially those in inner cities, are most neglected (*Promoting Health*, 1980; *Report . . . UNESCO*, 1978). Our recent plans for educational reform focus on improved competition in the international contest for scientific and technological supremacy, with proposals for longer school days, weeks, and years (New York *Times*, November

1983, Section 12). By September 1984, 23 states had mandated increases in instructional time (New York *Times*, September 9, 1984).

The purpose of this chapter is to explore the disappearance of the embodied child in U.S. education. It may be considered a case history of the way in which one human need — physical exercise — was identified and became a part of public policy. The cultural redefinitions of the need for physical exercise and the changes in educational practices are viewed against a backdrop of the shifting conceptions of sex differences. The first part of the discussion is historical and traces (a) the humanistic tradition, espousing the trinity of mind, body, and morals from the founding of the common schools through the early nineteenth century; (b) the rise of the athletic movement and its eclipse of the humanistic tradition in the 1930s; and (c) the women's educational stand for the humanistic tradition. The second part of the chapter deals with the political and scientific forces which brought about passage of the legislation for equality in education, the implementation of the policy, and the legal decisions which followed the legislation. Finally, the educational policies of the United States are contrasted with international developments, and the implications for policy formation are considered. Throughout the chapter, the roles of protoscientists and developmental psychologists emerge as they seek to influence and are influenced by wider social values. However, the body and those primarily responsible for health and physical training provide the prism through which scientific activity and social policy are viewed.

THE HUMANISTIC TRADITION: 1820–1889

European Influences on Social and Scientific Thought

The humanitarian reforms of the 1830s were rooted in the eighteenth-century conviction that human suffering was irrational and unnecessary. Education, aided and directed by enlightened philosophy and scientific achievement, could usher in a new (or, in the case of the romantics, recapture an old) era of personal and societal goodness through the cultivation of sound bodies and minds and the elevation of personal morality. While the revival of interest in the Greek ideals in education can be traced to the humanists, the links among the body, mind, and morals were forged anew in the writings of John Locke and Jean Jacques Rousseau.

Both Rousseau and Locke begin with the premise that human nature is good and malleable. In order to cultivate morality, the individual mind must be guided to discover natural moral laws given by the Creator. These laws are accessible to all people, without the intervention of orthodox religion, but the mind must be able to apprehend them. The physical senses play a primary role in the formation of the mind and in the acquisition of knowledge; hence, the path to the mind and to morality is through the body.

Locke advocates all manner of physical exercise, as well as a regime of dietary simplicity and hygiene, in his treatise on education. "A sound mind in a sound body, is a short but full description of a happy state in this world" (cited in Quick, 1880). Rationality is to be formed through self-discipline and orderly habits. In *Émile*, Rousseau argues that a "debilitated body enfeebles the soul" and urges educators to cultivate intelligence through the power of the body that it is given to govern (Rousseau, 1762/1966). Rousseau, however, gives an original turn of thought to the conception of childhood. Taking Locke to task for his emphasis on rationality, Rousseau writes, "It is no part of a child's business to know right and wrong, to perceive the reason for a man's duties. Nature would have them children before they are men" (Rousseau, 1762/1966, p. 54). "Let them run, jump and shout to their heart's content" (p. 50). Childhood is not an antechamber to adulthood, but a unique period in development. Education must take its cues from natural childhood. Émile was to have only a physical and sensory education until 12, then intellectual subjects were to be introduced. Moral education was to begin at age 15. The preparation of the good individual was, therefore, grounded in natural physical activities.

The European educational reforms of the late eighteenth and early nineteenth centuries bear the marks of both Locke and Rousseau. The knowledge of Greek gymnastics had been revitalized by the appearance of medical gymnastics books, increasingly buttressed by physiology and a new understanding of the skeleton and the muscular system (Leonard & Affleck, 1947). By the end of the eighteenth century, gymnastics systems for the "art of exercise" had been developed by Guts Muth and Christian Salzmann in Germany, Franz Nachtegall in Denmark, and Henrick Ling in Sweden. These systems were infused with romantic ideology and the promise to recapture the purity and vigor of earlier eras (Leonard & Affleck, 1947).[3] Ling's gymnastic exercises were based upon free or natural movements. Johann Bernhard Basedow opened his private academy, the Philanthropium, in Dessau in 1774, where mental and physical classes were taught. By the early 1800s, the highly influential Pestalozzi had written a tract on physical education and opened a gymnasium in his school in Switzerland. Emmanuel Fellenberg's school at Hofwyl emphasized gymnastics and outdoor exercise as well as agriculture and manual labor. Friedrich Froebel included gymnastics and a great variety of exercise and play activities at Yverdon (Hackensmith, 1966). In these widespread reforms which were to become models for American education, the body was given a significant place in efforts to raise the moral level of children from all social classes. Physical well-being and health were central to a belief in the perfectible human being and societal progress.

The influence of science was also brought to bear on the relationship of body, mind, and morals. There was a near reverential attitude toward science in the early nineteenth century. Advances in anatomy, physiology, and physics and applications in medicine and statistics supported enlightenment views that orderly laws of nature could be discovered, and taught. Franz-Joseph Gall's research in 1810 suggested not only that the brain is the "organ of the mind" but that functions are localized in the brain (Boring, 1929/1950). Johann Spurzheim, Gall's popularizer, dubbed the system "craniology," but T. I. Forster's term "phrenology" was the one to endure (Macalister, 1911). The implications were striking. Science could reveal the guidelines for individual improvement through rational means. The regulation of lower faculties and the development of higher faculties rested on an understanding of the laws of nature and the laws of health. George Combe, the most famous proponent of phrenology in England and the United States, presents in *The Constitution of Man in Relation to External Objects* (1835) the scheme by which the individual can find harmony with the whole order of creation: "Man, when civilized and illuminated by knowledge ... discovers in the objects and occurrences around him, a scheme beautifully arranged for the gratification of his whole powers, animal, moral, and intellectual; he recognizes in himself the intelligent and accountable subject of an all-bountiful Creator" (p. 11).

Combe, who was devoted to the ideal of progress, explains human evil as a lack of knowledge of the laws by which to control conflict between his noble and fiendish instincts or impulses. Although he never specifies these laws, he draws analogies to man's capacity to adapt to and control nature:

> Man cannot arrest the sun in its course, so as to avert the wintry storms and cause perpetual spring to bloom around him; but, by the proper exercise of his intelligence and corporeal energies, he is able to foresee the approach of bleak skies and rude winds, and to place himself in safety from their injurious effects. These powers of controlling nature, and of accommodating his conduct to its course, are the direct result of his rational faculties; and in proportion to their cultivation is his sway extended (p. 9).

The key to rational faculties was through the body. The brain (and the mind) are a part of the physical body; therefore, a healthy body is a necessity. In order to achieve bodily health, the laws of physiology must be followed. Physical exercise, activity in the fresh air, simple and nutritious food and so on must be provided for every schoolchild. The narrow curriculum must be expanded to include physical exercise and a variety of subjects in order to train the various faculties of the brain. Education was the chief social reform espoused by the phrenologists, and they were to exert a strong formative influence on developments in the United States (Curti, 1959).

A Moral Crusade for Common School Reform

By the 1830s, the new republic was beginning to face a myriad of problems which threatened realization of the democratic ideals set forth in the Constitution. The Northeast was feeling the impact of industrialization, rising immigration, and urbanization which had grave implications for both family life and health. Work in manufactories meant separation from family, and the crowded conditions of cities, foul air, and lack of sanitary provisions were causes of increasing alarm. Rapidly accumulating fortunes and conspicuous displays of wealth provided a stark contrast to the lot of the poor. The wave of immigration westward and the election of Andrew Jackson held not only a promise of new opportunity for the masses but the threat of an unruly populace with political power.

The inextricable relationship between education and national progress was repeatedly invoked by the pre-Civil War architects of universal schooling in their attempts to win public and political support (Cremin, 1961). Appeals to the public promised that universal education would result in economic progress and social harmony. To the affluent, mass education was presented as the only alternative to public disorder, crime, and an ignorant labor force susceptible to radicalism; to the middle class and poor, it was to be the "great equalizer" in the race for success and the foundation of popular power (Hofstadter, 1962). The unifying theme of the crusade was that education would bring about the moral regeneration needed to recapture what was widely believed to have been the purer form of democracy that existed during the Revolutionary period (Curti, 1959).

A belief that the Republic would be great or weak depending on the character of its citizens had been reiterated since the Revolution. The assumption that moral training was a private (family) and religious concern had been challenged by European thought and educational reforms. The powers of the "established" churches in New England had been greatly diminished by the abolition of laws requiring citizens to attend and maintain them (Douglas, 1977). Calvinistic tenets of predestination, infant depravity, and salvation only by grace had given way to a far more optimistic view of human nature, a belief in individual access to God, and a reliance upon the "dictates of the heart." Religious evangelism and the secular Sunday School Unions were flourishing (Hofstadter, 1962). In such a climate, the argument that the schools — relying upon "nonsectarian" reading of the King James version of the Bible and prayer — could provide the basis for a common morality found support. "Pan-Protestantism" was to become a plan in the moral model for the nation (Tyack & Hansot, 1982).

Thus was the public sphere to assume responsibility for shaping morality. But how could this development be reconciled with the belief that the foundations of national morality must be laid in private families? Both secular and religious thought contributed to resolving the conflict. Women, whose "domestic sphere" included responsibility for child rearing and morality training, were to provide the link between home and social institutions. The virtues of the home were to radiate throughout society. The good individual would contribute to the good society (Cott, 1977). Protestant clergy — faced with a voluntary flock, competition for members, and a female majority in attendance — became major spokesmen for the virtues of the family and the importance of women in shaping the morality of the nation (Douglas, 1977; Hofstadter, 1962). Secular thought emphasized the malleability of the child and the significance of early training, as well as women's "natural role" as teachers of morality. The crusade for common schools meshed with a social movement to educate women in order to fit them for this new interpretation of their responsibilities.

Catherine Beecher, a prominent educator, lays out the argument vividly in her *Treatise on Domestic Economy for the Use of Young Ladies at Home and at School* (1841/1846). While accepting woman's "subordinate position" to her chosen husband as part of a "system of laws which must be established, which sustain certain relations and dependencies in social and civic life" (p. 33), she emphasizes the significance of the part to be enacted by women in the great democratic enterprise:

> The success of democratic institutions, as is conceded by all, depends upon the intellectual and moral character of the mass of the people. If they are ignorant and wicked, it is only a curse, and as much more dreadful than any other form of civil government, as a thousand tyrants are more to be dreaded than one. It is equally conceded, that the formation of the moral and intellectual character is committed mainly to the female hand. The mother forms the character of the future man; the sister bends the fibres that are hereafter to be the forest tree; the wife sways the heart, whose

energies may turn for good or for evil the destinies of a nation. Let the women of a country be made virtuous and intelligent, and the men will certainly be the same. The proper education of a man decides the welfare of an individual; but educate a woman, and the interests of a whole family are secured (p. 37).

Her appeal is to women of all social classes, for each is to play a part in the "building of a glorious temple." Whether they are rich or poor, mistress or servant, "each and all may be animated by the consciousness, that they are agents in accomplishing the greatest work that was ever committed to human responsibility" (p. 38).

Beecher, as well as Emma Willard, Mary Lyon, and Zilpah Grant, provided leadership and organization in altering public opinion about the teaching profession (Curti, 1959; Scott, 1979). Women of all classes were "by nature" endowed with the sensitivity and self-sacrifice required of a teacher. Working-class women suffered at the hands of manufactories, and upper-class women were suppressed by social custom. Together, they could create a true and noble, casteless profession. Horace Mann and other prominent male educators agreed with the stance (Mann, 1842/1891), and the scheme had the additional benefit that women could be hired for less money. Gradually, between 1840 and 1880, women were to replace men as teachers in American schools (Sklar, 1973).[4] In both the private and public realms, women were to be guardians of morality.

Catherine Beecher's devout belief in the great work of American education was echoed by other educational reformers as they spoke from lyceum platforms and wrote tirelessly to obtain support. Reverend E. E. Hale reminisced about the faith in education that abounded in his boyhood: "Briefly, there was the real impression that the Kingdom of Heaven was to be brought in by teaching people what were the relations of acids to alkalies, and what was the derivation of the word cordwainer. If we only knew enough, it was thought we should be wise enough to keep out of the fire and should not be burned" (Hale, 1893, pp. 25-26). The introduction of phrenology into such a cultural Zeitgeist of optimism was little less than a scientific sensation.

During the 1820s, the publications of Gall, Spurzheim, and George and Andrew Combe were widely circulated among educated Americans. Spurzheim's successful lecture tour of 1832 brought popular acclaim as well. In the midst of a whirlwind of activities at Harvard, Spurzheim fell ill and died. Three thousand people, including the Boston Medical Society in a body, marched in the funeral procession. The arrangements were made by President Josiah Quincey of Harvard and a distinguished group of faculty members. On the evening of the funeral, the Boston Phrenological Society was formed (Davies, 1955).[5] George Combe assumed the mantle of leadership and was lionized on his extensive tour in the United States in 1838-40. Combe's best known book, *The Constitution of Man* (1828), sold 2,000 copies in ten days in England; it took more than 15 years for Darwin's *Origin of the Species* (1859) to sell 16,000 copies (Giustino, 1975). By 1838, more than 70,000 copies had been printed in English (Messerli, 1972). The first U.S. edition was published in 1829 and reprinted in many editions, including school editions until 1860 (Giustino, 1975). John Morley noted in the United States and Harriet Martineau in England that it was seen on shelves where there was nothing else save the Bible and *Pilgrim's Progress* (Davies, 1955; Giustino, 1975).

Phrenology must be viewed both as a science and as a philosophy or natural religion. The central scientific tenet, derived from the idea that the mind was located in the brain and involved localized functions, was that the mind could be investigated through observation and experimentation, quite apart from metaphysical speculation. More controversial was the proposition that there was a relationship between the exterior of the skull and the brain (Boring, 1929/1950). By the time entrepreneurs Fowler and Wells began their successful character readings in the United States, "orthophrenologists" were rejecting the "doctrine of the skull" (Bakan, 1966). Oliver Wendell Holmes was among those to recognize the scientific implications of phrenology while villifying the "bumps on the head": "Strike out the false pretensions of phrenology; call it anthropology; let it study man the individual in distinction from man the abstraction, the metaphysical or theological lay-figure; and it becomes the proper study of mankind, one of the noblest and most interesting of pursuits" (cited in Davies, 1955, p. 171).

The philosophy or natural religion of phrenology caught the prevailing winds of thought in the United States. While in England bitter disputes grew in magnitude over the atheistic and materialistic implications of phrenology (Giustino, 1975), U.S. advocates held fast to Combe's early claim that all sound philosophy and all true religion must harmonize (Combe, 1835).[6] "Human nature and the external world have both proceeded from the Creator, and it is impossible, in interpreting their constitution aright, to arrive at any conclusion at variance with a correct interpretation of Scripture" (Combe, 1835, p. 28). Phrenology could be characterized, according to Combe, as Christian morality as it exhibits the "natural foundations of the precepts taught only dogmatically in the New Testament" (Combe, 1835, p. 28). Religious instruction failed in the past to bring mankind and society to a high state of happiness and goodness because it lacked a suitable moral and physical science. Undreamed-of heights of virtue could be attained if natural moral laws were followed. No complicated metaphysical arguments were needed; a simple, natural course could lead to self-improvement and the realization of the "new millenium." While the scientific basis of phrenology was neglected and half-understood by the populace, the philosophical tenets provided the movement with its vitality (Curti, 1953; Davies, 1955).

The social thought of the phrenologists gave impetus to and gained support from believers in humanitarian reforms of all sorts. Whether or not people subscribed to "craniology," many thought, like Oliver Wendell Holmes, that phrenologists were simply preaching "good sense under the disguise of an equivocal system" (Giustino, 1975, p. 74). The phrenologists cast critical eyes upon the evils of society — slavery, alcoholism, infant mortality, child labor, disease, insanity, crime, and so on — and held out hope that these could be abolished through rational means. Health was the core about which a nexus of reforms grew. Andrew Combe, a distinguished physician and brother of George Combe, was a significant figure in health reform.[7] His highly successful *Principles of Physiology Applied to the Preservation of Health and to the Improvement of Physical and Mental Education* (1834/1842), from which he deletes phrenology, became a sort of Bible to reformers.[8] In an era of fads, quackery, tonics, and sorry medical practice, he preached preventive medicine. The burgeoning public health movement, campaign for parks and recreation areas for all classes, and drive for temperance were fanned through his writing (Giustino, 1975). Temperance, it should be noted, was advocated not because drinking was a sin, but because dissections of the brains of the insane and notorious criminals suggested the degenerative effects of alcohol (Combe, 1834/1842).

The health of women and the ways children should be cared for were major themes in Andrew Combe's writings. A plethora of books by physicians and educators appeared in America, directed to these themes (see Wishy, 1968, for a review of popular child nurture writers). Beecher's *Treatise on Domestic Economy* (1841/1846) was reprinted 15 times between 1841 and 1856 (Sklar, 1973). She cites Andrew Combe frequently throughout the book in decrying the fashions and conventions dictated to middle- and upper-class women, and the working and living conditions of laboring women which contribute to invalidism and poor health. Following Combe's example, Beecher included detailed chapters on the structure and functioning of the body from the skin through the nervous system. The premise shared by these writers was that knowledge of physiology could lead to adherence to natural laws of health, through which illness and many diseases could be prevented.

The urgency to improve women's health and their knowledge about health care was mandated by concern for women as the procreators and rearers of children. The concern was documented by Beecher's reference to the fact that one-quarter of the children born died before completing their second year (Beecher, 1841/1846) and Combe's citation of Dr. Granville's tables indicating that only 542 infants out of every 1,000 births among the poor survived the second year (Combe, 1834/1842, p. 326). The strong and abiding bonds between women's groups and health reforms, including temperance, become more understandable in light of the statistics of the 1830s and the conviction that they could be remedied. Education, of course, was the key to the dilemma.

The Constitution of Man could be considered, wrote George Combe, "an introduction to an Essay on Education" (Combe, 1835, p. 410). His message was to energize the work of some of the most influential educators in America, including Horace Mann, Henry Barnard, Cyrus Pierce, and George B. Emerson (Hinsdale, 1937). Horace Mann was converted after reading *The Constitution of Man* in 1837, and he became a lifelong friend of Combe whom he considered the greatest living man. He named his son in Combe's honor, and he spread the philosophical teachings of phrenology as an integral part of his campaign for common school reform (Mann, 1865).

Mann, like George Combe and a large number of American educational reformers, found in phrenology an antidote to a Calvinistic childhood. Moral elevation—the chief end of education—was to be achieved for all individuals, not merely the elect, through the teaching of natural moral laws. Sectarian creeds were like politics; they divide human beings and promote dissension. Neither was to have a place in the common school. Phrenology promised to bring individuals and society into harmony. Science could enhance and fulfill the New Testament precepts of love, concern for one another, and recognition of the common bonds among all humans (Mann, 1865).[9]

The prominence given to the body could not have been further removed from the Calvinistic denial of the physical being.[10] In the first issue of the *Common School Journal* (1838), Mann affirms his faith in the union of body, mind, and morals in education. Mental power will rise in proportion to physical power. If the race deteriorates physically, their bodies will be "wholly unfit to keep a soul in" (p. 11). The entire contents of his Sixth Report (1842) as secretary of the Board of Education of Massachusetts was devoted to a dissertation on the study of physiology in the schools. Physiology, as Mann used the term, meant the study of the "laws of life and hygiene, or the rules and observations by which health can be preserved and promoted" (Mann, 1842/1891,

p. 131). He strongly criticized the state of the schools and included a lengthy discussion of the effects of exercise on oxygenation of the blood, proper diet, purity of air, and cleanliness on health.[11] His argument, well buttressed by medical reports and Biblical quotations, was for the primacy of physiology in the school curriculum.

Mann's emphasis on the body in educational reforms was hardly radical. As early as the 1820s, the virtues of European gymnastics were discussed in such diverse journals and magazines as *The North American Review, Medical Intelligencer, American Journal of Education, The Gazette* (edited by the Pestalozzian, Francis Neefe), and *Ladies Magazine* (Betts, 1968). Two important German political refugees, with letters of introduction from Lafayette, arrived to spur on the interest: Charles Follen introduced gymnastics at Harvard, and Charles Beck joined the staff at the Round Hill School in Northhampton, Massachusetts, organized by Joseph Cogswell and George Bancroft (Leonard & Affleck, 1947). In the Round Hill Prospectus of 1823, the founders announced that they were "deeply impressed with the necessity of uniting physical with moral education" and said they were "the first in the new continent to conduct gymnastics with a purely literary establishment" (cited in Betts, 1968, p. 793). Catherine Beecher included calisthenics (adapted chiefly from Ling's system of free movements) in her teacher training school, and wrote *Suggestions Respecting Improvements in Education* in 1829 and *A Course in Calisthenics for Young Ladies* in 1831 (Betts, 1968). Influential reports appeared in the 1830s to give further impetus to the reforms Mann espoused: Victor Cousin's *Report on the State of Public Instruction in Prussia* in 1835, Calvin Stowe's *Report on Elementary Instruction in Europe* in 1837, and A. D. Bache's *Report on Education in Europe* in 1839 (Betts, 1968; Sklar, 1973).

Throughout the 1840s the common school crusade spread and gained momentum; and the body moved in tandem with the reforms as the doctrine of the unity of body, mind, and morals was advanced from podium and press. Andrew Combe's *Principles of Physiology* was known by teachers in "almost every school district" in New York (Betts, 1968). German immigrants, seeking refuge from political turmoil, arrived in large numbers. Many were professional men with families (known as Latin-Farmers) who brought with them high standards for state schools with an emphasis upon physical as well as mental education (Munrow, 1981). By 1848, the Cincinnati and New York *Turgemeinde* gymnastic clubs had been formed. Within three years, there were 25 or more Turner Societies, as they were called, with a membership of nearly 2,000, scattered from New York through the Midwest. By the late 1850s, the membership had risen to between 9 and 10,000 members (Leonard & Affleck, 1947). In many common schools in German communities, one to two hours were given daily to gymnastics (Gymnastics, 1861).

But the course of social reform was to be a slow and painful one. Catherine Beecher, in her unremitting campaign for education and health, indicates an acute sensitivity to political reality. In *Letters to the People on Health and Happiness* (1855) and *Physiology and Calisthenics for Schools and Families* (1865), she focuses forcibly on the deteriorating health of the people and their children, and the failure to provide the "proper education of the body" (*Letters*, p. 8). "In consequence of this dreadful neglect and mismanagement, the children of this country are every year becoming less and less healthful and good-looking." She recalls the "rosy cheeked" children, "full of health and spirits," of her own youth and contrasts them with the "sallow complexions" and "delicate looks of children now" (*Letters*, p. 9). She sets out a practical plan, which is "so short that even American men of business can be induced to read it" (p. 11). She calls for proper ventilation of school rooms and for at least one-half hour of every school session to be spent in a regular course of calisthenic and gymnastic exercise. Instruction in hygiene was also essential, and "Nothing can be made more interesting to children than information in regard to the curious construction of their own bodies" (p. 171). Teachers were needed whose "official duty is to secure the health and perfect development of the body," as were scientifically arranged and applied programs to train teachers (p. 171). (*Physiology and Calisthenics for Schools and Families* gained a larger circulation than her earlier volume for teachers, and her adaptation of Swedish gymnastics set to music was becoming well known [Van Dalen & Bennett, 1971].) In Beecher's view, all that was wanting in the effort to "transform the inhabitants of this land from the low development now so extensive to the beautiful model of the highest form of humanity" was public understanding and demand for a "universal course of training" (*Letters*, p. 171).

Beecher's warnings about the deteriorating health of the nation touched a wellspring of growing concern. For all of the bright hopes of the 1830s, the ills of industrialism multiplied. By the 1850s, factory workers had begun to agitate for a reduction of work hours, from 13 to 15 hours a day to 10. The New England Association of Farmers, Mechanics and Other Workingmen protested the brutal factory regime and stated that the threat to the health and morals of a rising generation of children in factories constituted "perhaps the most alarming evil that afflicts our country" (Betts, 1972, p. 45). A sanitary survey of the state of Massachusetts, proposed by the American Statistical

Association and supported by the Massachusetts Medical Society, resulted in two influential reports in 1850. The reports documented the plight of the laboring classes and called for reforms in hygiene and public parks and for more attention to be given to physical training (Betts, 1972). The American Medical Association instigated studies of the sanitary and general health conditions in many cities, including New York, Philadelphia, Baltimore, New Orleans, and Cincinnati (Betts, 1972). The dismal impression of public health was underscored by the Surgeon General's Report of 1856: Out of the 16,064 men who presented themselves for enlistment in the U.S. Army in 1852, only 2,736 were accepted. Eighty-three percent of the men were rejected for physical disqualification (Baxter, 1875). By 1857, a Sanitary Convention was held in Philadelphia to encourage the development of a public health movement — the National Health Association (Shyrock, 1929). Lay people, including a large representation of temperance workers, joined with physicians, statisticians, and legislators in making plans that were intended to benefit all classes of the population. One speaker expressed a commonly held belief of the time: "If the people would but seek health first, all other things from money to morality would be added unto them" (cited in Shyrock, 1929, p. 648).

By the outbreak of the Civil War, the unity of body, mind, and morals was a concept strongly insinuated into social thought. The mounting problems of society had strengthened arguments for the state's assumption of responsibility for health and morality. Women's duties in the public as well as private realms were clear. Education must not only reach all children, it must be revised to ensure the proper development of the whole person. Haphazard techniques employed by badly educated teachers would not suffice. The need for a new profession of physical trainers, guided by scientific precepts, was to become as apparent to other educators and physicians as it was to Catherine Beecher.

A New Profession

In 1861 Amherst College established the first department in hygiene and physical education, headed by a physician with faculty status. The physician was to be responsible for teaching physiology and hygiene, supervising student health, and providing instruction in gymnastics. That such an appointment would be made at Amherst some 20 years before other colleges and would provide a conceptual model for the nation must be considered in the light of the mission of Amherst itself and the remarkable scientists who guided the enterprise.

Amherst was founded in 1821 to revive and preserve the faith of the Puritans. Harvard had defected to the paths of the Unitarians, Williams was faltering, and the orthodox saw in Amherst an institution based on the "principles of charity and benevolence" for "the classical education of indigent young men of piety and talents for the Christian Ministry" (Hitchcock, 1863, p. 160). Edward Hitchcock (1793-1864), the third president of Amherst, like his predecessors was a minister committed to the unique responsibility of the college for the training of the young. In addition, he was a geologist of world fame, the first president of the American Association for the Advancement of Science (1840), and a charter member of the National Academy of Sciences (Lesley, 1867). He shared the conviction of other distinguished nineteenth-century scientists that science must not necessarily be reconciled with a literal interpretation of the Scripture, but that the principles of science are a transcript of Divine character. Hitchcock wrote in his inaugural address in 1845: "And it is the facts of the natural world that most strikingly discover to us the wonders of adaptation and design, and lead the mind irresistibly to infer a Superior Being" (Hitchcock, 1845, p. 19).[12]

Hitchcock was also concerned about the physical health of the students and published a book of lectures given to the students on temperance and the prevention of dyspepsy through walking and moderate exercise (Hitchcock, 1831). He believed that "no sciences have furnished so many and so appropriate facts, illustrative of natural theology, as anatomy and physiology" (1845, p. 26). But it is to Hitchcock's successor, Reverend William Augustus Stearns, that credit is given for the elevation of physical education to the regular curriculum. Stearns had stated in his inaugural address in 1854 that "of one thing I am certain; the highest intellectual efficiency can never be reached, the noblest characters will never be formed, till a greater soundness of physical constitution is attained" (Stearns, 1855, p. 87). In each successive annual report to the trustees he brought attention to the failing health of students, and by 1859 called for the building of a gymnasium and the procuring of its proper appointments. If moderate daily exercise could be provided to every student, "I have the deep conviction . . . that not only would lives and health be preserved, but animation and cheerfulness, and a higher order of efficient study and intellectual life would be secured" (cited in Tyler, 1895, p. 161). In 1860 the gymnasium was completed, and the trustees voted to create a new department. The first physician appointed was an accomplished gymnast, but he was to resign after only a few months due to ill health. The second person named to the position in 1861 was Edward Hitchcock, Jr., M.D. Young Hitchcock had graduated from Amherst College (1849) and from Harvard Medical School (1853), and studied comparative anatomy with Sir Richard Owen, England's most distinguished biologist, in 1859 (Leonard & Affleck, 1947). He taught natural sciences at the Williston Seminary and collaborated with his father in publishing *Elementary Anatomy and Physiology for Colleges, Academies and Other Schools* (1859). The philosophical tenet shared by father and son is that the amazing organization and harmony of the whole animal kingdom reveal the work of one Infinite Mind. The study of physical structures and the observance of "Nature's Laws" concerning the need for diet and exercise were crucial for health and morals (Hitchcock & Hitchcock, 1859/1864).

When Dr. Hitchcock assumed his new position, the problem to be solved was "How shall the man physically be made efficient so that the intellectual, moral and spiritual may at the same time secure its full development?" (Hitchcock, 1881/1962, p. 108). Hitchcock's approach was an empirical one, and he began to collect longitudinal anthropometric measurements of Amherst students in the fall of 1861. "This I did partly to enable the students to learn by yearly comparisons of themselves how they were getting on as regards the physical man. The ulterior object, however, was to help ascertain what are the data or constants of the typical man, and especially the college man" (Hitchcock, 1881/1962, p. 111).

Just when Hitchcock read the seminal book *Sur l'Homme et la Developement de ses Facultes* (1835) by the Belgian statistician Adolphe Quetelet is not known, but it was translated into English in 1842. Quetelet (1796-1874) provided a historical review of the quest of artists, anatomists, and mathematicians (cf. Giotto, Leonardo da Vinci, Durer) to determine the ideal proportions of the human body. Of most significance was his theory that human stature is distributed in populations according to the law of error. His data included surveys of the height and weight of children. His notion of "*l'homme moyen*" or the typical man was presented as an example of the laws of nature. M. Quetelet reasoned that if a typical figure or model of the human race existed, all variations from it in excess or defect would be due to accidental causes. The need for the collection of anthropometric data was clear for " . . . how can we study the modifications which the elements relative to man, as well as their laws of development, undergo in the different races, when we have not settled the point of commencement?" (cited in Boyd, 1980, p. 342). Quetelet's theoretical and empirical work was to have an enormous impact on scientists, military planners, and social reformers in many countries, and he was among the founders of the British Association for the Advancement of Science (Baxter, 1875).

Hitchcock says of his own work,

> I have no theory on the subject [the typical man] and have instituted
> but very few generalizations; but my desire has been to carefully
> compile and put on record as many of these observations as possible
> for comparison and verification of statistical work in this same
> direction by many other persons in America and Europe (Hitchcock,
> 1881/1962, p. 111).

Hitchcock's modesty is apparent, for although in 1881, when he provides a retrospective view of his contributions, anthropometric
research was flourishing, in 1861 there had only been a few cross-
sectional studies of medical students and army and police recruits in
the United States (Boyd, 1980). For 50 years Hitchcock served
Amherst as the chief medical supervisor and mentor to generations of
students and fostered the union of scientific endeavors and educational
policy (cf. Hitchcock, 1885, 1887). He was named the first president of
the American Association for the Advancement of Physical Education
(AAAPE) in 1885 and formed a committee on statistics and
measurements (Leonard & Affleck, 1947).

Although German gymnastics flourished and the Turners's
system was the best organized and largest in numbers and
geographical distribution in the United States, the normal school
established in New York in 1866 was not to become the model for the
new profession of physical trainers (Zeigler, 1979). Hitchcock labored
in splendid isolation for nearly 20 years, but his call for the union of
scientific measurement and exercise in order to better the health and
morals of each individual student was heard by educators and social
reformers (Hartwell, 1886).

In 1879 Dr. Dudley Allen Sargent (M.D. Yale University) became
assistant professor of physical training and director of the new Hemenway Gymnasium at Harvard University.[18] From the outset, he collected an extensive set of anthropometric measures on students. He
also evolved a series of strength tests, using the dynamometer which
anthropologist William T. Brigham had brought from Paris (Van Dalen
& Bennett, 1971). Sargent began with complete physical examinations
and photographs for future comparisons of each student, and repeated
his examinations and anthropometric measurements every six months.
Individual prescriptions for exercise were made for each student,
specifying the "movements and apparatus he may best use" (Sargent,
1889/1962, p. 155). More than 50,000 physical examinations were made
in his department at Harvard (Gerber, 1971).

The golden age of anthropometric measurement by physical
educators, ushered in by Hitchcock and Sargent, was between 1885

and 1900. In this period, Dr. Jay W. Seaver charted 2,700 students at Yale; Wood, 1,500 at Wellesley; Dr. Delphine Hanna, 1,600 at Oberlin; and Clapp, 1,500 women at the University of Nebraska (Van Dalen & Bennett, 1971). As noted earlier, Dr. Edward Hitchcock served as chairman of the newly established Department of Anthropometry and Statistics when the AAAPE was formed in 1885. Two years later a Committee on Vital Statistics was added, chaired by Senda Berenson of Smith College (Spears & Swanson, 1978). The direction of professional development was spurred by wider social concerns over the health of children and, for those who made a "benign" interpretation of Darwin and Spencer, a need for the public sphere to take measures to ensure the improvement and future of the human race.

Anthropometric research was to bind the disciplines of physical education, physiology, anthropology, and the child development movement. The distinguished Harvard physiologist, Dr. Henry Pickering Bowditch, persuaded the Boston School Committee to fund a growth study of public school children; the results, considered classics in the international growth literature, were published between 1877 and 1891 (Tanner, 1981). Bowditch also chaired the Committee on School Anthropometry of the AAAPE which was formed in 1897 (Spears & Swanson, 1978). Franz Boas, the eminent anthropologist, began his longitudinal study of growth in Worcester, Massachusetts, in 1881 when he was recruited by G. Stanley Hall to come to Clark University. Boas approached school authorities in Oakland, Toronto, Milwaukee, and St. Louis that year in his role as chairman of the section of Physical Anthropology for the World's Columbian Exposition to collect and pool data on physical growth. The results appeared in major publications between 1893 and 1900 (Tanner, 1981). G. Stanley Hall, credited with founding the child development movement, further strengthened the late nineteenth-century bonds. Hall, who studied physiology in Germany with Professor Ludwig (Hall, 1904), received a Ph.D. at Harvard in 1878 upon presenting a dissertation, supervised by Bowditch and conducted in his laboratory, on "The Muscular Perception of Space" (Wilson, 1914). The articles included in *Pedagogical Seminary*, the journal Hall founded in 1891, reflect his great and abiding interest in anthropometric measurement and physical health. He, like Bowditch and Boas, acknowledges the contributions of Hitchcock, Sargent, and other physical educators involved in anthropometric research (see Hall, 1904; Boyd, 1980).

Anthropometric measurements of children and students had important implications for public policy debate; the improvement in methods and standardization of techniques could yield information about some of the pressing social issues which had been gathering momentum for 50 years: the effects of child labor, social class, urban dwelling, diet, and exercise on growth and health. It is not a coincidence that measurement flourished with and supported all manner of "progressive" reforms and private acts of philanthropy from the boom in the building of parks and playgrounds to the creation of programs to distribute milk in urban areas (see Rainwater, 1922; Siegel & White, 1982).

Physical educators saw themselves at the very center of reforms for health and morality. Results of anthropometric measurement, as we have seen in Sargent's work, could be used to prescribe individualized exercise for children, to evaluate different forms of exercise,[14] to detect physical deformities, especially scoliosis (curvature of the spine) which was the focus of Dr. Delphine Hanna's research,[15] and to monitor healthy growth and development. Yet for all of the promise held by the profession, only California had passed legislation requiring instruction in hygiene and physical exercise in 1866.[16] Ohio followed suit, slowly, in 1892, and North Dakota in 1899 (Hackensmith, 1966). By the 1880s, laws requiring compulsory education and limiting child labor began to be passed, and school attendance soared (Hackensmith, 1966). These developments led to a resurgence of the major question of the 1830s—the effect of school attendance on health. Armed with the methods of anthropometry, researchers from America and Europe sought to provide data to effect reform of school regimes with their long hours of sedentary intellectual labor (see Hall, 1905).[17]

Educational reform hinged on rigorous teacher preparation. Dudley Allen Sargent saw teacher training as the most important part of his work (Sargent, 1881/1962). For 40 years, beginning in 1881, he conducted teacher training programs at the Sargent Normal School and the Harvard Summer School for more than 5,000 men and women (Gerber, 1971). Course work—in addition to practical classes in gymnastics, swimming, and so on—included anatomy, histology, physiology, anthropology, anthropometry and methods of prescribing exercise, visual and hearing tests, and conducting physical examinations (Sargent, 1881/1962). Mrs. Mary Hemenway founded the Boston Normal School of Gymnastics (BNSG) in 1889, modeled after the Royal Gymnastics Central Institute in Stockholm. Amy Morris Homans was appointed director, and Baron Nils Posse, a graduate of the Royal Institute, became the first teacher. The basic science courses, similar to those prescribed by Sargent, were taken at the Massachusetts Institute of Technology; lectures were also given by Harvard professors (Spears & Swanson, 1978). Dr. William G. Anderson and Dr. Jay Seaver began the Chautauqua Summer School of Physical Education (1886) in which sciences and anthropometry were taught (Van Dalen & Bennett, 1971). The direction of training was that of applied physiology.

In 1885, women physical educators in the public schools out-numbered men, as they did in teaching in general (Lewis, 1969a). The nexus of health, morals, and education attracted idealistic and able women to the new profession. They assumed positions of leadership in coeducational institutions and women's colleges as well as in profes-sional organizations (Spears & Swanson, 1978).[18] The most significant meeting of the post-Civil War period was called by a woman, philan-thropist Mary Hemenway. The Boston Conference of 1889 aroused such interest among physical educators that the AAAPE cancelled its scheduled convention for that year and its membership attended the Boston Conference (Weston, 1962).

The plan of the Boston Conference was to invite representatives of each of the leading gymnastic systems, including the Turners and the YMCA, to present summaries of their philosophies, programs, and research (see Weston, 1962, for the texts of the speeches). Although it may be assumed that Mary Hemenway and Amy Morris Homans were inspired in part by a desire to bring Swedish gymnastics to the atten-tion of the public, the conference served much broader professional and historical ends. There emerged no winner in the so-called "Battle of the Systems," but participants were exposed to different schools of thought and different emphases in teaching. Indeed, some of the par-ticipants (for example, Hitchcock and Sargent) had long advocated diversification of programs of exercise. Historically, the conference presentations are of interest because they reveal a robust research in-terest and a commitment on the part of all speakers to individual and mass health and to the unity of body, mind, and morals.

While the problem ostensibly facing the conference was how to build an integrated, organized approach to bodily training, a larger problem appears in ghostly form. No representatives of competitive athletics were invited; a "presence" was felt, however, and many of the participants referred to the popular student-run amusements or recreation. Dr. Edward Hartwell of Johns Hopkins University, among others, complained about the difficulty of regulating athletic sports and warned that they could only be seen as a single stage of training: " . . . they bear so indelibly the marks of their childish origin; they are so crude and unspecialized as to their methods as to render them in-adequate for the purposes of a thorough-going and broad system of bodily education" (Hartwell, 1889/1962, p. 128). Sargent, however, touched the nub of the great battle of the future: "Some of us believe it is more to the credit of a university to have one hundred men who can do a creditable performance in running, rowing, ball playing, etc. than to have one man who can break a record, or a team that can always win a championship" (Sargent, 1889/1962, p. 116).

THE COMPETITIVE TRADITION

Athletics and Elite Virtue

In the mid-nineteenth century, as European countries developed gymnastics systems for schools, the English public schools (that is, private) for boys gave recognition to the student-run games which had been practiced since the 1820s. Although Dr. Thomas Arnold, the famous headmaster of Rugby from 1828 to 1842, cannot be credited with the development of organized games in England, he gave an indirect but powerful impetus to their growth and endorsement by headmasters. P. C. McIntosh writes of Arnold:

> Public Schools at the beginning of the century were as notorious for their vices and lawlessness as they were famous for their classical education. At Rugby and Winchester, school rebellions reached such dimensions that the military had to be called out to quell them. Arnold set out in 1828 to infuse a new moral tone and a religious idealism into Rugby. He once said that what he looked for in a Christian school were first religious and moral principles; secondly, gentlemanly conduct; thirdly, intellectual ability (McIntosh, 1981, p. 192).

Arnold sought the support of the oldest boys, those in the sixth form, to secure reforms which included forbidding hare hunting and disbanding the boys' pack of hounds, and expelling uncooperative students; that support was won, in part, by recognizing the boys' authority in the area of athletics. Herein, according to McIntosh, lies the key to the acceptance of organized games as the pattern of physical education in public schools: the tradition of self-government. In that tradition, the boys hired the games master, a man valued for his skills in cricket or other games, and selected their own teams (McIntosh, 1981).

Tom Brown's Schooldays (1857), written by Thomas Hughes, gave a fictitious account of Rugby in the time of Dr. Arnold. In this best-selling novel worldwide, the cult of the games was given an ideological boost which was to have a great influence upon education in England and the United States (McIntosh, 1981). Cricket and football were not merely games; they were noble institutions, the birthrights of British boys, the formers of character.

In 1864 the earl of Clarendon, chairman of the Royal Commission on Public Schools, gave a more prestigious endorsement to the link between athletics and character:

> The bodily training which gives health and activity to the frame is imparted at English schools, not by gymnastic exercises which are

employed for that end on the continent—exercises which are undoubtedly very valuable and which we should be glad to see introduced more widely in England—but by athletic games which,
whilst they serve this purpose well, serve other purposes
besides. . . . The cricket and football field . . . are not merely places
of exercise and amusement; they help to form some of the most
valuable social qualities and manly virtues, and they hold, like the
classroom and the boarding house, a distinct and important place in
Public School education (cited in McIntosh, 1981, p. 186).

For the elite males who were the pride of the British Empire in
government, business, and military pursuits, competitive athletics
became mandatory. For the masses, however, a different course of instruction was suggested in the 1850s and 1860s: Gymnastics were seen
as a more suitable form of physical education because they would do
more for physical health in the comparatively short time these
children were in school. Women were allowed to assume leadership in
the development of physical education in the elementary schools, and
they waged a successful campaign to oust military drill and teach
Swedish gymnastics (see Posse, 1890). In 1878 Concordia Löfving, a
Swedish teacher of Ling's system, was invited to become lady
superintendent of physical education (McIntosh, 1981). Thus,
England's dual system grew. Athletics were taught by professional
male coaches and gymnastics by women educators.

The English games found fertile ground in America. By the 1840s,
student-run competitive athletics had created problems for educators
who complained about absences from class, injuries, and an injection of
professionalism into amateur pursuits (Van Dalen & Bennett, 1971).
The developing interest in athletics was marked by the appearance of
the first two sporting weeklies, *The Spirit of the Times* and the *National Police Gazette*. They featured news on horse racing, boxing,
cricket, and baseball (Betts, 1974).

After the Civil War, the British male ethos of athletics and
character building, and enthusiasm for competitive athletics fused in
American colleges and universities as well as the wider society (Van
Dalen & Bennett, 1971). The development of "manly" virtues was
celebrated by Horatio Alger in *Bound to Rise* (1873), in which "red-
blooded" replaced "pious" (the word of a generation earlier), for example, as the principal word of praise for the boy hero (Wishy, 1968).
Spencer's popularization of Darwin led to the common adoption of
catch phrases like "survival of the fittest" which were applied to competitive athletics, lending an evolutionary cast to the contests. The
qualities needed for athletic success were explicitly linked to those required for entrepreneurial contests (Hofstadter, 1944). If the weaker

dropped out along the way, so much the better for the future. As Andrew Carnegie, one of Spencer's enthusiastic supporters, declared, "All is well since all grows better" (Hofstadter, 1944, p. 44).

Athletic growth was not only compatible with laissez-faire interpretations of Darwin, but with social reform advocates as well. One of the most significant figures in promoting the cause and calling upon education to regulate the "manly" game of football was Theodore Roosevelt. (Those who advocated abolition of the sport he put in the "mollycoddle class"; cited in Hart & Ferleger, 1941, p. 183). He explicitly and on many occasions extolled the contributions of athletic competition to moral development and good citizenship (cf. Lewis, 1969b). Further, Roosevelt struck out directly at the physical trainers and made "superior" moral claims for competitive athletics:

> Granting that athletic sports do good, it remains to be considered what athletic sports are best. The answer to this is obvious. They are those sports which call for the greatest exercise of fine moral qualities, such as resolution, courage, endurance and capacity to hold one's own and to stand up under punishment. For this reason out-of-door sports are better than gymnastics and calisthenics. To be really beneficial the sport must be enjoyed by the participator. Much more health will be gained by the man who is not always thinking of his health than by the poor being who is forever wondering whether he has helped his stomach or his lungs, or developed this or that muscle. Laborious work in the gymnasium, directed towards the fulfilling of certain tests of skill or strength, is very good in its way; but the man who goes through it does not begin to get the good he would in a season's play with an eleven or a nine on the gridiron field or the diamond. The mere fact that the moral qualities are not needed in the one case, but are all the time called into play in the other is sufficient to show the little worth of the calisthenic system of gymnastic development when compared with rough outdoor games (Roosevelt, 1893, p. 1,236).

Roosevelt, always the astute observer of public sentiment, was well aware that athletics had become an integrating feature of college life in the 1880s. (By the 1890s, 50,000 or more people attended the Yale-Princeton game in New York on Thanksgiving Day; Lewis, 1972.) Newspaper coverage of athletic events had long since abandoned the green young reporters of the 1840s. Specialists were employed to write expert and imaginative articles on the national institution of athletic competition. From the New York *World* to the San Francisco *Examiner*, the best of writers were hired to analyze sports events (Betts, 1974). Further, agencies outside the schools had embraced athletics as a means of social reform. Muscular Christianity was preached from even elite pulpits (Douglas, 1977).[19] Churches formed athletic clubs which grew to become the widespread Boys Clubs of the 1890s (Van Dalen & Bennett, 1971). The Young Men's Christian Association, an early leader in gymnastic training, gradually revised its offerings to include, and later emphasize, competitive sports under the red triangle symbolizing the union of the physical, intellectual, and spiritual (Van Dalen & Bennett, 1971). The burgeoning parks and playgrounds created by reform movements also provided homes for athletic competition, explicitly seen in some circles as a means of preventing and curing juvenile delinquency (Schlossman, 1973).

The "moral" science of psychology both echoed and reinforced the association between athletics, for males, and morality or character building. G. Stanley Hall inspired support from journalists, educators, and community agencies for the adoption of athletic programs for boys (cf. Gould, 1977; Schlossman, 1973). This is, of course, the same G. Stanley Hall who admired and helped to foster the work of the anthropometrists and advocated a "gymnasium of the future," in which basic sciences should be taught, in the first part of *Adolescence* (Hall, 1904, vol. 1). But Hall's deeper conviction was recapitulation theory. The play activities of children were seen as primary evidence for the idea that individual development (ontogeny) rehearses the development of the species (phylogeny). The "basal powers old to the race" provide the best exercise, for they " . . . enforce those psycho-neural and muscular forms which race habit has handed down rather than insist on those arbitrarily designed to develop our ideas of symmetry regardless of heredity. The best guide to the former is interest, zest and spontaneity" (Hall, 1904, vol. 1, p. 207). Brutality, bullying, and so forth should not be stamped out (in some portions of the book) as they will "deplete the bad centers." And as a further corollary, undesirable impulses stimulate the "higher powers" for "An able-bodied young man, who can not fight physically, can hardly have a high and true sense of honor, and is generally a milk-sop, a lady-boy, or a sneak" (Hall, 1904, p. 217).

Hall, like Rousseau whom he acknowledged, would leave the prepubescent years to nature and "allow the fundamental traits of savagery their fling until twelve" (Hall, 1904, p. x). But after this time, during the critical years of adolescence, the foundations of male morality are laid down and athletics are seen as a school of ethics (Hall, 1904). Thus a remarkable ripple from Rousseau unites the British public school tradition with the edicts of G. Stanley Hall. Early education really doesn't matter; it can even be left to women, as nature's course should be followed. Older boys, however, need to be inducted into the paths of masculine character.

Hall's theory was important to Roosevelt's efforts to wrest morality from female clutches and to provide a "strenuous" example of the male reformers and "Stern men with empires in their brains" who were needed by America. The clarion call could not long be ignored by American educators.

The New Physical Education

The dilemma facing educators committed to individual and public health for boys and girls was a thorny one, with volleys coming from popular, governmental, and scientific advocates of athletics. But to make the situation even more complex, the humanitarian and romantic arguments of John Dewey must be added. Like Friedrich Froebel and George Herbert Mead, Dewey saw in play the foundations of a sense of self and community. Play was not the antithesis of work but an educational touchstone for responsible development. Natural activities, rather than adult interventions, were the guide to tapping interest and creativity in educational pursuits. Dewey spoke of young children and Hall of adolescents, yet "play" was the common term used by both men. Given the lack of distinction in terms, "play" was used for many purposes. In the speech of those reformers of physical education who strove to separate it from a reliance upon gymnastics, admittedly an adult intervention, "play" became a rallying point.

The "New Physical Education" movement, as first defined by Clark Hetherington (1910/1962) and Thomas Wood (1910), reveals the strong influence of Dewey and Hall. First, dualism of mind and body was rejected. This was hardly a new concept for physical educators, but a somewhat different hue was given to the argument. Physical education was to be physical only in the sense that the activity of the whole organism was the educational agent and not the mind alone (Hetherington, 1910/1962), and it would find itself in organic relationship with education as a whole (Wood, 1910). Second, the definitions of "play" were expanded. "We use the term general play to include plays, games, athletics, dancing, the play side of gymnastics, and all play activities in which the large muscles are used more or less vigorously" (Hetherington, 1910/1962, p. 160). The influence of Hall and Dewey is evident in Hetherington's comment that "better educational results in general and a broader and higher capacity to work are secured by organizing the child's natural self-sustaining activities than by forcing upon him those foreign to his nature" (cited in Gerber, 1971, p. 392). Hetherington also agreed with Hall that "play" activities were internally impelled (Hetherington, 1910/1962).

Hetherington shared the widespread belief of progressives that play experiences could help to fill the void appearing in methods of moral training in public schools. But the potential dangers of competitive athletics were well known:

> The most conspicuous thing about play is its character-forming power. Vices are learned in play, not in the classroom. In the anxiety of earnest parents concerning championship is seen the moral power of leadership. Criticisms of intercollegiate athletics are eloquent testimonials of the moral power of athletics and the quality of leadership. (Hetherington, 1910/1962, p. 163)

At the time Hetherington wrote this article, he had resigned from his unique post as "Professor of Physical Training and Director of Gymnastics and Athletics" at the University of Missouri. After building a model program for the nation at Missouri, including extension services for children and adults, the intercollegiate athletic reforms he instituted brought down the wrath of the alumni, who demanded the resignation of President Richard Jesse (Bronson, 1958).[20]

T. Tait McKenzie, M.D. (University of Pennsylvania) also endorsed the incorporation of athletics in 1910, although it cost him dearly as well:[21]

> This great surging tide of emotion . . . cannot be dammed; it must be directed, and it is we, as directors of physical education, to whom, as leaders in the work, is given the task of turning this great power for good or evil in the right direction that it may be used, not for the debauching but rather for the uplifting of the whole nation (cited in Gerber, 1971, p. 344).

The subtle shifts in the "New Physical Education" were to have wide repercussions that could not have been anticipated in 1910. The shifts of note are: the rejection of formal gymnastics and calisthenics as a basis for curricula, and a new emphasis on group interactions, the expanded definitions of play and physical education that led from physiology to education as a primary training discipline, and the suggestion that the moral potential of physical education might outweigh contributions to health within a total educational plan.

The Transformation of Physical Education

"Athletics are educational and character-building" were the words needed by advocates to transform and profit from the administration of these activities. College presidents, and their trustees and regents, had already become aware of the potential revenue to be gained from athletics. In 1889, for example, as the physical educators mapped a professional future, Yale alumni held a dinner at Delmonico's for over 400 people honoring its athletes. A few years later, Yale became the first college to organize annual alumni giving, and within ten years the endowment fund was doubled (Lewis, 1969a). Critics such as economist Thorstein Veblen and Henry S. Pritchett, president of the Carnegie Foundation, noted with concern the ties between higher education and commerce. Pritchett commented in 1905: "The American university, whether supported by private gift or by the state, is conducted under an administrative system which approximates closer and closer as time goes on that of a business corporation" (Pritchett, 1905/1972, p. 223).

By 1906 athletics began to be placed under the control of college authorities, and athletic coaches were increasingly named directors of comprehensive departments, which included physical education, and given faculty rank (to ensure "proper control") (Lewis, 1969a). The popularity of the sports programs sponsored by the YMCA during the First World War further strengthened the athletic cause, despite the fact that gymnastics and calisthenics were employed to train recruits (Lee, 1972b). Physicians, many of whom returned to medical schools for additional training following Abraham Flexner's critical report to the Carnegie Commission, saw little future for themselves in higher education after the war (Lewis, 1969a). Medical gymnastic expertise and research were no longer a first-order priority and were of no relevance to the prominent new coaches.

In 1908, 41 percent of the directors of physical training in colleges and universities had medical degrees, but by 1928 the Carnegie Commission Report found that "physical education" showed the largest number of members with the rank of professor who had only a bachelor's degree or no degree whatsoever. However, of the 177 directors, only 23 had majored in physical education and only four held master's degrees in either physical education or education. The typical director was a former varsity athlete, and 85 percent of the directors were football coaches (Lewis, 1969a). A similar transformation took place in the men's programs in secondary schools: 70 percent of the school administrators considered athletics and physical education part of one program, and in 52 percent of the cases the director of physical education was responsible for competitive athletics (Lewis, 1969a).

William T. Foster, one of the many critics of these developments, wrote a stinging indictment of intercollegiate athletics in the *Atlantic Monthly* in which he delineated the aims of athletics conducted for education and athletics conducted for business:

> The most obvious fact is that our system of intercollegiate athletics, after unbounded opportunity to show what it can do for the health,

> recreation, and character of *all* our students, has proven a failure. The ideal of the coach is excessive training of the few; he best attains the business ends for which he is hired by neglect of those students in greatest need of physical training (Foster, 1915, p. 578).

Foster also disavowed the high moral claims of the supporters of athletics and cited "lawlessness, dissipation and rowdyism." He saw no evidence that the discipline, responsibility, and self-sacrifice required to work for the "welfare of mankind" could be inculcated through athletics (Foster, 1915).

In a similar vein, Alexander Meikeljohn wrote in the *Atlantic Monthly* of the "radical blunder" in taking the management of games from students:

> ...much to their delight as they saw our more "efficient" administration. In their place we have established coliseums, have increased gate receipts, have aroused public interest, have "developed" teams, until the whole system has become an absurd travesty of the motive from which it sprang, the impulse to play which it was intended to serve (Meikeljohn, 1922, p. 663).

But no amount of protest seemed adequate to halt the growth of the Leviathan. The administrative marriage of physical education and athletics ensured that each wave of concern about health and fitness — for example, the devastating findings that one-third of American men were unfit for military service in World War I — benefitted athletics as well as education (Van Dalen & Bennett, 1971). Accommodation of varsity athletics was the "key factor in the transformation of the profession," according to G. M. Lewis, "The status of competitive athletics established the location of physical education in high schools and colleges; facilities, equipment, and staff secured for varsity sports determined the content of the curricula and the nature of the programs" (Lewis, 1969a, p. 42).

The rhetorical change to "sports for all" concealed the fact that "all," for many coaches, meant varsity athletes.[22] Without direct information about individuals and their activities, there was no way in which to distinguish between the two camps in men's programs. Professional titles and vocabulary had been hopelessly confounded. As legislative mandates for physical education and "character development" became nationwide realities, the shoe fit the progressive foot as well as the giant fin. It is hardly surprising to learn that the National Collegiate Athletic Association (NCAA) campaigned vigorously for physical education requirements (Lewis, 1972).

Women Educators and Athletic Competition

Women physical educators viewed the development of commercialized competitive athletics in education with deep concern. By 1919, it had become clear to many of the leaders in physical education that the popularity and proliferation of competitive athletics for women and girls was about to sweep this "component" of educational programs out of the hands of trained teachers into a commercial enterprise ruled by coaches, just as it had in men's programs. Basketball, in particular, was flourishing across the country with high school girls' teams, sponsored by businessmen, preceding boys' competition; at the college level, increased pressure was brought to bear on educators for intercollegiate competition in emulation of the male athletic model (Wayman, 1928).

Elizabeth Burchenal, chairman of the Committee on Girls' Athletics of the American Physical Education Association, articulated the common concern and stressed the common values in 1919: Athletics should be a part of health education for all girls — at least 80 percent should find a given sport accessible and enjoyable; intensive training of individual stars and crack teams, and all of the accompanying admission fees, newspaper coverage, and so on, were to be eliminated; trained women instructors and leaders should direct girls' athletics (Burchenal, 1919). Burchenal not only pinpointed the commercial aspects of male programs, but directed attention to the disembodiment of the person which could occur. An athletic position (for example, halfback or runner) could become more important than the individual child or student. Further, the exclusivity of male athletics violated the teacher's responsibility for all students. The term "coach," therefore, was dropped from the vocabularies of women physical educators (see Wayman, 1928).

The general alarm sounded in 1922 when the Amateur Athletic Union (AAU), which did not hold jurisdiction over women's track and field, accepted an invitation to the First Women's Olympic Games in Paris and named a man as coach! Physical educators protested vociferously but in vain, and it was clear that a crisis was at hand (Wayman, 1928). Leaders in the profession were politically astute enough to realize that national grass roots unification was the only way to preserve their ideals and educational autonomy (Wayman, 1928, 1932). Their efforts, in my opinion, form a unique chapter in the history of American education. Educators made educational policy!

Mrs. Herbert Hoover, a long-time supporter of health and fitness for girls and women, was approached; and in 1923 she convened a national meeting of leaders from education, health, industry, volunteer associations, and so forth. (It is worth noting that the large constituency of women who had supported suffrage in 1920 was still intact, as well as many coalitions championing the causes of public health and preventive medicine such as the Sheppard-Towner clinics and public nursing.) The Women's Division, National Amateur Athletic Federation (NAAF), was created at the convention. Mrs. Hoover was named permanent chairman, and "a strong group of physical educators" were appointed as executive committee, among them Ethel Perrin, Blanche Trilling, Dr. J. Anna Norris, and Agnes Wayman (Wayman, 1928). Wayman writes of their actions:

> The organization of this Women's Division was one of the most noteworthy forward and upward steps general education has witnessed in years. While general education probably knows little about it as yet, as time goes on, it cannot help but feel its influence. At the time, it meant that women were refusing to be towed longer behind a doubtful physical education scheme, that they were setting forth under their own sail with women at the tiller and mainly women propelling the craft. It meant that at last the women were united with certain definite ideals and were agreed for the most part on standards and procedures (Wayman, 1928, p. 25).

By 1932, the federation had grown to include over 700 organizations, institutions, and individuals representing nearly every influential group working with women and girls in the country, all of whom endorsed the resolutions concerning athletics and health adopted by the federation.[23] Leaders in public and private schools, the Red Cross, YWCA, Girl Scouts, settlement leagues and churches, the Children's Bureau, U.S. Department of Labor, and industrial groups such as the National Women's Trade Union League, to name but a few, supported the "stand" (Wayman, 1932).

The 16 resolutions (see Wayman, 1928) set out the standards by which the federation would control and promote competitive athletics. However, athletics were given less attention than was the total physical education program which supporters resolved to provide for every child, male and female. The framers of the resolutions, like Catherine Beecher nearly 100 years earlier, hoped to win national endorsement with an appeal to women, but the ethics and educational practices they espoused were meant to apply to both sexes.

By the late 1920s, women could point with pride to the leading colleges and universities that had abandoned intercollegiate competition and instituted intramural sports and "play days or sports days" in which large numbers of women from schools in close proximity could participate in a variety of activities.[24] Team composition typically was determined by lots drawn by all participants. Progressive elimination games, dancing, singing, and luncheon speakers were included, as well as times set apart for a tour of the host campus and social hours. Telegraphic meets were also sponsored, in which competition was held at individual colleges and the results were mailed to a designated institution for tallying of outcomes. Although in high schools it was more difficult to stem the tide of "crack teams," state championships were eliminated, "play days" increased, and more states employed girls' rules for basketball (Lee, 1931). Given the "sport-crazed" 1920s, the educational stand was no mean feat.

The legacy of the physical trainers, as we have seen, stressed health and individual differences. Dewey's emphasis on the significance of group interaction added to the responsibilities of physical educators but was by no means at odds with the design of diverse curricula and prescription of activities based on individual needs. Wayman wrote in *Education through the Physical* (1928): "It is a sad mistake to make a program and try to adapt every boy and girl to it" (p. 30). In the hands of many general educators, such a "progressive" posture often led to confusion and curricular disarray. Although there were certainly great controversies in the 1920s and 1930s about the relative weight to be given to components of the program (see Gerber, 1972), physical educators were in an enviable pedagogic position.

Activities existed that could be introduced to children who needed postural remediation or who were physically handicapped, obese, or "awkward." Some elements emphasized free expression and creativity, notably "free" gymnastics and dance. Other instruction, for example, individual and team sports, required rules and the acquisition of skill. The latter, however, were seen as an important preparation for the continuation of physical exercise in adulthood. Both instruction in hygiene and the social interaction involved in sports provided teachers with a realistic basis for discussions of individual and communal welfare. Physical examinations and repeated measurements furnished an empirical basis for individual prescriptions. While with perfect hindsight one might regret that the profession affiliated with education rather than becoming an applied branch of physiology or anatomy, at the time physical educators were able to identify their professional ideals and aspirations closely with John Dewey's views of the child, the school, and the society.

The Humanistic Tradition and Child Development

By 1919, designated by President Wilson as the Children's Year, the scientific activities directed toward children and a widespread social commitment to child welfare had gained momentum (Sears, 1975). The studies of the Children's Bureau, created in 1912 and headed by Julia Lathrope, revealed by 1918 that the United States had an unusually high rate of maternal and infant mortality, ranking seventeenth of 20 nations surveyed (Lemons, 1973). These data, in addition to the dismal state of recruits in World War I, served to spur the efforts of scientists and the support of private philanthropy, notably the Laura Spelman Rockefeller fund for research, teaching, and dissemination in the field of child development (Sears, 1975). A child development subcommittee in the Division of Anthropology and Psychology of the National Research Council was established in 1922, and by 1927 the first issues of the multidisciplinary *Child Development Abstracts* were published. In 1929, President Hoover called a White House Conference on Child Health and Protection to study the present status of health and welfare of children and to recommend what ought to be done and how to do it. The journal *Child Development* appeared in 1930, and by 1933 developmentalists from many disciplines formed an independent Society for Research in Child Development (SRCD) (Boyd, 1980).[25]

In many accounts of the 1920s and 1930s, the tension between positions on nature and nurture, generally pitting Gesell and Watson, achieved prominence. That tension, which Robert Sears has called the "San Andreas fault beneath child development," merits continuing attention. But for the scientific tradition traced from phrenologists through anthropometrists, the controversy was but the rumbling of an antiquated dualism. The relevant question for the founders of SRCD was one of how to study the complex interaction between individual growth and experience. They sought to bring scientific order and system to the approach.

Late nineteenth- and early twentieth-century studies by anthropometrists and physiologists had raised questions concerning the use of norms based on chronological age to reflect or predict the course of individual growth. Bowditch (1891) reported that prepubertal acceleration in growth and weight just before puberty came earlier in large children than in small. B. T. Baldwin corroborated these findings in 1916 (Dennis, 1946). C. Ward Crampton (1908), a prominent physical educator, reported differences in height and weight between prepubertal and postpubertal boys of the same chronological age and an increase in strength accompanying pubescence (Crampton, 1908a, b). During the 1920s and 1930s, serious efforts focused on achieving an adequate biological measure of maturity, for example T. Wingate Todd's pioneering efforts in the use of X-ray photographs and scales of skeletal age (Todd, 1937); Shuttleworth's identification of the prepubertal apex or the "age of maximum growth" (Shuttleworth, 1939); and Greulich's pubic hair and external genitalia standards (cf. Greulich, Day, Lachman, Wolfe, & Shuttleworth, 1938).

A clear statement of the importance of determining a measure of maturational age was made by Lucy Sprague Mitchell (one of the founders of the New School for Social Research), reflecting on her experience at the Bureau of Educational Experiments (1916):

> [Discussing the data collected on children in schools gave her] . . . a sort of perspective view of the organic, interdependent complexities within each child that made him a unique individual. They also gave me an appreciation that, though children pass through the same stages in developing, they mature in their own way and at their own rate. Maturity levels, as distinguished from age levels, become the important thing to understand about children (Senn, 1975, p. 13).

Myrtle McGraw's assessment of the period helps to pinpoint the major implications for theory and method:

> The prevailing thought operating in most of the early investigators was that individual differences in the development of children is so great that only norms or averages of achievement, based upon the study of groups of children within chronological periods, would be of scientific value. [She then refers to Gesell, 1925, and the Minnesota group, 1940, among others who published standardized scales of development during the preschool years.] . . . Such standardized measures provide information as to *when* particular behavior items are achieved, but they do not disclose *how* a function undergoes change as it progresses from inception toward optimum efficiency. It is also recognized that since children do not grow uniformly the average norms do not reflect the actual course of growth as represented by one individual. A child may be advanced in one respect of development and retarded in another.

McGraw continues by noting that longitudinal inquiry was demanded with the realization that

> in order to analyze behavior development as a process of change not only the child subjects but sequential changes in specific behavior phenomena would have to become the subject matter of investigation. The method of analysis calls for an appraisal of behavior, not as it deviates from some reputed average but as it compares to its own function at an earlier time (McGraw, 1946, pp. 357-58).

As noted earlier, the Rockefeller Memorial Fund, under the guiding spirit of Lawrence K. Frank, was crucial in enabling investigators to pursue longitudinal studies of children. Grants were made to Iowa, Minnesota, Yale, Teachers College, and the University of California, Berkeley in the late 1920s (see Tanner, 1981). The University of California's Institute of Child Welfare began studies in 1928. Herbert Stolz was the first director of the Institute and Harold Jones, the director of research (Jones, MacFarlane, & Eichorn, 1959). Three longitudinal investigations were begun (see Jones, Bayley, MacFarland, & Honzik, 1971); but in the present context, the Oakland Growth Study (also called the California Adolescent Study), initiated in 1932 by Stolz and Mary Cover Jones, is most germane.

After three years as a Rhodes Scholar at Oxford, Stolz obtained a medical degree from Stanford in 1914 and served as an assistant to Clark Hetherington, replacing him in 1920 as director of physical education for the State of California. Stolz had known Hetherington at Stanford and admired him greatly. They shared a humanistic view of the child and society, and it was at Hetherington's invitation that Stolz joined the staff (private communication from Dr. Lois M. Stolz). Stolz's activities during his years with state government reflect some of the values he brought to research. For example, in a teacher's manual for health supervision and instruction (1924), specific directions were given for individual health and development report cards. He elicited suggestions from children, parents, and teachers and disseminated information about child development and physical growth to them. The growth of knowledge was seen as a cooperative venture.

Stolz and Jones were joined by Lois Meek Stolz, former director of the Child Development Institute at Teachers College, Columbia University. In the 1940s and early 1950s, a series of publications dealing with the interrelations of physical development with changes in interests, self-perceptions, personality development, and social behavior began to appear, some addressed to researchers and some to teachers and parents (for example, *California Parent Teacher* and *Progressive Education*). The picture that emerged of a changing individual and changing expectations and demands by adults and peers (we now call this bidirectionality) gave vivid testimony to the inadequacy of chronological age in the study of human development. Jones (1948), for example, documented the way in which differing maturational rates of boys of the same chronological age affected long-standing constellations of social groups and patterns of friendships.

The Somatic Development of Adolescent Boys (Stolz & Stolz, 1951) was the culmination of the research relating to physical development which was Herbert Stolz's chief responsibility. The seven years of exacting measurement revealed four distinct phases of adolescent growth.

> These phases are defined by changes in the *rate* of growth. The tendency toward the four phase sequence pattern is apparent not only for each of the several skeletal measures but also for growth in weight and in muscular strength. Moreover, specific phenomena of sex-appropriate procreative ripening usually show coherent timing relations to these specific phases of somatic growth (p. 424).

The synchronic nature of the process of growth in each individual was striking:

> The systematic relatedness of growth phenomena *in the individual* becomes more impressive as evidence of differences in growth dynamics *among individuals* accumulates. The patterns of change in skeletal dimensions, subcutaneous tissue, muscular tissue, body hair, genitalia, muscular strength, and body weight show that whatever may be the similarities in growth achieved at the end of adolescence they do not mean identity or even similarity of growth experience (p. 429).

The case study of Ben (prepared by Lois Meek Stolz) is presented with rich detail to illustrate the way in which the four periods of development within adolescence might be used as a base line for studying changes in social behavior. Ben's diary, cumulative interviews, and personality inventories, for example, are integrated with information from his parents and teachers as well as naturalistic observations of his social behavior and peer ratings in each successive period. The case study, and the larger data base, gave convincing evidence that "the course of somatic growth during adolescence is an important thread in the pattern of personality development" (p. 496). Lawrence Frank of the Laura Spelman Rockefeller Memorial Fund was less modest in his appraisal of the "unique" study, which he thought marked a "turning point" in the field of child development (Senn, 1975).

Longitudinal studies also refined the ways in which sex differences could be viewed. The timing of physical maturation, the achievement of puberty, and the social meaning of certain activities had different significance for boys and girls. Athletics and strenuous sports participation are an excellent case in point.

Expertise in athletics by the 1930s had already become a powerful factor in peer acceptance for boys (Tryon, 1939). The early maturing boy, with his advantages in height and strength, was overrepresented on athletic teams (Jones & Bayley, 1950; Stolz & Stolz, 1951). The "transformation" of physical education programs for boys discussed earlier is documented by Dimrock's report (1935) of an increase in spectator activities and a decrease in participation in sports between the ages of 12 and 16. Athletics was, and has remained, the domain of the early maturing male (cf. Friedrich-Cofer, Johnson, & Tucker, 1980; Johnson & Buskirk, 1974).

For girls the findings were more complex. By the 1930s the average two-year gap in the physical maturation of boys and girls had been noted (cf. Shuttleworth, 1939). While girls as well as boys mature at widely differing chronological ages, the earlier maturation of girls provides a biological backdrop for the consideration of sex differences. Since gains in height and subcutaneous tissue are associated with normal maturation in girls, it is not surprising that tallness and fatness were reported as major sources of concern (Stolz & Stolz, 1943). The early maturing girl, unlike her male counterpart in maturational rate, did not reap the rewards of popularity with peers and leadership opportunities; indeed, she was rated by classmates and adult observers as less active and lacking in self-assurance, expressivity, and social poise (Everett, 1943; Jones & Mussen, 1958). Athletic success did not have the same prestige for girls as for boys (Tryon, 1939); further, longitudinal and cross-sectional research indicated that later maturing girls continued to demonstrate interest in strenuous sports while the interest of other girls declined after puberty (cf. Stone & Barker, 1939). Although some later investigators tended to interpret these findings as examples of simple differences in social norms for boys and girls, more recent evidence indicates the need for continued psychobiological perspectives (see also, Cairns & Cairns, Chapter 4, "On Social Values and Social Development: Gender and Aggression"). Late maturing girls are not only more linear in body build but are overrepresented on interscholastic, intercollegiate, and Olympic teams (Malina, 1983), report more sports activities in high school and college (Halpern, 1982), and are more favorable toward mixed-sex competition in a coeducational physical education setting (Friedrich-Cofer, 1981).

By the 1940s the implications of the findings on maturational timing for boys and for girls were brought to the attention of physical educators. Flexibility in curriculum and sensitivity to individual interests and abilities, particularly in mixed-sex groups in which late maturing boys and early maturing girls might feel conspicuous, were needed if physical education classes were to be of benefit to all children (cf. Meek, 1940).

Longitudinal research efforts in the United States came under sharp attack in the 1950s (Lomax, 1977), and the sweeping "atheoretical" charge launched at all such studies seems to persist in the literature. There were, of course, great conceptual differences among longitudinal researchers who were referred to as "organismic" in orientation. Although the Oakland Growth Studies were not guided by a thoroughly articulated theory of developmental psychobiology (see Cairns, 1983), the research represents a significant advance in theoretical conceptualization. That, at the time, the theoretical implications were not explored more fully may be accounted for in part by the fact that the investigators were not chiefly involved in training graduate students who would continue and refine the tradition. Moreover, the funding patterns and professional criteria for advancement supported short-term, cross-sectional studies of a normative nature. The "atheoretical" charges may also be translated as "not in accord with reigning theoretical positions."

The theoretical views which were to dominate child development as it became absorbed into psychology looked to the mind, not to the body. (Psychoanalytic theory, for a complex set of reasons, was not to become a part of the academic mainstream [Sears, 1975].) Learning theories of all varieties, as well as Piagetian theory as interpreted by American psychologists, posited a responsive or an active mind which seems to proceed without a body. (See Baldwin, 1968, for review of theories.) Adolescent study fell out of fashion as the reigning popular and scientific values converged on "early intervention." The interdisciplinary composition of SRCD diminished, and child psychologists assumed exclusive leadership, making program decisions and so forth. The collective "view" began to narrow.

As the individual child and adolescent with bodies faded from view, many of the humanistic ties which bound scientist, teacher, family, and child faded with them.[26] The collaborative efforts of all participants so evident in the Oakland Growth Studies gave way to "brief encounters" necessitated by the fact that schools had children who could serve as subjects and teachers and administrators needed to be convinced of the "scientific" importance of intrusions into school time. The thoughtful reporting of results of continuing study, as well as intimate knowledge of children and the important people in their lives, were often replaced by memos reporting mean results and findings which were statistically significant.

Educational Reforms: 1957–1972

The unity of body, mind, and morals was not a theme which animated the educational reforms, expansion of federal expenditures for education, or increasing federal involvement in education from the 1950s to the early 1970s (cf. Moynihan, 1975). These reforms looked to the mind.

The body, in education, meant athletics. The rapid spread of television brought professional and intercollegiate contests into millions of American homes; it also brought new revenues to higher education (Van Dalen & Bennett, 1971).[27] The fortunes of coaches rose or fell depending on the won/lost records of their teams; none were fired, as Harry Edwards points out, because they didn't teach well (Edwards, 1973). Interscholastic athletics caught the coattails of the athletic explosion. The policy recommendations set out in the mid-1950s by the Educational Policies Commission to abolish post-season championships and the receipt of revenues other than tax funds in interscholastic athletics went unheeded. Their recommendations in favor of play days and sports days, corecreational sports and activities for boys and girls, and the teaching of sports that could be played in adulthood were also ignored (Talmini & Page, 1973).

At the time of the Educational Policies Commission Report, President Eisenhower, engaged in an undeclared war in Korea, was concerned when the marked inferiority of American children compared to European children on strength tests was brought to his attention by John B. Kelley. Eisenhower responded by inviting a host of athletic celebrities to a White House luncheon in 1955. A year later, a President's Conference on Youth Fitness was created, chaired by Vice-President Richard Nixon (Van Dalen & Bennett, 1971). Athletes had become the symbols of American fitness, and their efforts provided some support to physical educators (Van Dalen & Bennett, 1971), but the deeper significance of the association of athletics and education was not appreciated by the public.

With the launching of the Soviet space satellite in 1957 and the threatened military and technological supremacy of an adversary, the body fell from the list of educational priorities. The National Defense Act, quickly enacted in 1958, specified funds for academically gifted children and improvement in the teaching of mathematics, science, and languages (Moynihan, 1975). James B. Conant testified at the hearings, and his influential reports (1960, 1963) stressing the need to upgrade the quality of American education dealt a serious blow to physical educators. Dr. Conant, like the general public by this time, failed to differentiate between physical education and athletics. He recommended the abolition of interscholastic athletics (at the junior high level) and graduate programs in "physical education," noting Football 1 and 2 as travesties. He suggested that wide reading in the humanities and social sciences are advisable, since "more likely than not, the man preparing to be a physical educator [sic] is, perhaps unconsciously, preparing to be an educational administrator" (Conant, 1963, p. 186).[28] The role of the body in education had been divorced from the pursuit of academic excellence.

The next wave of federal support for education (in the 1960s) was a major plank in the War on Poverty and an attempt to bring about equality between the races (Moynihan, 1975). The embodied and non-symbolic child remained in obscurity. Black athletes on television were touted as representing the egalitarian nature of the athletic enterprise and a sign of the vitality of individual ability to rise above hardship.[29] Social scientists assured policy makers of the ease with which the desegregation plans they recommended could affect the "self-image" and academic skills of minority group children.[30]

The black protest movement, in its many forms, revealed the contradictions between professed American values and the realities of American society (Tyack & Hansot, 1982). The parallels that many women activists saw between their own plight and that of blacks were to be sharply drawn in the women's protest movements (Degler, 1980). Women, who had entered the work force in unprecedented numbers during World War II, were recognizing that they were ill paid and denied access to professional training. Political activists identified a white male elite that controlled the structure of power in the nation, and they urged women to unite to claim a fair share of the privileges. In contrast to the earlier women's movements for educational and health reforms, a strong vein of individualism and explicit denial of the physical body was injected into the protests.

Simone de Beauvoir (1953), in *The Second Sex*, labeled the female body a hazard to creative and intellectual aspirations. While she celebrated the virility and power of men, she described women as the "victims of the species" (Beauvoir,1953). The rejection of the female body and of the embodied person is a theme of much feminist literature of the 1960s (see Elshtain, 1981). The sharp attack on psychoanalytic thought, particularly that of Helene Deutsch, was a corollary of the proposition. The idea that the mind and affective experience might be related, however complexly, to biological factors was villified. The "masculine" qualities compatible with individualistic pursuits and achievement in society were extolled. Despite the warnings of Rae Carlson (1972) and Jeanne Block (1973) that psychological inquiry into the organization of female personality structure might not be advanced through a rejection of the body and an acceptance of a narrow system of values, "androgyny" became the latest research fad. In the desire to provide a quick remedy for educational ills, psychologists and activists set out to bring about educational reforms which would guarantee "equality" through socializing girls and boys in the same way. Men's programs, however, were taken as a measure of the "good"; existing women's programs in education were ignored or devalued. The language used and the legalistic means employed to achieve their ends were to be fatal to many of these programs in public education (cf. Carnegie Commission Report, 1973; Howe, 1975; Walsh, 1983), not the least of which was women's physical education.

PUBLIC POLICY AND EDUCATION

Legislation and Implementation Regulations

The resolutions adopted by the Women's Division, NAAF, in the 1920s are worth mentioning again as "models" of public policy statements. Each group that endorsed them knew exactly what they stood for and what they opposed. Although the Ninety-first and Ninety-second Congress in the 1970s passed some important specific legislation to remedy inequalities in access to training and pay for women (many of them recommended by the Task Force for Women appointed by President John F. Kennedy and chaired by Mrs. Eleanor Roosevelt), the "sweeping" legislation—the Equal Rights Amendment and Title IX of the Education Amendments—were another matter. Both were well intentioned but vague in wording and legislative history, and both could win the endorsements of opposing constituents.

Senator Sam Ervin was one of the most articulate minority voices calling for specification in statute and legislative record:

> In the nature of things, lawmakers use words to express their purposes. Courts must ascertain from their words the purposes of the lawmakers ... [quoting Justice Oliver Wendell Holmes]: "A word is not a crystal, transparent and unchanged; it is the skin of a living thought and may vary greatly in color and content according to the circumstances and the time in which it is used." ... During my many years as a lawyer, a judge and a legislator, I have discovered that many words have many meanings, and that the purpose they are intended to express must be gathered from the context in which they are used. I have learned that the most difficult task which ever confronts a court is determining the meaning of imprecise words used in a scrimpy context (Senate Calendar No. 660-662, 92d Cong., 2d sess., p. 66).

Ervin's appeal for precision in the record of legislative intent did not prevail. It seems to have been a time for bold action promising to end sex discrimination forever. Title IX of the Education Amendments Act, 1972, states: No person in the United States shall, on the basis of sex, be excluded from participation in, be denied the benefits of, or be subjected to discrimination under any education program or activity receiving Federal financial assistance" (20 USC, sections 1681-1686

Supp. V, 1975). Significantly, the provision parallels Title VI of the Civil Rights Act of 1964 which prohibits racial discrimination in federally assisted programs (Cox, 1977).

Senator Birch Bayh introduced the amendment as a part of the higher education bill, and two major themes emerge from those hearings to provide some guidance as to legislative intent. First, a massive amount of data had been assembled to document widespread discrimination in hiring, salary, access to training programs, and so forth, within education. With many references to compatible psychological studies on sex stereotyping and "fear of success," these facts were intimately and repeatedly related to the number of women living below the poverty level, and especially to women who were single heads of households and either on welfare or likely candidates for welfare. Education was not only to mend its own sexist fences but to rid society of poverty. The second theme required a further leap from the documentation, but a scientific conviction in "socialization" was called to assist. If education would socialize boys and girls in the same way, the evils of stereotyping would vanish. The disparities in achievement between adult men and women were evoked to mandate a policy that would radiate throughout the entire educational system. Children were seen (when they were mentioned at all) as "nonsexist" steppingstones to adult equality. One may not agree with the assumptions of the witnesses and many of the legislators, but the intent to abolish discrimination in and through education is stated and restated (20 UCS, Supp. V 1975).[31] (See also Cavanaugh, 1971, and *Sex Discrimination and Intercollegiate Athletics*, 1979, for use of social science assertions in testimony.)

Ervin's fears were prophetic: Not only was the statute vague but there was no legislative record to guide the framers of implementation regulations. Physical education and athletics were never discussed or debated. The focus of the legislation — higher education — directed attention to academic preparation for professions, but the education provided for younger children and the possibility that their needs might differ from those of college students were ignored. The enforcing authority was to be the Department of Health, Education and Welfare (HEW), and within this department, the Office for Civil Rights (OCR) was given responsibility for drafting the regulations. Lawyers, relying on Title VI of the Civil Rights Act and the evolving (if contradictory) legislative record of the recently passed Equal Rights Amendment, were to make critical decisions concerning elementary, secondary, and college curricula.[32] (Caspar Weinberger, Secretary of HEW, was also an attorney.)

Advocates of legislation that has great symbolic importance often forget Felix Frankfurter's observations concerning the administration of public policy:

> Hardly a measure passes Congress the effective execution of which
> is not conditioned upon rules and regulations emanating from the
> enforcing authorities. These administrative complements are
> euphemistically called "filling in the details" of policy set forth in
> statutes. But the "details" are of the essence; they give meaning
> and content to vague contours (MacLeish & Prichard, 1939, p. 231).

By 1974, the first confidential draft of HEW's proposed Title IX
regulations was circulated, and the "neglected" part of the legislative
record and a small part of Title IX — intercollegiate athletics — became
the focus of a pitched and prolonged battle. The NCAA, as representatives of education, descended upon Washington to protest the
possibility of federal intervention in their programs. Amendments
were introduced to exempt "revenue-producing sports." Women's
groups were quick to point out that 95 percent of the NCAA college
athletic budgets ran in the "red," despite the fact that 51 percent of
them included fees collected during registration from all students.
Further, men's athletic budgets (on the average more than 22 times
larger than those of women) and opportunities for participation were
shown to be patently discriminatory (see Sex Discrimination Hearings,
1975). During the four-month comment period in 1974, after the implementing regulations were published, HEW received nearly 10,000
comments. The athletic regulations were the target of much of the
commentary (Fishel, 1976). Caspar Weinberger remarked, "I had not
realized until the comment period that athletics is the single most important thing in the United States" (Cox, 1977, p. 34).

The final regulations concerning physical education and athletics
were clearly expedient politically and indicative of prevailing values.
For example, contact sports were exempted from nonsexist guidelines
and budgets did not have to be "exactly" equal. Physical education
classes and intramurals, however, were to be integrated; and student
interest in determining offerings were deleted. (See Cox, 1977, for a
comparison of proposed and final regulations.) Deleting student interest eradicated, of course, a main plank of women's and girls' programs.

The controversy over athletics had threatened all of Title IX, and
the shaky victory (and unclear legislative record) led to a myriad of
legal disputes to be settled by the courts. These ranged from the question of breadth of coverage (that is, all programs or only those that
receive direct aid) to whether or not employees were covered or an individual had the right to bring suit, or HEW had the authority to issue
the regulations. (See Kuhn, 1976, for legal arguments for narrow interpretations; see also Supreme Court decision, 1984, in favor of the narrow interpretation of coverage.)

A Look at Consensus and Women's Groups

Recently, attention has been drawn to the middle-class constituency of the National Organization of Women (NOW) and the Women's Equity Action League (WEAL) and their inability to transcend class and racial differences (Degler, 1980; Elshtain, 1981). Looking at Title IX, the prominence of the contest with the NCAA has masked the deep divisions that were apparent among women in education. The "separate but equal" dilemma was, in some respects, the crux of the matter.

Representatives of NOW and WEAL testified before Congress both in the Equal Rights Amendment hearings and the Title IX regulations hearings that sex-segregated classes or schools were "relics" of the past and an anathema. At the same time, the Carnegie Commission on Higher Education (1973), as well as the American Academy of Arts and Sciences (see American Higher Education, 1974, 1975), were recommending the continuation and strengthening of diversity in higher education. The Carnegie Commission noted that the strongholds of administrative leadership for women were in black women's colleges and Catholic women's colleges, as deans of women were disappearing in coeducational colleges and universities and were not being replaced by women in other administrative positions. Jill Conway, president-elect of Smith, warned: "Up to the present, attention has been focused on the access of women to institutions of higher education, with little or no thought given to the relationship of women students to the curriculum, women scholars to research activity, or women graduates to the occupational structure of society" (Conway, 1974, p. 239). She predicted a revitalized and significant role for women's colleges in the future. (Unfortunately, and again significantly, neither the Carnegie Commission nor the American Academy publications devote a page to athletics or physical education—a commentary on how far the body has moved from the mind in higher education.)

A deep and abiding rift developed between female athletes and the spokeswomen for NOW and WEAL. Brenda Fasteau, an attorney, summarized the argument in 1973 that training would not bring women on a basis with men in high-level competition:

> Unfortunately, no American woman would have made the Olympics if the team had been integrated and if the same criteria of selection were applied to both sexes. The very best men ... are still better than the very best women .... It is debatable whether Billie Jean King would even make the top 10 if male and female professional tennis players competed against each other. (Fasteau, 1973, p. 58)

Athletics were absent from the works of leading feminists, "to be integrated only as a part of more general efforts" (*Sex Discrimination*, 1979, p. 1,267). Many of the leaders in the new associations for women in sports, for example, the Association for Intercollegiate Athletics for Women (AIAW), were also opposed to merger with male associations because of their distinct philosophical position—a resolve to extend competitive opportunities for women without being snared by powerful commercial interests (Hult, 1980).

For physical educators, the conflict with the NOW and WEAL position was a fundamental one. Katherine Ley, president of AAHPER, wrote in 1974: "The most unhappy aspect of Title IX, from a woman's point of view, is the impression one gets that what men are doing is the standard of excellence against which to judge the women's programs" (Ley, 1974, p. 129). She goes on to note that the AIAW policy against scholarships based on athletic ability was changed due to a threatened law suit, and that many colleges and universities had already merged men's and women's departments with a loss of influence for women in the decision-making process. "The greatest loss may very well be in the realm of philosophy, because the attitude of many women toward competition does differ from that of men.... Competitive achievement appears to have taken priority over ethics in many aspects of American culture" (Ley, 1974, p. 131). Ley endorsed "separate but equal" departments as she witnessed their demise. Her call for a participatory philosophy and activities in sports and athletic programs and her ingenious plan for achieving those ends have yet to be realized.

The NOW and WEAL support for coeducational physical education classes was also extremely unpopular with physical educators (Fishel, 1976). Corecreational activities had been a part of physical education programs since the 1920s. Teachers understood, if political activists did not, that mandating the same activities for adolescents would reduce interest if a diversity of offerings (for example, dance, gymnastics, or wrestling) were sacrificed for the simpler "sports" approach. One wonders if WEAL women had ever seen a physical education class, but this is the position:

> This requirement is absolutely key to assuring equal *sports* [emphasis added] opportunities for females, both in the long run and in the short. Sex segregated physical education has produced major inequities in physical training [sic] for males and females. Given these inequities, full integration of presently segregated physical education classes is the one fair solution. As long as our schools and colleges are permitted to treat male and female students as separate groups these institutions will continue to design different

programs for them based on traditional sex stereotypes surrounding sports (Fishel, 1976, p. 98).

And why were sports important? Margaret Dunkle's testimony on behalf of WEAL at the 1975 Title IX hearings is illustrative of the past and present position:

> Athletic competition is a powerful socializing agent in our society: to limit the athletic opportunities of girls is to limit their other options as well. Many of the same attitudes that lead people to belittle and scoff at female athletes also lead them to discount girls who aspire to other "nontraditional" fields—from business executive to college professor to physician to attorney (Hearings, 94th Congress, June 1975, p. 287).

The value system of NOW and WEAL was shared by the NCAA. Throughout the hearings and in subsequent publications concerning women and athletics, the "character building" or "personality enhancing" virtues of athletics are extolled. In addition, athletics could abolish the myths of women being weak and passive and pave the way to the advantages of "androgyny." The volumes of data used then and now to support the charge of continuing "discrimination" compare athletic budgets for men versus women and the numbers of male versus female participants. Nowhere in these documents (including those of the Office of Civil Rights) are the questions addressed of how much money is being spent on the "few" and just how "few" students of either sex participate. Indeed, it is seen as an obstacle to be overcome that more women participate in intramural activities than in varsity ahtletics. The Office of Civil Rights notes noncommittally that while intramurals allow more people to play, supervisory staff and playing fields are often not available, given the needs of competitive athletics (U.S. Commission on Civil Rights, 1980). (For additional "discriminatory" data, see also Dunkle, 1977, and Notes, Sex Discrimination, 1975).

There is support for Bella Abzug's representation of consensus with the WEAL position on Title IX by women concerning equal pay and access to training (Fishel, 1976). However, if the enactment of the regulations had depended upon a point by point analysis and vote, women would have been divided, and it is questionable that Congress would have allowed the regulations to stand.

The Courts and Education

The court precedents that developed between 1971 and 1981 concerning athletics, for all of the differences in individual cases, are consistent in two important respects for schools. First, athletic associations are found to be operating "under the color of state law" by virtue of their "symbiotic" relationship with schools. Schools, therefore, are responsible for (and liable for) the policies set by these bodies. Second, while education is not a federally guaranteed right (nor is athletic competition) as long as it is offered by the states, discrimination cannot be made on the basis of sex. (See, for example, *Yellow Springs, etc. v. Ohio High Sc. Ath. Assn.*, 647 F. 2d 651 [1981] for a comprehensive review of cases.)

If one views the judiciary record as an illustration of ethical myopia, it is a myopia shared by many others. Holmes observed in 1881 that judges are influenced by the "felt necessities of the time, the prevalent moral and political theories, intuitions of public policy" (p. 1). The adversaries and evidence presented focused attention on male interscholastic athletic opportunities versus deprivation for women. A suit over physical education has never been brought, and physical educators have never had a "day in court."

Virtually every judge in the more than 50 cases reviewed refers to *Brown v. Board of Education*, 1954, for the Supreme Court's view of the state's interest in education:

> Today, education is perhaps the most important function of state and local governments.... Today, it is a principal instrument awakening the child to cultural values, in preparing him for later professional training, and in helping him to adjust normally to his environment. In these days, it is doubtful that any child may reasonably be expected to succeed in life if he is denied the opportunity of an education. Such an opportunity, where the state has undertaken to provide it, is a right which must be made available to all on an equal basis (*Brown v. Board*, 347 U.S. 483, 493 [1954] p. 691).

To define the relationship of interscholastic athletic competition and education, each association has a creed. They are all variations on the same theme, employing the language of the progressives. The *National Federation of State High School Athletics Association Official Handbook* states:

> Interscholastic athletics shall be an integral part of the total secondary school education program ... [and will provide educational experiences which will] develop learning outcomes in the areas of knowledge, skills and emotional patterns and will contribute to the development of better citizens. Emphasis shall be upon teaching "through" athletics in addition to teaching the "skills" of athletics (cited in *Gilpin v. Kansas State High Sc. Ath. Assns., Inc.*, 337 F. Supp. 1233 [1974]).

Neither athletic plaintiffs nor association defendants dispute the "creed," and in many cases the judge arrives at the reasonable conclusion that these benefits are of no less value to girls than to boys. Frequently, they are seen to be more important for girls to compensate for previous social discrimination and stereotyping. Perhaps one of the most significant opinions of this persuasion, since it was rendered by a judge of the U.S. Court of Appeals, is that of Nathaniel R. Jones.

Judge Jones analyzes cases which have gone through lower courts in a thorough manner and cites the voluminous testimony given by women's "sports" advocates. (He appends the first chapter of the U.S. Commission on Civil Rights publication, *More Hurdles to Clear*, referred to earlier as strongly reflective of the WEAL position.) Jones writes:

> Equal participation in sports by female athletes would be a major step in overcoming the outmoded notions of female roles still prevalent in our society. I cannot overlook the impact of education and athletics as "a principal instrument in awakening the child to cultural values, in preparing him (or her) for later professional training and in helping him (or her) to adjust normally to his (or her) environment . . . [Cites *Brown v. Board*] . . . . Sex discrimination in sports is debilitating to the individual athlete whose development and career is stunted and to women as a whole who labor under the burden of traditional notions of their role in society (*Yellow Springs v. Ohio* [1981] p. 667).

Talmudic expertise is not required to see that Judge Jones has explicitly linked athletics and education before quoting from the Brown decision. Further, he omits the portion of that quote which refers to the need for the state to provide opportunity to "all on an equal basis." His omission is a crucial one for his purposes as he goes on to advocate that outstanding women be allowed to play on men's teams even if female teams are available. While segregation of activity may preserve opportunity for the "majority" of women, it "fails to accommodate the exceptional female athlete who would rather compete against men" (p. 667). The "all" and the "majority" shrink greatly in numbers in the espousal of such an individualistic philosophy.

The "separate but equal" cause had been heatedly debated in many of the cases, and judges tended to grant women access to male teams only if there were no female teams. Decisions in Pennsylvania, Massachusetts, and Washington opened the way for mixed-sex teams in all sports, contact and noncontact, citing their states' recently passed equal rights amendments. Women's athletic groups consistently opposed such decisions, arguing that only a few women could make such teams and that the newly formed women's teams would be inundated by men. (Two suits were brought by men to be allowed to play on women's volleyball teams.) Jones specifically refused comment on the issue of men on women's teams. (See Rose, 1978, for a summary of legal arguments, pro and con, on athletics and the Equal Rights Amendment.)

Judges found themselves caught up in the details of how many and what constellation of specific teams, and what kinds of rules, might satisfy equal protection considerations. (See Comment, Sex Discrimination, 1974; Stroud, 1973). Whatever the plans, they all entailed a significant increase in interscholastic teams which educators must find the money to support. The opinion of Judge Matsch, USDC, Colorado, stands out among the suits not only because of his unusually thoughtful and scholarly review of the level of scrutiny required in equal protection claims, but because he has looked beyond the specific case to the schools, from the one to the many:

> The importance of an opportunity for both sexes to participate in a total athletic program presenting a variety of choices for those with differing interests and abilities is far different from the importance of an opportunity for a boy to play volleyball or a girl to play football. The strength of the state interest and the character of the groups affected will also differ according to the scope of the total program (*Hoover v. Meiklejohn et al.* 430 F. Supp. 164 [1977] p. 171).

Looking from the court cases to the schools, interscholastic competition received a great deal of press coverage welding its identity to education and touting the "character building" presumptions. While a few judges, for example, Matsch, specifically noted that schools could discontinue interscholastic athletics or provide more teams for women, schools responded by increasing the numbers of teams as educational budgets were shrinking.

CURRENT NATIONAL AND INTERNATIONAL PERSPECTIVES

Physical Education and Athletics in the United States

Attempts to monitor the effects of the Title IX regulations on athletics and physical education have focused primarily on athletics. Advocates of reform have disseminated and commented upon the following statistics in defense of their position.

From 1972 to 1980, the percentage of girls participating in high school varsity athletics rose from 7 percent to 33 percent. High school athletic budgets are well disguised, but those for boys are estimated to be as much as five times larger than those for girls. In colleges, participation by women in intercollegiate athletics has increased 250 percent; but while more than one-third of the athletes are female, women's ahletics receive 20 percent of all athletic aid. The average athletic budget of large universities now allocates about 16 percent to women, rather than the 2 percent given in 1972, but the increase in total budgets of NCAA Division I schools has been twice the total allocated to women's programs (cf. *Alliance Update*, September/October, 1981; SPRINT clearinghouse of information on sex equity in sports, 1981).

Women's increasing participation and the continuing discrimination in financial support fuel the controversy. As early as 1981, the Reagan administration began its "examination" of Title IX athletic policies prompted, according to Vice-President Bush, by the large numbers of requests from college presidents to end costly and burdensome conformance to regulations (*Chronicle of Higher Education*, September 2, 1981). The "narrow interpretation" of Title IX may well result in athletic departments being able to exempt themselves from coverage if they can demonstrate that they receive no federal aid. There is every reason for deep concern on the part of those who looked for equality of opportunity for women in high-level athletic competition.

There are other reasons for concern which have not received the attention of critics. Physical education departments have "merged," resulting in a significant loss of female (and physical education) leadership and influence (Hoferek, 1980). Girls' rules have been largely abandoned, in some cases by court order.[33] The demand for coaches soared, and women were replaced by men, especially head coaches, as new teams were formed for girls and women (Holmen & Parkhouse, 1981). The certification requirements for nonteaching coaches, fought for by physical educators and teaching coaches, were eliminated by one state after the next with widespread adoption of a practice called "rent-a-coach." By 1981, only 20 states had any semblance of "certification": one course in first aid, despite the fact that the injury rate among secondary school athletes is about 25 percent, with the coach often assuming responsibility for treatment (Parsons, 1981). Perhaps of greater consequence is the threat to long-term health from training regimes and practices imposed by "coaches" whose responsibility is not to the student but to those who hired him to produce results that approximate professional standards of performance.

For boys and men, the potential dangers of specific intensive training have received some attention by physicians and exercise physiologists (cf. Martens, 1978). For girls and women, however, problems not only have been ignored but may be of a different order of magnitude. Leanness is contrary to physical development for girls, who gain more subcutaneous tissue than boys during the pubescent period (Faust, 1977). The relationship of low body fat and strenuous exercise regimes to amenorrhea was identified in the early 1900s. One of the reasons physical educators insisted upon female coaches was to be able to monitor menstrual functioning without embarrassing female students (Wayman, 1928). Their opposition to long-distance running and several other arduous sports stemmed from concern over amenorrhea and its unknown long-term health consequences (Wayman, 1928).

We now have a national health problem, sometimes put under the rubric of "eating disorders," of increasing dimensions for women. There is broad consensus that anorexia and bulimia have increased dramatically, perhaps doubled, in the last decade; one recent study reports 7 percent of the respondents acknowledged being anorexic and 10.3 percent reported bulimia. The latter percentage, projected to population figures for females, would yield 7.6 million American girls and women with a history of bulimia (Pope, Hudson, & Yurgelun-Todd, 1984). Only recently has the concern been expressed over the numbers of athletes, particularly runners, who have these illnesses (cf. New York *Times*, March 6, 1983). Not only are many coaches pressuring female athletic hopefuls to maintain an extremely low percentage of body fat, but amenorrhea has been seen by coaches and some physicians as a benign side effect which can be easily remedied when a woman wishes to become pregnant (Caldwell, 1984; Ullyot, 1981).

The national health problems, however, appear to have been underestimated as there is new evidence suggesting a link between athletic amenorrhea and osteoporosis. Osteoporosis, a condition in which bone density decreases, is the leading cause of bone fractures in postmenopausal women. Some 15 million Americans and one out of every four women over the age of 60 have osteoporosis to some degree (National Library of Medicine, 1984). In men and women after bone growth stops there is a period of consolidation until about age 35, when bone tissue density increases. Peak adult bone mass is about 30 percent higher in males than in females, although there are large individual differences. After menopause and the decline in estrogen production, there is a period of three to seven years in which women lose bone mass rapidly; by the age of 70, 45 percent of the total amount of bone has been lost. Men begin to lose bone approximately 20 years later, and at a rate less than half that of women (*Osteoporosis*, 1984). These striking sex differences are seen to be partly under genetic control; the lower calcium consumption of American women versus men after age 11 and inadequate exercise are also considered contributing factors. Although it was evident that athletic amenorrhea in young women resulted in the loss of estrogen, and that they were often malnourished, it was not until 1984 that two seminal articles appeared documenting the decreased mineral content in the bones of amenor-rheic runners (Cann, Martin, Genant, & Jaffe, 1984; Drinkwater, Nilson, & Chestnut, 1984). Drinkwater et al.'s results indicated that the mean bone density of the 25-year-old woman was comparable to that of a 50-year-old woman.

While "dispelling the myths about menstruation" is a major theme in "nonsexist" curriculum guides for teachers and coaches as well as in the court cases and anthologies of women and sports, amenorrhea is not mentioned. Nor is amenorrhea a topic suited to the current glorification of the "lean, hard, new women" in the media (cf. "Coming on Strong: The New Ideal of Beauty," *Time*, August 30, 1982, cover and lead story). Menstruation, of course, puts women in a "class" and challenges the smooth parallels of policy between blacks and women; between athletic records and competitive achievement in all areas of endeavor.

If the vision of equality of opportunity in education is extended beyond the confines of athletics, a different set of problems emerges. As more school funds were diverted to athletics, physical education re-quirements for all students and time allocations decreased after steady gains over a 20-year period prior to 1972.[34] In elementary schools, physical education suffered disproportionately, especially in inner-city neighborhoods (Report UNESCO, 1978). National Youth Physical Fitness tests, which exhibited significant gains during the period between 1958 and 1965, showed no improvement between 1965 and 1975 (Report UNESCO, 1978). Although the fitness data seem to contradict expectations, given the increased athletic opportunity for women since 1972, the numbers of participants must be considered rather than the ratio of men to women in varsity athletics.

The numbers of participants in interscholastic athletics are, however, nearly as elusive to determine as athletic budgets. Until 1979, the National Federation of State High School Association statistics were, and still are, quoted in the press as 10 million par-ticipants: 2.5 million girls and 7.5 million boys. But once Canadian athletes, haphazard counting of junior high participants, and multiple entries for one person in several sports were omitted, the figure dropped to about 5.5 million: 1.85 million girls and 3.7 million boys (*Alliance Update*, September/October, 1981; SPRINT, Fall 1981). Rainer Martens (1978) estimates that only 4 million youngsters are in-volved in school sports, including junior high participants. The U.S. Bureau of the Census figures for 1981 indicate that for high school enrollments alone, there are 13.5 million youths. A generous estimate would be that one-fourth of the students are accepted for athletic programs which cost in excess of $13 billion annually (Martens, 1978). The number of participants in athletic competition may well be less than the number of seriously obese children between the ages of 10 and 17 in the population (Report UNESCO, 1978).

Expansion of opportunities for participation in sports through extramural sports days and intramural sports, including those that can be played in adulthood, was strongly emphasized in the Educational Policies Commission report of 1954 and recommended by the President's Council on Youth Fitness as late as 1967 (Talamini & Page, 1973). The implementation regulations of Title IX, however, stated only that intramural sports must be integrated by sex. Those who have monitored changes attributed to Title IX have had little to say about intramural participation. The U.S. Commission on Civil Rights reports only that 56.1 percent of the players are boys and 43.9 percent are girls; participation figures are "not available" (More Hurdles to Clear, 1980). Even in this publication, as noted earlier, there is a cryptic reference to lack of supervision, equipment, and space available for intramural sports because facilities are needed by athletic teams. Physical educators, however, have been sharply critical of practices that are in conflict with widespread participation of students. Dr. Robert Leake, for example, notes that the emergence of the girls' competitive sports program has taxed facilities and staff beyond capacity and that competitive programs (for select boys and girls) in many high schools have come to dominate staff and facilities before and after school (Health, Physical Education and Recreation Newsletter, Utah State Board of Education, May 1979).

The numbers of children and youth in physical education classes and the decline in physical education requirements have also escaped the view of those monitoring "nonsexist progress." What has received attention is the lack of success in achieving instructional parity between the sexes, despite a plethora of "nonsexist" tracts that include elaborate methods of ascertaining and grading skills in sports which may be employed without reference to sex. The SPRINT survey of 1978 indicated that schools were trying to comply with what they thought was the letter of the law by offering coeducational classes, but they were often teaching single-sex groupings within those classes. A 1981 survey of secondary schools in Virginia indicated that only 29 percent of the teachers wanted all or the majority of instruction to be coed, and an additional 37 percent wanted some but not all coed instruction; only 27 percent of the students preferred coed physical education classes (Alliance Update, November, 1980). More militant critics have blamed teachers for these developments (cf. Geadelmann, 1980).

In the review of the controversy between female activists and physical educators over the implementation regulations of Title IX presented earlier, women educators feared that competitive sports would come to dominate instructional programs and that diversity of offerings would be diminished. No national survey exists of the 16,000 school districts which addresses these issues. A national file of news clippings supplied by SPRINT shows two clear trends. One, suggesting decreased interest in physical education, particularly by women, is represented by male and female teachers who watch students play jungle ball rather than providing instruction, and by elimination of dance and wrestling classes, for example, because enrollments were split along sex lines, along with other, similar developments that verify the reality of physical educators' concerns.[35] The other set of developments, called the "New Physical Education," can be viewed as a continuation and renewal of the humanistic tradition that we have traced. "New Physical Education" emphasizes individualized programs, physical fitness, and a large variety of activities that can be sustained throughout the lifespan. The American Alliance for Physical Education, Health, Recreation and Dance (AAPHERD) is a strong advocate of the curriculum.[36] Pockets of excellence can be found in various parts of the country where youth swim, play golf, learn paddleball, jump rope, do aerobic exercises, and so forth (see, for example, New York *Times*, Sunday, April 22, 1979). For male physical educators who believed in the priority of health and participation, the government mandates gave fresh impetus for reforms that they had long sought to introduce into programs for boys. The problem, however, is not with physical educators and their ability to provide activities for the many as well as for a select few. It is funding and the perpetual dilemma of the physical educator who is caught between the crossfires of the supporters (feminist or traditional) of athletics and the advocates of "rigorous" education in which "frills" are to be eliminated.

As noted at the outset of the discussion of school reform, the new press for "excellence" has not included the body; physical education has not been considered in the increases mandated for instructional time. On the other hand, athletics and the symbolic competitor have received an enormous boost from the Olympic successes in 1984. When Congress approved the Amateur Sports Act of 1977 and appropriated $10 million to assist in the development of national training centers for amateur sports, physical educators were cautiously optimistic that the funds might also benefit sports opportunities for all children in school, especially for the neglected young children. They argued that the national interest required providing instruction for lifelong skills and pointed to the comments of President Ford's Commission on Olympic Sports that amateur sports activity should emphasize opportunity and access for all citizens (Forker, 1978). But the funds have been restricted to elite athletic training. In addition, the funds required by the U.S. Olympic Committee of the sponsors of the 1984 Olympics were committed to teen-age sports. Peter Ueberroth commented that "athletic programs put all the emphasis on really young people. Then at the time when youngsters need direction, age 13 to 17, we take all the sports away!" (*Time*, August 8, 1983).

Ueberroth's statement seems a good reflection of the cultural zeitgeist. In evaluating the educational changes that have occurred between 1972 and 1982, a hierarchy of "compliance" becomes apparent. College athletics have received most coverage, followed by high school athletics; intramural participation and physical education have been given small notice. Kindergarten, primary, and elementary schoolchildren are absent from governmental and feminist reports and from media coverage. The adevelopmental stance of policy framers and implementers has, thus, extended to the monitoring of the effects of policy. To gain a developmental perspective on educational reforms, attention must be given to widespread international educational activities.

International Reforms

For the past 30 years, daily physical exercise programs for all children throughout the school years have been multiplying internationally (McIntosh, 1981). As early as 1964, a UNESCO Council's declaration on sport asserted:

> An individual, whatever his ultimate role in society, needs in his growing years a due balance of intellectual, physical, moral and aesthetic development which must be reflected in the educational curriculum and time table.... Between 1/3 and 1/6 of the total time table should be devoted to physical activity (cited in Bailey, 1973, p. 427).

The UNESCO declaration reflected, in part, the growing anxiety of the industrialized world over degenerative diseases, especially coronary heart disease, and the belief that habits of exercise established in school might well contribute to the "prevention of this scourge of the twentieth century"(McIntosh, 1981). Further, the declaration demonstrated the influence of the educational reforms undertaken in Vanves and Lyon, described at the outset of this discussion, which had spread by this time to Cuesmes, Belgium, and several other countries.[37]

After 1964, England, Denmark, West Germany, and Japan—to name but a few countries involved—instituted physical exercise in increased amounts for all schoolchildren and youth. Daily physical exercise was adopted in Sweden, Belgium, France, East Germany, USSR, and China (Bailey, 1973; McIntosh, 1981; Report . . . UNESCO, 1978). Although the East Germans and Soviets established elite sports schools, they also determined that every child in state schools should have physical education classes daily. In South Australia, 60 percent of all schools were offering daily physical education programs by 1980 (Physical Education Branch, 1981).

Educational Reform in Canada

The impressive educational reforms achieved in Canada during the 1970s merit scrutiny because of several parallels that can be drawn between Canada and the United States. Neither country has a single, unified governmental ministry that sets educational policies for the nation; great stress is placed on academic achievement; and there is a deeply engrained tradition of competitive athletics in schools and other sports programs for youth (cf. Bailey, 1979).

Some common features of the campaign waged by Canadian educators and advocates of reform are noteworthy.[38] First, the reforms were initiated primarily in elementary schools, grades one through eight or one through six; thus, the decisions not only were consistent with the developmental perspective advanced, but avoided confrontations with entrenched athletic powers at the high school level. The issue framed was one of the healthy growth and development of the child, not whether competitive athletics were good or bad. Second, the appeals for support relied only partially upon data indicating the improved cardiovascular condition of children who exercise; they also stressed the Vanves results, because this was much more than a "fitness" campaign. A unity of body, mind, and spirit was called for in citing the improvement in human relations as well as academic performance of children in the French schools (cf. Bailey, 1973). Rather than a call for improved physical training, therefore, it became an educational movement for the common good. Third, a participatory ethic runs through the descriptions of how programs began in various schools. Parents were given a good deal of information about the proposed programs, and their opinions as well as those of teachers and children were solicited throughout the trial periods and reported to the participants. "Subjective" impressions from students, teachers, and parents were given credence and, in one case, wide public exposure. When the CBC filmed the Sherwood School project in Regina,

Saskatchewan, nationwide interest was sparked by the program (Report, Regina Board of Education, 1975). Fourth, as in France and Belgium, costs were minimized by employing physical educators to train classroom teachers and serve as curriculum consultants, and full use was made of community recreation facilities.[39] Unlike the French and Belgian experiments, however, the Canadian school day retained North American hours. The Sherwood School revised its schedule from 9:00-4:00 to 8:30-3:30 (two hours less than the French and Belgian plans). In the three Canadian programs identified as following the Vanves plan, nonacademic subjects were offered in the afternoon, as well as 40-45 minutes of physical education per day. No provisions were made for supervised homework during school hours, and there is no mention of eliminating evening homework. Other innovative programs followed the relatively mild procedure of extending the school day by 15 minutes and paring 5 minutes from other instructional periods to achieve 30-45 minutes for physical activities. Although some additional equipment was required, additional budget requests were kept to a minimum (cf. Sommerville, 1979). The descriptions of changes refer to the Vanves project, but perhaps the most impressive feature of Canadian developments is that their implementation was far less radical than the educational innovation from which they drew inspiration.

A survey of daily physical education programs implemented in Canada since 1973 documents the vitality of the movement (Martens & Grant, 1980). Not all provinces are equally involved in promoting daily physical education (at least one-half hour), but Martens and Grant report that there is at least some activity in every province in both Catholic and public schools.

Martens and Grant also present an overview of the efforts being made to evaluate some programs. Most of the evaluations are of the "subjective" type; that is, enthusiastically favorable comments from the majority of children, teachers, administrators, and parents involved.[40] Despite the fact that more lesson preparation and training are required, the enthusiasm on the part of teachers is striking. It is interesting that the French and Belgian evaluations mention the same paradox and credit the new organization required with creating greater solidarity among teachers. The phrases "increased interest and involvement," "positive attitude toward school," "decreased behavior problems," "improved attitude" all emerge with great frequency in the brief reports obtained from schools. Although the language is richer, the observations of French and Belgians are similar: "We have spoken about the joy of the children. It is probably our best proof. The system pleases. We have lived at Cuesmes, another experience of 'a happy school'" (Study of an Interesting Initiative, p. 17). While many researchers in the United States have shunned affective realms of investigation—at least until recently—and some would prefer counts of "prosocial exchanges," the consistency of reports across countries and across the diverse school systems in Canada is impressive. Further credence to the validity of the reports is given by the fact that these educational reforms flourished at local levels during a serious recessionary period.

Where fitness and aerobic tests were given, Martens and Grant report generally significant positive results. Some schools also have reported significantly higher scores in reading, language arts, and mathematics for children assigned to experimental classes (Martens & Grant, 1980). The presentation of the survey data did not attempt to provide details of measures and other facts that would be needed to evaluate the research efforts. The purpose was to document the widespread adoption of daily physical education and to describe the positive momentum for change that arose across Canada. That such a momentum developed without federal directives or vast expenditures of funds is noteworthy. Too often we think of policy making at the federal level, ignoring the power of grass roots movements.

RETROSPECTIVE AND PROSPECTIVE VIEWS

The history that was selected for this discussion began with the movement for common schools reform, a movement that was animated by a desire to provide training for all individuals in the commonweal to enable them to become effective, contributing members of a democratic society. Ensuring the health of each child was the kernel of educational reform. Looking first to the body as the means to affect both intellectual and moral elevation was supported by European thought, most notably by the phrenologists who called for the study of individual physical development. The disparity between the ideals of health and the growing problems of an industrialized and urbanized culture provided a continuing target for advocates of reform. After the Civil War, fledgling professions in public and child health began to join with sectarian and nonsectarian volunteer organizations to better the lot of children. Clear strides were made. Gymnastics and hygiene were incorporated into higher education and began to make inroads in public schools, accompanied by more precise measurement of physical growth and fitness. By the 1890s, physical educators in colleges and universities had become leaders in anthropometric measurement and the study of physical growth. Strong scientific links existed among statisticians, anthropologists, physiologists, physical educators, and psychologists involved in the child study movement. The training of teachers in sophisticated gymnastics systems was flourishing, and the awareness of individual differences in physical growth and changes in patterns of growth over time led to early specialization for teaching children of different ages. Women were a significant source of public support for health reform in the community and in the schools. Scientific endeavors aimed at determining the maximum techniques for assuring healthy growth were intimately bound to a powerful political movement for health reform.

The course of events for physical education in the common schools was not, however, to take the direction that seemed so evident at the Boston Conference of 1889. English athletics, which had been administered by the students in the United States as well as in England, were taken over by higher education, in part to control undesirable excesses and professionalism and in part to furnish revenues and a sense of communality among students and alumni. In a few brief years, high schools followed suit and the transformation of physical education began. The claims of male virility and morality that were used to "rescue" the games from the students in times of imperialistic fervor reduced health to a secondary concern.

While we have traced an enduring interest in healthy individual growth and development and continuing research efforts directed to this end through the 1940s, the issue no longer was as starkly framed for educational policy as it once had been. Far more public attention was focused on athletic contests which were promoted as teams of healthy people cooperating for success; and the social sciences, including developmental psychology, became ever more concerned with group processes and models of learning rather than interactional models of development. Physical educators, while preserving their concern for individual development, nevertheless became separated from applied physiology and were more committed to creating a positive, noncommercialized, and participatory program for sports. Women's physical education programs slipped to last place in the bureaucracy of education and no longer were an integral part of a larger women's movement for health. Programs for boys and men emphasized group sports, and a hierarchy appeared of which varsity athletic performance was the peak. The profound and enduring public confusion between physical education and athletics becomes more understandable when it is seen as a matter of sex differences. Boys and men did one thing; girls, another. But what girls did, and why, failed to reach public attention. That boys who were not athletically talented were being neglected, in favor of the few who were, did not become a critical issue in defining educational policy. Even as noted an educator as Conant, for example, was apparently unaware of programs for students who were not male athletes and teachers who were not male coaches.

Although neither physical education nor athletics was discussed during consideration of the enactment of Title IX, it is understandable that athletics became the focus on a controversy over sexism in higher education. Athletics was, and remains, the province of the male physically elite. One of the positive outcomes of the Title IX regulations was that talented female athletes were granted at least a small piece of intercollegiate and varsity budgets, and public support of female athletes has risen. What is of more value—if physical health is the defining criterion—is the increased participation of both men and women in intramural sports at the college level. But as the adevelopmental mandates are traced downward through high school, junior high, and elementary school, there is less evidence of increased participation by boys and girls who are not athletically talented; indeed, there is support for the idea that staff, equipment, and playing field are dominated by select athletic competitors, and funds for the many, especially for young children, have been reduced.

One of the lessons of the Title IX athletics controversy is that the athletic enterprise in our secular society has assumed the proportions of a national religion. There are powerful financial interests at stake in promoting athletic contests of high quality and entertainment value for many millions of people. Without question, these contests continue to provide a sense of communality among a deeply fractured and diverse population. The interests of sound educational policy will not be enhanced by direct confrontation with the athletic establishment. Indeed, there should be no need for such a battle. Why a country as wealthy as the United States cannot fund physical education for all children and youth, and a broad intramural sports program as well as highly competitive sports, is the common question. The rest of the international, industrialized world seems to have been able to make such provisions. In the United States, however, public support for such action can come only if the educational policy issues are framed and presented differently than they have been in the last 40 years.

If the question addressed by policy makers were how public schools can contribute to healthy individual development and the prevention of illness across the lifespan, the assessment of national practices would follow a different course from that indicated by federal efforts to eliminate sex discrimination. The Children's Bureau, as noted earlier, focused on investigating and reporting child health; the health conferences it sponsored reached communities across the country; and, despite the retrenchment of the 1920s, an agenda of policy priorities was created and revitalized later in the New Deal (Lemons, 1973; Parker & Carpenter, 1981). It is time again to organize the scattered fragments of data and to collect and disseminate information on the status of child health and cultural practices that harm or promote healthy development.

The most recent estimates from the Bureau of the Census indicate that $322 billion, 393 million was spent on the national health in 1982. Of this total, the public expenditure was $136 billion, 830 million (*Statistical Abstracts*, 1984). The cost of osteoporosis, alone, has been estimated at $3.8 billion for 1984 (*Osteoporosis*, 1984). Companies spend as much as 25 percent of the total payroll on employee health costs (New York *Times*, October 14, 1984). Given the magnitude of the health problems, it seems incredible that the small funds needed for teacher training in physical education and hygiene — critical to educational reforms internationally — have not been appropriated, and that systematic assessments of physical development in children have not been undertaken.

From a developmental perspective the questions would begin with the assessment of the health of infants and young children who have not been admitted to public schools. Attempts have been made to regulate daycare facilities in a number of respects, but time for indoor and outdoor play, and the amount of television children watch, have not been considered and there are no statistics available. Once children enter school, the primary and elementary school programs are especially devoid of physical education specialists to screen health problems and to provide sound programs in physical training, despite the fact that there are millions of children who watch more than five hours per day of television (cf. Stein & Friedrich, 1975) and others who are confined to their homes after school as parents work and parks are unsafe for play. But there is no public record to document practices or reveal the health of inactive children. During the adolescent period, the issues become more complex as both sex and maturational timing need to be considered in monitoring efforts. The primitive profile that emerges is one in which early maturing boys and late maturing girls dominate the athletic teams, while more than 75 percent of the youths are excluded from participation. It is clear that state requirements for physical education at the junior high and high school levels have diminished in the last ten years, but the magnitude of the decrease is masked by inadequate reporting.

There is growing evidence that adolescence may be a crucial period for developing sound adult cardiovascular function (Bailey, Malina, & Rasmussen, 1978). Cross-sectional measures of the efficiency of the oxygen transport system in the United States are lower with older children than with younger; in the Scandinavian countries these measures increase with age (Bailey, 1973). Yet this is only one indicator of healthy functioning. Young female runners have superb cardiovascular records, but these measures tell us nothing about the mineral content of their bones. We need monitoring and reporting of the athletic and dietary regimes of women who have become involved in arduous athletic competition. Further, we need to record and disseminate information about the health of the millions of women who are at risk for the development of osteoporosis because of poor diets and lack of exercise during adolescence.

Throughout the history of school reform movements, proponents have noted the increased alertness, attention, and intellectual performance of children who exercise at school. Empirical data to support these observations are scattered and, in some cases, not very systematic, but the convergent evidence lends credence to the common-sense notion that healthy, active children are better students. Two hundred years of observation have affirmed the Greek idea that positive affective states are associated with physical exercise. The provocative new research on endorphins, the complex modulatory system of the brain which has focused largely on pain modulation thus far, also promises to yield information on the ancient Greeks' observation (Miller, 1983; Watkins & Mayer, 1982).

Framing the social policy question anew suggests that we have assigned millions of children in the United States to an educational experiment in physiological deprivation. Viewed in this light, it is not surprising that many symptoms that are at least in part physicologically based have emerged: inability to attend and listen, lack of enthusiasm and interest, lack of self-control. Good programs of physical training for every child would not provide a panacea, but the experience of other countries leads us to believe that rather marked improvements should be noted in many domains of human functioning.

A curious remnant of dualism has been associated with the periodic calls for academic rigor and excellence in the last 30 years. That dualism has, unfortunately, been supported by the efforts of a large cast of social scientists. The body, however, seems to be reappearing in theoretical formulation and research activity. The news media lead us to believe that our culture is enormously concerned with physical fitness. Perhaps the convergence of societal values and empirical research will once again focus educational policy-making efforts on the whole and healthy individual who can contribute to the commonweal.

ACKNOWLEDGMENTS

I should like to thank the following professors of physical education who helped me to understand the intricacies of their profession: the late Katherine Ley, Don Bailey, Barbara Forker, Angela Lumpkin, F. L. Martens, Terry Parsons, Jack MacKenzie, and Mae Timer. Lois Meek Stolz, Harriet Rheingold, and Charles Cofer reviewed the initial draft with great care, and I should also like to thank Francis Beech, Lloyd Borstelman, Charles and Isabel Eaton, Mary Cover Jones, Fred Keller, Greg Lockhead, and Robert Sears for their critical comments on the final manuscript. Preparation of the manuscript was funded in part by the Bush Foundation, University of North Carolina.

REFERENCES

American higher education: Toward an uncertain future. (1974, Fall; 1975, Winter). *Daedulus, 1,; 2.*

Bailey, D. A. (1973, October). Exercise, fitness and physical education for the growing child. *Canadian Journal of Public Health, 64,* 421-30.

Bailey, D. A., Malina, R. M., & Rasmussen, R. L. (1978). The influence of exercise, physical activity, and athletic performance on the dynamics of human growth. In F. Falker & J. M. Tanner, *Human growth* (Vol. 2, pp. 475-505). New York: Plenum.

Bailey, R. (1979, Summer). Physical activity vital for all children. *Health,* pp. 10-11; 22-23.

Bakan, D. (1966). The influence of phrenology on American psychology. *Journal of the History of the Behavioral Sciences, 2*(3), 200-20.

Baldwin, A. (1968). *Theories of child development.* New York: Wiley.

Baxter, A. M. (1875). *Statistics, medical and anthropological* (Vol. 1). Washington, DC: U.S. Government Printing Office.

Beauvoir, S. de. (1953). *The second sex.* New York: Knopf.

Beecher, C. E. (1846). *Treatise on domestic economy for the use of young ladies at home and at school.* New York: Harper. (Originally published, 1841.)

_____ . (1855). *Letters to the people on health and happiness.* New York: Harper.

_____ . (1865). *Physiology and calisthenics for schools and families.* New York: Harper.

Betts, J. R. (1968). Mind and body in early American social thought. *Journal of American History, 54,* 787-805.

Betts, J. R. (1972). Public recreation, public parks and public health before the Civil War. In B. L. Bennett (Ed.), *The history of physical education and sport* (pp. 33-52). Chicago: Athletic Institute.

_____ . (1974). *America's sporting heritage: 1850-1950.* Reading, MA: Addison-Wesley.

Block, J. H. (1973). Conceptions of sex role: Some cross-cultural and longitudinal perspectives. *American Psychologist, 28,* 512-26.

Boring, E. C. (1950). *A history of experimental psychology* (2nd. ed.). New York: Appleton-Century-Crofts. (Originally published, 1929.)

Bowditch, H. P. (1891). The growth of children studied by Galton's percentile grades. *Annual Report, Massachusetts Board of Health, 22*, 479-525.

Boyd, E. (1980). *Origins of the study of human growth.* University of Oregon Health Sciences Center Foundation (Portland, OR).

Bronson, A. O. (1958). *Clark W. Hetherington, scientist and philosopher.* Salt Lake City: University of Utah Press.

Burchenal, E. (1919). A constructive program of athletics for school girls: Policy, method and activities. *American Physical Education Review, 24*, 272-79.

Burnham, W. H. (1892). Outline of school hygiene. *Pedagogical Seminary, 22*(1), 9-71.

Cairns, R. B. (1983). The emergence of developmental psychology. In P. H. Mussen (Ed.), *Handbook of child psychology* (4th ed.): *Vol. 1. History, theory and methods* (pp. 41-102). New York: Wiley.

Caldwell, F. (1984). Light-boned and lean athletes: Does the penalty outweigh the reward? *The Physician and Sportsmedicine, 12*(9), 139-49.

Cann, C. E., Martin, M. C., Genant, H. K., & Jaffe, R. B. (1984, February). Decreased spinal mineral content in amenorrheic women. *Journal of the American Medical Association, 251*, 626-29.

Carlson, R. (1972). Understanding women: Implications for personality theory and research. *Journal of Social Issues, 28*(2), 17-32.

Carnegie Commission on Higher Education. (1973). *Opportunities for women in higher education: Their current participation, prospects for the future, and recommendations for action.* New York: McGraw Hill.

Cavanagh, B. K. (1971). Note. A little dearer than his horse: Legal stereotypes and the feminine personality. *Harvard Civil Rights-Civil Liberties Law Review, 6*(2), 260-87.

Combe, A. (1842). *The principles of physiology applied to the preservation of health and to the improvement of physical and mental education* (7th Edinburgh ed.). New York: Harper. (Originally published, 1834.)

Combe, G. (1835). *The constitution of man considered in relation to external objects* (2nd ed.). Edinburgh: Anderson.

Comment. Sex discrimination in interscholastic high school athletics. (1974). *Syracuse Law Review, 25*, 535-76.

The Common School Journal for the Year 1839. (1838, November). *1*, 11.

Conant, J. B. (1962). *Recommendations for education in the junior high school years* [note]. Princeton: Educational Testing Service.

———. (1960). *The education of American teachers.* New York, London: McGraw-Hill.

Conway, J. K. (1974, Fall). Coeducation and women's studies: Two approaches to the question of woman's place in the contemporary university. *Daedalus, 1*, 239-49.

Cott, N. F. (1977). *The bonds of womanhood.* New Haven, London: Yale University Press.

Cox, T. A. (1977). Intercollegiate athletics and Title IX. *George Washington Law Review, 46*(1), 34-64.

Crampton, C. W. (1908a). Anatomical or physiological age versus chronological age. *Pedagogical Seminary, 15*, 230-37.

_____. (1908b). Physiological age. *American Physical Education Review, 13*, 144-54; 214-27; 268-83; 345-58.

Cremin, L. A. (1961). *The transformation of the school.* New York: Vintage Books.

Curti, M. (1953). Human nature in American thought: The Age of Reason and morality, 1750-1860. *Political Science Quarterly, 68*, 354-75.

_____. (1959). *The social ideas of American educators.* New Jersey: Pageant Books.

Davies, J. D. (1955). *Phrenology fad and science.* New Haven: Yale University Press.

Degler, C. N. (1980). *At odds.* Oxford: Oxford University Press.

Demos, J. (1970). *A little commonwealth.* Oxford: Oxford University Press.

Dennis, W. (1946). The adolescent. In L. Carmichael (Ed.), *Manual of child psychology* (pp. 633-66). New York: Wiley.

Dimrock, H. S. (1935). A research in adolescence: The social world of the adolescent. *Child Development, 6*, 285-302.

Douglas, A. (1977). *The feminization of American culture.* New York: Avon Books.

Drinkwater, B. D., Nilson, K. L., & Chestnut, C. S. (1984, August). Bone mineral content of amenorrheic and eumenorrheic athletes. *New England Journal of Medicine, 311*, 277-81.

Dunkle, M. (1977). *Sex discrimination in education.* Report. National Coalition for Women and Girls in Education.

Edwards, H. (1973). *Sociology of sport.* Homewood, IL: Dorsey Press.

_____. (1983, August). Educating black athletes. *Atlantic Monthly,* pp. 31-38.

Elshtain, J. B. (1981). *Public man, private woman.* Princeton: Princeton University Press.

Everett, E. G. (1943). *Behavioral characteristics of early- and late-maturing girls.* Unpublished Master's thesis, University of California.

Fasteau, B. (1973, July). Giving women a sporting chance. *Ms. Magazine,* pp. 56-60.

Faust, M. S. (1977). Somatic development of adolescent girls. *Monographs of the Society for Research in Child Development, 42,*(1, Serial No. 169).

Fishel, A. (1976). Organizational positions on Title IX. *Journal of Higher Education, 47,* 93-105.

Forker, B. (1978). Opportunities for sports developments inherent in high quality programs of physical education. In *Report National Conference of Senior Officials to Consider UNESCO Recommendations on Physical Education and Sports* (pp. 71-76). Washington, DC: U.S. Government Printing Office.

Foster, W. (1915, November). An indictment of intercollegiate athletics. *Atlantic Monthly,* pp. 577-88.

Friedrich-Cofer, L. (1981, April). *Modes of psychological adaptation to puberty: Adolescent females in coeducation physical education classes.* Paper presented at the biennial meeting of the Society for Research in Child Development, Boston, Massachusetts.

Friedrich-Cofer, L., Johnson, L., & Tucker, C. (1980, March). The relationship of physical maturation in adolescent males to agency in a naturally occurring competitive situation. Paper presented at the Southwestern Regional meeting of the Society for Research in Child Development, Lawrence, KS.

Geadelmann, P. L. (1980). Physical education: Stronghold of sex role stereotyping. *Quest, 32*(2), 192-200.

Gerard, H. B. (1983). School desegregation: The social science role. *American Psychologist, 38,* 869-77.

Gerber, E. W. (1971). *Innovators and institutions in physical education.* Philadelphia: Lea & Febiger.

———. (1972). The ideas of McCloy, Nash, and Williams. In B. L. Bennett (Ed.), *The history of physical education and sport* (pp. 85-100). Chicago: Athletic Institute.

Giustino, D. (1975). *Conquest of mind.* London: Croom Helm.

Gould, S. J. (1977). *Ontogeny and phylogeny.* Cambridge: Harvard University Press.

Greulich, W. W., Day, H. G., Lachman, S. E., Wolfe, J. B., & Shuttleworth, E. K. (1938). A handbook of methods for the study of adolescent children. *Monographs of the Society for Research in Child Development, 3*(2).

Gymnastics. (1861, March). *Atlantic Monthly,* pp. 283-302.

Hackensmith, C. W. (1966). *History of physical education.* New York: Harper & Row.

Hale, E. E. (1893). *A New England boyhood.* New York: Cassell.

Hall, G. S. (1892). Editorial. *Pedagogical Seminary, 2*(1), 1-8.

———. (1904). *Adolescence* (Vol. 1). New York: Appleton.

Halpern, C. T. (1982). *Personality correlates of maturational timing in black and white females.* Unpublished doctoral dissertation, University of Houston.

Hart, A., & Ferleger, H. (1941). *Theodore Roosevelt cyclopedia.* New York: Roosevelt Memorial Association.

Hartwell, E. M. (1886). *Physical training in American colleges and universities.* Report to the Bureau of Education. Washington, DC: U.S. Government Printing Office.

Hartwell, E. M. (1962). The nature of physical training and the best means of securing its ends. In A. Weston, *The makings of American physical education* (pp. 124-29). New York: Appleton-Century-Crofts. (Originally published, 1889.)

———. (1894). A preliminary report on anthropometry in the United States. In *Papers on anthropometry* (pp. 1-15). Boston: American Statistical Association.

Hearings before Subcommittee No. 4 of the Committee on the Judiciary, House of Representatives 92d Congress First Session, on H. J. Res. 35, 208 and related bills proposing an Amendment to the Constitution of the U.S. Relative to Equal Rights for Men and Women. March 24, 25, 31; April 1, 2, 5, 1971 Serial No. 2.

Hetherington, C. W. (1962). Fundamental education. In A. Weston, *The making of American physical education* (pp. 159-65). New York: Appleton-Century-Crofts. (Originally published, 1910.)

Hinsdale, B. A. (1937). *Horace Mann and the common school revival in the United States.* New York: Scribner's.

Hitchcock, E. (1831). *Dyspepsy forestalled and resisted* (2nd. ed.). Amherst, MA: Adams.

_____. (1845). *The highest uses of learning:An address delivered at his inauguration to the presidency of Amherst College.* Amherst: Adams.

_____. (1852). *The power of Christian benevolence illustrated in the life and labors of Mary Lyon.* Northhampton, MA: Hopkins, Bridgman.

_____. (1863). *Reminiscences of Amherst College.* Northhampton, MA: Bridgman & Child.

Hitchock, E. [Jr.] (1881/1962). The first academic program of physical education in American education. In A. Weston (Ed.) *The making of American physical education.* (pp. 107-112). New York: Appleton-Century Croft.

_____. (1885). Athletics in American colleges. *Journal of Social Science, 20,* 27-44.

_____. (1887, November 26). *The need of anthropometry.* Paper presented at the second annual meeting of the American Association for the Advancement of Physical Education, Brooklyn, NY. (See also *Report of the Committee upon the Method of Physical Measurement.* Brooklyn: Rome, 1887.)

Hitchcock, E., Jr., & Hitchcock, E. (1864). *Elementary anatomy and physiology for colleges, academies, and other schools* (2nd ed.). New York: Ivison, Phinney, Blakeman.

Hoferek, M. J. (1980). At the crossroad: Merger or _____ ? *Quest, 32,* 95-102.

Hofstadter, R. (1944). *Social Darwinism in American thought.* Boston: Beacon Press.

_____. (1962). *Anti-intellectualism in American life.* New York: Vintage Books.

Holcombe, A. (1982, January). Hey, your values are showing. *Journal of Physical Education, Recreation and Dance,* pp. 60-63.

Holmen, M. G., & Parkhouse, B. L. (1981). Trends in the selection of coaches for female athletes: A demographic inquiry. *Research Quarterly for Exercise and Sport, 52,* 9-18.

Holmes, O. W. (1881). *Common law.* Boston: Little, Brown.

Howe, F. N. (1975). *Women and the power to change.* New York: McGraw-Hill.

Hult, J. S. (1980). The philosophical conflicts in men's and women's collegiate athletics. *Quest, 32,* 77-94.

Johnson, W. R., & Buskirk, E. R. (Eds.). (1974). *Science and medicine of exercise and sport* (2nd ed.). London, New York: Harper & Row.

Jones, H. E., MacFarlane, J., & Eichorn, D. (1959). A progress report of growth studies at the University of California. *Vita Humane, 3,* 17-31.

Jones, M. C. (1948, September). *Studying the characteristics of friends.* Paper presented at the annual meeting of the American Psychological Association, Boston, MA.

Jones, M. C., & Bayley, N. (1950). Physical maturing among boys as related to behavior. *Journal of Educational Psychology, 41,* 129-48.

Jones, M. C., Bayley, N., MacFarland, J. W., & Honzik, M. P. (1971). *The course of human development.* Waltham, MA: Xerox.

Jones, M. C., & Mussen, P. H. (1958). Self conceptions, motivations, and interpersonal attitudes of early- and late-maturing girls. *Child Development, 29*, 492-500.

Kuhn, J. L. (1976). Title IX: Employment and athletics are outside HEW's jurisdiction. *Georgia Law Journal, 65*, 49-77.

Lee, M. (1931). The case for and against intercollegiate athletics for women and the situation since 1923. *Research Quarterly, 2*, 93-127.

———. (1972a). Personal reflections on R. Tait McKenzie. In B. L. Bennett (Ed.), *The history of physical education and sport* (pp. 177-86). Chicago: Athletic Institute.

———. (1972b). The state of the profession from World War I to women's lib. In B. L. Bennett (Ed.), *The history of physical education and sport* (pp. 101-20). Chicago: Athletic Institute.

Lemons, J. S. (1973). *The woman citizen: Social feminism in the 1930s.* Urbana: University of Illinois Press.

Leonard, F. E., & Affleck, A. M. (1947). *The history of physical education* (3rd ed.). Philadelphia: Lea & Febiger.

Lesley, J. P. (1867). Biographical notice of Edward Hitchcock. In *Annual of the National Academy of Sciences for 1866* (pp. 129-54). Cambridge, MA: Welch, Bigelow.

Lewis, G. M. (1969a). Adoption of the sports program, 1906-39: The role of accommodation in the transformation of physical education. *Quest, 12*, 35-47.

———. (1969b). Theodore Roosevelt's role in the 1905 football controversy. *Research Quarterly, 40* (4), 717-24.

———. (1972). Enterprise on the campus: Developments in intercollegiate sport and higher education, 1875-1939. In B. L. Bennett (Ed.), *The history of physical education and sport* (pp. 53-66). Chicago: Athletic Institute.

Ley, K. (1974, October). Women in sports: Where do we go from here, boys? *Phi Delta Kappan*, pp. 129-31.

Lomax, E. (1977). The Laura Spelman Rockefeller Memorial: Some of its contributions to early research in child development. *Journal of the History of the Behavioral Sciences, 13*(3), 283-93.

Macalister, A. (1911). Phrenology. *Encyclopedia Brittanica* (11th ed.), vol. 21, pp. 534-41.

MacLeish, A., & Prichard, E. F. (Eds.). (1939). *Law and politics: Occasional papers of Felix Frankfurter.* New York: Harcourt, Brace.

Malina, R. M. (1983). Menarche in athletics: A synthesis and hypothesis. *Annals of Human Biology, 10*(4), 1-24.

Mann, H. (1891). *Life and works of Horace Mann* (Vol. 3). Boston: Lee & Shepard. (Originally published, 1842.)

Mann, M. P. (1865). *Life of Horace Mann.* Boston: Lee & Shepard.

Martens, F. L., & Grant, B. (1980, May/June). A survey of daily physical education in Canada. *CAHPER Journal, 46*(5), 30-38.

Martens, R. (1978). *Joy and sadness in children's sports.* Champaign, IL: Human Kinetics.

McGraw, M. B. (1946). Maturation of behavior. In L. Carmichael (Ed.), *Manual of child psychology* (pp. 332-69). New York: Wiley.

McIntosh, P. C. (1981). Games and gymnastics for two nations in one. In P. C. McIntosh, J. G. Dixon, A. D. Monrow, & R. F. Willetts (Eds.), *Landmarks in the history of physical education* (pp. 185-249). London: Routledge & Kegan Paul.

McKenzie, J. (1974). *One third time physical education.* Unpublished paper, Regina Public School Board, Regina, Saskatchewan.

Meek, L. H. (1940). The opportunity of physical education to influence the social development of boys and girls. *The Progressive Physical Educator, 23*(1), 16-22.

Meikeljohn, A. (1922, July-December). What are college games for? *Atlantic Monthly,* pp. 663-71.

Messerli, J. (1972). *Horace Mann: A biography.* New York: Knopf.

Miller, N. E. (1983). Behavioral medicine: Symbiosis between laboratory and clinic. *Annual Review of Psychology, 34,* 1-31.

Moynihan, D. P. (1975, Winter). The politics of higher education. *Daedalus,* pp. 128-47.

Munrow, A. D. (1981). Physical education in the United States of America. In P. G. McIntosh, J. G. Dixon, A. D. Munrow, & R. F. Willetts (Eds.), *Landmarks in the history of physical education* (pp. 156-84). London: Routledge & Kegan Paul.

National Library of Medicine. (1984). *Osteoporosis literature search,* January 1980 through March 1984, No. 84-3, Bethesda, MD.

Notes: Sex discrimination and intercollegiate athletics. (1975). *Iowa Law Review, 61,* 420-96.

Osteoporosis. (1984). Bethesda, MD: U.S. Department of Health & Human Services, National Institutes of Health, Office of Medical Research.

Parker, J. K., & Carpenter, E. M. (1981). Julia Lathrop and the Children's Bureau: The emergence of an institution. *Social Service Review, 55,* 60-77.

Parsons, T. W. (1981). *Position paper opposing Amended House Bill #251, Ohio.* Unpublished manuscript, Bowling Green State University.

Pope, H. G., Hudson, J. L., & Yurgelun-Todd, D. (1984). Anorexia and bulimia among 300 suburban women shoppers. *American Journal of Psychiatry, 141,* 292-94.

Physical Education Branch, Education Department of South Australia. (1981). *Physical education bulletin R#12.* South Australia: Woolman.

Posse, N. (1890). *The special kinesiology of educational gymnastics.* Boston: Lothrop, Lee & Shepard.

Pritchett, H. S. (1972). Shall the university become a business corporation? In L. Desaulniers (Ed.), *Highlights from 125 years of the Atlantic* (pp. 221-24.). Boston: Atlantic Monthly. (Originally published, 1905.)

Promoting health/preventing disease: Objectives for the nation. (1980). Washington, DC: U.S. Government Printing Office.

Quick, R. H. (1880). *Some thoughts on education by John Locke.* Cambridge: Harvard University Press.

Rainwater, C. E. (1922). *The play movement in the United States.* Chicago: University of Chicago Press.

Reiff, G. G., Kroll, W., & Hunsicker, P. (1978). The fitness of American youth: Program status and implications for physical education in the United States. In *Report National Conference of Senior Officials to Consider UNESCO Recommendations on Physical Education and Sport* (pp. 53-65). Washington, DC: U.S. Government Printing Office.

Report National Conference of Senior Officials to Consider UNESCO Recommendations on Physical Education and Sport. (1978). U.S. Department of Health, Education and Welfare, Office of Education. Washington, DC: U.S. Government Printing Office.

Report, Regina Board of Education. (1975). *Sherwood School Project, 1975.*

Rheingold, H. (1986). The first twenty-five years of the Society for Research in Child Development. In A. Smuts and J. Hagen (Eds.) *History and research in child development. Monographs of the Society for Research in Child Development. 50* (4, 5, Serial No. 211), 126-40.

Roosevelt, T. R. (1893, December 23). *Harper's Weekly*, p. 1,236.

Rose, C. L. (1978). The ERA and women's sport: A hypothetical trial case. In C. A. Oglesby (Ed.), *Women and sport: From myth to reality* (pp. 221-46). Philadelphia: Lea & Febiger.

Rousseau, J. J. (1966). *Émile.* London: Dent. (Originally published, 1762.)

Sargent, D. A. (1962). The system of physical training at the Hemenway Gymnasium. In A. Weston, *The making of American physical education* (pp. 113-17). New York: Appleton-Century-Crofts. (Originally published, 1889.)

Schlossman, S. L. (1973). G. Stanley Hall and the Boys' Club: Conservative applications of recapitulation theory. *Journal of the History of the Behavioral Sciences, 14*(2), 140-47.

Scott, A. F. (1979, Spring). The ever widening circle: The diffusion of feminist values from the Troy Female Seminary 1822-1872. *History of Education Quarterly*, pp. 3-25.

Sears, R. (1975). Your ancients revisited: A history of child development. In E. M. Hetherington (Ed.), *Review of child development research* (Vol. 5, pp. 1-73). Chicago: University of Chicago Press.

Senn, M. J. (1975). Insights on the child development movement in the United States. *Monographs of the Society for Research in Child Development, 40*(3-4, Serial No. 161).

Sewall, R. B. (1980). *The life of Emily Dickinson.* New York: Farrar, Straus & Giroux.

Sex discrimination and intercollegiate athletics: Putting some muscle on Title IX. (1979). *Yale Law Journal, 88,* 1,254-79.

Sex discrimination regulations: Hearings before the Subcommittee on Postsecondary Education of the House Committee on Education and Labor, 94th Cong., 1st sess. 206 (1975) (Rep. Schroeder).

Shuttleworth, F. K. (1939). The physical and mental growth of girls and boys age six to nineteen in relation to age of maximum growth. *Monographs of the Society for Research in Child Development, 4*(3, Serial No. 1).

Shryock, R. H. (1929, November). The origins and significance of the public health movement in the United States. *Annals of Medical History, 1,* 645-65.

Siegel, A. W., & White, S. H. (1982). The Child Study Movement: Early growth and development of the symbolized child. In H. Reese & L. P. Lipsitt (Eds.), *Advances in child development and behavior* (Vol. 17, pp. 233-85). New York: Academic Press.

Sklar, K. K. (1973). *Catherine Beecher.* New Haven, London: Yale University Press.

Sommerville, R. D. (1979, May/April). Daily physical education and the principal. *CAHPER Journal,* pp. 3-4; 41-42.

Spears, B. (1974). The emergence of women in sport. In *Women's athletics: Coping with controversy* (pp. 26-42). Washington, DC: AAHPER.

Spears, B., & Swanson, R. (1978). *History of sport and physical activity in the United States.* Dubuque, IA: Brown.

Stearns, W. A. (1855). *Discourses and addresses at the installation and inauguration of the Rev. William A. Stearns, D.D. as President of Amherst College, and Pastor of the College Church.* Amherst: Adams.

Stein, A. H., & Friedrich, L. K. (1975). Impact of television on children and youth. In E. M. Hetherington (Ed.), *Review of child development research* (Vol. 5, pp. 183-256).

Statistical Abstract of the U.S., 1984. (1984). U.S. Department of Commerce, Bureau of the Census, 104th ed.

Stolz, H. R. (1924). *Manual in health supervision and instruction.* California State Department of Education.

Stolz, H. R., & Stolz, L. M. (1944). Adolescent problems related to somatic variations. Chapter 5 (pp. 80-99) in National Society for the Study of Education, *Adolescence, 43* Yearbook, Pt. 1.

Stolz, H. R., & Stolz, L. M. (1951). *Somatic development of adolescent boys.* New York: Macmillan.

Stone, C. P., & Barker, R. G. (1939). The attitudes and interests of premenarcheal and post menarcheal girls. *Journal of Genetic Psychology, 54,* 27-71.

Stroud, K. M. (1973). Sex discrimination in high school athletics. *Indiana Law Review, 6,* 661-82.

Study of an interesting initiative. The Cuesmes experiment of the half and half pedagogic system. Unpublished manuscript.

Talmini, J. T., & Page, C. H. (Eds.). (1973). *Sport and society.* Boston: Little, Brown.

Tanner, J. M. (1981). *A history of the study of human growth.* Cambridge: Cambridge University Press.

Todd, T. W. (1937). *Atlas of skeletal maturation.* St. Louis: Mosby.

Tryon, C. M. (1939). Evaluations of adolescent personality by adolescents. *Monographs of the Society for Research in Child Development, 4*(4, serial No. 23).

Tyack, D. B. (Ed.). (1967). *Turning points in American educational history.* Waltham, MA: Blaisdell.

Tyack, D., & Hansot, E. (1982). *Managers of virtue: Public school leadership in America, 1820-1980.* New York: Basic Books.

Tyler, W. S. (1895). *A history of Amherst College.* New York: Hitchcock.

Ullyot, J. (1981, December). Amenorrhea: A sensitive subject. *Womansport,* pp. 46-47.

U.S. Commission on Civil Rights. (1980, July). *More hurdles to clear: Women and girls in competitive athletics.* Clearinghouse Publication No. 63. Washington, DC: U.S. Government Printing Office.

Van Dalen, D., & Bennett, B. (1971). *A world history of physical education* (2nd ed.). Englewood Cliffs, NJ: Prentice-Hall.

Walsh, J. (1983). Survey shows freshmen shift on careers, values. *Science, 219,* 822.

Watkins, L. R., & Mayer, D. J. (1982). Organization of endogenous opiate and nonopiate pain control systems. *Science, 216,* 1,185-92.

Wayman, A. (1928). *Education through physical education* (2nd ed.). Philadelphia: Lea & Febiger.

_____. (1932, March). Women's division of the National Amateur Athletic Federation. *Journal of Health and Physical Education,* pp. 3-7; 53-54.

Weston, A. (Ed.). (1962). *The making of American physical education.* New York: Appleton-Century-Crofts.

Wilson, L. N. (1914). *G. Stanley Hall: A sketch.* New York: Stechert.

Wishy, B. (1968). *The child and the Republic.* Philadelphia: University of Pennsylvania Press.

Wood, T. D. (1910). Physical education. Part I, Health and education. In *The ninth yearbook of the National Society for the Study of Education* (pp. 75-104). Chicago: University of Chicago Press.

Zeigler, E. (1979). *History of physical education and sport.* Englewood Cliffs, NJ: Prentice-Hall.

NOTES

1. French educational reforms have their own complicated history. (See, for example, Moody, J. N., 1978, *French education since Napoleon.* Syracuse: Syracuse University Press.) In the example cited, however, the long-standing health concerns meshed well with other prevailing reform movements, and led to a favorable political climate for the reception of research findings.

2. In the AAHPER 1974 Youth Fitness Survey, one of six boys aged 10 to 17 could not do one pull-up; conservative school population estimate, 2,319,712 children (Reiff et al., 1978). Preliminary results made available from the National Children and Youth Fitness Study, October 1984, indicate that in the sample of 8,000 children tested (aged 10-18), body fat measurements were significantly greater than those collected during the 1960s by the National Center for Health Statistics. Participation in daily physical education remained at about one-third of the sample. Girls' cardiorespiratory endurance measure (mile walk/run) showed no difference between the performance of 10- and 18-year olds (*Summary of the Findings from National Children and Youth Fitness Survey,* U.S. Department of Health and Human Services, October 1984). The 1984 Fitness Profile of American Youth by the American Athletic Union involved more than 4 million children from 6 to 17 in public and private schools. Only 36 percent met AAU standards for physical fitness (from 1979 to

1982, 42 percent of the youngsters passed the tests). Performance of adolescents, particularly girls, did not show the consistent improvement associated with physical maturation (New York *Times*, October 17, 1984).

3. Tanner (1981) writes that eighteenth-century Prussians were obsessed with physical size and based their belief in the inferiority of contemporary Germans in part on the writings of Julius Caesar and Tacitus who extolled the height and strength of the Germanic tribes. Ling, whose poetry and plays dealt with Norse mythology and history, was committed to the belief that the vigor of the Norse heroes must be revived in Sweden (Leonard & Affleck, 1947).

4. Women were paid about half the salary of male teachers (see Sklar, 1973, p. 312). Between 1840 and 1880, philosophical and fiscal arguments for women teachers merged. By 1888, 63 percent of American teachers were women; and in cities, 90 percent of the teachers were women (Sklar, 1973, p. 180).

5. Other members of the funeral arrangements committee included, for example, Nathaniel Bowditch, Harrison Gray Otis, Joseph Story, and Joseph Tuckerman. German professor Charles Follen, who introduced gymnastics to Harvard, gave the funeral oration. Reverend John Pierpont composed an "Ode to Spurzheim" which was sung by the Handel and Haydn Society. James J. Audubon and other artists made sketches of the deceased (Davies, 1955).

6. Throughout the 1840s George Combe moved further away from the Christian phrenologists, explicitly rejecting an afterlife and declaring that traditional Christianity was exhausted and the Bible a dead letter (see Giustino, 1975, Chap. 6).

7. Andrew Combe was a Fellow of the Royal College of Physicians (Edinburgh), Physician Extraordinary to the Queen in Scotland, and Consulting Physician to the King and Queen of the Belgians. His professional prominence, and the fame of the other physicians in Edinburgh's flourishing medical research center, not only lent prestige to phrenology but were important in attracting the attention of American physicians who studied abroad (Guistino, 1975).

8. While noting that his own sentiments concerning doctrines of phrenology were already before the public, Andrew Combe explained the omission as follows:

> My reasons are simply that, for the object I had in view, a special reference to them was not necessary; and that, in a work written for the general reader and for practical purposes, I was naturally anxious to avoid every contested point. Accordingly, in limiting myself to the statement that different parts of the brain perform different functions, without specifying those connected with any particular part, farther than they are all concerned in mental operations, I am not venturing beyond what most eminent anatomists and physiologists, in the past and present times have taught before me (Combe, 1842, p. 299).

9. Mann was plagued by the problem of the proper teaching of morality in the schools during his entire tenure as secretary of the Board of Education of

Massachusetts. He referred to himself as the poor rabbit being hunted by bloodhounds (Mann, 1891). He was sought out by orthodox Christians on the one hand and nonbelievers on the other for his firm stance against any "sectarian" teaching and in favor of prayers and reading from the King James translation of the Bible in the schools. He was mystified and appalled when, in reaction to his Seventh Report (1844) in which he wrote about the teaching of religion abroad, supporters of the provision to allow separate religious instruction for Catholics and Protestants attacked him (Mann, 1891).

10. In the correspondence between Mann and Combe, their poor adult health is frequently attributed to Calvinistic practices during boyhood (Mann, 1891). Catherine Beecher suffered from frequent bouts with illness during her adult life and cites both religious views and social conventions as major causes of debilitation among women in New England (Sklar, 1973).

11. Mann presents a chilling survey of the death rates in Massachusetts and states:

> About seven millions, or one-half of the free white population of the United States, are under eighteen years of age. Could we allow to these only an average period of twenty four or five years, after having reached majority, how important to the country would be their condition as to health and strength! How much more important, yet how much less regarded, than if they were an army of seven millions of men! And what significancy and impressiveness does it give to the fact, that half of mankind die before reaching the age of twenty years (Mann, 1891, p. 154).

Among the criticisms he launched at the schools is the following:

> So, in nine-tenths of the schools in the State, composed of children below seven or eight years of age, the practice still prevails of allowing but one recess in the customary session of three hours; although every physiologist and physician knows, that, for every forty-five or fifty minutes' confinement in the schoolroom, all children under those ages should have at least the remaining fifteen or ten minutes of the hour for exercise in the open air (Mann, 1891, pp. 139-40).

12. Reverend Hitchcock taught and lectured publically on all of the natural sciences and organized botanical and geological field trips for students and young people in Amherst. His lectures and poetry combine scientific expertise and observation, aesthetic sensitivity and deep religious conviction. For his influence on Emily Dickinson, see R. B. Sewall (1980). He was a great supporter of higher education for women and a mentor and devoted friend of Mary Lyon about whom he wrote a biography (see Hitchcock, 1852).

13. Ironically, despite Dr. Sargent's many publications and his international reputation, his five-year academic appointment was not renewed. From 1874 until his retirement in 1919, his title was simply "Director of the Hemenway Gymnasium" (Leonard & Affleck, 1947).

14. Lucille Eaton Hill, for example, conducted a study in 1893 at Vassar in which she compared students taking Swedish gymnastics with those in "scientific oarsmanship" (with a nonactivity control group, of course) over a five-month period. The data provided support for the importance of participation as well as diversification: no physical training, no improvement. Gymnasts gained more in lung capacity, but "overall rowers held their own" (reported in Spears, 1974, p. 33).

15. Dr. Hanna's research at Oberlin College led her to stress the significance of teacher training:

> There are various reasons why lateral curvature should be treated by the gymnasium teacher. At present physical education is carried on largely in connection with our schools. The initial stage of lateral curvature—that reached by preventive measures—corresponds to the time spent in elementary education. The stage of development requiring remedial measures, corresponds to the time spent in secondary or higher education. The number of cases presented to the gymnasium teacher is much larger than that presented to the orthopedic surgeon (Hanna, 1894, cited in Gerber, 1971, p. 326).

16. California, under the leadership of John Swett and support from the Turners and temperance organizations, passed legislation in 1866 stating:

> Instruction shall be given in all grades of schools, and in all classes, during the entire school course, in manners and morals, and the laws of health; and due attention shall be given to such physical exercises for the pupils as may be conducive to health and vigor of body, as well as mind; and to the ventilation and temperature of school rooms (cited in Gerber, 1971, p. 100).

Swett acknowledged the influence of Catherine Beecher on his thought and writings (Gerber, 1971).

17. The entire second issue of *Pedagogical Seminary* (1892) is devoted to health. In his introductory editorial, Hall writes that "Body and mind should be brought to the fullest and most complete maturity of which they are capable" (Hall, 1892, p. 7). A lengthy article appears in this volume by W. H. Burnham in which he discusses arguments for lengthening the school day and year and counters with Dr. Leo Burgerstein's Viennese data on the effects of fatigue on mental operation. Burnham concludes that

> short periods of study, alternating with periods of recreation and exercise, few hours of home study, and plenty of sleep are evidently the conditions of efficient mental work and it is likely soon to be demonstrated by experiment that only by regarding these conditions can the pressing problems concerning the curricula of the primary, grammar and high schools be solved (Burnham, 1892, p. 67).

G. Stanley Hall's esteem for Dr. Leo Burgerstein may be judged by the fact that Burgerstein was honored at Clark University in 1909, when Hall was president, along with Freud. In a group picture, Burgerstein stands at Hall's right hand, and Freud and Jung stand at Hall's left (Siegel & White, 1982).

18. Edward Hartwell, M.D., Ph.D., of Johns Hopkins University, refused to attend the 1885 meeting because "the profession was dominated by women with bees in their bonnets" (cited in Lewis, 1969a). The 1885 meeting resulted in the formation of the AAAPE. Hartwell attended the 1889 meeting!

19. Ann Douglas points out that in less fashionable quarters Bill Sunday was preaching that Jesus Christ was "no dough-faced, lick-spittle proposition. Jesus Christ was the greatest scrapper that ever lived" (Douglas, 1977, p. 397).

20. Hetherington returned to California and began, among other educational innovations, the highly successful Demonstration Play School at the University of California and a comprehensive plan of physical education for the state. In 1921, he resigned as superintendent of Public Instruction when pressures from athletic coaches deadlocked the vote over rigorous, science-based teacher certification requirements (Bronson, 1958).

21. McKenzie was a most unusual man — an orthopedic surgeon, rehabilitation training specialist, and sculptor of some note. At the University of Pennsylvania, however, he was to devote long hours and a good deal of his professional time charged with the task of devising a plan to "give sports back to the students" through a comprehensive department of health, physical education and intercollegiate athletics known as the "Gates plan." Gates was president of the university (Gerber, 1971). Another view of McKenzie comes from Mabel Lee, who acknowledges his great support for women colleagues: "It was Tait McKenzie who gave me the courage and inspiration to do what ever I was able to do as my share in the Women's Division of NAAF and in the Women's Athletic Committee of APEA to hold off the AAU" (Lee, 1972a, p. 182).

22. In the 1920s, President Garfield of Williams College reported: "In New England colleges, the average expenditure per student for athletic purposes was $170.00 with only 16 percent of the students participating. The figures of the country at large were $59.00 with only 17 percent competing" (Wayman, 1928, p. 19).

23. Women wrote and lectured tirelessly. One important article that was cited frequently was written by Mabel Lee in 1931 (see references).

24. Clark Hetherington had initiated such "sports days" at the University of Missouri some ten years earlier. He was also a firm and supportive colleague to women in their stand against the AAU (Bronson, 1958).

25. The early volumes of *Child Development*, and its editorial board, reflect the prominence and research activity of those interested in physical development. Anthropometry and physiology were among the disciplines that held meetings at the first and second biennial meetings of SRCD in 1934 and 1935 (Rheingold, 1986).

26. The articles written by investigators (for example, Herbert Stolz, Lois Meek Stolz, Mary Cover Jones, Carolyn Tryon, Stuart Stoke, Roger Barker) for *Progressive Education* under the editorship of James Hymes are as fresh and informative in 1984 as they were in the early 1940s. In course evaluations (LFC)

of adolescent development over a ten-year period, students rated these articles as among the most important and interesting readings assigned.

27. Radio and television stations and networks paid $55 million to broadcast professional and college football games in the 1967-68 season; this represented an increase of $6 million more than the previous year (Van Dalen & Bennett, 1971).

28. Lawrence Cremin has noted in *The Transformation of American Education* that the rapidity of the collapse of progressive education was due, in part, to the severance of ties, in the course of bureaucratic development, with lay support (Cremin, 1961). Women physical educators, and their ideological stance, had dropped from public view. Further, the old coalitions of women who had been so influential in health reform has dissipated.

29. Harry Edward's position that commercial educational interests exploit and dehumanize black (and white) athletes was and is an unpopular one (Edwards, 1973, 1983).

30. That the efforts to provide equality of educational opportunities to all children might have taken a less painful and more humane and realistic course is now a question for soul searching among social scientists (Gerard, 1983).

31. Senator Bayh's earlier amendment failed, and this one included some important exemptions for groups who could muster political support, for example, military schools, sororities and fraternities, single-sex private colleges.

32. William H. Rehnquist, at that time assistant attorney general, repeatedly remarked in his testimony before the House Subcommittee of the Committee on the Judiciary that those who had testified in favor of the equal rights amendment "do not appear to be in agreement as to the sweep of its language":

> Logically it would appear that legislative history would not be particularly persuasive unless it could be shown that not only the Congress, but the ratifying legislatures of three-quarters of the States were fully aware of an ambiguity in the language of the amendment, and of the legislative reports or debates which purported to clarify that ambiguity (hearings before Subcommittee No. 4, 1971).

The ambiguity to which Rehnquist referred, of course, was the fundamental question of equality and parity of treatment of the sexes. Some advocates of the equal rights amendment envisioned "reasonable" distinctions would be made between men and women, taking into account their dual role as wives and mothers as well as workers, and their present disadvantaged position in the job market; others saw the amendment as abolishing sex as a differentiating criterion altogether. (See *Harvard Civil Rights, Civil Liberties, Law Review*, Vol. 6, 1971, for constitutional arguments concerning the interpretation of an equal rights amendment.)

33. See, for example, *Dodson v. Arkansas Activities Association*, 468 F. Supp. 394 (1979), in which "split-court" basketball rules are determined to deprive girls of equal protection. (Note that these rules were adopted in order to allow twice the number to play on the courts at the same time and to make the game accessible to girls with varying levels of strength and endurance.)

34. President John F. Kennedy gave strong impetus to a national fitness program for all children. He appointed "Bud" Wilkerson, head football coach at the University of Oklahoma, as consultant to his Council on Youth Fitness and Theodore Forbes, supervisor of health and physical education of the Sacramento public city schools, to his executive staff as director of health, physical education and recreation, with intermediaries in government. Forbes was aware that 75 percent of the nation's schools had no daily period of physical education, and he advocated no less than 30 minutes per day for every student (Hackensmith, 1966). Despite the irony of having an athletic hero advocate fitness for the masses, Kennedy showed political astuteness in employing a popular media figure to arouse sentiment for educational reform.

35. The *News-Enterprise* (Elizabethtown, KY, October 7, 1979) reported that there were 80 fewer girls enrolled in high school physical education classes than there were when the program went coed five years earlier. Recommendations included reassessing girls' interests in activities.

36. See, for example, issues of the AAPHERD publication, *Journal of Physical Education, Recreation and Dance*, 1975-1983.

37. The French experiments did not, of course, spring fresh from the brow of Zeus. Before the Second World War, the persistent question of the 1830s and 1890s of the effects on health, affect, and learning capabilities of long sedentary hours in school had not been put to rest in Europe. In 1933, for example, Professor Latarjet of the Faculty of Medicine, University of Lyons, presented the results of a study to the International Congress of Sports Medicine in Turin, Italy. Female students, who were the "weakest physically and intellectually" were sent to special classes in which the schedule for intellectual study was reduced and physical education activities were increased. After 18 months, there was a noticeable decline in absences from school as well as an increase in general intellectual development. Other studies were begun but were interrupted by the advent of World War II (McKenzie, personal communication regarding the report of the Canadian Association for Health, Physical Education and Recreation, 1973). In England, the Peckham Health Centre served as a stimulus to many "positive health" endeavors and research efforts. The Nuffield Foundation, which funded academic chairs in child health, aided in establishing an Institute of Social Medicine to fund research in school auxiology and longitudinal studies of development (Tanner, 1981).

38. These comments are based on a review of a large amount of literature, questionnaires, and reports from many provinces in Canada addressed to parents, school board members, and the public at large, which were generously supplied by Jack McKenzie of the Regina Board of Education, Professor D. A. Bailey of the University of Saskatchewan, and Professor F. L. Martens of the University of Victoria.

39. Madame Boes, "principal" of the Vanves school, saw more than a financial argument for the involvement of classroom teachers in physical education activities. She believed their participation was critical to the formation of new relations between teachers and children and among teachers themselves.

40. In the Sherwood School, for example, 128 of a possible 152 questionnaires sent to parents were completed and returned; to cite a few examples of

the positive responses, 76 percent felt that their child's attitude toward school had improved, 80 percent believed that the child's physical health had improved, and 73 percent thought that academic work had improved (Report, Regina Board of Education, 1975).

II
Adventures in Contemporary Efforts to do Relevant Research

4

On Social Values and Social Development: Gender and Aggression

Robert B. Cairns and Beverly D. Cairns

[B]y the very constitution of society itself, we are all duty
bound to occupy ourselves with the conditions of our fellow
citizens, and especially of the less fortunate among them.
A. Binet and T. Simon (1914, p. 1)

In keeping with the themes of this volume, we begin with comment on the relations between development study and social values,
and how they are inextricably linked. But the inclusion of social values
in the scientific process, while imperative, continues to present special
dilemmas for the researcher. Accordingly, we address some of the
hazards raised by this dual allegiance to science and society, and sum-
marize the guides that we have adopted in dealing with them. Then we
describe some of the pertinent findings on the development of aggressive patterns in girls and boys, and comment on their implications
for theory and application.[1]

ON SOCIAL QUESTIONS AND DEVELOPMENTAL PSYCHOLOGY

Alfred Binet was arguably the first significant experimental child
psychologist. He was also vitally concerned about social policy. Binet
and his colleagues had labored to initiate the special school movement
in Paris for the benefit of learning-disabled children. So he was under-
standably upset when academic entrepreneurs threatened to obscure
the concepts and cash in on the activity. On this score, he (with Simon)
wrote with some irony:

Ever since public interest has been aroused in the question of
schools for defective children, selfish ambition has seen its opportunity. The most frankly selfish interests conceal themselves
behind the mask of philanthropy, and whoever dreams of finding a
fine situation for himself in the new schools never speaks of
children without tears in his eyes. This is the everlasting human
comedy (1914, p. 10).

The "mask of philanthropy" has many guises. Nowadays there are fewer tears shed than there are solemn assertions about social significance. Nonetheless, Binet's pedagogical movement survived, and so did some of his ideas about cognitive assessment.[2]

The broader lesson is that social values and social machinations have been interwoven historically with the activities and institutions of developmental psychologists. Three more illustrations from the past may help clarify the point:

1. The first university chair in psychology in America (filled by G. Stanley Hall at Johns Hopkins University in 1893) was created in large measure because of the desire to integrate the findings of the "new science" with educational practice and training (Ross, 1972).
2. The child study movement began in 1895 as a grass roots activity among parents, mother's clubs, and teacher's organizations in their search for better ways to rear and train children. A direct line may be drawn between the child study movement and the formation of the basic institutions of child development, including: the original research institutes at Iowa and Merrill-Palmer; federally supported parent training programs; parent magazines; large-scale foundational support; and the founding of the Society for Research in Child Development.
3. The major research efforts involving children over the first part of the twentieth century were stimulated by vital societal concerns about the rearing of children. These include (among others) the Hartshorne and May (1928) inquiry on the development of conscience, morality, and altruism; the Peterson and Thurstone (1933) investigations on the effects of motion pictures upon children's beliefs and attitudes; and the Terman (1925) studies of gifted children and their longitudinal development.

As Elshtain observes in this volume, the historical intermingling of social values, social policy, and developmental psychology may reflect the common ground between political theory and the goals of the science. Every citizen — not merely parents and grandparents — has a vested interest in the transmission of societal institutions and values to the next generation. Accordingly, scientific prescriptions or advice on how to rear a child are as much the business of society as of parents.

But can a "real" science exist under such constraints? Binet, for one, thought it could. His thoughts on the matter are still instructive. He offered his work as "a guide — imperfect no doubt, but still useful — for the organization of some of those social inquiries conducted in a strictly scientific spirit, which are becoming more and more necessary for the proper management of public affairs" (Binet & Simon, 1914, p. 10). His investigations reflected the assumption that "we are all duty bound to occupy ourselves with the condition of our fellow citizens, and especially of the less fortunate among them" (p. 1). Binet and Simon (1914) add:

> "The consequence is that the very people who up to the present time have kept themselves most aloof from the social problem are being brought into contact with reality. It is a curious thing to see how scientific men, who for the past fifty years have never stirred a foot outside their laboratories, are showing a tendency to mingle in affairs. In spite of the diversity of the forces at work, there is one general fact which is undeniable. Pure and disinterested science retains its votaries, but the number is increasing of those who are turning to science for useful and practical applications; albeit, they are thinking less of science than of society, for it is those social phenomena which are capable of amelioration which scientifc men are now studying by the most exact methods for the benefit of men of action, who are usually empirics" (pp. 1-2).

Developmental research in the 1980s could be productively guided in its selection of issues toward those social problems which are "capable of amelioration." These might include, for instance, childhood problems of learning and behavior, the effects and prevention of parental abuse and neglect, the emergence of the child's violence toward others, and self-abusive habits and how they might be prevented or ameliorated. To this list, J. B. Watson added (in 1913) the problems of development in infancy, assessment of the psychological effects of drugs and other substances, the effects of advertising, and investigations into the organization of justice and legal reform.

What, then, is the dilemma presented by the introduction of social values into scientific inquiry? The main problem is that two masters must be served and strong pressures may be introduced which are antithetical to the spirit of science. Scientific work requires, among other things, a dispassionate and objective weighting of the empirical evidence. In the case of socially relevant questions, a competing set of beliefs may be employed to determine the meaning and value of the work. These criteria may tyrannize the data. The penalties for disagreeing with deeply held theoretical beliefs in science are severe enough in themselves, and the additional penalities for social heresy can be crippling. Conversely, the rewards for conformity can be substantial and enduring, at least for the tenure of the investigator.

The problem of how to buffer developmental research from the intrusion of well-meaning but destructive biases has been a major concern for the area in its brief history. Many of the conventions of scientific inquiry that have been adopted were designed to protect the integrity of the discipline and prevent some of the obvious methodological abuses. These include the high standards for the reliability and objectivity of measurement, conventions for statistical analysis, guides for rules of inference (following pre-established probability criteria), and built-in guards against the suggestibility and biases of investigators.

Some guides have been less clearly structured, however, and therein problems arise. For example, it has been difficult to establish firm standards for interpretations that would prevent the selective sampling of data or glossing over "discrepant" findings. More subtly, the conventions that have been adopted for publication in modern psychological journals make it difficult to reject any sane hypothesis. The problem is that most phenomena of social import are determined by multiple factors. With large numbers of subjects, the null hypothesis is a relatively impotent guide to truth. The problem for developmental psychology is not merely to determine whether or not variables have "significant" effects but to determine how these variables are organized and weighted over ontogeny.[3]

How can one go beyond the constraints of the social context in which developmental research is conducted yet preserve its relevance? Although we are reluctant to offer any general guide on the matter, a resolution of the science-social dilemma was essential so we could get on with our own work. Following Binet and Simon (1914), our solution can be covered in the following five points:

1. Regardless of the values that may lead to the initiation of an investigation, there can be no substitute for the adoption of the highest standards of objective inquiry in its execution.
2. The goal of analysis should be understanding the organization of the effects within individuals over a meaningful segment of their lifetimes. This implies, among other things, that the identification of a given variable as "statistically significant" is only the first step in the analysis, not the last. It also requires a commitment to developmental study and the organization of behavior over time.
3. As a corollary of the last point, investigators should seek convergent evidence for any conclusion of primary significance. This convergence may involve replication, adoption of different forms of measurement of the same characteristic (behavioral,

cognitive), employment of alternative research designs (experimental, naturalistic), and/or extension to different forms of analysis (individual case, parametric). Even more compelling forms of convergence involve comparative methods, where parallels and differences may be sought in different cultures and/or in different species. Such comparisons may be invaluable in providing a bridge to sister disciplines (including anthropology, evolutionary biology, and ethology).

4. The investigator is committed to accepting the results of the total data set, or explicitly accounting for the omission of findings from the interpretation. In other words, investigators should be willing to believe their data, even when these outcomes create serious problems for their own interpretation or acceptance by colleagues.

5. To the extent that applications are proposed, investigators are themselves responsible for determining the adequacy of the proposals in order to ensure that misapplications are not encouraged.

All this is to say that the enterprise of child development research is not beyond science, but the standards for the work must be uncompromising. Nor should research be limited to phenomena that can be studied under the highly controlled laboratory conditions. To the contrary, questions of social significance require innovation as well as rigor. The solution of complex problems demands respect for their ecological and organismic relativity. Hence the initial stages of the research are often productively addressed to phenomena in the conditions under which they normally occur.

THE ROLE OF GENDER IN AGGRESSIVE BEHAVIOR PATTERN DEVELOPMENT

The Relevance of Development

Doubtless one of the most important—and most bitterly debated—areas of gender difference concerns the expression of aggressive patterns. In sexual stereotyping, one of the first gender differences to be identified by young children is the difference between boys and girls in aggressive acts (Best, Williams, Cloud, Davis, Robertson, Edwards, Giles, & Fowles, 1977). Further, this area of difference is considered by Maccoby and Jacklin (1974) to be one of the two most reliable dimensions of gender difference. On the other hand, Frodi, Macaulay, & Thome (1977) raise questions about the reliability of the difference in men and women, and Block (1976) questions the nature of the difference in children. Although a number of issues are involved—both methodological and conceptual—it does appear that this dispute is one that might be clarified, and perhaps resolved, by a developmental analysis of the phenomena.

Beyond the discrepancies that have been identified in studies of children and experimental studies of adults, two general findings stand out. First, demographic investigations of the incidence of violence, including murder, show consistent age by sex differences in the victims and in murderers. Although boys and girls up to ten years of age show virtually no differences in either victim or victimizer, a sharp difference in the trajectory of increase may be observed at the onset of puberty. The incidence of violent offenders begins to rise in both boys and girls, but the rise for males is nearly vertical over the six-year period from 12 to 18 years. Young men of 18 years of age are without contest the most violent persons in the United States. For females, rise in rate of violent crime is rather modest compared to males, so at age 18 years there is a 10:1 difference in the male:female rate of being arrested for murder (Crime in the U.S., 1982). Is this an aberration of the 1980s? Probably not, in that the same sex differential in homicide was observed in thirteenth-century England (Given, 1977). Nor is the effect limited to a given segment of the present century, in that virtually identical trajectories may be described in each of the past 20 years that adequate age/sex offense records have been kept by the FBI. Further, the effect is not limited to inner-cities or to rural states: parallel curves have been found in all of the major regions of the United States.

One other domain of evidence suggests that it should be useful to apply a developmental analysis to the understanding of sex differences in the expression of aggressive patterns. In comparative-developmental studies of attacks and fighting in nonhuman species, certain reliable trends have been consistently reported. For instance, in studies of the development of aggressive patterns in mice—where extraordinarily violent creatures can be produced through selective breeding and selective rearing—male-female differences in attacking emerge at puberty, even among the lines selectively bred for the behavior. The trajectory of difference is remarkably similar, in form and perhaps function, to that observed in the demographic analysis of violence in humans. That is to say, there is a sharp increase in the most violent forms of attack from the onset of puberty until early adulthood in males. This developmental curve then begins a slow decline to late maturity and senescence. For females, tested under the appropriate circumstances, the increase is neither as sharp nor the absolute level of performance as high as obtained in males (Cairns, MacCombie, & Hood, 1983; Cairns & Hood, 1983). One methodological feature that seems to have obscured male-female similarities in animal studies should be noted, however. It is that the genetic similarities between females and males, to be identified, require different experimental assessment conditions. The conditions appropriate for maximal expression of attacks in males turn out to be different than the conditions appropriate for females, and vice versa. Only when these "optimal conditions" are employed does one find evidence for a common genetic background for aggressive performance in males and females. When they are not employed, investigators have erroneously concluded that male and female aggressive patterns reflect the operation of separate genetic pathways (Hyde & Ebert, 1976; Oorstermenn & Bakker, 1981).

Recent Findings

With this background in mind, a few years ago we initiated developmental studies of children and adolescents. We were concerned with gender differences in the development of aggressive behavior, and we had a special interest in girls and boys who were at high risk for subsequent violence. Consistent with the above guides for research, the work has been multimethod and longitudinal. We felt it important to identify convergences — and lack of convergence — within a network of closely related studies, and between our work and those of other investigators. Two other considerations should be mentioned. One involved the age of the persons we studied. The subjects were, for the most part, between 9 and 17 years of age. This is the age period where youth, on theoretical and social grounds, seemed to be most vulnerable for serious problems in aggressive behavior. It was also the period where our comparative studies suggested the integration of psychobiological and interactional factors should be most informative. A second consideration was methodological. Because the total number of subjects in the primary study was relatively large (that is, N = 660), we chose a dual focus. Some comparisons involved the total sample, and other, idiographic analyses involved a smaller number of "high-risk" individuals within that set. The in-depth behavioral analyses, for instance, involved comparisons between the risk groups and their matched controls (N = 80; 40 "high risk" and 40 "control"). Most of the work was conducted in natural settings, primarily the child's school or residential institution, although certain experimental studies of interchange processes have been completed (for example, Hall & Cairns, 1984).

Our aims in the work have been straightforward. To begin, we wanted to achieve an adequate description of the development of the various forms of behavior that might be called 'aggressive' in girls and boys, and in normal and risk populations. Surprisingly little information has been obtained on this fundamental matter, particularly for girls. On this matter, the assumptions of the discipline have changed little over the past 25 years. As a second step, we planned to go beyond description to determine which aspects of the behavior could be predicted over development, and which could not. We were especially interested in whether the stabilities found in young, "normal" children would be replicated in the socially and clinically relevant risk samples. Our third goal involved amelioration and developmental change. We hoped to identify factors in development—including characteristics of the children, their social experiences, and their social circumstances—that contributed to the behavior and to its developmental change. This was a step toward our final objective. We envisioned the formulation of practical guides for introducing enduring modifications in behavioral organization of children, so that some of the more personally disastrous consequences could be averted.

To this point we have achieved reasonable progress toward the first two objectives, and we are continuing work on these and the rest. The details of method have been described in technical reports, so they need not be repeated here (see Cairns & Cairns, 1984; Cairns, Cairns, & Ferguson, 1984; Hall & Cairns, 1984, for accounts of the methods). For the questions we outlined earlier in this chapter, the most relevant findings can be summarized in five general points.

First, in unselected samples of boys, there is an age-related increase in physical abuse as a means for expressing anger and dealing with other males. This phenomenon has been called the "brutalizing" effect by Ferguson and Rule (1980). In our work, the outcome appears in two primary measures: self-reports and behavioral observations. Boys show an increasing, age-related change from the fourth grade to the seventh grade in reports of physical violence when citing recent conflicts with other boys, and there is a comparable increase in the direct observation of hostile conflicts among males.

For unselected girls over the same age range (that is, fourth grade through seventh grade), there is little or no increase in the same measures. This means, among other things, that a gender difference in physical "brutalization" appears in the unselected samples in early adolescence. One other finding on gender difference requires comment. Among boys, there is a "dual standard" in the reports of conflicts, with quite different outcomes reported for conflicts with girls than conflicts with boys. That is, adolescent boys less often report conflicts with girls than boys, and they rarely report physical violence toward girls. With females, there is less evidence of a dual standard, either in the preadolescent years or in early adolescence. These self-reports are consistent with observations of the children's and adolescents' behaviors. They are also consistent with our earlier findings obtained from studies of adolescents in maximum security facilities (Perrin & Cairns, 1980) and affluent private schools (Cairns, Perrin, & Cairns, 1982).

Second, among the high-risk males and females, gender differences in observed aggressive behaviors have been negligible and generally unreliable. This relative absence of gender differences in observed conflicts is found in both late childhood (fourth grade) and, again, in early adolescence (seventh grade). The few differences between the male and female risk samples that emerge in early adolescence, however, are consistent with general gender expectations. For instance, in early adolescence, the proportion of girls in the public school population who are considered to be "at risk" is reliably smaller than the proportion of "at risk" boys. In the fourth grade, there is no such gender difference. Nonetheless, the girls who do qualify as being "at risk" in early adolescence demonstrate a remarkable capacity for destructive and interpersonally harmful behavior, and are virtually indistinguishable from their male counterparts on this dimension.

Third, the predictability of individual differences in aggressive expression over a one-year period is moderate-to-strong, depending on the measure employed. In general, the highest levels of prediction are obtained when the measures—predictor and outcome—are in the same domain. Hence teacher ratings in the fourth grade are the best predictors of teacher ratings in the fifth grade, are moderately strong predictors of peer nominations, and are poor predictors of self-assessments. Conversely, self-reports in one year predict self-reports in the next year, but little else. These findings are consistent with the recent reviews of Olweus (1979), Loeber (1982), and Pulkkinnen (1982).

Fourth, gender differences in predictability are, like developmental changes, relative to the persons' risk status. Consistent with the early report of Kagan and Moss (1962) and the recent one of Eron and Huesmann (in press), we find some evidence for somewhat greater individual-difference stability in boys than in girls. This difference, though small, was statistically reliable and it was restricted to a single measurement domain (that is, teacher ratings of aggressive patterns).

Quite a different picture of gender differences in predictability is obtained if one restricts the analysis to the persons in the "risk" groups. In this clinically relevant sample, the aberrant behavior of girls is as predictable as that of boys, at least over the short-term longitudinal period of assessment. Why the difference as a function of risk? On this score, we suspect that the "risk" girls are more deviant from the normal population than are their male counterparts. Given their extreme status, the deviant girls might be expected to have greater difficulties being reassimilated into a normal group than boys, despite the advantages of adolescent growth changes (see also Eron & Huesmann, in press).

Fifth, social network factors play a role of increasing importance in the manipulation and control of aggressive expression as the children develop from late childhood to adolescence. Among other things, the forms of aggressive expression become increasingly sex-differentiated with age in the normal population. In early adolescence, girls rely increasingly upon techniques of social control, and manipulation of the social network. Such social control strategies include attempts to ostracize and alienate the offender. Among males in the same age range, there is scant use of such social network strategies. One interactional advantage of social network controls is that they are relatively hidden and not susceptible to immediate reciprocity and escalation. This outcome suggests that females may be developmentally advanced not only in physical maturation but, as well, in social manipulation.

One additional social network factor requires mention. Coie, Dodge, and their colleagues (e.g., Coie & Dodge, 1983) recently observed that aggressive adolescents tend to be rejected by peers in the social system. Their measures involved sociometric ratings generated by peers in the school. Our findings on the phenomena of the social network influences suggest an extension and revision of that conclusion. It is accurate that highly aggressive adolescents, both male and female, are not usually popular with classmates in general. Few of them are elected cheerleaders or selected as class presidents. Nonetheless, it does not mean that they are inevitably isolated. To the contrary, they tend to cluster with peers who have similar problems, hence gain mutual support for their disruptive behaviors. "Popularity" and "rejection" are relative terms; they depend upon whom one is popular with, and for what reasons.

Finally, some comments on developmental change and prediction are in order. It is a minor irony that successful amelioration is deemed, for statistical purposes, a failure in prediction. In tracking individuals, we had hoped for a large number of such "failures," and we have found some. Along the way, we were reminded of some old lessons, and learned some new ones. The old lesson was that there is likely to be, over time and space, considerable specificity to the changes that are introduced in the person's lifestyle. For instance, we have found various cases of "failure" in prediction of persons in the risk groups—in one year, but have been disappointed to find that they revert to old problems the next year. What happened? In some instances it was a case of the child's having had a masterful and sensitive teacher or counselor. But when the adult support was withdrawn, because the child graduated, moved, or was placed in another class, the improvement ceased or was cancelled out. In other cases, the changes have been more enduring. Again, a variety of circumstances contribute to such "permanent" modifications, including a total change in the person's living circumstance (through having moved to another state), or social and athletic opportunities. Given the dynamics of human development, the judgments of "success" or "failure" are relative to the time at which the assessment is made, and the conditions of assessment.

Just as we find some shifts from the risk groups to the "normal" population, we have found an unhappy number of instances where children develop problems with aggressive expression in early adolescence. Given the information that we have already discussed, it should not be surprising that the newly identified "aggressive" subjects are mostly males. This group we consider to be *real* failures in prediction. Beyond the individual characteristics involved in change, several ecological, instructional, and setting factors provide powerful immediate controls for aggressive behavior. For instance, classroom structure and organization (as determined by evaluations of "freedom of movement") are highly correlated with the incidence of observed conflicts (that is, r's = .80 to .95). Outbursts are rare in one classroom, but recurrent in another, despite the fact that the same students are involved. Microbehavioral differences in handling conflicts and their prevention provide the stuff out of which proposals for amelioration and change can be offered.

Toward a Developmental Account of Gender Differences

Developmental psychologists have an advantage over their colleagues in other areas of psychology. The issues of the field demand focus on individuals and how they accommodate over time (see also Carlson, Chapter 8, "Affects, Ideology, and Scripts in Social Policy and Developmental Psychology"). This orientation can be contrasted with a focus on variables—pet or otherwise—that are divorced from the matrix of events in which they normally occur. Hence most of the enduring advances in the field have been associated with the intensive study of individual development by Binet, Preyer, Baldwin, Gesell,

Lewin, Piaget, Barker, and, of course, Freud. Given this history of advances, it is ironic that the advantages of individual study must be rediscovered with each generation. One conceptual advantage that comes from the study of individuals as units over time is that the configuration of determinants can be kept under scrutiny, so that significant modifications can be identified and their consequences tracked. Such a strategy also seems essential if one aspires to assign differential weight to a given set of determinants, and to examine how this weight might change as a function of the total configuration.

So far, we have had few such systematic investigations of individual children over a significant portion of their lifetimes. Thus, it should not be surprising that we have to be tentative about key questions of how the component factors in the configuration are weighted, and how these weights might change over time. Nonetheless, there is a convergence of evidence that permits at least some speculations on the matter, albeit tentative ones. For our present purposes, these speculations concern the integration and multiple roles of psychobiological, social learning, and peer/ecological factors in the emergence of gender differences. A comment on each of these "roles" is in order.

Psychobiological contributions.

Some contributions are so obvious from a common sense perspective, they are ignored in a scientific formulation. That is a pity, because our job is not necessarily to transcend common sense; it may be just as important to explain it. In any case, the biological machinery of males and females, prior to puberty, are nearly identical in terms of potential for action. There are some differences — as in length of forearm and in height — but these differences are trivial compared to the similarities across sex and the differences within each sex. On this count, the points made by Plomin and Foch (1981) are applicable and well taken. But it is also the case that almost universal changes in form and function are observed at adolescence. Lest we overplay these changes, it should be noted that a 10 percent to 13 percent difference is significant, but there remain ample within-sex differences and capabilities for across-sex overlap. (For instance, 99.5 percent of living males would be ill-advised to compete with Mary Decker in the 1500 m run or Martina Navratilova in tennis.)

Overall, age-paced differences in behavioral form and function not only qualify males and females for different kinds of interchanges, they are associated with the rise of motivational patterns at different times in development. With the emphasis on early- and late-maturing girls and boys, it should not be overlooked that the vast majority of girls are "early-maturing" with respect to boys. Shifts in needs and values, concomitant with psychobiological changes, contribute to a sex-differential in the trajectory of their behaviors. Some of the major sex differences may be attributable as much to sex differences in the timing of development as to sex differences in content (Cairns, 1976; Tanner, 1962).

From the foregoing, it seems clear that there is scant basis, prior to puberty, for expecting psychobiological factors to produce gender differences in behavior. Hence the ubiquitous differences in play patterns, reciprocal activities, and reputations for aggressiveness must, in children, be assigned to other, nonbiological determinants. There is ample evidence from the anthropological literature that some of these supports for gender difference may anticipate economic role differences that the person will fill at maturity (for example, Whiting & Edwards, 1973). Similarly, there are clear differences in parental expectations for male and female behavior patterns, regardless of the child's actual capabilities (for example, Fagot, 1974). But if the child is exposed to different local norms, or rejects the ones to which she/he is exposed, the potential for behavioral similarity in boys and girls seems to be great indeed.

Social norms are not the only processes that help produce behavioral discontinuities at adolescence (Kagan & Moss, 1962). The norms are supported by changes that occur with the adolescents themselves. Three sorts of "internal" change seem to be of particular importance, namely:

1. Girls become at puberty increasingly disadvantaged, on the average, in direct physical combat with boys. Hence the techniques that might have proved to be highly effective at age 10 become ineffective at age 14. This discrepancy in growth/strength/configuration development is general, and its implications for negative social interchanges are direct and robust.

2. Hormonal changes associated with puberty introduce a new set of behavioral controls, including enhanced sexual motivation. Not only do girls find it less productive to fight with boys, they find it less rewarding than other sorts of intimate interactions. In any case, there is abundant evidence in interviews and in behavior that sexual concerns and flirtation become increasingly dominant in female-male relationships in the seventh grade. There is virtually no overlap with the attitudes and behaviors observed in late childhood (that is, fourth grade).

3. The gender stereotypes adopted by both boys and girls at adolescence tend to be more extreme and pervasive than those observed at an earlier age (for example, Best, Williams, Cloud, Davis, Robertson, Edwards, Giles, & Fowles, 1977). This outcome is ironic, given the presumed heightened cognitive relativity of these adolescents relative to young children. But it is wholly consistent with fundamental changes in morphology, and in the form and functions of social interchanges distinctive to the two sexes. Fighting and dominance, for instance, seems to be one key for enhancing the sexual attractiveness of males, but exactly the opposite for females.

To sum up, the problems of gender differences in aggressive behavior are likely to prove as confusing in humans as in nonhumans, if age-developmental considerations are overlooked. But if these considerations are taken into account, the picture becomes reasonably coherent, though never simple.

Social learning and social extinction.

In modern developmental theory, it has seemed entirely reasonable to use learning concepts to account for relatively stable dispositions and patterns that cannot be readily assigned to temperamental or organismic factors. J. B. Watson (1926) provided the field with an extreme statement of the position, and B. F. Skinner (1953) managed to step beyond Watson. But recent social learning statements have been made more plausible by the integration of concepts of learning with advances in the study of social cognition and social interaction (for example, Bandura, 1977; Patterson, 1982). However, there is a basic problem with the theoretical proposition that enduring individual characteristics of persons can be explained solely in social *learning* terms. The problem is, in a word, extinction. What has been learned is presumably susceptible to be unlearned. More generally, it would be maladaptive to fail to forget most of the specific lessons of socialization. The social patterns that worked exceedingly effectively in infancy and childhood would, for the most part, be absurd or psychopathological if retained into adolescence or adulthood. Indeed, a strong case can be made for the proposition that the primary function of learning — social and otherwise — is to facilitate local, time-bound accommodations that cannot be achieved as effectively by less plastic structural or genetic changes.

Now let's return to the problem at hand; the acquisition and change of gender-specific behaviors, values, and norms. Within the present analysis, it would be expected that social learning experiences could play a significant role in forming relationship patterns, styles of responding, and conditions for affective expression. Hence at any given developmental stage, social learning effects should be readily produced and these, in turn, should be linked directly to the supporting ecological and social conditions. But the very processes that make social learning useful in fitting the organism for the exigencies of local/time-bound contexts and relationships should render it less useful as a mechanism for long-term constancy. As the contexts and relationships change, so should social learning experiences.

We might thus anticipate significant changes in those gender-specific behaviors that are based on individual learning experiences, if the conditions for social/physical/physiological adaptation change. And to the extent that such conditions remain constant, there should be an impression of the "permanence" of social learning. All this is to say that there should be much plasticity in the lessons that are acquired via social learning. So those aspects of gender role that are indeed "learned" might be expected to undergo relatively rapid transition, if the person is assimilated into a social ecology where the values, behaviors, and characteristics of others are markedly different from that to which she/he had been previously exposed. Hence the faddishness of styles, in clothing and in behavior.

From a developmental perspective, social learning experiences serve a distinctive function in facilitating accommodation to disparate surroundings and relationships. So the apparent weight of this set of processes would be maximal under conditions of contextual/relational change, and this capability for change would not be limited to infancy, childhood, adolescence, or maturity. To be developmentally useful, the organism should remain capable of such accommodations throughout the lifespan, including changes in gender-specific behaviors. In Baldwin's (1897) terms, personality development is after all a never ending thing. So should be many aspects of gender role and gender behavior.

Social Structure and Social Ecology

The third major factor to be considered here is in fact a number of sets that may be subsumed as social structure and social ecology. It might also be called society or culture. In any case, the factor(s) refer to enduring aspects of the social and nonsocial environment that provide the conditions for individual accommodation. Within a developmental perspective, these determinants are necessarily represented in the configuration of events that contribute to gender similarities and differences. As the person's age-developmental status changes, she/he may be qualified for new roles and new expectations with those social structures of which she/he is a part. These roles, in turn, provide the occasion for new social learning experiences and values/behaviors that correspond to the role. Again, the normal state of affairs is such that roles, physiological changes, and styles of interpersonal responding are coordinated. The behavioral outcomes are bi- or multi-directional, in that changes in one significant feature of the configuration are likely to contribute to changes in other features. So it becomes difficult to disentangle which set has priority in behavioral determination and change. It is only in the case of sharp discontinuities — such as shifts from one social setting or group to another, or retardation/acceleration of growth relative to chronological age and social status — that the weight of one factor becomes pitted against the rest. Precisely what compensatory mechanisms are brought into play at that juncture are likely to reflect the individual's circumstances and the range of compensatory adjustments that are possible.

Of special concern for understanding gender differences in behavior are the support groups provided by clusters of peers. Indeed, one of the most pervasive trends in social behavior, from early childhood to late adolescence, is the increasing tendency to form groups of two or more peers. Once established, these groups serve as potent guides for behavioral reciprocity, norm formation, and the ostracization and control of others. Recent observations indicate that it is a mistake to view peer cliques as a teen-age invention; they are identifiable in preschool (Strayer & Strayer, 1976) and elementary school (Cairns, Perrin, & Cairns, 1982) as well as in adolescence. But it does appear that such groups take on new and powerful functions in adolescence, especially for girls. Since these adolescent groups — like the childhood ones — are for the most part sex-segregated, it seems likely that they act as a catalyst for the consolidation of gender differences in values and behaviors. They also seem to provide exceedingly effective "attack groups," through the isolation and ostracization of other girls who are in disfavor (Youniss, 1980; Cairns, Perrin, & Cairns, 1982).

To sum up, the developmental perspective is necessarily an organismic one. Single variables or single factors, taken alone, are likely to be misleading. The problem is that behavior is the outcome of a dynamic process. An adequate description of this process requires attention to the integration of influences. This sort of feedback system, complex in the abstract, works effectively and efficiently in the lives of individual children. Indeed, the understanding of gender differences in social development is tantamount to the understanding of social development.

SOCIAL APPLICATIONS AND SOCIAL REALITY

Moving from data to application is like taking a stroll down the Grand Canyon, or a saunter up the Matterhorn. The passage is none-theless an essential one for investigators who aspire to address social questions in the context of developmental science. Writers as different in outlook as Watson (1913) and Binet (1909) have held that studies of application are critical to the progress of the science itself. But re-searchers who become involved in the data → theory → application transition discover the pitfalls described elsewhere in this volume by Scarr in Chapter 5, Cofer in Chapter 2, Friedrich-Cofer in Chapter 3, Carlson in Chapter 8, and A. and C. Baldwin and Cole in Chapter 6.

Beyond the practical and methodological obstacles, we find a ma-jor difference in perspective that must be considered in any transition from research programs to social applications. The perspective dif-ference is between a focus on variables as in most research and a focus on persons as in most applications. For instance, even if one succeeded in identifying the range of variables that contributed to violent behavior in adolescence, the problem remains to describe how these variables are organized, combined, and integrated in the life of an in-dividual youth. At best, regression equations provide group solutions, not individual accommodations. But personal integration is the point where applications begin. Accordingly, an essential theoretical issue for developmental approaches lies beyond the delineation of signifi-cant variables; it involves the definition of rules for describing the organization and adaptive integration of influences within persons.

It is in the solution of the integration problem that developmental scientists may have much to learn from the reversal of the accepted data → theory → application sequence. By virtue of having to deal with individuals who are embedded—or mired—in a complex of en-vironmental and social circumstances, practitioners must arrive at a workable procedure for integrating information and predicting in-dividual behavior. They then must take responsible action. Small wonder, then, that experienced clinicians and teachers are usually unimpressed by the "exciting" results of research on the effects of a particular set of variables. Such information, if useful for analysis and prediction, has doubtless already been recognized in their subjective equations (Cairns & Green, 1979). It is likely for this reason, for exam-ple, that we have found teacher judgments to be among the most pow-erful predictors of future antisocial aggressive activity (see also Olweus, 1979). Teacher ratings are imperfect, to be sure. They are plagued by biases and prejudices, and suffer from idiosyncratic errors of perception, memory, judgment, and reconstruction. But it would be a bigger error to overlook their primary strengths. In the course of dealing with the several problems presented by individual children, teachers (and parents and clinicians) must integrate information from multiple sources in order to arrive at informed assessments, including ratings.

We suspect that a key to forming a successful bridge between data and application is to begin with the expertise and experience of the practitioners. When this happens, we find that the most pressing needs expressed by professionals cover questions of amelioration and change that lie at the limits of the research available, including our own. In the course of addressing these concerns, we have also found it useful to use the research information at hand to identify, build upon, extend, or modify the strategies that are being employed by the professionals. In actual application (in workshops and training conferences), this ordinarily involves work in six specific areas, including:

1. Identification of interactional dynamics, including aggressive reciprocity and escalation and the conditions under which they are most likely to occur (see also Patterson, 1982).
2. Specification of techniques for establishing relationships with problem children. Training, or retraining, in interview techniques has proved to be beneficial, as are suggestions for dealing with children during the times that they are not in stress.
3. Focusing attention on the supportive or destructive role of social groups, including strategies for enhancing (or diminishing) the child's role in it. The role of the adult/teacher/parent in orchestrating such "peer group" influences has been useful to review.
4. Covering ways to enlist the support of parents or guardians in the amelioration of specific problems.
5. Training in procedures for systematically recording information about particular children, and ways to use this information for dealing with him/her productively.
6. Developing strategies for preventing conflicts as opposed to handling them after they have occurred. These include procedures of classroom management and organization, and the communication of expectations to children as well as rewards for their fulfillment.

We find the benefits from conducting such "applied" workshops flow in both directions. The investigators must not only sharpen their insights about the nature of interactional dynamics, they must also formulate systematically the reasons why some procedures work and others do not. Such "grass roots" work may seem a modest contribution compared to social policy at the state, national, or international level. It may be the case, however, that some of the flaws of social policy adoption would be prevented if greater attention were paid by researchers to the details of science ⇄ application transitions in their initial development.

Up to this point, we have discussed problems of social application rather than social policy. We suspect, however, that many of the issues apply to both areas. Our most recent professional involvement in social policy matters follows from efforts to contribute to the implementation of a unique state-supported treatment program for highly aggressive children. The State of North Carolina has, over the past three years, been engaged in a large-scale effort to identify and treat violent minors. The program was the outcome of an out-of-court settlement of a suit brought against the State of North Carolina ("Willie M." et al., vs. Governor J. Hunt, et al., 1980). The class-action complaint was that North Carolina provided no adequate program to meet the legitimate needs for the treatment of one highly aggressive boy ("Willie M.") and three other children like him. The settlement required that the State identify all children who fit the "Willie M." aggressive-violent category, and provide treatment for each child so identified in a community setting (that is, outside custodial/residential facilities). Because of an ambiguity in the definition of the "Willie M." category, the original expectation that only 200 to 300 children would qualify proved to be a gross underestimate. In late 1983, over 1,200 children had been certified after extensive psychological and psychiatric evaluation as falling within the "Willie M." class. The state therefore was obligated to provide special individualized treatment for all of the children. In 1984, $17 million was appropriated by the state legislature for the support of the program.

Because of the nature of the original agreement, virtually no funds were provided to determine which programs would be most efficacious, or even what alternatives were available. Moreover, little information was at hand concerning the fate of children who might have been classified as "Willie M." subjects but who were not (for example, because of a failure of parental consent or a fear of extensive psychological/psychiatric assessment). Finally, scant attention has been given to the possibility of developmental changes, including the likelihood that children assigned to the "Willie M." class at one age might not qualify subsequently, or vice versa.

Our own research began before the establishment of the program, and has since been conducted concurrently with it. Because of the design of our research, we have obtained information on such critical issues as the longitudinal development of "at risk" children, the age-related increase in the vulnerability of unselected children, and the differential predictability of "risk" females as opposed to normal girls. The task of the researcher, as we see it, is to establish mechanisms for direct communication of those findings that might enhance the programs and treatment policies. As in the case of individual application, the key is to view the problem from the perspective and expertise of the policy makers. With the encouragement of state administrative personnel, we are presently working toward that goal.

To sum up, social responsibility and scientific commitment would appear at times to be engaged in a tug-of-war. Hence the implementation of our fifth guideline is not so simple as it might first appear. But there are foreseeable benefits. To the extent that researchers take greater responsibility for applications of their work, there should be better social programs and a stronger developmental science.

REFERENCES

Baldwin, J. M. (1897). *Social and ethical interpretations of mental development: A study in social psychology.* New York: Macmillan.

Bandura, A. (1977). *Social learning theory.* Englewood Cliffs, NJ: Prentice-Hall.

Bandura, A., & Walters, R. H. (1959). *Adolescent aggression.* New York: Ronald.

_____ . (1963). *Social learning and personality development.* New York: Holt-Rinehart.

Best, D., Williams, J. E., Cloud, J. M., Davis, S. W., Robertson, L. S., Edwards, J. R., Giles, H., & Fowles, J. (1977). Development of sex-trait stereotypes among young children in the United States, England, and Ireland. *Child Development, 48,* 1,375-84.

Binet, A. (1909). *Les idées modernes sur les enfants.* Paris: Schleicher.

Binet, A., & Henri, V. (1895). La psychologie individuelle. *L'Anneé Psychologique, 2,* 411-65.

Binet, A., & Simon, T. (1914). *Mentally defective children.* (W. B. Drummond, Trans.) London: Edward Arnold.

Block, J. H. (1976) Debatable conclusions about sex differences. *Contemporary Psychology, 21,* 517-22.

Cairns, R. B. (1961). The influence of dependency inhibition on the effectiveness of social approval. *Journal of Personality, 29,* 466-88.

_____ . (1973). Fighting and punishment from a developmental perspective. In J. K. Cole & D. D. Jensen (Eds.), *Nebraska Symposium on Motivation* (Vol. 20, pp. 59-124). Lincoln: University of Nebraska Press.

_____ . (1976). The ontogeny and phylogeny of social interchanges. In M. Hahn & E. C. Simmel (Eds.), *Evolution of communicative behaviors* (pp. 115-39). New York: Academic Press.

_____ . (1979). *Social development: The origins and plasticity of social interchanges.* San Francisco: Freeman.

Cairns, R. B., & Cairns, B. D. (1984). Predicting aggressive patterns in girls and boys: A developmental study. *Aggressive Behavior, 10*, 227-42.

———. (1985). The developmental-interactional view of social behavior: Four issues of adolescent aggression. In D. Olweus, J. Block, & M. Radke-Yarrow (Eds.), *Development of antisocial and prosocial behavior* (pp. 315-42). New York: Academic Press.

Cairns, R. B., Cairns, B. D., & Ferguson, L. L. (1984). Aggressive behavior in elementary school children: Gender similarities, differences, and developmental continuities. Paper read at the Eighth Biennial Meeting of the Southeastern Conference on Human Development, Athens, Ga.

Cairns, R. B., & Green, J. A. (1979). How to assess personality and social patterns: Ratings or observations? In R. B. Cairns (Ed.), *The analysis of social interaction: Methods, issues, and illustrations* (pp. 209-26). Hillsdale, N.J.: Erlbaum.

Cairns, R. B., & Hood, K. E. (1983). Continuity in social development: A comparative perspective on individual difference prediction of aggressive behavior. In P. B. Baltes & O. G. Brim (Eds.), *Life-span development and behavior* (Vol. 5, pp. 301-58). New York: Academic Press.

Cairns, R. B., MacCombie, D. J., & Hood, K. E. (1983). A developmental-genetic analysis of aggressive behavior in mice: I. Behavioral outcomes. *Journal of Comparative Psychology, 97*, 69-89.

Cairns, R. B., Perrin, J. E., & Cairns, B. D. (1982). The self, the other, and the real. Paper read at the Seventh Biennial Meeting of the Southeastern Conference on Human Development, Baltimore.

Coie, J., & Dodge, K. (1983). Continuities and changes in children's social status: A five-year longitudinal study. *Merrill-Palmer Quarterly, 29*, 161-81.

Crime in the United States. (1982). Washington, DC: Government Printing Office.

Eron, L. D., & Huesmann, L. R. (in press) The control of aggressive behavior by changes in attitudes, values and the conditions of learning. In R. J. Blanchard & C. Blanchard (Eds.), *Advances in the study of aggression.* (Vol. 2). New York: Academic Press.

Fagot, B. I. (1974). Sex differences in toddlers' behavior and parental reaction. *Development Psychology, 10*, 554-58.

Ferguson, T. J., & Rule, B. G. (1980). Effects of inferential set, outcome severity, and basis for responsibility on children's evaluations of aggressive acts. *Developmental Psychology, 16*, 141-46.

Frodi, A., Macaulay, J., & Thome, P. R. (1977). Are women always less aggressive than men? A review of the experimental literature. *Psychological Bulletin, 84*, 634-60.

Given, J. B. (1977). *Society and homicide in thirteenth-century England.* Stanford: Stanford University Press.

Green, J. A. (1978). Experiential determinants of postpartum aggression in mice. *Journal of Comparative Psychology, 92*, 1,179-87.

Hall, G. S. (1904). *Adolescence: Its psychology and its relations to physiology, anthropology, sociology, sex, crime, religion, and education* (2 vols.). New York: Appleton.

Hall, W. M., & Cairns, R. B. (1984). Aggressive behavior in children: An outcome of modeling or social reciprocity? *Developmental Psychology, 20*, (5), 739-45.

Hartshorne, H., & May, M. A. (1928). *Studies in the nature of character*: Vol 1: *Studies in deceit*. New York: Macmillan.

Hyde, J. S., & Ebert, P. D. (1976). Correlated response in selection for aggressiveness in female mice. I. Male aggressiveness. *Behavior Genetics, 6*, 421-27.

Kagan, J., & Moss, H. A. (1962). *Birth to maturity: A study in psychological development*. New York: Wiley.

Loeber, R. (1982). The stability of antisocial and delinquent behavior: A review. *Child Development, 53*, 1,431-46.

Maccoby, E. E., & Jacklin, C. N. (1974). *The psychology of sex differences*. Stanford: Stanford University Press.

Olweus, D. (1979). Stability of aggressive reaction patterns in males: A review. *Psychological Bulletin, 86*, 852-75.

Oortmerssen, G. A., & Bakker, T. C. M. (1981). Artificial selection for short and long attack latencies in wild Mus musculus domesticus. *Behavior Genetics, 11*, 115-26.

Patterson, G. R. (1982). *Coercive family process*. Eugene, Ore.: Castalia Publishing.

Perrin, J. E., & Cairns, R. B. (1980). Aggressive patterns in adolescent offenders. Paper read at the Sixth Biennial Meeting of the Southeastern Conference on Human Development, Alexandria, VA.

Peterson, R. C., & Thurstone, L. L. (1933). *Motion picutres and the social attitudes of children*. NY: Macmillan.

Plomin, R., & Foch, T. T. (1981). Sex differences and individual differences. *Child Development, 52*, 383-85.

Pulkkinen, L. (1982). Self-control and continuity from childhood to late adolescence. In P. B. Baltes & O. G. Brim, Jr. (Eds.), *Life-span development and behavior* (Vol. 4, pp. 63-105). New York: Academic Press.

Robins, L. N. (1966). *Deviant children grown up*. Baltimore: Williams and Wilkins.

Ross, D. (1972). *G. Stanley Hall: The psychologist as prophet*. Chicago: University of Chicago Press.

Skinner, B. F. (1953). *Science and human behavior*. New York: Macmillan.

Strayer, F. F., & Strayer, J. (1976). An ethological analysis of social agonism and dominance relations among pre-school children. *Child Development, 47*, 980-99.

Tanner, J. M. (1962). *Growth at adolescence*. Oxford: Blackwell Scientific Publications.

Terman, L. M. (1925). *Genetic studies of genius* Vol. 1.: *Mental and physical traits of a thousand gifted children*. Stanford: Stanford University Press.

Watson, J. B. (1913). Psychology as the behaviorist views it. *Psychological Review, 20*, 158-77.

Watson, J. B. (1926). What the nursery has to say about instincts. In C. Murchison (Ed.), *Psychologies of 1925* (pp. 1-35). Worcester, MA.: Clark University Press.

White, J. W. (1983). Sex and gender issues in aggression research. In R. G. Geen
& E. I. Donnerstein (Eds.), *Aggression: Theoretical and empirical reviews*
(Vol. 2, pp. 1-26). New York: Academic.
Whiting, B. B., & Edwards, C. P. (1973). A cross-cultural analysis of sex dif-
ferences in the behavior of children three through eleven. *Journal of
Social Psychology, 91*, 171-88.
Youniss, J. (1980). *Parents and peers in social development*. Chicago: Univer-
sity of Chicago Press.

NOTES

1.   Why aggression and why gender differences? The problem of
how aggressive behavior becomes established and how it can be changed
and modified has been a matter of long-term professional interest to
both writers. But until recently, we approached the matter from quite
different perspectives.

For one of us (BDC), understanding aggressive behavior initially
was more a matter of social survival than it was of social duty. As a
newly trained teacher, she accepted a position teaching a fifth-grade
classroom comprised of children who had been deservedly labeled "in-
corrigible." Although the area in California was then (as now) affluent,
the school was not. The teaching position became open because of the
abrupt departure of two of the teachers who had earlier been assigned
to the class. The classroom — boys and girls, students and teacher —
had been dominated by the threats, coercion, and blatantly aggressive
behaviors of one of the girls, Diana. Already large and strong, Diana
had been retained in grade because of overwhelming academic difficulties and behavioral problems. Normal teaching activities had
become impossible because of the girl's frequent and unpredictable
outbursts, as well as her orchestration of the aberrant acts by other
members of the class. Dismissal, suspension, or transfer were out of
the question in part because of parental neglect and because of the
girl's intimidation of the principal and other school authorities. The
details of how the school year was completed will not be recounted
here. There was, in brief, a marked improvement in Diana's academic
performance and a near-reversal of her behavior problems. For Diana,
this was accomplished by establishing a close positive relationship
with the child, identifying areas of accomplishment that could be used
as the basis for further progress and development, and employing
Diana's influence as a facilitative (as opposed to disruptive) factor in
classroom organization.

Diana became the first of a series of "problem" girls assigned to
the classroom in succeeding years. Although the difficulties presented
by the girls were rarely as severe as Diana's, comparable levels of

improvement were typically achieved. Three comments may be offered on what we learned from these early experiences with deviant girls in the public schools. First, contrary to expectations we had obtained from accounts of development and behavior, preadolescent and early-adolescent girls provided as many problems in aggressive acting out as did boys. Second, we could not divorce the children's behavior from the context in which it occurred, including the social network of the classroom and the child's living circumstances. Third, short-term remediation was no guarantee for long-term change. In the case of Diana, her subsequent academic performance was dismal; she soon dropped out of school and began work as a prostitute. Follow-up information obtained on the subsequent behavior of other girls who showed extreme acting-out behavior indicated a range of unhappy outcomes, including one murder conviction.

So much for case histories. While hardly a substitute for scientific analysis, they provide the stuff out of which social concerns grow and social values are formed.

For the other writer (RBC), professional exposure to the problems of aggressive development occurred in a safer environment; namely, the Alameda County (Calif.) Probation Department. It was there that he collaborated in the conduct of an early investigation of adolescent aggression (cf. Bandura & Walters, 1959), and completed a dissertation on the matter (Cairns, 1961). In the course of this work, he developed a respect for the utility of social learning concepts, and formulated some ideas quite beyond those that appeared in the published reports. One concerned the range of ecological and social network variables that had been eliminated in the first stages of the social learning analysis. These social and demographic factors seemed more important for some purposes than were the variables that had been measured and manipulated. Another concerned the importance of gender similarities. In the light of the preceding case histories, it is ironic that both the project and the dissertation were limited to the study of males. This gender bias reflected the prevailing view—still alive in the 1980s—that aggressive behavior was either irrelevant for girls or too rare to be systematically investigated.

In large measure because of the unresolved (and, at the time, unresolvable) gap between social learning concepts and social reality, we spent several subsequent years exploring the problems of aggressive behavior at new levels of interactional and developmental analysis. This work included attempts to determine how biological and experiential factors are interwoven over the lifespan, and attempts to manipulate experimentally the presumably key factors of aggressive control in nonhuman species (Cairns, 1973; 1979; 1984). Comparative studies of males and females were conducted as were investigations of the effects that could be produced over the lifetimes of individual animals and over successive generations of related individuals. This work indicated, in brief, that a powerful and coherent account of aggressive behavior is possible, at least for the behavior in nonhuman species. It also underscored the need to adopt a developmental perspective in order to understand the organization of biological and social learning processes, in animals or humans.

The investigations we report here were initiated some six years ago. As such, they represent a return to the problems that we initially confronted.

2. But Binet's critical insights on cognitive development and change did not travel as well to the U. S. as the test procedures, leading to a misapplication of the tests and misunderstanding of the concepts. The present-day commercial exploitation and misuse of Binet's essential procedures give us another view of the 'human comedy'.

3. This problem in contemporary research is not unrelated to the one identified by Binet and Henri (1895) on the error of attending to the individual components of intelligence rather than their organization.

5

Cultural Lenses on Mothers and Children

Sandra Scarr

INTRODUCTION

All the world's a stage, but the play is not *As You Like It*; it is *Rashomon*. Each of us has our own reality of which we try to persuade others. In this chapter I hope to explain how this should change our claims about research, not discredit them.

If one adopts, as I do, a constructionist position on epistemology, then knowledge of all kinds, including scientific knowledge, is a construction of the human mind. Sensory data are filtered through the knowing apparatus of the human senses and made into perceptions and cognitions. Further, what we know is colored by how we feel and what we want — emotional and motivational components of human knowledge. The human mind is also constructed in a social context, and its knowledge is in part created by the social and cultural context in which it comes to know the world with its assumptions and values. Knowledge of the world is therefore always constructed by the human mind in the working models of reality in the sciences. If this is not evident, one need only consider for a moment the vast differences in our concepts of the world before Galileo, Darwin, Einstein, and Freud.

We do not discover scientific facts; we invent them. Their usefulness to us depends both on shared perceptions of the "facts" (consensual validation) and on whether they work for various purposes, some of them practical and some of them theoretical.

Material in this chapter, including the nine figures reproduced herein, is taken from "Constructing psychology: Making Facts and Fables for our Times," by Sandra Scarr in *American Psychologist*, Vol. 40, No. 5 (1985). Copyright© 1985 by The American Psychological Association. Reprinted by permission of the publisher and author.

The Construction of Science

It is also true that we cannot perceive or process knowledge without the constraints of belief. One example of the personal constraint on knowledge is found in eyewitness accounts of crimes (Loftus, 1979). Fleeting impressions of criminal behavior are elaborated by individuals into complete accounts that they believe to be "true." The wrong people are identified as the criminals, and events are construed in ways that are consistent with the observer's emotions and prejudices. When such events are videotaped and reviewed repeatedly by observers, a different consensus of the event emerges, one that is not consistent with the eyewitness account of the observer at the scene. The problem is that the eyewitness to such a criminal, or other emotional, event gleans only partial knowledge from the immediate experience. The eyewitness fills in the gaps in his or her knowledge by plausible constructions of what "must have" or "should have" happened to make sense of the scene. Unfortunately, the eyewitness account is often at variance from that of observers who can review the event more than once in the calm of a videotape viewing room. Emotional responses and personal prejudices color knowledge of such events.

Should we accept the eyewitness as an analogue to scientific knowledge? I argue that there are only quantitative differences between scientific inquiry and the eyewitness account. Each scientist approaches scientific problems with a theoretical viewpoint, whether explicit or implicit. Theory guides inquiry through the questions raised, the framework of inquiry, and the interpretation of the results. Each scientist seeks to find "facts" to assimilate to his or her world view. Thus, each of us is biased by the human tendency to seek "facts" that are congruent with our prior beliefs.

In everyday life, the biases of information seeking and interpretation are personal. In science, these biases are shared preferences for one theoretical perspective or another — social and cultural biases in the "facts" gathered and believed. But they can be seen as very much the same kind of biases as those of everyday life, except that they are shared beliefs among members of the scientific community. Their common acceptance in science may seem to give them status in reality that they do not have.

Socio-cultural Biases in Knowledge

Although I am in sympathy with most of the current cultural ethos, let us be clear that we change our scientific lenses with the social and cultural myopiae. Knowledge of human behavior is constructed and interpreted through our biases. We pose questions to fit our place and times; we get answers to fit our theoretical niches. Information gained from research is likely to be assimilated to current views. It is unlikely that current views will be challenged by any need to accommodate to discrepant information, because the "facts" gathered will not be construed as challenging to our current perspective.

One example from developmental psychology will illustrate this point. Since the Second World War the divorce rate has risen to proportions that some consider intolerable. Currently in the United States, half of the children born will live some of their developing years in a single-parent family. The rate of illegitimacy is now such that about one-fourth of all births are to unmarried mothers. Scientists are not immune to cultural views. Thus, in the 1950s and 1960s, many social scientists looked for evidence of damage to children from "broken" homes. Families without fathers at home were studied extensively for their bad effects on son's masculinity, poor mathematical skills, and poor personal adjustment. Daughters were considered at risk for poor psychosocial development. The implicit, or sometimes explicit, assumption of the investigators of the period was that families without a masculine presence were doomed to inadequacy as rearing environments for children.

Like the eyewitness to a crime, the investigators of father-absent families filled in the gaps in their constructed knowledge by construing outcomes as unfortunate, whatever they were. Thus, sons who were less stereotypically masculine were lamented, as were daughters who were less stereotypically feminine.

Along came the women's movement, and the scientific assumptions about father-absent families changed. Now, we have alternative family forms, or nontraditional families (Lamb, 1982) that are not assumed, a priori, to be deficient versions of the nuclear family. Our scientific assumptions are that women are capable of working outside of the home and being adequate parents for their children. It is no longer a virtue for sons to be super-masculine; they should be able to cook and clean, as well as work outside of the house, because their adult roles will include shared responsibilities for the home. Daughters who are competent at occupational skills, as well as at homemaking, are approved as the women of the future. Suddenly, the single-parent family has strengths that were "overlooked" by a previous generation of investigators. Such virtues as androgyny (having the good characteristics of both sexes) are applauded by social scientists, not because they have been discovered but because they have been invented. Androgyny is the summative virtue of the 1970s, wrought by the women's movement and the Vietnam War.

This example is not intended to parody developmental psychology, which is no more or less susceptible to the foibles of the human perceiver than any other field. Inquiries into the nonhuman subject matter of physics and chemistry may seem less biased by the human observer because the subject matter seems less directly related to the human condition. But the leaders of research in the physical sciences have been the most vocal commentators on the powerful effects of the human observer on "discovered fact." No, we all share the problems of the human knower.

We should not be disturbed that science is constructed knowledge. Rather the recognition of our own role in scientific knowledge should make more modest our claim to Truth as the discovery of everlasting Natural Laws. Science construed as procedures of knowing and persuading others is only one form of knowing by the rules of one game. There are other games in town, some like art more intuitive, some like religion more determined by authorities. In science there is a more democratic competition of ideas at any one time with rule of fairness in the procedures that govern the scientists. Unlike religion, there are no revealed truths with claims of unchanging verity.

Science as Rules of Knowing

In my definition science is an agreed upon set of procedures, not constructs or theories. At any one time there are prevailing views with favored constructs, which are inventions of the scientists to "explain" and make consistent the "facts" as we construe them. But it is the procedures for gathering observations (sensory data) that are the rules of the scientific enterprise. The observations become facts only when interpreted within a theoretical frame.

Psychology has developed good techniques to avoid the personal biases of knowers through requirements for reliability and validity. At least knowers have to agree on phenomena. The "facts" must be reproducible across some units of time, across similar populations, and situations. Thus, the single eyewitness problem of personal bias and limited perception can be reduced. Observations that are shared among observers and that prove useful can be separated from those that are idiosyncratic, based on limited experience, and that do not prove useful.

The admission that reality is a construction of the human mind does not deny the heuristic value of the construction. Indeed, we get around in the world and invent knowledge that is admirably useful. But the claim that science and reality are human constructions denies that there is any one set of "facts" that is absolute and real. It asserts instead that there are many sets of "facts" that arise from different theory-guided perceptions.

PERSUASIVE IMAGES

Scientific theories are judged by their persuasive power in the community of scientists (Rorty, 1979). Scientific theories advance and decline through discussions among scientists. Scientists conduct theory-ridden searches for new kinds of observations that become facts more easily within their theories than in the perspectives of competing theories. By this process of invention and fact building, scientific ideas evolve. By evolve, I mean change, not necessarily progress; every era has its pet variables that may replace those that precede. Rather than accumulate, scientific knowledge may undergo metamorphoses of interpretation, as when the sun replaces the earth as the center of our universe and the motivation of young children is reinterpreted as basically benign rather than evil and willful; mothers become essential to children's mental health. The sociocultural-historical context of the investigator is clearly a major determinant of what is likely to be believed by the investigator and by colleagues. The most persuasive views of the era form the working assumptions of most scientists of that time.

In this chapter, I examine two kinds of evidence for my assertion that knowledge is invented and that facts are only theory relevant. First, I examine changing conceptions of mothers and children in this century; second, I dispute current ideas about mother-child interaction.

Changing Ideas about Mothers and Children

It seems natural to believe that mothers are important to their children's development, but the notion that mothers have special and irreplaceable roles in children's lives is an invention of the nineteenth century. The image of women as mother, rather than as a household manager who also had children, is rather new. From the Renaissance to the mid-nineteenth century, children evolved psyches that required special maternal care. Ministers stressed the importance of mother's example and her wise training of little ones. By the mid-nineteenth century, mothers were told that they also had an important psychological role to play in their children's lives. Why did psychologists and other experts begin to stress a special bond between mothers and children, one that required her full-time devotion? In this chapter, I trace the evolution of ideas about mothers and children through the advice of child-rearing experts. What have the experts told parents about children and their responsibilities to them?

If we believe that children develop more or less by themselves with reasonable protection and guidance, the obligations of parents are far less demanding of their time and energies than if we think that babies require intensive interaction and instruction for optimum development. The parents of the laissez-faire child can relax and watch their child develop, but the parents of the interventionist child must be constantly involved in programming their child's environment. Theories about children and what they need make a big difference in how we see our roles as parents.

Current conflicts and guilt about being a woman who is a mother and a person in her own right are a socially defined malaise, not an individual problem. In my view, current dilemmas of motherhood arise from a mismatch between ideas about mothers and children that suited the late nineteenth and early twentieth centuries and the current realities of family life. The conflict is not between being a mother and having a career; it is between nineteenth century ideas about children and today's women.

The Nature of The Child

Each era invents its own child. The ideas that society holds about children express broader beliefs about social, economic, religious, and political issues, and beliefs about the prospects of the society itself (Borstelmann, 1983). Optimism about the society's future usually goes with optimism about child nature; pessimism with pessimism. Over the past 500 years, conceptions of the child changed gradually from an ill-formed adult, who must be subjugated to society's goals, to a precious being, who must be protected from unreasonable social demands. Childhood has come to be seen as a special period of life, rather than as a temporary state of no lasting importance for adulthood (Kessen, 1965).

Two major themes are woven through all discussions of children and child rearing: Is child nature basically good or evil? And, do children need careful and detailed nurturance, or is their growth basically programmed by nature? At some times children have been regarded as naturally evil and in need of salvation by wiser, more godly adults. Stern training and even physical abuse could serve to improve the chances of their eventual redemption. At other times, children were thought to be basically good and trustworthy to grow up according to their own natural development. All they needed was protection from the evils of the world.

Democratic optimism has tended to produce an image of children as good by nature and redeemable through training and education. This child is badly affected by poor environments, including inept parenting. The good child who could be trusted to grow up largely on his own is the Darwinian vision of an evolved little primate, whose genetic heritage assured his place in the natural order. A third child, seething with potentially ruinous impulses, owes his nature to evolution and his perfectibility to parental management—repressive or sensitive, depending on the era. We shall meet all three children in the twentieth century.

Children Get Psyches

Beginning in the early years of the nineteenth century children assumed an individuality never before known. They were no longer given the names of their parents or a dead sibling; they were given unique names. In divorce petitions, children began to be mentioned. With improvements in public health and medicine in the later nineteenth century, infant survival improved and so did interest in them as individuals. Although many parents in earlier eras mourned the deaths of their children, death was not unexpected.

Child labor laws in Europe and the United States took children under 13 out of the factories and mines. Compulsory schooling was introduced in France, England, and the United States for children around the turn of the twentieth century, thus making childhood a protected period of learning. Young adolescents from poor families still went to work in the factories and mines, and basic literacy was still unknown to many. But children had been recognized as special people in need of protection.

Along with the change in physical and social conditions of children came a new concern with their psyches. Mothers were put in charge of the delicate construction of nurturant environments for the newly prized little ones. By their good example, mothers were to shape the minds and hearts of the next generation. The ideas that children have feelings of any lasting importance for their development is a very recent invention (or insight, if you wish). Two of the experts we consider in the chapter spoke little of children's emotions; only Freud stressed the lasting import of children's emotional fantasies about their parents and children's vulnerability to distortions in relationships with their parents.

Mothers Front and Center

Ideas about mothers have swung historically with the roles of women. When women were needed to work the fields or shops, experts claimed that children didn't need them much. Mothers, who might be too soft and sentimental, could even be bad for children's character development. When men left home during the Industrial Revolution to work elsewhere, women were "needed" at home. One reason they were needed was to tend the children, but there were other reasons as well. In my opinion, the "cult of domesticity" (Cott, 1977) and motherhood became virtures that kept women in their place.

In the mid-nineteenth century experts stressed the importance of mothers as household managers. Mothers had primary responsibility for their children, but they also had responsibility for providing a refuge for their husbands from the corruption of the commercial world (Lasch, 1977). Women were the moral fiber in the family diet. They were responsible for making the home peaceful, harmonious, and uplifting for the husbands and their children.

From the mid- to late nineteenth century, home management and child rearing were of balanced importance, part and parcel of a woman's domestic role. Beginning in mid-century, however, a new element of romanticism focused on children. Romantics, such as Jean Jacques Rousseau, had in the previous century emphasized feeling over reason, primitive over sophisticated, natural over contrived, and simple over complicated. Romantics stressed children's need for love and the responsibility of mothers to rear them lovingly. As romantic ideas caught the nineteenth century imagination, children became increasingly precious and mother more and more responsible for rearing them (Degler, 1980, p. 73). Mother love began to be promoted as the salvation of children.

At the same time, child rearing came to be considered an increasingly difficult and responsible task. Motherhood replaced domesticity as a cult, but love was not enough. The new idea was that mothers could not trust their instincts to rear children, they needed *knowledge*. The goal of motherhood was to train the young properly to inherit the earth—or at least their corner of it. Mother's psychological relationship with her child was not so important as her proper example and consistent training efforts to mold him.

The Ideology of Educated Motherhood

In the last quarter of the nineteenth century, ideal womanhood was guided by feminine virtue. Middle-class women were supposed to embody an inherently feminine kind of morality, chastity, and sensibility for the good of their families and the larger society. As motherhood became the focus of feminine virtue, however, a new kind of ideal woman emerged—one who learned and practiced the science of child development.

Near the end of the nineteenth century, mothers joined together to share information about their crucial tasks. The National Congress of Mothers was founded in 1897, following on the Society for the Study of Child Nature, founded in 1888. In 1910, the mothers' movement was absorbed into the National Congress of Parents and Teachers (the PTA). From a laywoman's organization founded on mother love, mothers were swept into a professional movement that proclaimed a scientific basis for child-rearing advice and knowledge of children's nature. The era of scientific child study was begun. It was begun by mothers but soon coopted by child-rearing "experts."

Such expert guidance was forthcoming from the scientific child-study movement, begun in the late nineteenth century. The domestic science of the early and mid-nineteenth century that concerned itself with homemaking skills was transformed into child science. Children now held front and center stage in the family drama, having upstaged cooking, sewing, cleaning, money management, and fathers. Some mothers even wished to live with their children in boarding houses so that their full attention could be on the children, undistracted by household duties.

G. Stanley Hall, the first U.S. psychologist and president of Clark University, was enormously influential with the mothers' movement. He also addressed experts with studies of children and claims of scientific knowledge (we discount his studies today). Hall was the guru of the child-rearing experts in the early century. It was Hall who brought Freud to America for his first visit and Hall who wrote more than a dozen books on children and child rearing. He stressed children's developmental stages and the importance of maternal management. In addition, Hall urged mothers to take copious notes on child development, to be (unpaid) research assistants in the grand new adventure — exploring the mind and souls of children. With the scientific blessing of Dr. Hall, children became invested with importance and childhood emerged full-blown into what we know today.

The battle to keep women out of higher education was lost, but women's education could be turned to children's advantage by demanding education for proper motherhood. G. Stanley Hall said that the hand that rocks the cradle has more responsibility than the corporate executive. Because children change over development, the demands of educated parenthood are very complicated and need education to be done well. Now women could be college graduates and mothers, too. What could be better? College presidents agreed that their graduates would bring grace and education to their homes, a more important task than any other. As M. Carey Thomas, president of Bryn Mawr College stated in 1908:

Women cannot conceivably be given an education too broad, too high, or too deep to fit them to become the educated mothers of the future race of men and women born of educated parents. The pity is that we only have the four years of the college course to impart such knowledge to women who are to be the mothers (Rothman, 1978, pp. 107-8).

The president of Wellesley echoed similar sentiments, extolling the virtues of doing everything "right," from setting tables and trimming hats to teaching children to read. College-educated mothers could do it all better.

Nothing was more important than motherhood, President Theodore Roosevelt told a gathering of women:

The good mother, the wise mother—you cannot really be a good mother if you are a not a wise mother—is more important to the community than even the ablest man; her career is more worthy of honor and is more useful to the community than the career of any man, no matter how successful he can be.

But the woman who, whether from cowardice, from selfishness, from having a false and vacuous ideal shirks her duty as wife and mother, earns the right to our contempt, just as the man who, from any motive, fears to do his duty in battle when the country calls him (Ehrenreich & English, 1979, p. 190. For her own good; a speech to the First International Congress in America on the Welfare of the Child, under the auspices of the National Congress of Mothers, March 1908, Washington, DC).

Why the cult of motherhood? Part of the explanation can be found in romanticism, part in the better survival rates of children, part in Darwin and evolution, which made development an important part of scientific theory. Darwin's major work on *Origin of Species* was published in 1859. Parallels between evolution and development focused attention on children. Just as species were thought to represent a progression from simple animals to the complex, moral human, so was the development from infancy to adulthood considered a progression of ever more complex adaptations. Post-Darwinian philosophers, such as John Dewey, emphasized the child's educability, an idea similar to the earlier moral redemption through training, with the addition of romantic notions about the unspoiled goodness of child nature (Borstelmann, 1983). Whenever children were seen as redeemable and educable, mothers had a special role to play.

The most important political force to promote the cult of motherhood was the Progressive Movement. Progressives introduced new ideas about children's welfare that spawned public, state-supported programs to guard the health and development of children. The Progressive agenda was child centered and protective. Child and maternal health clinics, kindergartens, and protective legislation attempted to remove children and women from the labor force.

> Beginning in the twentieth century, with the coming of Progressivism, a new definition of proper womanhood emerged, a model of "educated motherhood." Focusing with a new intensity on the needs of the child, the ideal looked to train women to the tasks of motherhood. Women's insights into child development were now to take precedence over their virtuous and maternal instincts (Rothman, 1978, p. 5).

The mother and the state were dedicated to pursue the best interests of the child. Few were interested in mother as a person. And mother was assisted in her child-rearing tasks by a wealth of opinion about the nature of the child and proper upbringing. Mother had a special role but she needed expert guidance. Three experts, each with his own assumptions about the child, came forth to tell parents how to rear their children.

THREE EXPERTS ON CHILD REARING

The study of child behavior began a new phase in the early twentieth century. To illustrate the different children that one can invent, depending upon one's predilections, let us consider the developmental psychologies of Arnold Gesell, John Watson, and Sigmund Freud. Each of these men held different views about child development. Their common attitude, which followed the child-study movement, was that child development could be the proper object of scientific study. Of course, science proceeds from values and assumptions, so that each created a child and child-rearing advice to fit his own theory.

All were influential child experts from the 1920s to the 1940s, and their influences pervade our current cultural assumptions about children's natures and parents' responsibilities. Their assumptions and advice to parents are profoundly different, but each speaks to a major stream in American culture.

Arnold Gesell

Gesell and Watson represent the two polarities on each of the issues described earlier. Gesell's child is good by nature and endowed with self-propelled maturation; she is largely unaffected by details of parental caregiving, as long as it is not abusive or terribly neglectful.

It is the hereditary ballast which conserves and stabilizes the growth of each individual infant.... If it did not exist the infant would be the victim of flaccid malleability which is sometimes romantically ascribed to him. His mind, his spirit, his personality would fall ready prey to disease, to starvation, to malnutrition, and worst of all to misguided management (Gesell, 1928, p. 378).

Gesell's child is not so malleable as to be thrown off course by parents' "misguided management," because he has internal direction. Gesell's child is shaped by nature to grow up without much fuss by the parents. Child development is in fact so predictable that Gesell was able to publish norms or standards for behavioral development, much like those for physical growth—height, weight, and head circumference. Norms for language, motor, social, and adaptive (self-help, practical skills) development told parents that the average six-month old could reach for objects, nine-month-olds babble in consonent-vowel combination (ma-ma, ba-ba), two-year-olds stack blocks, and three-year-olds name many parts of the body. Although Gesell respected individual differences, his average developmental norms were used by parents to judge the progress of their children, without regard for the range of individual differences.

Gesell's descriptions of normal development were so successful that they formed the basis for his developmental test, which is still used today. The *Bayley Tests of Mental and Motor Developments* and the *Denver Development Screening Test*, used by nearly all pediatricians, follow Gesell's ideas closely and even use many of his items. The tests serve well to identify at early ages children who lag seriously behind 90 or 95 percent of their age mates.

Gesell recognized and respected individual differences. His norms were meant to convey a description of average development. Children within a normal range but ahead or behind their peers are not necessarily advantaged or disadvantaged. The baby who walks first will probably not be the first across the finish line at the New York Marathon. The child who talks first is not likely to become the state debating champion. Children who walk and talk later have just as good a chance of winning. Children have different developmental patterns that deserve respect from parents and others.

The inborn tendency toward optimal development is so inveterate that he benefits liberally from what is good in our practice, and suffers less than he logically should from our unenlightenment. Only if we give respect to this inner core of inheritance can we respect the important individual differences which distinguish infants as well as men (Gesell, 1928, p. 378).

Gesell had so much confidence in children's inborn tendency to the best development possible that he even proposed that children profit a great deal from good parenting but suffer little from parents' mistakes. The contrast with Watson could not be greater.

John Watson

Unlike Gesell's robust maturer, Watson's child is shaped entirely by nurture, as a passive recipient of detailed training. Watson's newborn is a "lively squirming bit of flesh, capable of making a few simple responses... parents take this raw material and begin to fashion it to suit themselves. This means that parents, whether they know it or not, start intensive training of the child at birth" (Watson, 1928, p. 46).

Gesell's robust child matures as the genetic program directs, while the environment plays a supporting role. Gesell reassured parents that they could hardly go wrong, because his child will blossom in many different gardens. Watson's fragile child is a blank page to be inscribed by carefully programed, detailed training. In the same year (1928), the two experts offered parents totally different guidance.

Watson impressed parents with the importance of their responsibilities and the many ways they could spoil their children's development. First and foremost, they must train the child to be a proper adult. Training the baby took many forms. Strictly scheduled feedings were intended to shape the child to the parents' will. Never, never, feed the baby when she demands it, or she will get the idea that she controls the parents. Never pick the baby up when she is crying, only when she is being pleasant. Early toilet training, beginning in the first months of life, was similarly designed to bend the child to the parents' will. Later table manners and other social graces were to be taught to make sure that the child was properly shaped.

Watson's ideas were attractive to parents because he promised that one can make of one's child whatever one wishes. This idea fit nicely with democratic ideals of everyman, latent genius, and millionaire. Better than Horatio Alger who had to make it on his own, Watson's child's future could be determined by diligent parents. Anyone, he said, could shape a child into a mathematical genius or a lyric poet, if only one tried hard enough and was consistent enough in training. Latter day Watsonians include the gourmet baby trainers, who promise a Harvard graduate, if only you will buy their products and follow their prescriptions.

In addition to the rigor, Watson insisted on objective and impersonal management of children. None of this mawkish sentimentality that led parents to forget long-term goals that could be achieved only with rigorous training for the temporary pleasures of affection.

> There is a sensible way of treating children. Treat them as though they were young adults. Dress them, bathe them with care and circumspection. Let your behavior be always objective and kindly firm. Never hug and kiss them, never let them sit in your lap. If you want, kiss them once on the forehead when they say goodnight. Shake hands with them in the morning. Give them a pat on the head if they have made an extraordinarily good job of a difficult task. Try it out. In a week's time you will find how easy it is to be perfectly objective with your child and at the same time kindly. You will be utterly ashamed of the mawkish, sentimental way you have been handling it (Watson, 1928, pp. 81-82).

Watson's child-rearing advice came out of a Victorian era of stern habit training. Although he does not dwell on sexuality, the regimen he sets up for parents would preclude any pleasure seeking on the child's part. The parents must dominate the child and direct his interests in profitable directions.

Parents a la Mode.

Parenting Gesell's child is like planting a tulip garden. You plant the bulb in good soil, water it, and wait for spring. Each flower will emerge with a predetermined color, size, form, and substance. There is nothing you can do to change the flower's development except to make it larger or smaller by tending it carefully or carelessly. The basic pattern of the tulip's development is set in the bulb. With the joining of the human sperm and egg, the preset developmental pattern of a human individual begins. Parents' good care serves to make the child the best version of himself.

Parenting Watson's child is like building a house. The builder can design it to be small or large, Colonial or Tudor style. The amount of investment the builder makes in its size, architectural details, and furnishings determines how grand a house it is. Once the blueprints are set, however, the builder cannot deviate from the plan, or the building may fail. Suppose that one wall were longer or higher than the corresponding wall—the roof would not fit. Suppose he changed his mind about the bathtub and bought one two feet too wide for the bathroom. The plan for the house can be almost anything a couple would want, but once set must be rigorously followed. And so Watson said it was with child rearing.

Gesell believed the child to be a biological organism, shaped by evolution to develop into a normal adult, with a little support from the parents. Watson believed the child to be a ball of clay to be molded as the parents wish, if they were determined enough to shape the child to their wishes. Whereas Gesell stressed that parents should enjoy observing their child's development, Watson stressed the parents' responsibility to shape the child into a proper adult. No more diametrically opposed views of child rearing could have been offered at the same moment in history—until Freud came along.

Freudian Revolution: Infantile Sexuality

At the same time that Gesell and Watson were promoting their opposite views of children and parenting, a new era was dawning in Vienna. Sigmund Freud invented a child whose image was to infiltrate much of the mid- to late twentieth century writing on children and parenting. Freud's child was neither a trustworthy, well-endowed maturer nor a blob of putty that required molding. Freud's child was a surging mass of conflicts set in time bombs.

> Unlike Watson who brought the hope of Everyman pianist, poet, and king; or Gesell lauding Growth as essentially benign, Freud's picture of the child was uncompromisingly a picture of conflict. No matter how strong the forces of growth or how well-intentioned and informed his parents, Freud's child must inevitably face the confrontation of his wishes, unbearable to his parents and eventually unbearable to him, with the facts of the world (Kessen, 1965, p. 269).

Freud's child was sexually driven and inevitably in conflict, both with adults who seek to curb his excesses and to socialize him, and with himself. Through mysterious processes of learning, called identification and internalization, the child comes to accept social standards and to control his own behavior, but never without eternal conflicts among what he wants (Id), what he believes to be Right and Wrong (Super-ego), and what he considers the most adaptive course (Ego).

The notion of dangerous infant impulses did not start with Freud. The Victorian era was full of preachments about the dangers of unbridled lust, in children as well as adults. It was a period of fearful fascination with sexuality. As we shall see, the U.S. official child-rearing doctrine advised parents to beware of the natural depravity of children, who seek sexual pleasures that will ruin them if allowed to develop unchecked.

Freud focused on the origins of sexuality, which in his view began at birth. Infantile sexuality shows itself in the oral behavior of the infant. Sucking and mouthing were evidence of the sexual drive seeking gratification through the mouth. Too much or too little oral gratification leads to personality disturbance. Weaning is the child's first of many inevitable conflicts with social norms. In Freud's view, infants desire to be suckled forever, which comes into conflict with the social norm of weaning around a year of age. As mother enforces weaning, the baby feels rejected by the only love in his life. Later, toddlers' sexuality was said to be invested in the anal region. Toddlers inevitably come into conflict with parents over toilet training — society's will over the baby's sexual gratification. Both lack of training and harsh training were said by Freud to be sources of personality disturbance.

Finally in the preschool period, the male child becomes phallic, his sexuality expressed through his penis. He wishes to express his sexuality directly toward his mother (Oedipal conflict), but is fearful of the wrath of his overpowering father, who owns mother's body. To avoid a terrifying confrontation and loss of father's love, the little boy renounces his desire for mother's body and vows to become big and strong like father so that he can have a woman like mother when he grows up. The family triangle is more like a noose for the Freudian boy.

Freudian girls were supposed to fall in love with their fathers (Electra complex), experience penis envy, and decide to identify with their mothers after all. Contemporary experts disagree in their assessment of Freud's theory of women's development. In my opinion, he had no satisfactory theory of women's development, which is understandable in an era that cared so little about women.

No longer Gesell's innocent evolved little primate who would inevitably become human, or Watson's pleasingly malleable putty. Freud's child surged with perverse energies that must be controlled. Inherent in the struggle to curb the child's dark nature was a catch-22 — neurosis came from too much control, character defects from too little. Few parents could produce mentally healthy children, because child rearing was made a nearly impossible task.

Although Freud began to publish on psychoanalysis in the late 1890s, the implications of his theory for child development did not dawn on American experts until 1909, when he spoke for the first time in the United States. Even then, Freud's child was not popular. Only a minority of American psychologists embraced Freud's vision of children, so that popular child-rearing advice was less saturated with the child-in-conflict than with Watson's habit training and Gesell's developmental norms with which to gauge your child's progress. Not until mid-century did Freud's conflicted child gain prominence in the press and in clinical circles. The Great Depression and the Second World War were barren ground for the growth of permissiveness and introspection.

Making Freud's Child American.

Furthermore, Freud's child was Viennese and Victorian, not a thoroughly American vision. Watered-down versions of psychoanalytic theory appeared in the 1950s under the guise of permissiveness, the view that children would be free of conflict if their good little natures were allowed to develop undistorted by society's demands. (Ironically, no view could have been further from Freud's. He certainly did not believe that children's natures were good or that they should be given permission to vent their raw feelings.) By mid-century, unsocialized monsters who dominated the household with crayoned walls and jam-smeared furniture appeared as cartoons in newspapers and magazines. Parents cowered in corners, fearful of daunting the child's spirit. Although the social upheavals of the 1960s and 1970s were often blamed on young people alleged to have been reared too permissively, it is unlikely that many parents followed this advice any more literally than the strict habit training Watson proposed.

In a more serious assimilation, the sexual nature of Freud's child was reinterpreted to a more pallatable psychosocial model by Erik H. Erikson (1950). The child was still in conflict, but psychological misfortune was not inevitable, if parents gave love and understanding to the struggling child. Developmental tasks of learning to trust, to be autonomous, and to take initiative in one's own life were important milestones in infant and preschool years; these psychosocial steps replaced Freud's oral, anal, and phallic stages, respectively.

Although he was a German refugee, Erikson had a wholesome vision of children that was compatible with the prevailing American bias toward perfectibility. With competent and humane management children could resolve their conflicts and develop healthy personalities. Bad outcomes were certainly possible, even frequent, but Erkison's American child had a stronger and more resilient Ego than Freud's Viennese child. The optimism of America in the 1950s gave psychoanalysis a new intellectual setting.

A stern father, who reigned over his submissive wife and cowering children in a darkened, velvet-draped parlor, typified the Victorian family of the Freudian child. The New World at mid-twentieth century transformed the ideal family into a backyard baseball team, gathered around the outdoor barbeque. Family members were almost equal partners. Children were cheeky, not cowed. And father cooked — at least outdoors. Rather than cowering in fear of parental reprisals and developing neurotic conflicts, the American Freudian child ran wild and developed an antisocial personality. Children were transformed, even if mothers had not yet metamorphosed from suburban housewife to employee.

FEDERAL ADVICE TO PARENTS

An excellent map for the exploration of changes in child-rearing advice is what the U.S. government tells parents. Since 1914, the U.S. Children's Bureau has published a booklet, *Infant Care*, to advise parents on the right ways to rear their children. Needless to say, the advice changed dramatically from the early years to the present. Martha Wolfenstein (1963), a psychoanalyst, analyzed the official U.S. position on the nature of children and the necessities of their care. She found remarkable changes in 1929 and 1942 from previous advice. I group the advice into three categories:

Pre-1929. Children were seen as having strong and dangerous impulses that had to be repressively curbed. As in the Freudian view, the child was seen as sexual. But, unlike the child-rearing advice that Freud would have given, the U.S. government advised the parent to do everything possible to prevent any erotic satisfactions for the child. Thumbsucking was to be stopped at all costs by sewing mittens over the sleeves of the nightgown and by pinning the child's arms to the bedsheets. Evidently mothers accepted this advice quite readily, because the government pamphlet had to warn mothers against too great restriction of the baby's mobility. "The mother's zeal against thumbsucking is assumed to be so great that she is reminded to allow the child to have his hands free some of the time so that he may develop legitimate manual skills; 'but with the approach of bedtime, the hands must be covered'" (Wolfenstein, 1963, p. 169).

Masturbation was a serious threat that could get dangerously out of control. Advice to parents was to tie the infant's feet to opposite sides of the crib so that he could not rub his thighs together. With arms bound, of course, there was no danger of manual stimulation. The child of the early century had evil erotic impulses that were to be curbed by careful parental management.

The 1930s. Under the influence of Watson, the 1929 version, and subsequent manuals of the 1930s, advised parents to beware of their infant's attempts to dominate them. The baby who was picked up when he cried quickly became a tyrant over his parents. Careful training in the objective ways advised would prevent this disaster. Don't pick them up when they cry; only when they are behaving nicely. And so forth, according to Watson's doctrine.

1940s and 1950s. The impulsive, evil, pleasure-seeking child has been transformed into a baby who is interested in exploring his world. Babies may incidentally touch their genitals or suck their thumbs, but there are far more interesting things for them to do, if parents will only provide distractions. Give them a toy and they will forget about autoerotic activities. In this period, babies need to be picked up, because adequate indulgence "makes the baby less demanding as he grows older" (Wolfenstein, 1963, p. 171).

Further, the 1940s baby was trusted to regulate the amount of stimulation and food he could take safely. In the early period, babies could not tell how much they needed to eat or how much excitement they could take; after 1942 infants are good judges of what stimulation and nourishment they can manage safely. The baby of the mid-century is to picked up when she cries and played with when she wants, or the parents want.

Consonant with the changed nature of the child, the conception of parenthood changed. In the 1914 era mothers' characters were supposed to be strong, persistent, patient, and full of self-control. Later, in the 1930s mothers were exhorted to know how to do a good job of training, in keeping with the Watsonian message. "The parents had to use the right techniques to impose routines and to keep the child from dominating them" (Wolfenstein, 1963, p. 173).

In the mid-century, parenthood and childhood became sources of joy. Father was much more involved than before, and the dictum was to enjoy the baby. Infants enjoy breast feeding, baths, food, and play with parents. They enjoy social contact and conversations with their parents. Parents enjoy the same activities (or else!). Gone are the fears that the baby's erogenous zones will overwhelm him and his parents. Gone are parental fears about training the infant to be a proper adult. Enter the trustworthy child, the sensible being whose impulses are acceptable and who needs supportive, attentive parenting. This is the contemporary child, yours and mine, who owes his nature to Gesell, with a little Freud for spice.

It is hard to imagine that parents ever followed Gesell's, Watson's, or Freud's advice literally. Children reared in the casual Gesellian manner make modern parents nervous—are they doing enough? Children reared according to Watson's doctrine would have no hearts, and those reared by American Freudian dictates would be thrown out of kindergarten for misconduct. I suspect that most parents of this century gave their children affection, training, and freedom in moderation—the advice of contemporary experts.

The full-fledged Freudian child never made his way into official American child-rearing advice. But Freud influenced child rearing through popular articles written by psychoanalysts, and in the concept of attachment. Freud influenced American parents through Dr. Spock, who by 1950 minimized training in favor of moderate permissiveness. In an Americanized version of the message, Dr. Spock advises parents to recognize the surging feelings of their children, but he also urges parents to be self-confident, to trust themselves and their child, and everything will turn out all right (Zuckerman, 1975). Like most popular, contemporary experts, Spock enlivens the trustworthy Gesell child with a dash of Freudian conflict to achieve the child for our times.

CONTEMPORARY PROBLEMS WITH LENSES

Let us now turn to the psychological lenses of the day and contemplate the problems of inference from our current research on mothers and children. The psychological world in which we conduct research is, in my view, a cloud of correlated events, to which we as human observers give meaning. In the swirling cloud of interacting organisms and environments, most events merely co-occur. As investigators, we construct a story (often called a theory) about relationships among events. We select a few elements and put them into a study. By so doing we necessarily eliminate other variables a priori from possible analysis, and we preconstrue causal relationships among the events. One cannot avoid either the theoretical preconceptions or the selection of variables to study, but one can avoid exaggerated claims for the causal status of one's variables.

The smartest paper I have ever read on the problems of causal inference was by Feldman and Hass (1970) on experimental versus correlational research. Each kind of design has virtues and deficiencies in the direct and indirect inferences that can be made. Correlational studies sample *existing* groups and describe their differences on one or more dependent variables. From correlational studies one can make direct inferences about naturally occurring differences between groups but only indirect inferences about the causes of those differences. Thus, from the studies of children with low to moderate lead exposures one can make direct inferences about existing differences but only indirect inferences about the "underlying" causes of those differences. Experimental studies can make direct inferences about the situations in which differences *can* occur but only indirect inferences about how they *do* occur in existing populations.

Plausible and Implausible Models

Suppose that an investigator decided to study the effects (beware already!) of parental management techniques on children's intellectual and emotional development. The investigator has read Richard Bell and Diana Baumrind and is prepared to think that children may have some reciprocal effects on their parents as well. To avoid the more obvious problems of correlational studies, in which the direction of effects is hopelessly muddled, the investigator chooses temporal priority to order the variables. The study will be longitudinal, to show the relative impact of parental behaviors at Time 1 on child behaviors at Time 2, and the effects of children's behaviors at Time 1 on parental behaviors at Time 2—the familiar cross-lag analysis.

Now suppose that the investigator decided to take both proximal measures of the interactions of parents and their children and more distal measures of parent and child characteristics that are not bound by the interactional situations. Having been influenced by trait theories of intelligence and personality, the investigator tests cross-situational traits and situational variables in explanatory models of parent-child reciprocal influence.

Parental Predictors

First, we look at a couple of proximal parental variables, maternal control of child rated from a 15-minute observation of a teaching situation and scores from an interview with mothers about their methods of disciplining their children in the face of typical misbehaviors, in Figure 5-1. Both measures have suitably high reliabilities and have been scored to yield a positive to negative dimension of parental management techniques. At the positive end are reasoning, explaining, and other verbal ways of dealing with young children. At the negative end is physical punishment. In the middle are various moderate to severe forms of admonishment.

The prediction of children's Stanford-Binet IQ scores over an 18-month period (Time 1 to Time 2) is quite good. Both positive control techniques observed and positive discipline scored from the discipline interview significantly predict child IQ concurrently (r's = .42 − .49) and 18-months later, with an R-square of .23.

Psychologists who favor proximal variables might stop there, write their papers and "prove" that positive parental management has a beneficial effect on intellectual development. The inference usually drawn from this sort of result is that parents who do not manage their children in positive ways could have more intelligent children if they

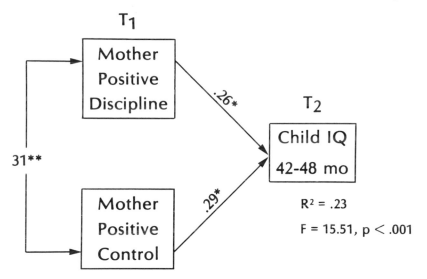

FIGURE 5-1. Proximal Maternal Behaviors as Predictors of Child IQ.

did. The implications for intervention with parents are implicit, if not explicit. If only psychologists could help all parents behave positively toward their children, their children would turn out to be brighter. As the editor of a developmental journal, I receive many papers of this sort.

As an investigator, however, I cannot resist examining the following result, in Figure 5-2. When two more distal variables, mother's WAIS vocabulary score and her education, are put into the equation, mother's IQ dominates the prediction of her child's IQ. Mother's IQ determines in large part how she behaves toward her child in the teaching situation, and contributes to her discipline techniques. Her educational level is of little importance to her behavior or to her child's IQ, once her own IQ is estimated from her vocabulary score. The only significant predictor of the child's IQ at three and a half to four years of age is mother's WAIS vocabulary score.

Perhaps, this result is peculiar to IQ. Let us look at child's communication skills, a score from the Cain-Levine Social Competence Scale (Cain, Levine, & Elzey, 1963), answered by the mothers. Again, mother's positive control and discipline techniques at Time 1 predict the child's communication skills at Time 2. If *only* all mothers would manage their children in more positive ways, their children would be better able to carry messages, remember instructions, answer the telephone, and tell stories.

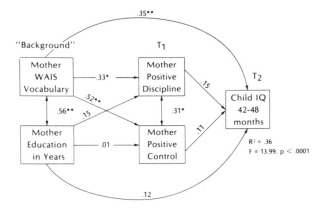

FIGURE 5-2. Proximal and Distal Maternal Predictors of Child IQ.

But again, the importance of these proximal predictors pales in comparison to mother's vocabulary score, as shown in Figures 5-3 and 5-4. Children with good communication scores have mothers with high WAIS vocabulary scores. Any importance of maternal management techniques is mediated by maternal IQ. Mothers who are smarter

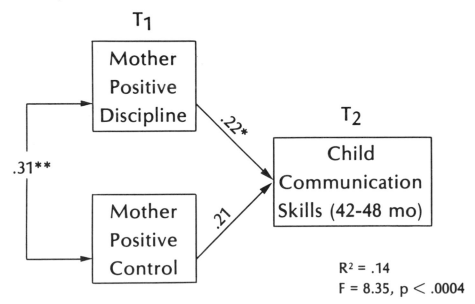

FIGURE 5-3. Proximal Maternal Predictors of Child Communication Skills.

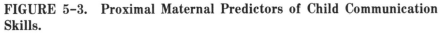

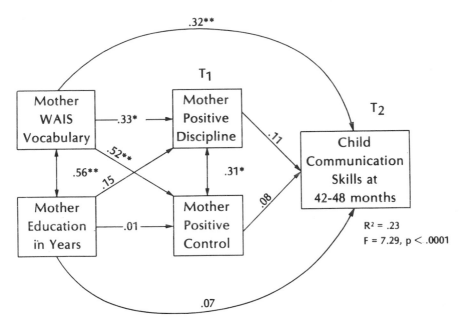

FIGURE 5-4. Proximal and Distal Maternal Predictors of Child Communication Skills.

behave in more benign ways toward their children, and their children have better verbal skills.

Perhaps, these results apply only to cognitive outcomes for children. Let us look at social adjustment. The *Childhood Personality Scale* (Cohen & Dibble, 1974) was rated by both mothers and observers. The average of their scores was entered into a principal components analysis, which resulted in one, large dimension of social adjustment—high expressiveness and attention and low apathy and introversion—as shown in Table 5-1.

TABLE 5-1. Social Adjustment Factor: Combined Ratings of Mothers and Raters.

	Childhood Personality Scale First Principal Component
Attention	.61
Expressiveness	.76
Introversion	− .81
Apathy	− .80
Eigenvalue 2.26	

Source: Compiled by author.

Figure 5-5 shows that positive maternal discipline predicts a well-adjusted child. Mothers who handle their children in benign ways have children who are more expressive and attentive and less withdrawn. The relationship between positive maternal discipline and child adjustment is sustained after the two maternal IQ and education variables are entered into the equation. This model is shown in Figure 5-6. Maternal vocabulary does not make a statistically reliable contribution to child's social adjustment, apart from its contribution to her discipline techniques.

Thus, we can see that the proximal variables of maternal control and discipline techniques can mask the relationships between maternal IQ and child's intellectual skills but contribute directly to the child's social adjustment. With a theoretical model that included only proximal variables, we could not have perceived a difference in the prediction of children's social and intellectual outcomes. Without testing proximal versus distal variables, we would not have invented differential models for social and intellectual development.

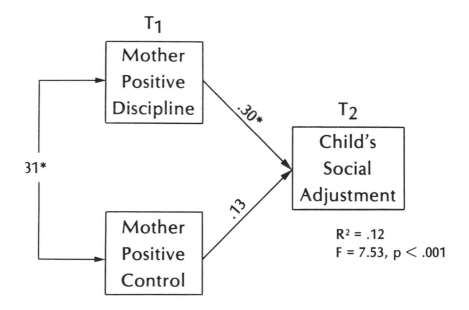

FIGURE 5-5. Proximal Maternal Predictors of Child Social Adjustment.

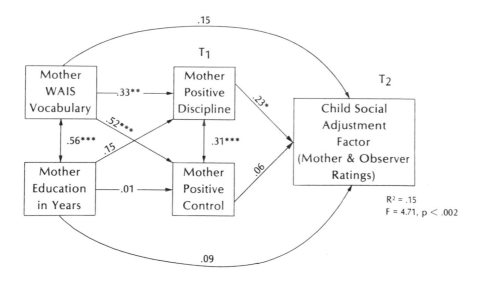

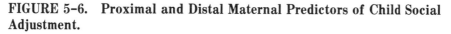

FIGURE 5-6. **Proximal and Distal Maternal Predictors of Child Social Adjustment.**

Child Predictors

Now let us examine children's effects on parents, again longitudinally. What effects do what characteristics of children have on their parents' behaviors toward them? I present only the full models to save space. First, one can see in Figure 5-7 that cooperative children are also those who score higher on the Stanford-Binet and have better communication and adaptive, self-help skills. Second, in the model with only proximal variables, one might have "found" that children's cooperation in the teaching task was very important in "determining" how their mothers control them while teaching the toy sort ($r = .37$ over 18 months from test to retest). In the full model, however, one can see that intelligent children "cause" their mothers to behave in positive ways toward them.

Children who are intelligent also have mothers who discipline them in positive ways, according to their mothers in interviews consisting of 15 vignettes of typical child misbehaviors (Figure 5-8). The correlation of child IQ with mother's discipline techniques is .40, both when the child is 24 and 48 months of age. Nothing the child is observed to do proximally controls this much variance in mother's behavior toward him/her. Although there are positive and statistically reliable relationships between children's proximal behaviors and

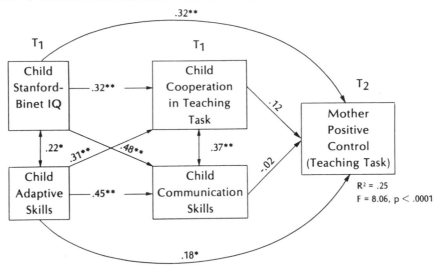

FIGURE 5-7. Proximal and Distal Child Predictors of Maternal Control Techniques.

maternal handling, they are better explained, one might say mediated, by the child's IQ. Little variance is explained by the proximal effects of children's behaviors on their mother's behaviors.

Actually, I don't believe that intelligent children directly cause their mothers to behave more positively toward them, because the

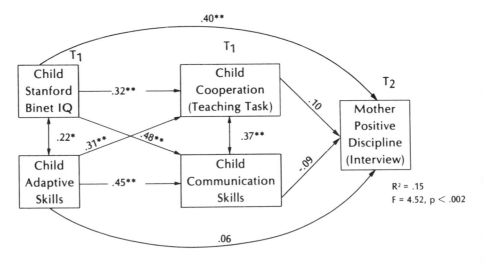

FIGURE 5-8. Proximal and Distal Child Predictors of Maternal Discipline Techniques.

model does not take into account the mother-child IQ connection, or the connection between maternal intelligence and maternal behaviors. Mothers who are intelligent have children who are intelligent; intelligent mothers behave in more benign and positive ways toward their children, who may also evoke more positive handling from their mothers. The world of parent-child interaction is fraught with inferential pitfalls.

I can "demonstrate" with the same data that bright children cause their mothers to be better educated! As Figure 5-9 shows, high-IQ two-year olds with good communication skills produce mothers with higher educational levels, regardless of whether or not the children cooperate in a teaching task. Implausible, you say! I agree that this model is implausible, because we have independent information about the educational histories of adults that make it very unlikely for a mother to obtain more education or to drop out of school according to her preschooler's IQ score. To imagine that preschoolers' intelligence determines their mothers' educational levels violates both criteria of plausibility, temporal and directional.

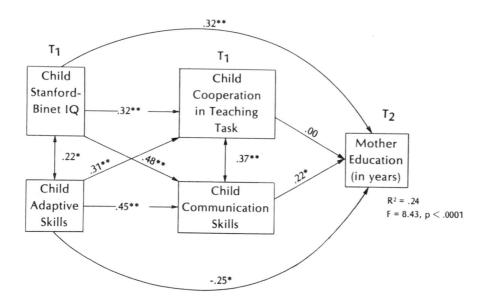

FIGURE 5-9. Proximal and Distal Child Predictors of Maternal Educational Levels.

Confounded Truths

What would our inferences be if we could randomly assign discipline techniques to mothers and cooperation levels to children? Perhaps, an experimental design would permit direct inferences about the effects of discipline per se on children and the effects of cooperative and uncooperative children on mothers' behaviors, without the confoundings of background variables and the co-occurrence of maternal and child characteristics. Unfortunately, such an experiment would not be feasible, ethical, or desirable. An experiment that divorces behavior from context would not generalize to the population of parents and children in the real world, where all of these variables co-occur in a cloud of correlated events. The system in which parental and child behaviors occur is, in my view, intrinsically confounded. The truth about this world cannot be simulated by the isolation of single variables, because I am fairly sure that there are nonadditive effects of parent and child characteristics (see Scarr & Weinberg, 1978; Scarr & McCartney, 1983). Bright parents have intellectually responsive children and provide a more stimulating rearing environment for them, and the children evoke and generate for themselves more intellectual stimulation than less bright children. One plus one about parents and children do not equal two.

As Feldman and Hass (1970) indicated, experimental and correlational studies provide different kinds of direct inferences. There are causal statements about socially important issues, such as how mothers and children affect each others' behaviors, about which we can make only indirect inferences. I believe that in studies of such events we are limited in the causal inferences we can draw from the cloud of correlated events that appear to us as sensory data. We must make inferences about their meaning, but we should be mindful that our "facts" are products of our own theories, and they must compete with others' "facts." Our problems with inference will not be solved by reliance on the complementarity of experimental and correlational studies. Our problems reside in the theoretical lenses of our theories that invent some "facts" and not others. We are blind to others' theories and "facts," even those based on the same observation.

PLAUSIBLE MOTHERS AND CHILDREN

Why do we find the models that claim that parents' and children's behaviors affect each other more plausible than the idea that children's intellectual traits affect their mothers' educational levels? Do we have independent information about the effects of parental and child behaviors on one another? I think not. What we have are pet variables that have a status in our affections that other theoretically invented "facts" do not.

I believe that we judge as plausible the models that specify parent-child behavioral influences because alternative formulations have not been considered, or have been thought evil, until recently.

Today's Child

Most contemporary developmental psychologists espouse the view of the robust, biologically organized child (Cairns, 1983). Today's child is sensitive to good and bad environments — but is resilient. Bad experiences do not necessarily have permanently damaging effects, nor good experiences permanently beneficial ones. A bad childhood can be overcome by later, good experiences; a good childhood cannot innoculate one against the traumas of an unfortunate adulthood.

According to most contemporary views, the development of our present-day child proceeds smoothly according to the internal biological plan, as long as the environment is supportive. But just how supportive and how specific do good influences have to be to promote optimal development? Arguments among child development experts center on the degree to which development is influenced by the details of everyday life — a version of the Watson-Gesell debate. Some experts are convinced that specific environments have very important effects at some periods of development (Wachs & Gruen, 1982). Language, for example, may be influenced by the amount of dialogue between adults and young children, so that children who do not experience a lot of conversation with adults may not develop as complex speech as those who do. Because correlations among good events are often confused for causation, other experts are dubious about the importance of the details of a child's upbringing. More Gesellian experts, such as Edward Zigler and myself, stress the importance of the child's biological organization and individual differences in developmental patterns that determine most of the ways children develop, as long as they have reasonable environments. We argue that parents can and do have important effects on their children but that most middle-class families provide adequate care for their children to develop normally, even optimally.

Current conceptions of children and mothers are rooted in the contemporary cultural ethos. Today's child requires less intense parenting to achieve optimum development than the pure Watsonian child. But today's child needs more attention to detail than the pure Gesellian child. Given the continuing concern with children's welfare and the legitimate concern with women's rights and roles, the semi-Gesellian child seems a good image of the 1980s offspring. There are no timeless truths here—just appropriate ways to rear children in our own times and places.

Models of proximal, behavioral effects of parents on their children, and vice versa, have reigned virtually unchallenged over models with more distal determinants. It has been unpopular to consider the possibility that most of what we observe about parent-child effects may be determined more by the parents' and child's characteristics, especially by genetic variation in their behaviors, than by mutual behavioral influences. Recently, a new wave of theories have (re)appeared.

Although mute on the subject of genetic variation in behavior, both Lerner (1979, 1983) and Wachs (Wachs & Gruen, 1982; Wachs & Gandour, 1983) propose theories of organism-environment interaction, in which people evoke and experience different environments, based on their own physical and behavioral characteristics. Lerner's and Wach's views are discrepant from the prevailing psychology-of-main-effects, in which everyone is affected in the same way by the same, observable events. I predict that their views, forecast by Bem (Bem & Allen, 1974; Bem & Funder, 1978) will become the dominant psychological lens of the 1980s. Psychological studies will focus on person-situation interactions and invent new "facts" about the differential effects of environments on individuals.

A more radical challenge to current theory focuses on genetic variation in behavior. Consider the possibility that the behavior of most parents has little influence on their children's intellectual development. In the absence of neglect and abuse, perhaps children merely develop, according to their own genetic blueprints, in a supportive environment. Ronald Wilson's (1978, 1983) description of a genetic blueprint for intelligence, following Waddington's idea of a growth path, accommodates such "facts" quite well. According to Wilson, the ebbs and flows of intellectual development from infancy to adolescence can be far better explained as features of individual patterns of growth than as the result of any pattern of environmental influence.

Perhaps, parents respond to the characteristics of their children in the only way they know how, and bright parents have more benign strategies than others. If one entertains this model, then parental behaviors are more or less correlated with those of their children as an epiphenomenon. If the parents' own characteristics are expressed in their parenting techniques and transmitted to their children genetically, then a correlation of parent and child behaviors can arise without any proximal influence of parents on their children or vice versa. This is an extreme view of the nature of parent-child effects, but is it any more one-sided than other theories based entirely on proximal variables? I do not think so.

The theory of genotype → environment effects that Kathleen Mc-Cartney and I presented (Scarr & McCartney, 1983) predicts that children's intellectual and social experiences are largely of their own making. Different people at different ages evoke and actively seek different experiences. In this view, what people experience cannot be indexed by observations of environments to which they are exposed. What people experience in any given environment depends on what they attend to, how much they learn, how much reinforcement they feel they get for what behaviors. And what they experience in any given environment is a function of genetic individuality and developmental status. The additional lens in this theory is one of genetic individuality and developmental program that changes the active genotype across the lifespan, which in turn changes the experiences that people glean from their environments.

The plausibility of theories such as those put forth by Lerner, Wachs, Wilson, and Scarr and McCartney will be judged by the community of psychologists. We will discuss and judge their plausibility, not on any grounds of logical priority but on how consonant such theories are with our historical times and cultural places. To be plausible they must correspond to other theories of reality and be coherent by the criteria of plausibility. In addition, theories must make sense — intuitively — to both scientists and policy makers to have any impact within science or politics.

Making Plausible Models

The remarkable feature of this process of making plausible models is that the same observations that were "facts" under the previous theories easily become different "facts" under the new. "Facts" about people's robust individuality in the face of different environments are invented by naturists from the same observations that have been used by nurturists to make "facts" about people's exquisite sensitivity to variations in their environments. One theory's china child can be broken by any environmental blow. Another theory's child is a magic plastic who bends under unusual environmental pressures but does not break. Rather than suffer permanent damage from bad experiences, this child resumes her shape when released and continues to function without too many dents. Each set of "facts" is theoretically determined — necessarily so. The nature of the scientific enterprise is to persuade one's colleagues of the plausibility of one's theoretically derived "facts."

IMPLICATIONS FOR SCIENCE AND INTERVENTION

Some may fear that the constructivist view of science leads to nihilism and withdrawal from efforts to improve human lives. Are we immobilized by the realization that what we perceive are "facts" of our own making? Can we no longer be agents of change, because we recognize the boundedness of our own constructions? I do not think that such pessimism is required by this view. Rather, I think we are obligated as citizen-scientists to make the best theories we can and to act on their implications for intervention.

A constructivist view does imply that diagnoses of problems and intervention strategies are products of their own times and spaces in the same way as any other construction of reality. But that does not make them bad or useless. On the contrary, interventions, like other forms of reality, must be theory-driven and must have contexts — social, cultural, and historical. Without a theory of the importance of early experience, we would not have had Head Start. If we had a theory about the importance of adolescence, we might have Teen Start — probably not a bad idea, if it had occurred during the baby boom glut of adolescents on the school and job scene a few years ago. With a theory about the fixity of genetic traits, we had the Eugenics Movement. With a theory about genetic variability of a probabalistic sort, we could have more respect for individual differences in behavior. With this theoretical lens, we would blame parents less for their problem kids and praise them less for their wonderful ones.

If we had recognized the time-boundedness of the father-absence problem, we might have acted differently toward black families and teen-age mothers. Intervention programs with mother-child families were driven by deficit theories. What if we had viewed father-absent families as blessed by mother-child integration, without the distractions of a sexual partner for mother? (Could this be another kind of sainthood?) Could one conceive of the mother-child household as beneficial for children?

Suppose we had considered alternative theories about early experience and the permanence of everyday traumas. We might have spent less time looking for far-flung sequels of temporary maternal separations and more time looking at children's current living conditions. Suppose we thought, like our ancients, that children's sensibilities began at the age of seven. We might have worried less about mother-infant bonding and more about the emotional effects of peer group rejection. If we had considered more distal variables, we might have put more money into effective public transportation than into job training for the unemployed, who could not reach potential jobs even if trained. If we had conceptualized the school and job problems of blacks in the 1970s as ignorance of the norms of the majority culture, rather than as racial discrimination, we might have launched second-culture programs rather than affirmative action.

Is the scientific enterprise, then, a cockpit of competing claims? That is one way to look at it. A more positive view is that science has a distribution of ideas that evolve through competition (Toulmin, 1973). The idea of evolution applied to ideas does not imply that a single view will dominate, however. On the contrary, well-adapted populations of animals and ideas are individually variable. There is no need to choose a single lens for psychology when we can enjoy a kaleidoscope of perspectives. In our own intellectual population we should construct the richest account we can of human behavior, which will include variables from several levels of analysis and alternative theoretical accounts. The effectiveness of the theory-spawned interventions will be judged in the same cultural context that generated the theories in the first place. How can we go wrong? Or right?

Let us examine the disadvantages and the advantages of a constructivist view of science and intervention. The disadvantage of this view over the current realism is that one may feel less certan of what one is doing. How can one know what is right, if there is no right? The feeling can resemble the loss of faith in a familiar and comforting religion. Theories make conflicting claims that cause one to have to think and choose—uncomfortable processes for many people. One is thrown onto one's own resources to invent a plausible story in the face of certain ambiguity.

The advantage of this view is that one can make more modest one's claims about the ultimate Truth, which leaves one with less egg on the face when other theories replace one's favorite view. A second and more important advantage is that one can modify one's ineffective attempts to change others' behaviors more easily, because one recognizes that one may have constructed the problem inappropriately for the time and space. It makes easier the invention of other questions and other approaches to a perceived problem.

Fortunately, however, both scientists and policy makers share one big view of mothers and children, as part of the larger social, cultural, and historical context of our times. Few today believe that children are born bad or that they require Watson's draconian regime to develop into normal adults. Most policy makers and scientists see mothers and children as having a close, not symbiotic, relationship; children as self-propelled maturers; and the environment as playing an important but supporting role in the drama of development. Therefore, arguments concern variations on the commonly held beliefs of the larger culture.

The implication of this appraisal of science and policy is that arguments about intervention strategies are constrained within discussable limits. Conversations about what to do to improve people's lives can take place within a framework of shared images of the nature of mothers and children. This is not to say that important variations are not present in the current cultural ethos. Indeed, vigorous advocates of infant programs compete for funds with others who advocate adolescent interventions, parent education, and other means by which they optimistically intend to change people's lives for the better. But no one of any influence calls for public whippings of little children, isolation of babies from their mothers, the reinstatement of child labor, or a return to the orphanages of yesteryear. No, our current views of children preclude such popular ideas from the past.

Any given theory and the intervention it launches are of limited usefulness — limited by the sociocultural time and space in which they occur. Why should we expect more? Why should we want more? The major disadvantage of realism in science is that it deludes believers into searching to discover facts that exist apart from theories about them. It seems to me much harder to be flexible in one's theory construction and intervention strategies if one believes there is a reality out there to be mirrored (Rorty, 1979). A constructivist view frees one to think the unthinkable, because one's view of "reality" is constrained only by imagination and a few precious rules of the scientific game. The problem is to persuade one's scientific peers and policy makers that one's variation on the cultural theme is the wave of the future. Because we *do* construct science and reality, we might as well give it breadth, depth, and some excitement.

ACKNOWLEDGMENTS

1. My appreciation to Carol Fleisher Feldman for many stimulating discussions on these and many other issues.

Research on mother-child interaction is part of a larger project in collaboration with Kathleen McCartney, J. Conrad Schwarz, Elizabeth Hrncir, Barbara Caparulo, David Furrow, Conchita Ming, the staff of the Child Development Project of Bermuda, and Dr. Michael Radford, consultant to the project.

The 125 families from whom the data were collected are 94 percent of all eligible families with young children in the parish of Devonshire, a representative sample of Bermudian families. Additional information about the project can be obtained by writing to Dr. Scarr for the government report.

Research on mother-child interaction was supported by the Bermuda government, Ministries of Health and Social Services and Education. I am grateful for support during the writing of the chapter from the W. T. Grant Foundation and the Center for Advanced Study at the University of Virginia.

REFERENCES

Bem, D. J., & Allen, A. (1974). On predicting some of the people some of the time. The search for cross-situational consistencies in behavior. *Psychological Review, 81*, 506-20.

Bem, D. J., & Funder, D. C. (1978). Predicting more of the people more of the time: Assessing the personality of situations. *Psychological Review, 85*, 485-501.

Borstelmann, L. J. (1983). Children before psychology: Ideas about children from antiquity to the late 1800's. In P. Mussen (Ed.), *Handbook of child psychology, Vol. 1*, (pp. 1-40). New York: Wiley.

Cain, L. F., Levine, S., & Elzey, F. F. (1963). *Cain-Levine Social Competency Scale*. Palo Alto, CA: Consulting Psychologists Press.

Cairns, R. B. (1983). The emergence of developmental psychology. In P. Mussen (Ed.), *Handbook of child psychology, Vol. 1* (pp. 41-102). New York: Wiley.

Cohen, D. J., & Dibble, E. (1974). Companion instrument for measuring children's competence and parental style. *Archives of Psychiatry, 30*, 805-15.

Cott, N. (1977). *The bonds of womanhood: "Woman's sphere" in New England, 1780-1835*. New Haven: Yale University Press.

Degler, C. N. (1980). *At odds: Women and the family in America from the Revolution to the present*. New York: Oxford University Press.

Ehrenreich, B., & English, D. (1979). *For her own good: 150 years of the experts' advice to women*. New York: Doubleday/Anchor Press.

Erikson, E. H. (1950). *Childhood and society*. New York: Norton.

Feldman, C. F., & Hass, W. A. (1970). Controls, conceptualization, and the interrelation between experimental and correlational research. *American Psychologist, 25*, 633-35.

Gesell, A. (1928). *Infancy and human growth*. New York: Macmillan.

Kessen, W. (1965). *The child*. New York: Wiley.

Lamb, M. (1982). Parental behavior and child development in non-traditional families: An introduction. In M. Lamb (Ed.), *Non-traditional families: Parenting and child development*. (pp. 1-14). Hillsdale, NJ: Erlbaum.

Lasch, C. (1977). *Haven in a heartless world: The family besieged*. New York: Basic Books.

Lerner, R. L. (1979). A dynamic interactional concept of individual and social relationship development. In R. L. Burgess & T. L. Huston (Eds.), *Social exchange in developing relationships*, (pp. 271-305). New York: Academic Press.

_____. (1983). *Developmental psychology: Historical and philosophical perspectives*. Hillsdale, NJ: Erlbaum.

Loftus, E. F. (1979). *Eyewitness testimony.* Cambridge, MA: Harvard University Press.

Rorty, R. (1979). *Philosophy and the mirror of nature.* Princeton: Princeton University Press.

Rosenberg, R. (1982). *Beyond separate spheres: Intellectual roots of modern feminism.* New Haven: Yale University Press.

Rothman, S. M. (1978). *Woman's proper place.* New York: Basic Books.

Scarr, S., & McCartney, K. (1983). How people make their own environments: A theory of genotype - environment effects. *Child Development, 54,* (2), 424-35.

Scarr, S., & Weinberg, R. A. (1978). The influence of family background on intellectual attainment. *American Sociological Review, 43,* 674-92.

Toulmin, S. (1973). *Human understanding.* Chicago: University of Chicago Press.

Wachs, T. D., & Gandour, M. J. (1983). Temperament, environment, and six-month cognitive-intellectual development: A test of the organismic specificity hypothesis. *International Journal of Behavioral Development, 6,* 135-52.

Wachs, T. D., & Gruen, G. E. (1982). *Early experience and human development.* New York: Plenum.

Watson, J. D. (1928). *Psychological care of infant and child.* New York: Norton.

Wilson, R. S. (1978). Synchronies in mental development: An epigenetic perspective. *Science, 202,* 939-48.

_____. (1983). The Louisville twin study: Developmental synchronies in behavior. *Child Development, 54,* 298-316.

Wolfenstein, M. (1963). Fun morality: An analysis of recent American child-training literature. In M. Mead & M. Wolfenstein (Eds.). *Childhood in contemporary culture,* (pp. 168-78). Chicago: University of Chicago Press.

Zuckerman, M. (1975). Dr. Spock: The confidence man. In C. E. Rosenberg (Eds.), *The family in history,* (pp. 179-207). Philadelphia: University of Pennsylvania Press.

6

Differential Stresses of Family Life on Mothers and Fathers

Alfred L. Baldwin, Clara P. Baldwin,
and Robert E. Cole

INTRODUCTION

Professor Cofer's chapter outlined the history of attempts to describe human nature (see Chapter 2, "Human Nature and Social Policy"). One of the motives for such descriptions was to understand how societies were held together. Human nature for some was a list of individual egocentric motivations that had to be governed in some way in order for society to function effectively. For others, human nature included some prosocial motivations that contributed to social stability, as well as more self-interested motives. For some people society functioned to transmit and enforce the rules to the common people who constituted the governed. Democracy allowed for a certain amount of reciprocal influence of the people upon the central government through elections, but was in daily functioning a top down set of influences.

During this same time the family was pictured as a sort of miniature society in which the father alone (or the father and mother jointly) was the government who were responsible for the behavior of the children and for their socialization into responsible adults who could play their roles in the social system. The influence was tacitly assumed to be unidirectional from parents to children, or teachers to children.

With the growth of sociology, the society was pictured as a social system which encompassed many kinds of reciprocal influences. In principle every person influenced every other person. In order to describe the stability of this social system over generations, the elements of the social system were not actual people but rather social rules that were taken by different people over time but the basic description was the relations of various social roles to each other. This study of social systems has a long, distinguished history. Sometimes the social system was described as the relationship between roles, like the role of predatory hunter is related to the role of food gatherer or farmer. Generally the hunter role was held by males, the food-gatherer role along with child rearing was held by females. At other times the sociologist investigated the properties of the social system, like class or caste differentiation, autocracy or democracy, or the separation or unification of the roles of priest and doctor. These global wholistic descriptions of the system as a whole versus the detailed interplay of each role with every other role is a continued controversy. The so-called "group mind" (see Allport, 1968) represents conception of the society as a sort of organism.

In developmental psychology the influence of the parents was tacit-ly assumed to be unidrectional until the 1950s, when reciprocal in-fluences of each person on each other person in the family began to be described. Sears (1951) in his presidential address in 1951 described the mutual influence of the members of a dyad on each other and how it could lead to a stable relationship of cooperation, or dominance-submission. Bell (1968) in his landmark article described how each of known facts about the consequences of child rearing could be described as the influence of the parent on the child or equally well as the influence of the child upon the parent. Aggressive parents produce aggressive children, or aggressive children provoke aggression in the parents. By now this reciprocal influence of each person on each other person is thoroughly accepted. It is easy to demonstrate the existence of reciprocal influences, but it is very difficult actually to map the sequence of reciprocal influences that trace it to a stable equilibrium outcome.

Whether these reciprocal influences result in a behavior adapta-tion of two people to each other, but with each person maintaining a relatively constant temperament, or whether these reciprocal in-fluences actually change the personalities of the people involved rather than merely their behavior is also an open question.

Having accepted reciprocal influences of one person on another, developmental psychology still must face such questions as whether a complicated set of interpersonal exchanges is the most profitable way to look at the developmental process, or whether it would be more pro-fitable to describe families in terms of system variables like degree of differentiation of subsystems (Minuchin, 1974) and power differential within the family, (Parsons & Bales, 1955). Is the family a group of in-teracting individuals or is it a kind of organism or can it sometimes be thought of as one and sometimes the other?

Of course, the same problem arises in the arguments over reductionism in the functioning of the individual. The behavioral acts of the organism were described and understood long before the same acts could be described in terms of communication and interactions of neurons or in terms of a computer program.

My own belief (ALB) is that both the interpersonal-interactional approach and the family system approach are useful ways to conceptualize the process of child development, but that developmental psychology has not given enough effort to exploring the possibilities of the family system approach.

The marital system is certainly upset or disequilibriated by the birth of a first child, and takes some time to reach a stable equilibrium in which the various roles are stabilized, and family interaction is reasonably rewarding to mother, father, and child (which is described in system terms as low frequency of disagreements and conflicts). This family system is again disequilibriated by the child learning to locomote and new family policies must be developed to achieve a new equilibrium and requires a new qualitatively different equilibrium to become stable. The same process can be described in interpersonal terms, and perhaps the causal sequence can be detailed with the development of new methods of investigation, but the system approach does put the process into a different perspective and may indeed be a profitable conceptualization in which the family rather than the child is viewed developmentally.

If developmental psychologists have tended to be individualistic rather than wholistic in looking at the child's life, Roger Barker is clearly an exception. His description of the difference between large schools and small schools in terms of the scarcity of performers for the many roles in a small school leading to pressure on pupils to take many roles rather than specialize is a very illuminating picture that would be hard to achieve without a social system approach to the school (Barker & Gump, 1964). His picture of the availability of community settings to children of various ages and the differences between Midwest in the United States and in England is another example of how the social system approach leads to new and interesting perspectives (Barker & Schoggen, 1973). The values of both approaches can be appreciated without getting entangled in the reductionist argument about which perspective is the ultimate explanation.

Nearly 20 years ago we began our first study of mother-child interaction. There were three reasons for beginning this study. One was the belief that the influence of one person on another must be mediated by the minute by minute interaction between them. A second was that we had a dream of an efficient method of recording and coding interpersonal interaction through a computer program. The third was a discontent with some of the assumptions underlying compensatory education for young children from lower class black homes. A number of people at that time pictured the lower class home as very impoverished in terms of parent-child interaction.

It was said, for example, that in the typical lower class black home there was never more than a minute of continuous interaction between the mother and the child. The basis for intervening was to compensate for the impoverishment of the home. We believed that we needed much more data about the mother-child interactions in a homelike atmosphere to determine empirically whether and how much lower class homes were impoverished. Much of the work on mother-child interaction up to that time had been in laboratory situations or in such settings as a doctor's waiting room.

Accordingly we set up a free play situation in the laboratory but told the mother that we wanted her to play with the child as if they were at home with time free to play together. We compared lower class black mothers from Harlem (who were part of Frank Palmer's sample) with a sample of upper middle class mothers recruited from around the Washington Square area. Many of them were professionals or wives of professional men. We found that there were significant differences between the two groups in the complexity of the grammer used by the mother in talking with the child, but that there were no differences in the amount of interaction or in the warmth of the interaction (Baldwin & Baldwin, 1970).

Thus we began the study of family interaction partly in response to a social policy that was being implemented at the time and a policy we mistrusted.

While we were collecting these mother-child interactions, we had an opportunity to observe also the interactions of mothers with children who were seriously disturbed. These children were enrolled in a therapeutic nursery school at the Department of Psychiatry at the Cornell Medical School. We found the interactions of these mothers and children strikingly different from those we had observed in the other two samples.

By this time we were at Cornell in Ithaca. Dr. Norman Garmezy was at Cornell on a year's sabbatical and during that same year he was working with a group of psychiatrists and psychologists who were planning a prospective study of a small group of families in which the mother had been hospitalized for schizophrenia. This small study was funded by the Scottish Rite Foundation and was headed by Dr. John Romano, the chairman of the Department of Psychiatry at the University of Rochester. They invited us to participate in the study and to study the mother-child interaction of these children at genetic risk for schizophrenia. We were to use our narrative method for recording the interaction of the mother and the child. Then Lyman Wynne accepted the chairmanship of psychiatry at Rochester and convinced us that we should try to use our methods to study the interactions of the mother, father, and the child. He had been studying families of schizophrenic patients at NIMH and was eager to make the family rather than just the mother the focus of the investigation at Rochester. We found to our very great pleasure that we could narrate the interactions of a three-person group without getting hopelessly lost and that our computer program for coding the interactions could be modified to count the interactions of every dyad in the mother-father-child triad.

This has been the history of our involvement in the University of Rochester Child and Family Study (called URCAFS for short). We have been part of URCAFS for about 13 years. This publication gives us an opportunity to sit back and view our research from a somewhat detached vantage point and to ask what tacit assumptions may have influenced the design of the research and the interpretation of the findings. In particular we will focus on the tacit assumptions about mothers and fathers that shaped the research project.

Since the first objective of this book, as we understand it, is to put developmental research in a societal and historical perspective, we will begin with a case study of the research project as it evolved from 1970 to 1983. This project was designed collaboratively by developmentalists, psychiatrists, and clinical psychologists and as such is one statement of the thinking of these social scientists regarding mental illness in the 1970s, its causes, and the role of the family in its etiology.

A CASE HISTORY OF THE UNIVERSITY OF ROCHESTER CHILD AND FAMILY STUDY

The University of Rochester Child and Family Study began about 1970 when a research team of a dozen psychologists and psychiatrists began to plan a prospective study of children who were at risk for the development of schizophrenia because at least one of their parents had been schizophrenic. It was not the first such study, but it was one of the early prospective ones and differed from the others in its emphasis upon family interaction as a major variable that might ameliorate or exacerbate the development of psychopathology.

The commitment to a family system viewpoint, was largely due to the influence of Lyman Wynne. He introduced the consensus Rorschach into the project and in that setting the interaction of the mother, father, and all the children was observed. This procedure broadened the small group observed in most family research on schizophrenia from the mother-father-child triad to the entire functional family.

In addition to its emphasis upon family interaction, URCAFS was exciting because it put family research in psychopathology into a prospective framework. There were several prospective risk studies of children but not of families; most family research in schizophrenia had studied families in which the child was already a diagnosed patient; so no one could distinguish between the family patterns that were part of the etiology of the disease and those that were responsive to the children's disturbances.

Another important research objective was to search for behavioral evidence of the child's vulnerability to mental illness. Even the most thoroughly genetic theory does not predict that all children of an ill parent will become ill, just as not all children of a color-blind father are color-blind. The children we studied were at genetic risk in a statistical sense, but not every one of them had the genes for mental illness, whatever they may be. Therefore one objective of the project was to contrast the children of schizophrenics with the children of nonschizophrenics on a battery of psychophysiological and cognitive measures that had been found to differentiate schizophrenic from nonschizophrenic adults. For example, the smoothness of visual eye tracking, and the differential responsiveness to censure and praise. If we could show that the children of schizophrenics were on the average different from those of nonschizophrenics, even in the absence of any overt behavioral pathology, then we might be able to pick out the individual children of schizophrenics who were genetically vulnerable to the disease, and thus be able to target interventions more efficiently.

A third part of our plan was to study the social competence of the child as a major dependent variable. We viewed this as an intermediate outcome, to be sure, but one we could investigate. We knew that there would be a 35-year wait before all the vulnerable children would or would not have developed a full blown psychosis — the risk period being adolescence to middle-age for schizophrenia. At the same time there is plenty of evidence that a certain proportion of mentally ill adults have a long premorbid history of social ineptness, so the intermediate outcome was not irrelevant to the long-term goal of the study.

Finally, we were all intrigued by the idea of the invulnerability of some children. Perhaps some even capitalized on their vulnerability to become creative and innovative. Heston (1966) made a rather casual observation that the children of the schozophrenic mothers he studied, who were not schizophrenic, were more interesting people than the children of the control sample. Even more importantly, we know that some children weather crises with a great deal of strength and even profit from them. Finding the antecedents of this strength in families' functioning was a goal for all of us. Norman Garmezy imbued us with this enthusiasm and he has since built his own research upon the concept of stress resistance.

On the background of these hopes, ambitions, convictions, and enthusiasms, we proceeded to design the actual research project. The objectives of the study put some severe constraints upon the design. If we were to study family interaction, we had to select parents of an intact family — at least at the beginning of the study — who had children of the right age and sex. We selected male children because they were known to be more at risk for childhood disorders in early years than girls. And we selected the ages of four, seven, and ten as transitional ages because of existing developmental literature (Piaget and others).

Next we planned to contrast a group of schizophrenics with a group of families in which one parent had been hospitalized for a neurotic depression. We preferred such a contrast group to a normal control group. They would contrast the presence and absence of genetic factors for schizophrenia and would be more comparable than a normal control group because in both groups a parent had been hospitalized for a psychiatric disorder.

At this point our planning ran afoul of the changing fashion in the diagnosis of schizophrenia. In our final sample of 146 families, 60 of the patient parents had been diagnosed as schizophrenic when they had been hospitalized. But by the time we saw these families and reviewed the hospital records, only 18 met our restrictive criteria for schizophrenia. The differences between DSM II and DSM III also indicate that psychiatrists in general were defining schizophrenia much more narrowly than they did earlier. It was important to be restrictive in the diagnosis to ensure that the child was truly at genetic risk. The trouble was that we could not find enough cases of schizophrenics with an intact family to make a reasonable study — we felt that 30 cases in each cell of our eventual design were about as few as we could live with.

We resolved this problem, not to everyone's satisfaction, by deciding to include families in which a parent had been hospitalized for any psychiatric disorder. For some of us, this shift from a emphasis on schizophrenia to a more general definition of mental illness was a welcome one. Instead of having just one contrast group, we could then set up several different contrasting groups based upon diagnosis. For example, we could contrast families and children of psychotics with those of nonpsychotics, affective disorders with nonaffective disorders, etc. The only diagnoses that were excluded were traumatic psychoses due to brain injury, mental illness primarily due to drugs (including alcohol), and postpartum illnesses, defined as those beginning within six months of the birth of a child. This last exclusion is very interesting for the present discussion because it tacitly presumed that a postpartum illness was some sort of an exogenous biochemical disorder qualitatively different from a functional mental illness and was not a reaction to the psychological stresses of pregnancy, delivery, and the changes in the family introduced by a new baby. In other words, a postpartum psychosis did not involve the same genetic factors as other functional illnesses.

Looking back upon this decision, we think the study should have included postpartum illnesses in the sample. In clinical interviews with the URCAFS mother patients, nearly half of them traced their original disturbance back to the birth of some child even though the key hospitalization occurred after the six-month deadline.

The scarcity of eligible subjects also created an imbalance in the sex of the patient parent. The decision to include father patients as well as mother patients in the sample had been debated. There were arguments for making the sample as homogeneous as possible, and perhaps some remnant of the belief in the schizophrenigenic mother still influenced our thinking. Once we decided to include father-patient families, however, we expected to equalize the numbers of father and mother patients. We knew that the general sex ratio among the major mental illnesses was about equal, although for particular diagnoses we expected to find sex differences.

If we had had an unlimited supply of subjects, we would undoubtedly have worked until we were able to equalize the cells representing the two sexes and what we now view as a puzzling discrepancy would not have occurred. The restrictive criteria, particularly for patients with intact families and at least one male child of the proper age made it difficult to fill all the cells in the design. Table 6-1 shows the final numbers of subjects in the six cells of the design.

We could find by all our efforts only one-third as many father as mother patients. When we kept finding more mother than father patients, psychiatrists furnished us with several answers. One was merely that the fact that the sex discrepancy was not expected. Mednick Mura, Shulsinger & Mednick (1971) had found in a consecutive sample of 9,006 patients that there were about twice as many schizophrenic mothers as schizophrenic fathers.

TABLE 6-1. Number of Families Categorized by Age and Sex in the URCAFS Sample.

Sex of Patient	Male Children Age 4	Male Children Age 7	Male Children Age 10	Total
Mother	28	38	42	108
Father	9	9	20	38
Total	37	47	62	146

Source: Compiled by authors.

Three explanations of the discrepancy were proposed. One was that women with schizophrenia found it easier to become married and to have children than men patients. Schizophrenics tend to be withdrawn and passive. Withdrawn and passive women could be courted, married, and impregnated, but withdrawn and passive men would not have the initiative to take their normal active role in wooing a woman.

A second related explanation also made the sex difference an artifact for our research. Women marry earlier than men and tend to develop schizophrenia later than men. So they have a longer period of effective fertility than men. This explanation tacitly assumes that people do not have children after they become schizophrenic and that schizophrenia is permanent. Both of these explanations are applicable only to schizophrenia and in the end schizophrenics formed only a minority of the URCAFS sample.

The third explanation was that women are hospitalized with less severe illnesses than men. Therefore, while the incidence of the illnesses were equal, women were hospitalized more frequently. Because men were the breadwinners in the family, psychiatrists hesitate longer before hospitalizing them. And men, themselves, because of their position in the family, resist hospitalization more than women. Along with this argument was the tacit assumption that hospitalization for women might often be a refuge from their troubles, rather than being a treatment for an actual illness. The fact is, however, that there was no difference in the severity of mental illness at the time of the hospitalization of the mother and father patients in the URCAFS sample.

Whatever the reasons, we did not seriously entertain the hypothesis that this inequality of the mothers and fathers reflected a genuine psychological phenomenon that deserved explanation, or that the discrepancy reflected greater stress on mothers than on fathers in the family interaction. It is very curious that we did not entertain this hypothesis since we were especially interested in family interaction. Had we been alert to the situation, we could have built in codes for family interaction that would possibly measure how stressful the interaction was on the mother and the father. In our narrations we frequently noticed how in some families the patient is ignored and almost prevented from interacting with the child while in other families the patient is actively encouraged to enter into the interaction. While we were careful to include measures of parental support for the child, we did not seriously try to measure how much support each parent received from the spouse and the children.

Review of the literature on sex differences in hospitalization for mental illness

Walter Gove (Gove & Tudor, 1973) reviewed 17 investigations on sex differences in hospitalizations and in psychiatric visits and had concluded that unmarried men (single, widowed, or divorced) were more likely to be hospitalized than unmarried women, but among the population of married people, wives were more likely to be hospitalized than husbands. Marriage is a protective factor for men, but the opposite for women. He did not report on any differences between wives and mothers.

Gove proposed three factors to account for the prevalence of psychiatric hospitalization for married women: (1) That married women generally have only one major role, child care and housekeeping, while men have an occupational role outside the home which may ameliorate a family-centered disturbance. If this reason is valid, then we would expect an even greater discrepancy between the fathers and mothers of intact families than between husbands and wives in general. (2) That housekeeping and child rearing is frustrating because it is not socially prestigious. In addition, child rearing is not a well-structured job. It is unclear and never-ending. (3) That even if the woman is employed outside the home, her job is probably less prestigious and less well rewarded than a man's. One might add that for many women success on her job is less important for her self-esteem than men's occupational success is for his self-esteem.

One implication of Gove's arguments is that men's mental illnesses are more likely to be connected with difficulties in his job, while women's are more likely connected with homemaking and child rearing. Indeed our findings confirm that hypothesis. Since job difficulties for men are not concentrated on the group who are fathers, psychiatric hospitalizations may be spread evenly across all men. With women, however, the frustration of homemaking and child rearing are concentrated on wives and mothers. Thus our large discrepancy between fathers and mothers of intact families may reflect the special vulnerability of mothers.

Gove's article in 1973 initiated a lively controversy about sex differences in psychopathology. Dohrenwend and Dohrenwend (1969) had concluded that there were no sex differences in the frequency of mental illness apparent either in hospital admissions or in community surveys. The dispute between Gove and the Dohrenwends revolved around the definition of mental illness. Gove defined mental illness as "a disorder that involves personal discomfort (distress, anxiety, depression, etc.) and/or mental disorganization (as indicated by confusion, thought blockage, motor retardation, and in the more extreme cases, by hallucinations and delusions) that is not caused by an organic or toxic condition." This definition includes neurotic disorders and functional psychoses, transient situational disorders, and also psychophysiological disorders, that is, somatic symptoms that appear to be the consequence of emotional tension. What are not included are the personality disorders because personality disorders are not accompanied by distress. The symptoms are ego-syntonic rather than ego-alien. Personality disorders are more frequent among men and neuroses are more frequent among women so Gove's definition seemed to load the dice to find more mental illness among women. There seems little point in arguing about whether or not a personality disorder is a mental illness, but nevertheless Gove (1972) and the Dohrenwends (1972) argued vehemently about it in a couple of articles.

Gove's main point, and this seems to be confirmed, is that marriage is more protective to men than to women. Gove's review found that the hospitalization rate for married women is higher than for married men, but the rate for single women is lower than for single men. He found similar results for widowed and divorced people as for singles. More recent studies have not confirmed the results for divorced men and women, but in general the protective effects of marriage for men is established; whether marriage actually makes women's lives more stressful or merely no better than the unmarried state is not clear.

Durkheim in his classic study of suicide (1951) calculated a *coefficient of preservation* as the ratio $\frac{\text{Rate for unmarried}}{\text{Rate for married}}$. A large ratio indicates that the effect of marriage is protective. Gove reviews the literature on rates of suicide; mortality involving overt social acts (like homicide or automobile accidents); mortality connected with socially approved drugs (for example, lung cancer and smoking); and mortality from diseases requiring prolonged medical treatment (tuberculosis, for example) as well as mental illness. For all of these categories the coefficient of preservation is higher for men than women. On the contrary the coefficient is not different for diseases like leukemia, which Gove argues is not affected much by psychological state.

There are three alternatives to the hypothesis that these findings reflect actual sex differences in the frustrations and pressures on married people. One is the selection hypothesis, that less fit people have a lower probability of getting married. Second is the social labeling hypothesis, that women are more likely to be labeled ill. Third is the hypothesis that women are more expressive and show their symptoms, seek help, and label themselves ill more easily than men. Without going into all the arguments about these hypotheses they do not seem sufficient to account for all these data.

Whether women have a higher rate of mental illness in general is not clear, but there seems little disagreement that they have a higher rate of depression. Klenman and Weissman (1980) report data about depression in women.

The URCAFS sample were intact families with at least one child. One hypothesis is that it is not so much marriage as motherhood that is stressful. There are very little published data that bear on this question. One study by Kramer (1967) indicates that admission rates to psychiatric facilities are higher for parents (both husbands and wives) with large families than families with no children or only one child. While mothers had higher rates than fathers, the difference between living with children and not was about the same in the two sexes. Radloff (1980) reports higher depression scores for parents living with children in contrast to those having no children or not living with their children.

Several studies of life satisfaction have found that life satisfaction is higher after children grow up and leave home. Pauline Sears (1979), in her follow-up on the women in Terman's sample, found that among gifted women without a career, those without children reported higher life satisfaction than those with children.

If we take one representative figure from Kramer, the rate of hospital admissions for mothers living with two or three children is 257 per 100,000 while the comparable rate for fathers is 237 per 100,000. Thus, if we sampled 100,000 of each sex, we would have a discrepancy of 257 to 238, which is much smaller than we found in URCAFS, 106 to 38. It is also much smaller than Mednick reports (1971). In his sample of 9,006 consecutive births in a Copenhagen hospital he found 57 schizophrenic mothers and 26 schizophrenic fathers. Probably Kramer's figures are more representative, but the discrepancy between the rates for mothers and fathers is generally confirmed.

Let us turn now to another set of findings about the ratio of hospitalized mothers and fathers of children who are mentally ill. Mothers are more frequent than fathers. For example Rutter (1966) began with a sample of 922 children who had come to Maudsley Hospital for any reason in 1955 or 1959. Of these 839 were disturbed and 147 were nondisturbed. Of the 839 disturbed children, 137 had parents with mental illness and of these 48 had been first seen at Maudsley. There were two comparison groups, taken from 200 adult patients at Maudsley. Of these, 137 have children 17 or younger who were well and 31 had children who were known to have psychiatric difficulties.

In these three groups, the ratio of mothers to fathers was 72.9 percent and 77.4 percent for the group with disturbed children and 50.9 percent for the group with undisturbed children. Rutter (1966) concludes that "psychiatric illness in the mother was therefore more often associated with disorder in the child than was illness of the father."

We now hypothesize that in the average family the mother occupies a more central position than the father. We use the term "central" in the Lewinian topological sense. A central region is the one region that is most easily influenced by what happens anywhere in the system and one whose influence is felt most by all the other regions in the system. Thus, we would hypothesize that in the average family the mother occupies a central position. She influences other people more and what they do influences her more. Thus she is both more vulnerable and more influential than the father in the usual family. Obviously this position would be modified if the mother had a career outside the home or if the father carried a great deal of responsibility for homemaking and child rearing.

Further, we hypothesize that the effect of mental illness on the parent is to reduce the patient's resources for interpersonal interaction and to make them withdraw from interaction. Other factors may also reduce a person's resources, like carrying a full-time job and running the house at night, worrying about financial difficulties, or being preoccupied by one's dissatisfaction with the marriage.

Further, but much more tentatively, we hypothesize that when the father is ill, his spouse tends to be supportive and tries to involve him in family interaction while when the wife is ill, the spouse tends to isolate her and exclude her from family interaction.

Relevant data from URCAFS

The first assessment of the family in URCAFS involved a total of 40 hours and included a clinical assessment of the patient parent, a clinical assessment of the child, extensive psychological testing of the child, and a number of psychophysiological measures and cognitive measures of the child to test hypotheses about the differences between children of a schizophrenic parent and children of parents with other diagnoses. We will not report on any of these psychophysiological or cognitive measures.

Then we observed family interaction in a number of different settings. They will be described shortly, but first let us describe the major variables describing the patient.

Diagnosis.

The patient parent was diagnosed on the basis of the hospital records, and a psychiatric interview. The diagnosis is made at the time of URCAFS but it applies to the patient at the time of hospitalization, or more accurately, at the time when he/she showed the most severe symptoms. The diagnosis does not describe the patient as observed in URCAFS. At that time he or she might show no mental illness, residual symptoms that have subsided since the most acute phase of the illness, or the patient might be flagrantly ill at the time of URCAFS.

The assessment of mental health of the patient.

The instrument used to give the patient's mental status a quantitative score was the Global Assessment Scale (Endicott, Spitzer, Fleiss & Cohen, 1976). This scale runs from 0 (least healthy) to 100 (most healthy). A score of less than 40 usually indicates a disturbance that requires hospitalization. A score of less than 60 or 70 indicates some clinically apparent problem. A score of 100 is an ideally healthy person, a tower of strength and fount of wisdom. The GAS score is judged on the basis of the hospital records and the clinical interview. Three GAS scores are available for each patient, one for the time of hospitalization, a second for the time of URCAFS 1, and a third at the time of the follow-up (URCAFS 2).

The Chronicity of the illness.

If the patient showed an absence of symptoms for a two-year period, the illness was classified as episodic, in some cases only a single episode. If the patient was never free of symptoms for any two-year period after the key hospitalization he was classified as chronic. Patients with chronic illnesses tended to have children who functioned less well than patients with episodic illnesses. We found that in the

URCAFS study the actual number of hospitalizations was not a useful measure of chronicity.

Measures of the child's functioning.

Teacher's rating.

Each child was rated on a battery of scales by his teacher and his score was recorded relative to the mean of the entire class. The teacher did not even know which child in her class was an URCAFS child, so these scores are completely independent of any URCAFS evaluation. She might or might not be informally aware of the parent's disturbed behavior, if the parent was overtly disturbed at that time.

Peer rating.

Again each child in the entire class containing an URCAFS child was rated by the other children on a sociometric instrument. The mean peer rating is again made relative to the rest of the children in the class.

COPE scores.

The clinical assessment of the child was based upon an interview with his parents, a study of his psychological tests, and an interview with the child. The clinical judgment was made on a nine-point scale by an experienced clinician after a review of all this information.

Family Interaction Measures

We will report findings from two different observations of the family. First is the observation of the mother, father, and index child in a 30-minute free play session. Each session was narrated by one of the three of us and was coded and scored by a computer program that analyzed the narration. The most useful measures that come from the free play observations: (1) The amount of interaction between each parent and the child. (2) The balance of initiations, that is, whether the parent made many more initiations to the child than the child did to the parent, whether the reverse was true or whether the ratio of initiations was close to equal. (3) The expressions of warmth by each parent to the child. Balance, that is, a proportion near 50 percent and the warmth are both related positively to the child's functioning in school and to COPE.

A second observation of the family interaction was in a consensus Rorschach, where the family had to come to an agreement about the percepts found in a Rorschach card (Card Ten to be specific). All the children living at home above the age of three were included in the consensus Rorschach. We also have observations of the mother and father alone in a consensus Rorschach task — called the spouse Rorschach.

From an analysis of the transcript of the interaction we derived some useful measures: the activity level of the family; the equality of participation of the parents and the children; expressions of positive and negative affect; a measure of communication deviance for each parent devised by Singer and Wynne (1966) and adapted to the consensus task; and a measure of healthy communication, (Wynne, Jones & Al-Khayal, 1982) which is not just the flipside of communication deviance.

All of these measures were repeated in a follow-up after three years and in addition we have information about rehospitalizations of the patient during the three-year period, and information about separations or divorces during the three-year period.

The first finding relates to the hypothesis that mental illness results in a withdrawal from family interaction. The patient parent has a lower rate of interaction with the child than the spouse. This difference is highly significant, it is larger if the patient had been hospitalized for a psychotic rather than a nonpsychotic illness, it is larger if the patient had been more recently discharged from the hospital and it is higher if the patient's GAS is less than 70.

This finding is remarkable in some ways because these patient parents were not necessarily symptomatic at the time we observed them. One of the early surprises, for everybody on the project, was how healthy the families appeared in the free play and the consensus Rorschach. We observers were deliberately blind to the sex of the patient and the diagnosis when we observed the family, and we tried to judge which spouse had been the patient and what had been the diagnosis. Unless the patient was clearly on medication, we were generally quite unable to do so. Even the most sophisticated psychiatrists were frequently unable to recognize the patient from a tape of the family interaction. In one instance a whole psychiatric seminar thought the mother had been the patient when in fact the father had been flagrantly schizophrenic less than a year previously. I can think of only two instances in which the patient actually looked blatantly ill in free play interaction.

Dr. John Romano impressed us with the fact that an active psychosis need not seriously damage parent-child relationships. One mother had been actively hallucinating for 20 years, listening to voices tell her that her children were not hers, that she had water rather than blood in her veins. Yet she was raising a family of children reasonably competently. It is as if her schizophrenia was a disability laid on her, with which she was coping in much the same way as other people cope with blindness or cerebral palsy.

As we said, it was a surprise to us how much the URCAFS sample of families looked like samples of normal families with which we were familiar. There were tremendous differences between families on many dimensions and we thought we could make some judgment about how well the child would function in school, but we expected somehow that if a parent was currently diagnosable it ought to be apparent in family interaction as emotional liability, or hostility, or overdependence or complete withdrawal. We saw all of these characteristics in some families, but they were not apparent in one parent rather than the other. For example, in one family the father was somewhat withdrawn, but not completely inactive; he participated in the consensus Rorschach. Yet while watching the child play, he described to his wife the answers he had given to the comprehension items of the WAIS. The observer detected suddenly that he was listening to a serious thought disorder.

I think probably we were better able to discern a severe personality disorder than a severe psychosis. We became more aware of just what is meant by ego-alien symtoms, which the person feels are not part of his true self, and ego-syntonic symptoms that are part of the personality but do not seem strange to the patient himself.

Despite our inability to recognize the patient, the difference between the activity level of the patient and the spouse is highly significant. We believe that the presence of psychotic symptoms even if not apparent in symptomatic behavior does tax the person's resources. They use up cathexis and prevent the full cathexis from being invested in family interaction. The schizophrenic mother who was raising her family in the presence of hallucinations was coping admirably with her psychosis, but at a cost and she was less active in the free play than her husband.

There is yet another factor that may play a role in the patient-spouse difference. Perhaps in some families the patient is cast into a patient role and is ignored or even excluded by the family. This role may last longer than the illness.

Regardless of the reasons, the patient is on the average significantly less active than the spouse in the free play interaction — although this is not true of every patient. On the average, the mother patients in particular were much less active than their husbands (86.4 vs. 116.90 social interactions between parent and child), while the father patients were only slightly less active than their wives (98.4 vs. 109.0). In the URCAFS sample, this created a statistically significant sex difference, independent of the patient-spouse difference. There may be such a sex difference, particularly in an experimental session in which the father is having a special opportunity to interact with his son. Some mothers deliberately set up the situation to encourage the father to play with the child.

On the other hand in a later study of normal families, that is, ones in which neither parent has been hospitalized, we found no difference between the rate of interaction of the mother and the father with the child. So perhaps the sex difference in patient-spouse differences is reflective of the different roles in the family played by the mother and the father patient.

The Relation of Mother's and Father's Mental Health to Family Conditions

In order to consider the hypothesis that the mother patient is more central to the family than the father patient we will examine the correlations between family variables and the patient's mental health, and also the patient's rehospitalization.

The mother's mental health as measured by the Global Assessment Scale is correlated significantly with the following variables:

1. Family warmth in the free play ($r = .19 \ p > .03$).
2. Family warmth in the consensus Rorschach ($r = .17 \ p > .05$).
3. Healthy communication in the consensus Rorschach ($r = 17, p > .05$).
4. The degree to which all the family members participate actively and equally in the consensus Rorschach ($r = .18 \ p > .04$).
5. The children's social functioning as described by the parent in a clinical interview ($r = .19 \ p > .04$).
6. The child's rating by the teacher ($r = .35 \ p > .0002$).
7. The child's social functioning judged by peers ($r = .32 \ p > .003$).
8. The child's COPE score ($r = .15 \ p > .001$).

In contrast the father's mental health is related only to the following variables. Because the number of fathers is small, there are many fewer significant correlations but the following list includes all correlations greater than 25, significant or not.

1. Negative affect expressed in the consensus Rorschach ($r = -.34 \ p > .02$).

2. The amount of communication deviance in the consensus Rorschach ($r = -.29, p > .04$).
3. The child's COPE score ($r = .62$ $p > .001$).

These correlations may reflect causation in either direction or a relation due to some third variable. These findings are consistent, however, with the hypothesis that the mother's mental health is more responsive to the functioning of the family, while the father's mental health is a function of other variables such as his job.

We have informal evidence from URCAFS that support this interpretation. Nearly half of the mothers who were hospitalized trace the disturbance that culminated in hospitalization to the birth of one of their children. If we had admitted mothers with a postpartum illness, this proportion would have been even higher. On the other hand, more of the fathers trace their disturbance to job-related variables. Since few of the mother patients were employed outside the home they did not implicate job-related variables.

These data also support the hypothesis that the mother's mental health as reflected in her behavior in the family is also more influential, but this interpretation is not supported as strongly. The actual behavior of the mother in the family interactions is not strikingly more related to the child's functioning outside the family than is the father's behavior. The father's activity and warmth in the free play are related more to the child's school functioning than the mother's, although both are significant. In the consensus Rorschach the mother's interaction tends to be more strongly related to the child's functioning than the father's. The difference between the parents is much less clear, however, when actual parental behavior rather than parental mental health is investigated.

We are inclined to the hypothesis that the mother's mental health is more influenced by family variables than the father's, but not that her behavior is more influential upon the child's social competence than the father's.

There are similar trends when the patient's rehospitalization is studied. Thirty-five of the URCAFS patients were rehospitalized during the three years following the initial assessment. Of these, 30 were mothers and 5 were fathers. This translates into about 14 percent of the fathers and 28 percent of the mothers. The difference is not statistically significant, however.

Fathers' rehospitalization is largely a function of his illness. Psychotics are rehospitalized more frequently than nonpsychotics ($p > .08$). Rehospitalization is also a function of chronicity of the illness ($p > .06$). The only relation with family interaction is a positive correlation with the mother's warmth ($r = .35, p > .07$) in free play and ($r = .51, p > .01$) in the family Rorschach.

Mothers rehospitalization however is less related to the illness itself—neither psychosis nor chronicity are significantly correlated. But the mother's rehospitalization is significantly correlated with the child's psychiatric rating ($r = .40, p > .03$), with her communication deviance ($r = .31, p > .01$) and her balanced activity with the child ($r = -.31, p > .01$).

We can also examine the correlations of the mother's and father's mental health scores at URCAFS 2. Father's mental health at follow-up is significantly related to his mental health at initial evaluation ($r = .46, p > .03$). His rating is stable but not related to any of the measures of the family or children at URCAFS 1.

The mother's mental health at URCAFS 2 however is not only related to her URCAFS 1 score ($r = .48, p > .02$) but also to the child's social functioning at URCAFS 1 and to the support she receives from the father at URCAFS 1. These latter correlations are all significant even after the correlation between URCAFS 1 and URCAFS 2 has been partialled out.

As a final note and an indication of the substantial differences between the interactions of mother- and father-patient families, it should be noted that in the father-patient families, the fathers' rehospitalization is positively related to his wife's warmth ($r = +.35$) and his mental health at follow-up is negatively related ($r = -.32$) to his wife's expression of warmth. This is the exact opposite of what is found in the mother-patient families.

We believe that two very different processes are underway in the mother-patient and the father-patient families. In mother-patient families the mother responds directly to her children and her husband. She is a barometer of the family; everyone's functioning improves and declines together. In the father-patient families we speculate that the mothers act to compensate for their husband's illness. Her warmth is a response to his illness and thus negatively related to his later mental health.

Manfred Bleuler (1978) from some of his data suggests much the same hypothesis. He found that a well mother of a sick father is better able to hold the family together than a well father of a sick mother. We also observed several instances of the well mother actively supporting her patient husband, while most of the cases in which the spouse seemed to be rejecting the patient, were instances of a sick mother.

Sex Differences in Divorce.

Since we studied these families three years after the original assessment we know whether they were separated or divorced during those three years. We have this information on all 145 families. We can examine some of the relationships between the assessment variables and later separation.

Based on Blueler's findings, we might expect the divorce rate for mother-patient families to be higher than for father-patient families. There is such a difference, (23 percent to 15 percent) but it is not significant.

In fact, the relationships are much more complicated. The expected difference in divorce rate occurs only among the families in which the patient at the time of URCAFS 1 is functioning very well (GAS more than 70).

We will not seriously advance an explanation for these findings. The interpretation depends very much on the initiation of the divorce. Our hypothesis would suggest that men divorce their wives when they are the sickest, that is, the most burden, but that the women patients who recover and function well may get out of the marriage that was so frustrating.

Obviously, divorce involves numerous factors and we are in no position on the basis of our data to draw even tentative conclusions.

All of these findings are statistical ones, searching for homogeneous correlates of the sex of the patient parent. While they are interesting, they do not seem to capture what we found most interesting in the analysis of the URCAFS data.

After we had collected all of the data blindly in order not to contaminate our raw data with information about the sex, diagnosis, and mental health of the patient parent, we then met regularly with other members of the URCAFS team to review the video tapes and the research records of individual families. These families were selected to represent some family pattern. Some of the families were extreme on particular measures, others were families in which the patient parent was very ill but the child was developing very well, or the reverse.

These case studies were very revealing of the diversity of patterns representing the family's coping or failing to cope with the stress of the parental illness, with economic hardship, or with marital discord. Some of the children seemed to develop a real empathy and understanding of the parental illness; others seemed to adapt by distancing themselves from the ill parent; still others were constantly fearful of the recurrence of the illness. One child said, "Every time I see grandma's car in front of the house I am afraid that mom had to go back to the hospital."

In several families an adaptation was found through joining a religious group, often a fundamentalist one. In some cases the child seemed to have been spared the more serious consequences of the parental illness because of the presence of some stable, warm figure, perhaps the grandmother, perhaps someone else. John Romano spoke of these children as having a "saving grace."

Throughout these careful studies of individual families we kept feeling that our statistical analyses had failed to capture many of the factors that played an important role in the development or the disintegration of the family. Most of the case studies did confirm our general findings—that is why the findings were statistically significant—but every family showed some idiosyncratic characteristics that greatly influence the outcome.

With hindsight, we felt that we could have included other variables which would have captured some of the variance, but in many instances we knew that we would have had such a small subgroup—that joined a religious sect, for example—that even the introduction of such a variable would not have lead to an improvement in our statistical predictions.

In Chapter 8, "Affects, Ideology, and Scripts in Social Policy and Developmental Psychology," Rae Carlson writes about the role of personology in the study of families. Our clinical analyses of these families points to the importance of incorporating this type of analysis into the scientific study of family functioning. Some of the methods for objectively analyzing individual lives might prove valuable if we had complete enough records. These methods search for statistical regularities in the individuals' reactions to events over a long period of time. But even such methods seem inadequate for capturing much of the richness of the family development that is obtained through careful case studies.

CONCLUSIONS

The first conclusion is the well-known one that it is difficult to search a body of data for answers to questions that the investigators did not have in mind when they collected it. While we did not completely neglect the mother-father relationship in the analysis of the data, we were clearly focused upon the relations between the parents and the child. It would be possible to reanalyze the video tapes of all these interactions and extract variables that would measure such variables as the support of one parent by the other and parental encouragement of the children's support for the other parent. We could count a number of triadic interactions, like the mother telling the child to obey the father or the mother suggesting to the child that he ask the father to help him. I think we could estimate how much the family of each patient viewed the patient as sick or weak or vulnerable. It would have been better, of course, to incorporate those questions in the interviews with the mother and father.

A much broader question, however, is how much our data are dated by the fact that these families were recruited nearly 15 years ago. We deliberately chose a sample of white, middle-class, intact families because that group was not represented in the literature on developmental psychopathology. Yet the sample might have been very different were we to assemble it in 1983 instead of 1970.

Our original sample was a group of quite traditional families. The father was the major source of support, mothers took care of the children. There were very few professional women. Some of the women before marriage had had traditional women's jobs like nursing, social work, and teaching school but there were no doctors, lawyers, professors, or business executives among the sample of mothers. This might be partially the result of the fact they had been mentally ill, but among father patients there were many examples of professional men. In fact it seems likely that even in 1970 the women in the URCAFS sample were more homemakers than the general population of mothers at that time.

The contrasting normal group which we have briefly mentioned was recruited in 1980. This new sample has a higher educational level of mothers with professional jobs and two-career families. Whether it is the time at which they were recruited, or the fact that there was no mental illness that makes the difference is impossible to say.

But we believe that if we recruited the sample today we would find more families where both parents were working, more families in which the wife established a career before becoming a mother, more families in which fathers carry a real share of the homemaking and child-rearing responsibility.

If one speculates about the stresses of family life on families nowadays, we can certainly picture a diverse sample of families. Some are traditional, that is, the father is the sole breadwinner. In some families the mother is employed but without any great personal investment in the employment but in some families there are genuinely two careers. We can also picture a variety of patterns for homemaking and child care. In some the traditional role division is maintained, in some there is a genuine attempt to share homemaking and child-rearing responsibilities. Rarely, even in the 1980s, is there a real role reversal.

What would be the consequences in these various patterns for stress and mental health of the father and the mother? There is evidence that single-parent families are very stressful on the parent who is usually the mother, but economic well being must be partialled out of the stress of a double role. We might expect, however, that two-career families, if the traditional role division is maintained in the home will be even more stressful upon the mother than the traditional family pattern. If there is a genuine sharing of both the breadwinning and home-making roles, then we could expect more equality of stress on the two parents, but the stress on each parent might either be reduced because of the sharing of responsibilities or increased because of the divided loyalties to family and career. At any rate a study of family interaction in these various modern patterns of family life would be fascinating and rewarding.

IMPLICATIONS FOR SOCIAL POLICY

Let us assume, for the moment, that the conclusions of the empirical findings are correct—something that we would not be willing to accept on the basis of such a small set of findings—then what are the implications for social policy?

We could all agree that it would be better if mothers did not become mentally ill because of the frustrations of family life. On the other hand it is not obvious that every pattern of family organization that reduced the stresses of family life on the mother would be desirable. Probably the mother would find family life less stressful if she were less emotionally invested in her family, but there is evidence that that emotional investment is essential to the development of a socially competent child, the maintenance of the marriage, and also the well being of the mother.

Furthermore many mothers, despite the fact that child rearing is not all a bed of roses, would not trade their way of life for one without children. The frustration of family life is to some degree the *other side of the coin* from the satisfaction of family life; to some extent the two go together.

In addition, the vulnerability of mothers to disturbances in family life is partly a consequence of the mother's greater influence on the family. It would not necessarily improve the situation for the mother to be more peripheral in family affairs.

On the other hand, it is not necessarily true that the only way a mother can be influential in family life is to be vulnerable to mental illness. It is the counsel of despair to believe that all the ills in a situation are necessary correlates of the satisfactions and that therefore nothing can be done to improve the situation.

Parsons and Bales (1955) in their analysis of the dynamics of socialization in the family recognize that socialization of the child inevitably produces frustrations for the child, for the parents, and for other children in the family. To change a child's behavior from an immature pattern to a more mature one requires the child to relinquish some satisfactions that he enjoys. This is necessarily frustrating to the child. The child's frustration and resentment in turn makes the parent's interaction with him less than rewarding to the parent, particularly to the one on the firing line. In American society this person is usually the mother. Hetherington (1979) colorfully describes this persistent nagging over minor irritations that mark the interaction of children and their divorced mothers as "being bitten to death by ducks" and both child and parent suffer from it. Patterson's analysis (1975) of the family interactions of aggressive children emphasizes how parent and child are both architects and victims of this interactive process.

Parsons and Bales (1955) describe some of the mechanisms they have found in the functioning of social systems that help the family system adapt to these strains. For one thing the child is not only frustrated but rewarded for becoming more grown up as well as reproved for being babyish. The parent who is primarily responsible for the socialization—usually the mother—is emotionally supported by the other parent and perhaps even some of the older children in the family. Parsons and Bales report that in small groups there is a period of celebration after the successful completion of a task which reestablishes a feeling of social solidarity. In the family this might take the form of some sort of recognition when the child, for example, goes for a week without wetting the bed.

Parsons and Bales describe these adaptive mechanisms of the social system as if they occurred almost automatically; in a well-functioning family they probably do. From the point of view of the individuals in the family, however, they are not automatic. They are the expressions of the feelings of empathy with the child by the mother and the empathy of the father with the mother and his recognition of the difficult position she is in. In some families however these corrective adjustments do not occur. In such families the child may not get any reward for complying with the parents' demands for maturity or the mother may not get any support to help her through the difficult time. The Parsons and Bales formulation of the dynamics of socialization makes it very clear how the mother, if she is primarily responsible for child rearing, is subject to stress and strain that may lead to pathological reactions.

If there were some sort of social policy that would ensure the existence of these supports it would certainly improve the quality of family life, but this picture of the complexities of the adaptation process makes it clear how difficult it would be to conceive of a social policy that would operate effectively. Obviously one cannot legislate humane and empathetic feelings toward other people.

It might seem that if the parents were jointly responsible for child rearing some of these problems might be alleviated, but the trouble is that there are many different ways that a family can function effectively. In some families the father and the mother may indeed share child-rearing responsibilities and thus find themselves collaborating in solving the problems that arise. But in other well-functioning families, the mother carries the major responsibility for child rearing, but the father supports her firmly in whatever decision she makes. Joint child rearing requires a commonly agreed upon policy if it is to be effective and this may not be easy to achieve. In view of the individual differences among well-functioning families who resolve these problems effectively but in very different ways, we can hardly picture what general across-the-board social policy would be helpful.

The implication of these considerations is that any attempt deliberately to change family life should be undertaken very cautiously because of two considerations: the possibility of unexpected side effects that may be worse than the problem that we are trying to correct and the fact that many different patterns of family interaction can be effective in one family but not in another. There are certain times when the best social policy is no policy at all.

These arguments do not imply that in a particular family in which the burdens of family life are very heavy on the mother or on any other member of the family, there is no wisdom in trying to improve the situation. Very often some change in family policy will produce a real improvement without deleterious side effects and seldom are the unexpected side effects disastrous. Perhaps it will take several tries to bring about the desired result. Changes in the family policy of an individual policy are tailored to the individual family and usually the rewards and problems emerge quickly. Families are very different from each other as we know very well and what works smoothly for one family might be a dismal failure in another family. It is precisely because of these differences among families that a broad social policy change may be ineffective and perhaps even dangerous.

REFERENCES

Allport, G. H. (1968). The historical background of modern social psychology. In Gardner Linzey and Elliott Aronson (Eds.), *Handbook of Social Psychology* (pp. 1-80). Reading, Mass: Addison-Wesley.

Baldwin, A. L., & Baldwin, C. P. (1970). *Cognitive content of mother-child interactions*. Final Report of OE Project No. 6-1341, ERIC No. ED041996.

Barker, R. G., and Gump, P. V. (Eds.) (1964). *Big school, small school*. Stanford, Calif.: Stanford University Press.

Barker, R. G., and Schoggen, P. (1973). *Qualities of community life: Methods of measuring environment and behavior applied to an American and an English town.* San Francisco, Jossey-Bass.

Bell, R. Q. (1968). A reinterpretation of the direction of effects in studies of socialization. *Psychological Review, 75,* 81-95.

Bleuler, M. (1978). *The schizophrenic disorders: Long term patient and family studies.* New Haven: Yale University Press.

Dohrenwend, B. P., & Dohrenwend, B. S. (1969). *Social status and psychological disorder.* New York: Wiley.

————. (1972). Sex differences in psychiatric disorders. *American Journal of Sociology, 181,* 1,447-54.

Durkheim, E. (1951). *Suicide, a study in sociology.* Translated by J. A. Spaulding & G. Simpson. Edited by G. Simpson. Glencoe, Ill.: Free Press.

Endicott, J., Spitzer, R. L., Fleiss, J. L., & Cohen, J. (1976). The global assessment scale. *Archives of General Psychiatry, 33,* 766-71.

Gove, W., & Tudor, J. (1973). Adult sex roles and mental illness. *American Journal of Sociology, 78,* 812-35.

Gove, W. R. (1972). The relationship between sex roles, mental illness and marital status. *Social Forces, 51,* 34-44.

Guttentag, M., Salasin, S., & Belle, D. (Eds.). (1980). *Mental health of women.* New York: Academic Press.

Heston, L. L. (1966). Psychiatric disorders in foster home reared children of schizophrenic mothers. *British Journal of Psychiatry, 112,* 819-25.

Hetherington, E. M. (1979). Divorce: A child's perspective. *American Psychologist, 34,* 851-58.

Klenman, G. L., & Weissman, M. M. (1980). Depressions among women: Their nature and causes. In M. Guttentag, S. Salasin, & D. Belle (Eds.), *Mental Health of Women* (pp. 57-92). New York: Academic Press.

Kramer, M. (1967). Epidemiology, biostatistics and mental health planning. In R. R. Monroe, G. Klee, & E. B. Brody (Eds.), *Psychiatric epidemiology and mental health planning* (pp. 1-26). Washington: American Psychiatric Association.

Mednick, S. A., Mura, E., Schulsinger, F., & Mednick, B. (1971). Prenatal conditions and infant development in children with schizophrenic parents. In I. Goottesman & L. Enlenmeyer-Kimling (Eds.), Differential reproduction in individuals with mental and physical disorders. *Social Biology, 18,* S103-S113.

Minuchin, S. (1974). *Families and family therapy.* Cambridge, Mass.: Harvard University Press.

Palmer, F. H., & Siegel, R. J. (1977). Minimal intervention at ages two to three and subsequent intellective changes. In M. C. Day & R. K. Parker, (Eds.), *The preschool in action: Exploring early childhood programs* (pp. 3-26). Boston: Allyn and Bacon.

Parsons, T., & Bales, R. F. (1955). *Family, socialization and interaction process.* Glencoe, IL: Free Press.

Patterson, G. R. (1975). The aggressive child: Victim and architect of a coercive system. In L. A. Hamenlynek, E. J. Marsh, & L. C. Handy (Eds.), *Behavior modification and families: I. Theory and research, II. Applications and development* (pp. 13-35). New York: Brunner Mazel.

Radloff, L. S. (1980). Risk factors for depression: What do we learn from them. In M. Guttentag, S. Salasin, D. Belle (Eds.), *Mental Health of Women* (pp. 93-109). New York: Academic Press.

Rutter, M. (1966). *Children of sick parents: An environmental and psychiatric study.* London: Oxford University Press.

Sears, P. S. (1979). The Terman genetic studies of genius 1922-1972. In A. H. Parson, (Ed.), *The gifted and the talented: Their education and development.* The seventy-eighth yearbook of the National Society for the Study of Education. (pp. 75-96). Chicago: University of Chicago Press.

Sears, R. P. (1951). A theoretical framework for personality and social behavior. *American Psychologist, 6,* 476-83.

Singer, M. T., & Wynne, L. C. (1966). Principles for scoring communication defects and deviance in parents of schizophrenics: Rorschach and TAT scoring manuals. *Psychiatry, 29,* 260-88.

Walsh, F. (1982). *Normal Family Processes.* New York: Guilford Press.

Wynne, L. C., Jones, J. E., & Al-Khayal, M. (1982). Healthy family communication patterns: Observations in families "at risk" for psychopathology. In F. Walsh (Ed.), *Normal Family Processes* (pp. 142-66). New York: Guilford Press.

III

What Kind of Science Can We Expect to Help Us to Manage Complicated, Changing Social Arrangements?

7

The Family's Changing Past: Myths, Realities, and Works-in-Progress

John Demos

In effect, this chapter is a "report from the trenches" in a field of research that was unexplored, not to say unimagined, as recently as two generations ago. The field is (what has come to be called) "family history." The trenches are as yet only half-dug; hence they are shallow in many spots, ragged along most of their edges, and littered with loose dirt throughout. But rough and unfinished as every part of this seems, it is possible to discern the contours, the proportions, and design of the whole. And since the work is very much ongoing, it is reasonable to look for further progress just ahead. In fact, the field *and* the trenches are swarming with eager diggers, whose enthusiasm alone must count for something.

The diggers, of course, are professional historians, drawn to the lure of new discoveries. They dig for themselves and for each other, but would be pleased to interest a wider audience. In fact, the results of their labors hold real importance for social scientists of several kinds, not least for developmental psychologists. Social science (including psychology) has long maintained a variety of historical assumptions — for example, about household size and structure, and the various stages of the life course — based on intuition, guesswork, or popular folklore. Many of these can now be evaluated in the light of the findings of the new family history. Moreover, a greater historical sophistication may directly assist the "reconstructive" enterprise so evident nowadays in academic psychology (and in the pages of the present volume). Psychology is the study of human beings and human experiences that are themselves in temporal motion. And psychology can ignore this element of motion only to its considerable peril.

A "Map" to the Field of Family History

For a territory so recently brought under investigation, no one "map" can be regarded as definitive. But the map to be presented here aims, nonetheless, for general coverage. And it does so by way of four principal sectors or subdivisions — each of which merits separate consideration.

The first sector one comes to — at least the first that family historians came to — is clearly marked as *demography*. The work in this area began some three decades ago, and has continued without pause to the present day. The initial advance came from a pioneering band of French demographers associated with the so-called Annales school. Their lead was soon communicated to a group of English scholars — the Cambridge Group for the Study of Population and Social Structure — and then, as the news spread farther west, across the Atlantic to the Americas. The result is that we now know a great deal about the demographic contours of family life in virtually every part of modern history, and not a little about the premodern situation as well. We know, for example, all about "mean household size" through a full four centuries of English history. The gist of the story there is a remarkably stable mean of five to six persons per household until the onset of the Industrial Revolution, and a very gradual decline thereafter (Laslett & Wall, 1972).

Actually, mean household size is not by itself a very interesting datum — except, perhaps, insofar as it serves to confute a stubborn piece of historical mythology. Folklore and science have long clung to the notion of the "extended family" — as the allegedly characteristic family form until just a few generations ago. If by "extended" we mean three (or more) generations, including married siblings and their various children, all living under one roof — that has *not* been the shape of Western family life for as far back as the records allow us to see (Laslett, 1965). Instead, the simple "nuclear" unit (husband, wife, and their natural-born children) has always been with us — admitting only of limited add-ons (a servant, an apprentice, and aging grandparent or two) in particular times and places (Demos, 1970). To be sure, many premodern communities supported a density of kin-contacts unknown in our own day; for siblings and cousins and in-laws frequently did inhabit the same village or parish neighborhoods. But not the same household. Thus, if co-*residence* is the defining factor, the concept of "extension" seems misapplied.

Mean household size is the net product of other demographic indexes — age of marriage, frequency of remarriage, rates of fertility and mortality. And the latter hold much interest in their own right. They also hold some surprises for "conventional wisdom" in this area. The present writer can recall his own surprise, in a graduate seminar project 20 years ago (Demos, 1965), upon discovering that most New

England colonists of the seventeenth century married in their mid- to late twenties. (That range has, in fact, been found typical for many other pre-modern populations as well.) He can also recall his astonishment at the sheer longevity of his "Puritan" study sample: nearly 70 years, on average, for those who survived the special health hazards of early childhood (Demos, 1970; Demos, 1978). (In this respect early New England turns out to have been very remarkable; most contemporaneous settings supported a far lower standard [Wrigley, 1969; Tate & Ammerman, 1979].) Other results have been unsurprising, though not unimportant: for example, high rates of fertility (eight or ten completed pregnancies per married couple), and thus (where mortality was not equally high) large complements of children (Demos, 1970; Greven, 1970).

These summary comments can hardly do justice to the richness and complexity of recent research. For, in addition to establishing the quantitative boundaries of family life, demographic analysis has thrown light into some of its most private corners. For example, we can now discover, from evidence of birth spacing and "age specific maternal fertility," the point at which given populations first began to practice birth control (Henry, 1956; Wrigley, 1966; Wells, 1971). This development—a veritable sea-change in family history—is inaccessible to all other methods of study, since the people involved would not ordinarily document their practice in such intimate matters.

Much of this demographic work raises questions of comparative—that is, transhistorical—psychology. To wit: What are the implications, for psychological life, of precontraceptive attitudes? (Perhaps some lessening of internal pressure and conflict?) And what is the impact, on personality development, of growing up in very large families? (More—or less—or simply different—"sibling rivalry"? A diluted experience of the Oedipus complex?) And how might "separation" issues be construed in a setting where death is a common experience for people of all ages and every social station? (A special range of "mourning reactions"? A certain degree of "psychic numbing"?)

It seems necessary to stress that these last are *questions* only, to which demography by itself cannot supply direct answers. There has, in fact, been some tendency among enthusiastic practitioners of the demographic art to leap from numerical *quantities* to psychological *qualities*. Thus, for example, high levels of early-life mortality have led some scholars to infer low levels of parental concern for infants and young children. (The implicit, sometimes explicit, premise is that parents would not allow themselves to become much attached to offspring whose prospects of survival are at all in doubt.) Similarly, rates of illegitimacy and of what demographers call "bridal pregnancy" have been taken as a measure of power relations within the family. In certain communities of eighteenth-century America, 30 to 40 percent of all brides were going to the altar pregnant: that much one can demonstrate by comparing their wedding dates with the birthdays of their eldest children (Demos, 1968). But can one then assume—as some scholars *have* assumed—an absence of "control" by the older generation, and a high degree of "autonomy" in the younger one (Smith & Hindus, 1975)? Prudence would supply a negative answer. And prudence would further suggest that demographic study be seen as setting the stage and not writing the script for the vital inner dramas of family history.

It is to the inner dramas that we must turn next. The division of power, the demarcation of roles and responsibilities: thus the family in its "structural" aspects. Here, too, history unfolds a long and changeable story, which scholars are only beginning to understand. The concept of "patriarchy" has served as an entering wedge. In premodern times, so the argument often goes, *fathers* ruled families with a more or less iron hand. Later (roughly the nineteenth century?) their grip was progressively loosened by all the trends of economic and cultural modernization (Shorter, 1975; Weinstein & Platt, 1969). Most scholars would be willing to accept this very rough model of historical change, but the particulars are so enormously variable that the model by itself does not mean a great deal. "Patriarchy" in relation to whom? and by what means? and to what specific ends? And how does one measure "power" and "responsibility," in the first place? Such questions suggest a need to disassemble the family structure, the better to see its constituent parts. One can study the marital pair—husband and wife—as a structure of power in its own right. One can study parents and children as another kind of structure—with further refinements that distinquish fathers and mothers, daughters and sons. One can even bring grandparents and grandchildren into view, where there are long-term issues of "lineal descent."

With the structural lines at least roughly identified, attention turns to the substantive contexts in which power relations are most fully expressed. Here, too, there is much room for historical flux and change. For example: in many premodern communities inheritance was a vital nexus of power in the family. Fathers might try to constrain the behavior of their maturing children by granting (or withholding) family properties (Greven, 1970). Unfortunately, it is not enough in these matters to study the set phrases of wills and other probate documents; a man who is left out of his father's will may be unusually rich or rebellious, or may simply be living far away. In order to "read" such materials aright, other evidence is needed — evidence on the particulars of that family's experience.

A second flashpoint of power between the generations is — at least, was — the issue of "mate selection." Typically, in premodern times, parents were much involved in the courtship and marital decisions of their grown children. But the picture is easily overdrawn. Few children anywhere were obliged to marry against their personal inclinations; indeed, positive inclination was seen as one of the requisites of a good marriage (but not the only one). In some premodern families parents would initiate a match and seek to bring it to fruition, while the young people involved might exercise a kind of veto; in others, the young initiated and the parents vetoed (Demos, 1970; Morgan, 1966). As time passed, the balance moved strongly in favor of the second pattern — and eventually parental influence might be circumvented altogether (Smith, 1973b). Here, surely, was a power shift of great historical consequence.

And yet it is necessary to sound a note of caution. The closer one gets to the details of power relations within the family, the more complicated — and the less amenable to summary formulas — they come to seem. Consider a specific historical case: one John Dane, born in England in the opening years of the seventeenth century, son of a tailor and himself trained as a tailor, and, in sum, a quite ordinary specimen of premodern humankind. The only *extra*-ordinary thing about Dane is a little autobiographical memoir, which he wrote near the end of his life and which has been fortuitously preserved to our time. Thus we have, in his own words, some revealing information on his relation to his parents.

> Being ... about eight years old, I was given much to play and to run out without my father's consent and against his command. Once when my father saw me come home, he took me and basted [i.e., beat] me. ... My father and mother ... told me that God would bless me if I obeyed my parents, and what the contrary would issue in. I then thought in my heart — oh that my father would beat me more when I did amiss!
>
> When I was grown to eighteen years of age or thereabouts, I went to dancing school to learn to dance. My father, hearing of it, ... told me that if I went he would baste me. I told him that if he did, he should never baste me again. With that my father took a stick and basted me. I took it patiently and said nothing for a day or two, but one morning betimes I rose and took two shirts on my back and the best suit I had, and put a Bible in my pocket, and set the doors open, and went to my father's chamber door, and said "good-bye, father, good-bye, mother." "Why, whither are you going?" "To seek

my fortune," I answered. Then said my mother, "go where you will, God will find you out." This word, the point of it, stuck in my breast; and afterward God struck it home to its head.

I thought my father was too strict . . . I thought Solomon said "be not holy overmuch," and David was a man after God's own heart and he was a dancer . . . [And so] I went on my journey and was away from him half a year before he heard where I was. (There followed a period of some two years when John Dane practiced his trade, on his own, in several different English towns.) But at last I had some thoughts to go home to my father's house; but I thought he would not entertain me. But I went, and when I came home my father and mother entertained me very lovingly.

(In time he left again, and married—no mention of consulting his parents about this—and settled with his bride in still another part of the country. And then, in about 1635, he made the fateful decision to emigrate to New England:) When I was much bent to come, I went to my father to tell him. . . . My father and mother showed themselves unwilling. I sat close by a table where there lay a Bible. I hastily took up the Bible, and told my father that if where I opened the Bible, there I met with anything either to encourage or discourage, that should settle me. I opening of it, . . . the first line I cast my eyes on was: "Come out from among them, touch no unclean thing, and I will be your God and you shall be my people." My father and mother never more opposed me, but furthered me in the thing, and hastened after me as soon as they could (Dane, ca. 1670/1972).

How shall we evaluate this little vignette as an instance of the politics of family life long ago? On the side of "patriarchy" we may count the father's readiness to "baste" his young son for misbehavior (and the son's acceptance of that procedure); the father's assumption that he can prevent his son (by then, 18 years old) from going dancing; and the son's assumption (though by this time he was married and a fully independent tradesman) that he must obtain his parents' consent before moving to America. On the other side—against patriarchy —there is the son's pursuit of his own aims and wishes from a very early age; the son's declaration of independence when (again at age 18) he leaves home to "seek his fortune;" and the clever way in which the son maneuvers around his parents' opposition to his plan to emigrate. (To be sure, he does get a timely assist from the Bible!) Where should the greatest emphasis be placed? This is a question on which reasonable scholars may well disagree.

In fact, power is an especially problematic issue, given the always imperfect record of centuries past. Role, by contrast, is much easier to study. Usually there are some prescriptive materials (for example, laws, sermons, advice books) to indicate the predominant values, and sufficient personal documents to exemplify behavior. Consider productive life, for example. Throughout the premodern world family members (save only the youngest) produced for their common good, in visibly direct and meaningful ways. Of course, most premodern families were rooted to farms, a situation which even today promotes a degree of work-sharing (Demos, 1970; Ulrich, 1982). In early America — as before, our leading case in point — there was some division of labor: men in the "great fields," plowing and planting; women in the orchards and dairies (or indoors by the hearth); older children helping out as needed (mostly, with their same-sex parent). But each could appreciate, could see the contributions of the others; and all could feel the underlying framework of reciprocity. (Moreover, in certain "crisis" periods, for example, the harvest, all worked side by side for days on end.) With the advent of urbanization and modern commerce and industry, this framework broke apart. Men were now "providers," "breadwinners," producers *par excellence* (Dubbert, 1979; Rotundo, 1982). Women were literally domesticated; their role became that of "homemaker" in a newly exclusive sense (Cott, 1977; Bloch, 1978; Degler, 1980).

These developments carried, in turn, important implications for child rearing. In the colonial period the primary parent had been father. Books of child-rearing advice had been addressed to him; the law had preferred him (to mother) in the matter of child custody; and all parties affirmed his superior "wisdom" in understanding and nurturing the young. (Women were considered too irrational and unsteady to take the lead here.) In the nineteenth century the pattern was rapidly, and radically, changed. Father's obligation to "provide" left him little time and energy to nurture (at least in a personal sense). Mother's duties, meanwhile, became virtually all encompassing. ("All that I am I owe to my angel mother": thus a favorite period cliche.) These forms of role separation have continued largely intact to the present day. But with some new winds just now beginning to waft through American family life, it may be instructive to remember the earlier period. Our own forms of fatherhood and motherhood are not writ in the stars or in our genes. All such forms — history reminds us — are cultural inventions. And they, too, shall pass (Demos, 1982).

Consideration of family structure has led, inevitably, to the related topic of gender. And gender itself makes a lively center of study. Indeed "women's history" (so called) has become one of the most lively of all research subfields in the past 10 or 15 years. The substance can be sampled in a plethora of books and articles; the spirit is evident in some of their titles: *A Heritage of Her Own* (Pleck & Cott, 1980); *Clio's Consciousness Raised* (Hartman & Banner, 1974); *The Majority Finds*

Its Past (Lerner, 1979); and so on. But although the spirit is broadly feminist, it is not (for the most part) overtly polemical. And the resultant gains for historical understanding are of the first importance.

The earliest forays in women's history — antedating the recent upsurge — expressed what now seems a rather narrow concern with politics. The origins of organized feminism; the struggle for the suffrage; the activity of women reformers more generally: such were the leading questions (Flexner, 1959; O'Neill, 1969). But as one work led to another, the boundaries widened and the questions deepened. There emerged a rough outline of women's past experience — at least, American women's past experience — which went approximately as follows. In colonial America women were defined as being inferior to men ("He for God, and she for God in Him"); but, practically speaking, they retained considerable scope for initiative and self-assertion. As previously noted, they made important contributions in household agriculture; and some of them also worked as tradespeople, physicians, innkeepers, and the like. They could not vote or be otherwise active in public affairs; but their influence was exerted, was *felt*, in countless informal ways. Then came the nineteenth century, with its massively transformed human ecology — and, for women, a severe loss of status and function (Welter, 1966; Demos, 1974; Demos, 1979). "Homemaking" was a form of domestic imprisonment; "polite culture" meant vapidity; and public life remained (more than ever) off limits. When, at midcentury, organized feminism was born, it expressed an anguished cry from the depths of oppression. And the plot-line of women's history ever since has been a stop and go effort to escape from those depths or, stated in less extreme terms, to push back the limits of traditional constraint.

But this historiographic overview is now being reconsidered, and at least partially revised. Its advocates are charged with having fabricated a "golden age" of women's history (the colonial period) and, concurrently, with having ignored certain positive features of the succeeding period (Norton, 1980; Smith, 1973a). Indeed, recent scholarship very nearly reverses the balance. Colonial women are still seen as "active," to be sure, within the family and elsewhere, but always under the heavy dominance of men. Nineteenth-century women had, at least, a place that was primarily theirs (home), and a vocation that was theirs alone (child rearing); thus within some confines they knew "autonomy" and made the most of it.

The debate thus (too briefly) summarized is still heating up, and will not soon be resolved. One must recognize, however, that "autonomy" has both a social and a psychological aspect. Unfortunately, historians are not always clear about the distinction; too often they stress the former, while ignoring (or misunderstanding) the latter. Indeed, this whole territory quivers with subterranean resonance, some of which links women's history directly with psychiatric history. The first important cohort of psychiatric patients—including Freud's early patients—was composed of troubled women from the "comfortable classes" of the late Victorian era. "Hysteria," "neurasthenia," "breakdown"—whatever the appropriate diagnostic category, their symptoms reflected strikingly on their life situation. The prevalent cultural values declared that women should be submissive, selfless, ceaselessly effective on behalf of others ("ministering angels," in the argot of the time). But *these* women, in their illness, managed to be *in*effective, *self*-absorbed, and tacitly dominant over friends and family members. The illness, in short, seemed to mock the cultural values, and may plausibly be viewed as a form of protest (Wood, 1973; Smith-Rosenberg & Rosenberg, 1973).

Many of these patterns and tendencies can be organized around the concept of "identity." Simply put, women's identity and men's seemed to diverge so radically in the nineteenth century that all human communication across the gender boundary was impaired. Experience differed, of course (again, the work/family dichotomy); but feelings, intelligence, sensibility, and moral inclination also differed in elemental ways. As a result courtship was heavily burdened with anxiety and doubt (Rothman, 1980; Degler, 1980); and women, in particular, underwent a characteristic "marriage trauma" (Cott, 1977). There must have been redeeming, even rewarding, aspects of Victorian marriage in many individual cases; but they are not easy to locate from our own vantage point a century later in time. Sexuality was one part of the problem—cultural standards defined women as "passionless," (Cott, 1978) and the standards were frequently enforced by the surgical procedure of clitoridectomy (Barker-Benfield, 1972)—but it was not the only part. Women expected understanding and sympathy only from other women; together they created what one scholar has called a "female world of love and ritual" (Smith-Rosenberg, 1975). Men did something similar in their own world (substituting "animal energy" for love); and social experience of all kinds seemed to divide on same-sex principles (Rotundo, 1982).

These male/female questions lead on endlessly, and there is no need in the present context to follow their trail any farther. Instead, we turn to age and aging—a topic of equally large importance. For every family is (and was) both a system of gender relations *and* a system of age relations. Power, status, and responsibilities within the family are defined by the second no less than the first.

But in order to put age relations in historical perspective one has to know how the people involved have defined and demarcated the aging process. The verdict of scholars in this area, while still very tentative, has at least an underlying coherence. In general, history has brought a greater and greater differentiation of the life course, and a sharper experience of its constituent parts. One of the earliest and most influential books in all the literature of family history presented a remarkable picture of childhood over time (Aries, 1962). In premodern times childhood was barely recognized as such; young people appeared chiefly as "miniature adults." Only in the seventeenth and eighteenth centuries — and then only in elite groups — did children begin to receive special consideration for their distinctive needs and interests and vulnerabilities. By some accounts, adolescence is an even more recent invention. In fact, it was a famous American psychologist, Professor Granville Stanley Hall, who put adolescence on the map (so to speak) of modern popular culture (Kett, 1977; Demos and Demos, 1969).

But these developmental categories themselves expressed fundamental changes of experience. And the experience is what counted most of all. To some extent, modern adolescence expressed an altered balance of social circumstance — the decline of apprenticeship, the growth of mass public education, the development of new living situations for young people exiting from their families of origin (Kett, 1977; Katz, 1975). But also there was an innerlife aspect — the growth of "identity diffusion" (in Erik Erikson's terms) in the face of ever-widening life choices.

The later parts of the life course are also historically variable; recent scholarship has, for example, produced a boomlet of studies on the history of old age (Achenbaum, 1979; Demos, 1978; Fischer, 1977; Stearns, 1977). But for present purposes it seems best to hold the focus on childhood and, in particular, on child rearing. We have already noticed the matter or responsibility for child rearing — the shift in the balance between fathers and mothers. But what of the goals and methods, and finally, the outcomes? Historians have been much intrigued by these questions, too, though somewhat handicapped in their source materials. (Often enough one finds abundant evidence of prescription, but precious little of practice [Mechling, 1975].) Still and all, certain broad trends do come clear. In early America child rearing was framed by the doctrinal standards of evangelical religion. "Original sin" was associated with all of humankind — and not least with its youngest specimens. Infants came into the world as carriers of a "diabolical" tendency, and right-thinking parents must react accordingly. The tendency was identified with "pride" and "self," and above all with "will." Thus the advice-literature urged the "breaking" and "beating down" of will, those were the favorite verbs, from the earliest possible age (Demos, 1970; Greven, 1977).

It took many generations for such advice to disappear altogether; but by the early nineteenth century the emphasis, and certainly the tone, had shifted. Children of that era were viewed as being morally neutral, or even "innocent." "Nurture," not will-breaking, became the touch stone of the advice-literature; parents were urged to mold their young by the "gentle arts of persuasion," and by their own good example (Wishy, 1968; Degler, 1980). In fact, the ends of child rearing had changed along with the means. There was a new and growing emphasis on qualities of independence, resourcefulness, initiative—a whole expressive mode. Only thus would a young person be prepared to seize the main chance and "go ahead" in the open society of modern America. At the same time, the same authorities stressed the need for an inner "compass" that would hold behavior within morally acceptable bounds.

Translated into the language (and concepts) of our own time, the nineteenth century seems to have replaced an old child-rearing regime based on shame with a new one based on guilt. Parents in the colonial period had frequent recourse to scolding, humiliation, and edicts of temporary banishment. (The famous "Puritan" preacher Cotton Mather wrote as follows about his own practice: "The first chastisement which I inflict for an ordinary fault is to let the child see and hear me in an astonishment, and hardly able to believe that the child could do so base a thing. . . . [And] to be chased for a while out of my presence I . . . make to be looked upon as the sorest punishment in the family" [Mather, ca. 1700/1911; Demos, 1970].) Nineteenth-century parents, by contrast, stressed the hurt given to others—especially to *themselves* —by the child's misbehavior.

Moving right along, one comes to a third major area of "trench-digging" within the larger "field." To be sure, it is not always recognized as a separate area by the diggers themselves, and it does adjoin (overlap?) some of the turf previously described. Yet it should be distinguished from the others as clearly as possible. And it should be identified, in big, bold letters, as "emotional experience"—or, more simply, as "affect."

The failure to identify this area properly has meant that historians have not studied it with much care or effectiveness. Indeed they have *assumed* and *inferred* more than they have studied. And what are their reigning assumptions? First, the affective experience was *generally* impoverished in the past; second, that families, in particular, knew only a fraction of the emotional rewards that we look for (and sometimes find) in our domestic life today; and, third, that individuals possessed little capacity for emotional sharing with others. Premodern marriage—so the argument goes—was a matter more of "convenience" and "instrumental advantage" than of loving care. And premodern child rearing was full of indifference, callousness, and outright brutality. In this regard the reigning view is a "progressive" view: family life, over time, has (allegedly) been getting better and better (Shorter, 1975).

And yet, one wonders. Indeed one wonders more about this part of the work of family historians than about any other. To be sure, it is not difficult to find evidence that appears, by the light of our own values, to support the progressive view. But do notice the qualifier: "by the light of our own values." The larger issue here may be illustrated *via* a particular aspect of the progressive view — the aspect that has to do with attitudes toward children. "A very large percentage of the children born prior to the eighteenth century, writes one scholar, "were what would today be termed 'battered children'" (Stone, 1977). "The history of childhood," declares another, "is a nightmare from which we have only recently begun to awake" (deMause, 1975). And how have such conclusions been reached? Here are some pieces of evidence and inference, which serve to exemplify the larger *corpus*.

- Parental reference to children in diaries, correspondence, and other personal documents from premodern times was sparse, brief, sometimes laconic. Evidently this reflected an attitude of profound indifference to the fate of one's own offspring.
- Two children, within a single family, were sometimes given the same name (usually after the older one had died). This implies a lack of individualized attachment to either one.
- Premodern child rearing included, among its favored techniques of discipline, whipping, threats of death and damnation, invocation of ghosts, goblins, witches, and the like. There was, then, no appreciation of the tender sensibilities of the young.
- A reliance on "child labor" (most shockingly, during the early phases of the Industrial Revolution) was well nigh ubiquitous. Here we observe an attitude not just of indifference but of rank exploitation.
- In at least some places, at some points in history, infanticide seems to have been practiced, even "accepted," on a fairly broad scale. This evinces a callousness of the most extreme sort.
- In certain premodern settings, for example, those associated with "Puritanism," infants were viewed as inherently corrupt; and (as noted previously) parental duties were framed in terms such as "breaking the (child's) will." Hence the underlying disposition toward children was unfriendly, to say the least.

Such numerous and varied materials seem at first glance to offer powerful support for the nightmare view of the history of childhood. Yet a second (longer) look gives reason for pause. Personal documents, for example, are probably the wrong place to look for signs of affect toward children; for premodern diarists and correspondents did not often write about *any* sector of their affective experience. The practice of naming new born children for deceased siblings may have reflected a deep sense of loss—and a corresponding wish for "replacement." Much of premodern child rearing does indeed seem harsh by our standards; but it was not incongruous, and certainly not capricious, given then-prevalent views of human nature and society. (Moreover, the chill undercurrents in traditional fairy tales may have served the most basic developmental needs of children; such at least is the argument of the psychoanalyst Bruno Bettelheim in his recent and fascinating book *The Uses of Enchantment* [1976].) Child labor was, before the Industrial Revolution, a relatively benign affair. Admittedly, the development of the factory system introduced new and dangerous elements; but the involvement there of children was (historically speaking) of limited duration. The practice of infanticide appears to have been closely associated with illegitimacy; in many of the more fully documented cases, it was the desperate recourse of unmarried mothers faced with both material privation and social stigma. Finally, the beliefs that emphasized the inborn wickedness of children also furnished hope for their redemption; in a sense, parental repressiveness would redound to the eternal benefit of the "little sinners."

Taken altogether, these considerations underscore the importance of context, in the evaluation of any given piece of social behavior. The overall demographic regime, the material facts of life, the prevailing system of beliefs and values, the intrinsic limitations of the evidence itself; all this and more must be carefully weighed in the interpretive balance. Almost certainly, similar questions could be raised about other parts of family history (for example, the marriage relation). But the larger point is already clear. Family historians have much work to do in the area of affective experience. And the work they have done already may be seriously flawed.

With demography, structure, and affect each noticed in their turn, one large territory yet remains. In a sense, all the issues discussed thus far have a point of reference *in*ternal to the family (its size and shape, its distribution of power and responsibility, its emotional qualities). And, in the same sense, what is left to discuss has an *ex*ternal reference: the family viewed from the standpoint of its individual members, on the one side, and of the larger community, on the other. How, in short, are we to construe the overall pattern of relations between the family and its constituency as history moves along?

This is, of course, an immensely large and complicated question, with as many different answers as there are family historians. The answer presented here is one of the many: a three-stage "model" of continuity and change, based entirely on research in American history, though applicable at least in part to other Western countries as well. It should, in any case, flag important issues which could be followed right across the board.

In colonial America—stage one of the model—family life was notable most especially for its manifold interconnections to the life of the wider community. The boundaries between families, and the boundaries that separated family and village, family and church, family and state, were rather thinly drawn. One crossed back and forth with relative ease and great frequency. The *functions* of the family, for individuals and also for the community, spanned a very broad range. The family was a school, in which children received learning of all kinds; a hospital, in which the sick were cared for; and (by the same principle) an old-age home, an orphanage, a poorhouse, even a penitentiary, and so on. "A family is like a little church, or a little commonwealth," wrote a well-known seventeenth-century preacher. Indeed the premodern family *was* a commonwealth—the basic cell of group life, from which all other social organisms were fashioned (Demos, 1970). Thus an apt summary description for it might be, simply, *the family as community*.

In the nineteenth century, as the inside aspects of family life were altered, so, too, was its relationship to society at large. Of course, society itself was massively reorganized by all the forces of modernization; farms and villages yielded steadily to the growing dominance of industrial cities. The urban family was a tightly bounded unit, a unique and carefully articulated portion of social space. Domestic life was set off from "the world" in the minds of countless new urban-dwellers and, it would seem, in their experience as well. The world (that is, factories, offices, public places of all kinds) was boisterous, chaotic, menacing; by turns the family was, or should be, orderly, peaceful, stable, nurturant. In short, the one setting reversed the qualities and values of the other (Jeffery, 1972). "Home" became idealized, sentimentalized, an object of enormous psychic investment. Ironically, home was losing some of its ancient *social* functions—to schools and to a whole panoply of formal institutions. But as foil to the world, as buffer *against* the world, it seemed more vital and "functional" than ever. And our caption for this second stage can be fashioned accordingly: *the family as refuge*.

A good deal of these two earlier patterns has survived into our own time. We tend still to view families as "building blocks" for the larger community, and we still seek refuge in our families from the slings and arrows endured elsewhere. And yet the temper—the inner meanings—of family life has altered once again. In fact, the context has altered, too: experience outside the family seems (on balance) less dangerous and disordered, but *more* flat, routine, monotonous. Thus we look to family life for a kind of compensatory stimulation; we want excitement and "growth," an antidote to the blahs of "mass society." Families must, above all, provide the setting for vibrant personal encounters: hence this caption for stage three, our own stage: *the family as encounter group.*

As noted at the outset of this essay, the research in family history is very much ongoing. No single question can be considered as finally resolved, and new questions are popping into view all the time. Nonetheless the results so far have considerable shape and structure; and at several points they refute, or revise, well-known elements of conventional wisdom. Moreover, they set some limits around what all of us (whether historians, psychologists, or simply concerned citizens) may reasonably expect of our future. Is the family likely to transform itself with something radically new and different, or even to disappear entirely? Not likely, given its impressive record of historical durability. Might gender roles alter such that parental and household responsibilities are no longer predominantly assumed by women? Quite possibly, considering the variable patterns, in this matter, of the past several centuries. Will childhood itself wear a different aspect (for example, more "hurried," as one recent prognosticator has put it) in times to come? Yes, insofar as childhood responds to cultural circumstances; but probably no, where innerlife development is concerned.

To raise these questions is to spotlight the unceasing traffic between our past, our present, and our future. And it is also to conjure up another kind of traffic — one that crosses the boundaries of disciplines, like history and psychology. From such imaginative journeys we all stand to profit.

REFERENCES

Achenbaum, A. (1979). *Old age in the new land: The American experience since 1790.* Baltimore, MD.: Johns Hopkins Press.

Aries, P. (1962). *Centuries of childhood: A social history of family life.* (R. Baldick, trans.). New York: Alfred A. Knopf.

Barker-Benfield, G. J. (1972). The spermatic economy: A nineteenth century view of sexuality. *Feminist Studies, 1,* 45-74.

Bettelheim, B. (1976). *The uses of enchantment: The meaning and importance of fairy tales.* New York: Alfred A. Knopf.

Bloch, R. (1978). American feminine ideals in transition: The rise of the moral mother, 1785-1915. *Feminist Studies, 4,* 98-116.

Cott, N. F. (1977). *The bonds of womanhood: Woman's sphere in New England, 1780-1835*. New Haven, CN.: Yale University Press.

──────. (1978). Passionlessness: An interpretation of Victorian sexual ideology. *Signs, 4,* 219-36.

Dane, J. (1972). A declaration of remarkable Providences in the course of my life. In J. Demos (Ed.), *Remarkable Providences: The American culture, 1600-1760.* (pp. 80-88). New York: Braziller. (Originally published, ca. 1690.)

Degler, C. N. (1980). *At odds: Women and the family in America from the revolution to the present.* New York: Oxford University Press.

deMause, L. (Ed.). (1975). *The history of childhood.* New York: Psychohistory Press.

Demos, J. (1965). Notes on life in Plymouth Colony. *William and Mary Quarterly,* 3rd series, *22,* 264-86.

──────. (1968). Families in Colonial Bristol, Rhode Island: An exercise in historical demography. *William and Mary Quarterly,* 3rd series, *25,* 40-57.

──────. (1970). *A little commonwealth.* New York: Oxford University Press.

──────. (1974). The American family in past time. *The American Scholar, 43,* 422-46.

──────. (1978). Old age in early New England. In J. Demos and S. Boocock (Eds.), *Turning points: historical and sociological essays on the family* (pp. 248-87). Chicago: University of Chicago Press.

──────. (1979). Images of the American family, then and now. In V. Tufte and B. Myerhoff (Eds.), *Changing images of the family* (pp. 43-60). New Haven, CN: Yale University Press.

──────. (1982). The changing faces of fatherhood: A new exploration in American family history. In S. H. Cath, A. R. Gurwitt, and J. M. Ross (Eds.), *Father and child: Developmental and clinical perspectives* (pp. 425-45). Boston: Little-Brown.

Demos, J., & Demos, V. (1969). Adolescence in historical perspective. *Journal of Marriage and the Family, 31,* 632-38.

Dubbert, J. L. (1979). *A man's place: Masculinity in transition.* Englewood Cliffs, NJ: Prentice-Hall.

Fischer, D. H. (1977). *Growing old in America.* New York: Oxford University Press.

Flexner, E. (1959). *A century of struggle: The woman's rights movement in the United States.* Cambridge, MA.: Harvard University Press.

Greven, P. J., Jr. (1970). *Four generations: Population, land and family in Colonial Andover, Massachusetts.* Ithaca, NY.: Cornell University Press.

──────. (1977). *The Protestant temperament: Patterns of child-rearing, religious experience, and the self in early America.* New York: Alfred A. Knopf.

Hartman, M., & Banner, L. (1974). *Clio's consciousness raised: New perspectives on the history of women.* New York: Harper and Row.

Henry, L. (1956). *Anciennes famillies Genèvoises.* Paris: Mouton.

Jeffery, K. (1972). The family as utopian retreat from the city. *Soundings, 55,* 21-41.

Katz, M. (1975). *The people of Hamilton, Canada West.* Cambridge, MA.: Harvard University Press.

Kett, J. (1977). *Rites of passage: Adolescence in America, 1790 to the present.* New York: Basic Books.

Laslett, P. (1965). *The world we have lost.* New York: Charles Scribner's Sons.

Laslett, P., & Wall, R. (1972). *Household and family in past time.* Cambridge, Eng.: Cambridge University Press.

Lerner, G. (1979). *The majority finds its past: Placing women in history.* New York: Oxford University Press.

Mather, C. (1911). Some special points relating to the education of my children. In W. C. Ford (Ed.), *The Diary of Cotton Mather,* Massachusetts Historical Society, *Collections,* (pp. 534-37.) *7,* 7th series. (Originally published, ca. 1700.)

Mechling, J. (1975). Advice to historians on advice to mothers. *Journal of Social History, 9,* 45-63.

Morgan, E. (1966). *The Puritan family: religion and domestic relations in seventeenth-century New England.* New York: Harper and Row.

Norton, M. B. (1980). *Liberty's daughters: The Revolutionary experiences of American women, 1750-1800.* Boston: Little-Brown.

O'Neill, W. L. (1969). The woman movement: Feminism in the United States and England. Chicago: Quadrangle.

Pleck, E. H., & Cott, N. F. (1980). *A heritage of her own.* New York: Doubleday.

Rothman, E. K. (1980). *"Intimate acquaintance": Courtship and the transition to marriage in America, 1770-1900.* Unpublished Ph.D. dissertation, Brandeis University.

Rotundo, E. A. (1982). *Men and masculinity in 19th century America.* Unpublished doctoral dissertation, Brandeis University.

Shorter, E. (1975). *The making of the modern family.* New York: Basic Books.

Smith, D. S. (1973a). Family limitation, sexual control, and domestic feminism in Victorian America. *Feminist Studies, 1,* 40-57.

_____. (1973b). Parental power and marriage patterns: An analysis of historical trends in Hingham, Massachusetts. *Journal of Marriage and the Family, 35,* 419-28.

Smith, D. S., & Hindus, M. (1975). Premarital pregnancy in America, 1640-1971: An overview and interpretation. *The Journal of Interdisplinary History, 5,* 537-70.

Smith-Rosenberg, C. (1975). The female world of love and ritual: Relations between women in nineteenth-century America. *Signs, 1,* 1-29.

Smith-Rosenberg, C., & Rosenberg, C. (1973). The female animal: Medical and biological views of woman and her role in nineteenth-century America. *Journal of American History, 60,* 332-56.

Stearns, P. N. (1977). *Old age in European society: The Case of France.* New York: Holmes and Meier.

Stone, L. (1977). *The family, sex, and marriage in England, 1500-1800.* New York: Harper and Row.

Tate, T. W., and Ammerman, D. L. (Eds.). (1979). *The Chesapeake Society in the seventeenth century: Essays on Anglo-American society and politics.* New York: Norton.

Ulrich, L. T. (1982). *Goodwives: Image and reality in the lives of women in Northern New England, 1650-1750*. New York: Alfred A. Knopf.

Weinstein, F., and Platt, G. M. (1969). *The wish to be free: Society, psyche and value change*. Berkeley, CA.: University of California Press.

Wells, R. V. (1971). Family size and fertility control in eighteenth-century America: A study of Quaker families. *Population Studies, 25,* 73-82.

Welter, B. (1966). The cult of true womanhood, 1820-60. *American Quarterly, 18,* 151-74.

Wishy, B. (1968). *The child and the republic: The dawn of modern American child nurture*. Philadelphia: University of Pennsylvania Press.

Wood, A. D. (1973). The fashionable diseases': Women's complaints and their treatment in nineteenth century America. *Journal of Interdisciplinary History, 4,* 25-52.

Wrigley, E. A. (1966). Family limitation in Pre-Industrial England. *Economic History Review, 19,* 82-109.

_____. (1969). *Population and history*. London: Weidenfeld and Nicolson.

8

Affects, Ideology, and Scripts in Social Policy and Developmental Psychology

Rae Carlson

The mutual wariness that once existed between policy makers and scientists seems to have evaporated, at least in the field of psychology. A regular feature of *The American Psychologist* devoted to "Psychology in the Public Forum" exhorts psychologists to contribute to policy formation concerning children and families. But the language of discourse is that of policy making and politics. We are asked to improve the clarity of our findings, to accept analysis of issues in cost/benefit terms, and to report our work in ways that are assimilable by busy legislators, administrators, and influential members of the lay public. Only rarely does a scientific community find — or create — an occasion for thoughtful self-examination of its potential contributions to the realm of public policy.

What frameworks should we use for such a self-examination? If the concerns of policy makers often seem alien to those of psychologists, we may be equally led astray by the conventions of our own discipline. Ultimately, developmental psychologists want to know how human beings develop as individual persons. Social policy is ultimately concerned with the impact of social directives on individual lives. Yet we seem to have lost our proper focus on *persons*, while embracing inquiry on "variables" that survive quantitative analyses of groups of subjects.

In this Chapter, I argue that we need the corrective vision supplied by a theory of personality, and sketch an approach to the topics of this conference by invoking the contructs of Tompkins's (1979) script theory. Unfamiliar to most investigators, Tomkins's theory is rooted in the personological tradition, but transcends its heritage with a "contructivist" notion of science, and a firm grounding in knowledge of the biosocial endowments of human beings and their embeddedness in sociocultural contexts.

THE PERSONOLOGICAL PERSPECTIVE: REFLECTIONS ON RECENT HISTORY

Nearly a half a century ago we enjoyed a vision of a scientific psychology of personality offered by Henry A. Murray and his colleagues at the Harvard Psychological Clinic. *Explorations in Personality* (Murray, 1938) presented both a theoretical perspective grounded in psychodynamic theory (Freud and Jung) and innovative, sophisticated methods of personality assessment. Essentially, this was a program for an "ego psychology" that would comprehend both the episodes of a life and an entire life history; its scope included ways of understanding how every person is like *all* other persons, like *some* other persons, and like *no* other person. Concurrently, Gordon Allport (1937) published the first textbook on personality, Kurt Lewin (1935) offered a vision of personality in "interactional" terms, and Murphy, Murphy, and Newcomb (1937) presented an elegant and comprehensive review of a vast literature. Prior to the end of World War II, we had every reason to expect the development of exciting work in personality psychology.

An account of the failure of so promising an intellectual movement is a task far beyond the scope of this chapter. Nonetheless, it is worth summarizing some of the intellectual trends that resulted in the stagnation of personological inquiry and the reasons to expect a rebirth of the personological tradition. Three trends in the postwar era seem crucial. First, the creation of professional training in clinical psychology (the Veterans' Administration's anticipation of mental health problems resulting from wartime experience) drew potential personologists away from inquiry and into clinical practice. Second, the end of World War II coincided with the beginnings of an experimental social psychology and an influx of bright new students (veterans entering academic life via the G. I. Bill) that culminated in a quarter-century of "cute" laboratory analogs of real-life social psychological phenomena. Third, the social programs of the 1960s — particularly the War on Poverty and the inauguration of the Headstart program — led to the spectacular growth of cognitive-developmental psychology. Piaget was rediscovered, and the tracking of intellectual development commanded the efforts of hundreds of talented investigators.

This historical message may be summarized briefly. Notice, first, that events in the larger society — wars and their aftermath, provision of training for professionals and intervention for clients — turned out to shape our disciplinary identity in ways that are rarely given explicit recognition. The rise of psychology as a "career" in academic settings brought other contraints on inquiry, most notably the demand for quantifiable evidence of "productivity." This, in turn, inflated the importance of the positivistic mystique: clean studies (experimental, when possible; correlational when necessary) of uncontaminated sources of variance. A scientific psychology eschewed any concern for individuals in the rush to establish orderly relationships among variables. Programs of persons could be left to the clinicians or to the self-help literature.

One serious consequence of historical trends was the abandonment of personological inquiry. Only lately has our disenchantment with positivism led to any serious reorientation of psychological inquiry. Current trends ("dialectical," "interactional," "transactional") cast doubt upon our guiding assumptions, but rarely produce new knowledge. It seems possible that *only* via thorough disenchantment with our customary ways of doing science will we rediscover the need to understand how part-processes function in individual lives. How are we to assimilate recent knowledge of part-processes into a coherent vision of a developing and functioning person?

Happily, we are now offered a comprehensive new theory of personality in the work of Silvan Tomkins (1962, 1963a, 1963b, 1979, 1981a, 1981b). Tomkins's theory, partially grounded in his work with the Murray group at Harvard, combines close study of individuals with far-ranging work in general psychology and the analysis of comparative civilizations. From this rich array of theoretical constructs, I will focus on three basic formulations as a framework for this chapter: (1) affects, (2) ideology, and (3) scripts as the most helpful ways of understanding the personological foundations of our efforts in developmental psychology and social policy.

This chapter is organized in four parts. First, I offer a brief summary of the basic notions of affect, ideology, and scripts. Second, these contructs are applied to current knowledge about men, women, children, and families as potentially useful guides to future inquiry. Third, the same constructs enable a critique of current social policy and the processes of policy-formation. Finally, the same basic constructs are invoked as a critique of contemporary developmental psychology and as suggesting more profitable lines of relevant inquiry.

BASIC CONSTRUCTS: AFFECT, IDEOLOGY, SCRIPTS

Any policy-relevant formulation of individual psychology must be prepared to answer three questions: (1) What are the fundamental motivations of individuals? (2) What larger world views govern their lives? (3) How are the particularities of experience organized into some program-for-living? These questions apply equally to those who make policy and those who are served (or not served) by it. We need an intellectual framework applicable to conditions of our post-modern/pluralistic society that is grounded in solid notions of human endowments and the various ways in which basic endowments lead to such diverse outcomes.

Affect Theory

In Tomkins's theory, the affect system lies at the heart of human motivation. Among the several subsystems produced in the evolution of the human being (affect, drive, memory, motoric, perceptual, etc.) only affects (emotions) possess the abstractness, flexibility, and generality required to guarantee the survival of the human being as an invention of nature. Unlike drives, the affects are general across time, place and objects. (Hunger is motivating, but can only be appeased by nutrition, and only at times. Sex is motivating, but is easily canceled by disgust, fear, or satiety, and may be endlessly elaborated or denied.) Affects are prior to and necessary for cognitive development. Tomkins (1962) has discussed the role of interest-excitement in the development of perception and thought; Haviland (1983) has shown that our assessment of infants' intelligence is heavily dependent on their "looking smart"—the visible manifestations of interest-excitement. Only the affects seem capable of rendering experience so urgent as to demand that we do something about it.

Tomkins's (1962, 1963a) affect theory differs from currently received ideas about emotions in ways that should be made explicit. First, the theory posits discrete affects (not simply positive or negative affect) as innately endowed programs. Enjoyment and excitement are intrinsically rewarding; anger, contempt/disgust, distress, fear, and shame are intrinsically punishing. These primary affects have their distinctive patterns of neural firing that "imprint" affect-dominated responses. (For example, contrast the upswing of excitement with the "slow burn" of anger; or the slow, relaxed mode of enjoyment with the muted dysphoria of distress.) Second, the primary affects, present at birth, are very soon subjected to modulated expression. Consequently, we can only observe affects through the filters of socially directed patterns of modulation. Third, it is important to distinguish between the innately endowed primary affects and the diversity of cognitive-affective complexes we observe in adults (cf., Tomkins, 1981a). Failing to recognize the developmental nature of affective life, we may either oversimplify (positive versus negative emotions) or overcomplicate (by confusing primary affects with their elaborations).

Ideological Polarity Theory

Underlying the most controversial issues recurring through centuries of Western thought—in domains as separate as mathematics, government, philosophy of science, or child-rearing practices—Tomkins (1963a, 1965) has identified a basic polarity. One's ideology in any domain rests on a more primitive "ideo-affective posture": a loosely organized set of feelings and ideas about feelings that establish one's resonance to any organized ideology.

The core issues constitute a polarity extending from an extreme humanistic position through a middle-of-the-road position to an extreme normative position.[1] Essentially, the polarity describes the humanist's faith in the intrinsic value and reality of human potentialities and experience as contrasted with the normative's belief that the human being can attain his full stature by struggling to meet an ideal essence basically independent of human frailties. In science, a humanistic ideology emphasizes discovery, while a normative ideology is concerned with verification of ideas. In child rearing, the contrast is between appreciating and molding the child. Illustrations in many fields of controversy could be multiplied.

The assumptions underlying humanistic and normative positions are rarely made explicit, yet they pervade our basic feelings about life. Are people basically good, or must their evil propensities be guarded against? Are values that which human beings wish, or do values exist independent of our wishes? Should people maximize satisfaction of their affects and appetites, or should they be governed by norms that in turn modulate appetites and affects? Is human weakness to be tolerated and ameliorated, or forbidden and punished?

Tomkins (1963a, 1965) has shown that these issues recur in the literature of our moral, philosophical, political, and scientific controversies. Their importance lies in the ubiquity and generality of underlying ideo-affective postures; for these should enable us to predict how a person will respond to new ideologies. Empirical studies of ideological polarity have shown its influence on conceptions of self and others (Carlson & Levy, 1970), moral judgments (Lieberman, 1982), quasi-judicial judgments (Williams, 1983), and even facial expressions (Vasquez, 1975).

Consideration of ideological polarity is germane to our immediate problems for at least three reasons. First, because origins of the polarity lie in the "socialization of affect" in family contexts, we need to study how children develop their basic outlooks on life. Second, social policies concerning children and families are highly ideological in nature; we need to understand the ideological bases of policy making and public resonance to policy issues. Third, our very science of developmental psychology is influenced by ideological postures. Our choice of problems, our methodological criteria, and such wisdom as we are prepared to offer in the domain of public policy will reflect subtle, underlying world views. These three issues are elaborated in later sections of this chapter.

Script Theory

Perhaps the most significant of Tomkins's theoretical innovations is the provision of a "dramaturgical" model that offers a radically different way of looking at personality.[2] Tomkins argues that our basic units of analysis must be more complex and more dynamic than the dimensionalized "traits" or "processes" familiar in psychological research. The basic unit of analysis in script theory is the *scene*: an idealized "happening" that includes actors, actions, affects, time, place, and psychological functions. The minimal definition of a scene is that it includes at least one affect and at least one object of that affect. *Scripts* are formed as one co-assembles a "family" of related scenes and formulates rules for interpreting, responding to, defending against, or creating further scenes. Originally, scenes determine scripts; over time, script-formation so consolidates experience that scripts come to determine scenes. Very roughly, scenes describe what is happening, and scripts tell us what to do about it.

Not all scenes and scripts are equal. Transient events, however affect-laden, that do not become interconnected with other scenes "disappear' in personality. Habitual scripts are complex organizations that have become so highly practiced and skilled as to evoke no new thought, feeling, or consciousness. "Commitment" scripts capture dedication to positive goals that enable absorption of much punishment and negative affect. "Nuclear" scripts deal with the individual's most urgent, unsolved, and unsolveable problems. "Addictive" scripts govern adaptations in which means-preempt-ends in a segregated closed system. This is but a partial taxonomy of scripts.

The fundamental point of script theory (and its most radical departure from received notions of personality) is the insistence on recognizing the complexity and heterogeneity of personality, the temporal organization of personality structures, and the cognitive-affective dynamics implicated in generation of scenes and scripts.

While Tomkins's script theory is primarily a theory of personality, its constructs may be applied to social and historical events by noting those affect-laden scenes that are most significant to a cohort or a social group and the socially shared scripts that dictate how prototypic scenes are to be constructed and dealt with.

Taken together, the three constructs of affects, ideology, and scripts suggest ways of organizing our current knowledge of women, children, and families, the ways in which social policy is formulated, and how developmental psychologists investigate problems in this domain.

MEN, WOMEN, CHILDREN, AND FAMILIES

Risking the charge of overgeneralization inevitable in any discussion of whole groups of people, let us consider what we know — or believe — about men, women, children, and families in terms of our three guiding constructs.

Affects

All human beings are born with approximately equivalent sets of innate affect programs. How, then, do we account for the discovery that men in general seem to be less comfortable in the realm of "feeling" where women in general are specialists? The answers will be complicated, but will surely have to take account of three interacting processes. First, there are innate biological sex differences (for example, in musculature, metabolic rates, perhaps cerebral lateralization, as well as in reproductive functions) that may "tilt" affect profiles differently for males and females. Second, every society implicitly acknowledges such innate differences and selectively emphasizes some of them in law, mythology, and socialization to further bias the affect profiles. Third, the individual, endowed with a particular temperament and born into a particular social cultural setting, further selects (mainly unconsciously) the affective experiences that will prove fateful in his/her personal development. One should wonder less at the diversity of findings across societies than at their astonishing convergences.

Of course societies differ in their degree of gender-specialization of affects, as anthropologists have demonstrated. But our immediate concern is with contemporary Western society and the Judeo-Christian tradition. Here the *kind* of specialization is amazingly consistent. When we look at the positive affects, we see that males are specialized for excitement, females for enjoyment. Among negative affects, masculine anger and contempt/disgust are counterpoised to feminine distress, fear, and shame. Profound consequences follow from this specialization alone. Excitement-oriented males are more attuned to daring, exploration, and risk; enjoyment-oriented females are more likely to savor familiar, sharable experiences. The anger/distress contrast suggests that men administer punishment, while women absorb it. The contempt/shame contrast specialization leads men to reject what is unworthy in self or others, and women to tolerate shame while retaining a wish to restore relationships.

Does this sound too stereotyped to be plausible? Not only is it borne out by trends in history and contemporary life, but also by recent empirical studies. For example, a recent study (Carlson & Carlson, 1984) asked college students to sketch plots for television dramas dealing with human emotions. Among several significant findings (most of them confirming general formulations of script theory), women introduced "interpersonal" themes, not only for the "social" affects of joy and shame, but also for the "nonsocial" affects of excitement and fear; men did so only for the social affects. Outcomes of negative-affect plots were happy for women, unhappy for men. Fear seemed especially taboo for men, in that they frequently introduced supernatural agents in devising fear plots, while women almost never did so. (A more recent unpublished study with a large group of undergraduates suggests that these trends hold in acknowledging emotional experiences in recent everyday life.) Such findings support what we already knew about gender differences, but they also go beyond such knowledge to suggest the power of affect, per se, underlying phenomena.

Children pose an interesting issue. As young, dependent creatures, they are like women in being expected to adapt to the directives of more powerful others. As Jeanne Block's (1973) longitudinal and cross-national studies have shown, socialization begins relatively early to encourage "masculine" affects in boys, while insisting on control and suppression of other affects. Girls are supported in both the expression and interpersonal connectedness of affective experience. The role of affects in gender-socialization has been obscured because psychologists tend to ignore affects in favor of other conceptual formulations. Such culturally valued goals as "achievement," "competence," "independence," and the like mask our endorsement of excitement over enjoyment, anger over distress, contempt over shame. Valuing affect *only* when it is successfully invested in individual achievement, we tend to ignore (or explain or excuse) the realm of feeling as somehow an unfortunate disruption of goal-directed action.

Taken together, these two phenomena—gender-specialization in the socialization of affect and the failure to recognize the ubiquity of affect—have produced affects of enormous consequence in both intellectual and social life. Insofar as the masculine pattern captures qualities "officially" valued by males and females alike, the triad of excitement, anger, and contempt/disgust is fostered throughout society. Insofar as this pattern is not recognized as affective in nature, only the "feminine" affects of joy, distress, fear, and shame are considered truly "emotional."

Thus what we know about males and females is strongly influenced by (masculine) values that pervade both our society as a whole and the conceptual language in which we consider the phenomena. For example, the instrumental/expressive polarity has been quite serviceable in capturing gender specializations, "sex roles," and the like. But notice the connotations of the terms: "instrumental" implies effective, goal-directed action; "expressive" implies a more aesthetic, amorphous, soothing mode. The women's movement prompted a vast amount of inquiry on psychological androgyny as an alternative (to "sex role adaptation") vision of psychological well-being. Yet when one examines an immense and inconclusive research literature, it is the masculine component of androgyny that appears to yield positive correlations with indexes of well-being. Such illustrations could be multiplied. My general point is that the very language of our social science, when devoid of the perspective of affect theory, abets the denial of the affective basis of our dominant value system.

Ideology

We have long been familiar with pendulum swings of opinion and ideology about child-rearing practices noted in several other contributions in this volume. The polarity between loving and controlling the child recurs throughout our history from the conflicting messages of Old and New Testaments through the most contemporary of child-rearing manuals. Rather than considering ideology *about* the family, it may be more useful to consider the family as the cradle *of* ideology. This is not a novel idea. Freud derived much of social and political life from the dynamics of the nursery; political scientists relate political attitudes to parental models (whether in agreement or Oedipal protest) and use family-mediated demographic variables in their predictions. What may be novel is the suggestion that we consider affect, per se, as the key feature of family socialization.

Basic to ideological polarity theory is the concept of ideo-affective postures: the "loosely organized set of feelings and ideas about feeling" (Tomkins, 1965, p. 74) that determine one's resonance to ideologies and that have their origins in one's history of socialization.

Humanistic ideology is promoted by a "rewarding" socialization of affect in which the child's feelings are explicitly valued, maximized, and made manageable. A normative ideology is based on parental concern for modulating affect in the service of some other norm. More commonly, a middle-of-the-road ideological position tempers humanistic ideology with normative constraints, or vice versa. Tomkins has outlined rewarding/punitive socialization of each specific affect in detail. The flavor of the discussion may be conveyed by a simple illustration of the handling of distress. What happens when a child cries? Does the parent emphathize with the feeling, verbalize empathic distress, and only later assist in dealing with its source? Does the parent reject the distress? ("Don't be a crybaby!" "Stop that crying or I'll give you something to cry about!") Or does the parent elide the empathic response by rushing to distract the child and deal with the source? ("There, it's all better now!") Such minutiae of parent-child interactions around affective episodes are not so trivial as they may appear at first sight. Long-term consequences of affect-socialization turn out to be important (if not necessarily fatal) for how the child comes to view the claims of feeling in personal and political life.

Ordinarily, the more or less casual episodes of affect are embedded in a context of ideology manifest in parents' words and deeds. Youngsters arrive at a sense of whether forgiveness or revenge is the right way to deal with wrongdoers, what qualities of human beings are most worthy of emulation, and what larger goals make sense of transient experiences. Identification with parental models in the domain of ideo-affective postures may turn out to be considerably more important than the "sex role identification" that has been more thoroughly investigated.

My impression is that Tomkins's treatment of the socialization of affect (and consequences for ideology) rests on a model of a traditional, middle-class nuclear family in which both parents are heavily invested in the child's socialization. While I believe the theory both correct and powerful, its implications need to be studied in nontraditional families (or even traditional ones) in periods of drastic social change. In a society where most mothers are in the labor force, most children will experience some disruption of the family (for example, via separation or divorce) and some alternatives to family care during childhood, the study of the roots of ideology will become both more difficult and more urgent.

Two illustrations may suffice. In attempting to analyze detailed portrayals of family life in the "culture of poverty," I have been struck with the absence of any consistent attention to the socialization of affect. Carmen Santana, in Susan Sheehan's (1976) *A Welfare Mother*, seems to live for affective turn-ons, since little else brightens her life. But the apparently casual/chaotic nature of her socialization practices defies systematic analysis in terms of any extant theory of child development. Her children's exposure to schools and other public agencies is so fleeting as to pose no competition to the street as the major source of affect and ideology. If the Santana children seem embarked on self-defeating patterns of promiscuity, drug dealing, and early death, they may have developed an ideological posture of sorts: one based on remnants of a Caribbean culture transplanted into the alien world of New York City bureaucracy in which magnification of affect (mainly excitement) is a major value. Such a pattern is a caricature of "humanistic" ideology, far from ideological in any conventional sense.

At the other end of an urban socioeconomic spectrum, we find upwardly mobile couples enrolling their infants in various programs for "forcing" intellectual development via elite nursery schools, home instruction, and the like. This is a caricature of "normative" ideology: one that combines genuine concern for children with frantic efforts that they "measure up" to parental visions of transcending any limitations in a competitive world. Both examples suggest that children have become objects of parental projections, accessories or instruments of parental ideology. Perhaps this has always been the case in some sense. However, the strains on the social fabric increase, and the need to comprehend ideological bases of socialization become more critical.

Scenes and Scripts

Our most difficult task is that of decoding the scenes and scripts that describe gender roles and family life. Historical change over centuries, and the extraordinary pluralism of contemporary life complicate the problem. "Childhood" is itself a relatively recent invention, as Aries (1962) has shown, and family life, as we conceive it, awaited the development of "affective individualism" (Stone, 1979) in the seventeenth century. John Demos, in Chapter 7, "The Family's Changing Past," has sketched at least three models of the family in American history: "a little commonwealth", a "haven", and an "encounter group" as these have unfolded in our national experience.

But the contemporary scene is still more confused. The variety of "nontraditional families" (Lamb, 1982) is particularly daunting when we realize that vastly different problems—and attempted solutions—underlie the experiences of househusbands of the professional class, unwed teenage mothers, migrant workers, communards, and children of divorce. It may be possible to extract from the very recent literature on nontraditional families *some* useful generalizations about development; but we are very far from that goal. Matters that were once taken for granted have become problematic. Even the most traditional middle-class nuclear family may find its children, when grown, reluctant to make marital commitments, unable to find employment, forced to "come home." Our young women anxiously watch the biological clock, hoping to have children, but unable to find suitable life partners. Children know at close range the stresses that lead to divorce, and may be cast prematurely into roles as confidants and supporters of parents. Giving our children physical protection and education is not so simple as it seemed a decade ago. How do we protect them from dioxin? Or (to cite a recent news item) from having "creationism" taught in their textbooks because publishers "go" with demands of their largest customer—the state of Texas?

Pluralism of contemporary society produces a turbulent intellectual field in which it becomes difficult to define our basic terms. What is a child? (A neonate, a toddler, a dependent, a potential litigant?) Who is a parent? (New technologies of reproduction—artificial insemination, surrogate mothers, test-tube babies; new adoption procedures—new patterns of kinship and custodial rights complicate matters once "understood".) What is a family? (Households no longer consist of nuclear families, but include shifting living arrangements devised by various combinations of adults and children.) Ready or not, we are confronted with the task of reexamining basic problems in a shifting social context.

I have no insights to offer beyond restating the issues in a slightly different way. Rather than assuming some "standard" portrait of family life, we need to conceptualize the different scenes and scripts that actually govern people's lives—recognizing that these are no longer contained within the family, but are very much a product of wider social forces. Some problems call for national policies that affect all children; others will require closer study of alternative ways of life that call for particular kinds of help.

Three general goals might motivate our inquiry. First, we need to recognize that childhood has its own claims, independent of adults' aspirations and confusions, that must be honored. Second, we need to identify the features of family life (however defined) that promote scripts in which positive affects predominate over the anxieties, confusions, and humiliations of childhood. Third, we have an urgent need to identify the strengths that people can mobilize in coping with the inevitable stresses of contemporary life. How can we best help design public policies needed to preserve an eroding heritage of civility and community, and a sharable vision of a "good life" based on as much psychological insight as we can summon?

ON CONTRIBUTING TO POLICY MAKING

Just as public policy involves more than legislation and executive orders, psychologists' contributions go well beyond our formal testimony or mission-oriented researches. Freud surely influenced the socialization of children more than any developmental psychologists (but see Sandra Scarr, Chapter 5, "Cultural Lenses on Mothers and Children," for an account of Gesell and Watson); consultants to the computer industry have modified educational praxis as much as have our contemporary educational psychologists.

Given the dual task of capturing how we *have* influenced policy and how we might do so in the future, the notions of scripts and ideology seem the most useful tools.

Scenes and Scripts

Behind the definition of any social problem is an implicit scene: a bit of dramatic action, usually best captured by our political cartoonists.[3] But who are the actors in such scenes, and what is the action? Food stamps. What does that bring to mind? One scene portrays bulging granaries and starving children. The optimal script told us to rescue youngsters and poor people (while reducing storage/subsidy costs) by feeding our own hungry people. Another scene is a supermarket checkout stand where arrogant-looking hippies are using food stamps to buy steaks, while a modest working-class housewife waits in line to buy spaghetti. The implicit script says that liberal social policies only encourage cheaters and oppress deserving, hard-working folks. How one constructs a "food stamps" scene involves ideology — a problem discussed below. The immediate point is that any social policy is "about" some idealized scene, and that actors may be cast in partial or incompatible roles in one or another of such scenes.

Perhaps it is inevitable that policy issues are fragmented and packaged in ways that fit the mind-sets of legislators, administrators, and special-interest groups. Family policy tends to remain segregated from other, equally problematic issues thought to engage other constituencies. Obviously the quality of family life is altered by policy decisions concerning armaments, taxation, trade, and the like. Yet if a senator were to introduce legislation diverting funds for the MX missile into a family-assistance program, she would be dismissed as mad or menopausal. (This example is vulnerable to immediate trends when candidates for national office are largely de-escalating "defense" expenditures. But the basic point endures: when "armaments" are competing with "social" programs, the value choice is either masked or voiced in a masculine baritone.)

When we consider the potential conflicts between "women's rights" and "child welfare," the scene/script properties become clearer. We are properly outraged by the scene of a talented woman denied equal pay, job security, and advancement potential, as compared with a male colleague. When we consider children's rights, the plight of the "latchkey" child no longer moves us as it did once. A bit of day-care legislation ought to take care of the problem, along with a pious resolution that fathers ought to be made more responsible, fiscally and emotionally, for their progeny.

Common to both scenes — and to others that I elide here — is a subtle difference between "social" and other policies. Social policies deal with whatever underclass is at issue: poor people, the aged, needy children, ethnic minorities. (Once a formerly powerless group attains political influence, it ceases to present a "social" problem; witness the current courting of women in political life.) Social issues, depending on the complexion of the administrative/judicial/legislative bodies in power at a particular time, may call for exhortation, nurturance, or punishment. But such issues tend to be segregated from the "important" matters that command the whole-hearted attention of policy makers.

My immediate point is that psychologists ought to recognize the type-casting underlying the definition of social problems. By accepting "expert" status on particular social problems, we may be abdicating the possibilities of enlarging the terms of discourse. My larger point is that our most valuable contribution might consist in the analysis of the scenes (the people and problems at hand) and the scripts (potential ways of solving the problems) that derive from our understanding of the human condition.

Ideology

Almost by definition, social policies are ideological in Tomkins's (1963b, 1965) sense. They deal with centuries-old value controversies that recur throughout Western history; they deal with "...any organized set of ideas about which human beings are at once both articulate and passionate and about which they are the least certain" (Tomkins, 1963b, p. 389); and they cease to become "ideological" when the accumulation of sheer "facts" turns burning questions into settled knowledge. Like any citizen, the psychologist who ventures into the ideological domain (whether in mathematics, science, literature, or our immediate concern with family life and child-rearing practices) is dealing with passionately held uncertainties.

What is distinctive and potentially helpful in Tomkins's ideological polarity theory is the explicit recognition of "ideo-affective postures" underlying formal ideologies. Armed with an understanding of the *affective* bases of ideological commitments, we are better prepared to decode the powerful, implicit appeals embodied in our approaches to social policy issues. We can move beyond labeling in terms of liberal/conservative political stances to understand the more abstract and subtle bases of ideological resonance.

Let us return to the example of "food stamps," examining it from the standpoint of ideology. The scene of bulging granaries/hungry children, and the attendant script of providing for need from stockpiles of grain, exemplified a humanistic ideological posture. There is a recognized human need, and a way to fulfill it; the appropriate legislation follows. Now consider the contrast-case: welfare cheaters enjoying themselves and the insidious comparision with the modest, deserving housewife. Here the normative message is that it is "wrong" to be dependent, to enjoy one's appetites without earning the right to do so, and that such "greediness" exploits others. Where the first scene evoked distress and (vicarious) enjoyment, the second scene is based on anger and contempt.

Potentialities for misunderstanding should be anticipated and corrected. Tomkins's theory does *not* imply that humanistic ideology is based on positive affect, normative ideology on negative affect. The point is more abstract. Essentially, Tomkins's theory focuses on what is "valuable" — and thus more "real" in a world where such issues are not settled. A humanistic posture leads us to celebrate the reality and value of any human potentialities; a normative posture insists that reality and value exist beyond the sphere of human frailties, and that human wishes are suspect *unless* one is striving to live up to an external norm. Tomkins's theory does *not* argue for an extreme humanistic posture (as might be exemplified by either irresponsible hippies or ultra laissez-faire libertarians) any more than for an extreme normative posture. A "middle-of-the-road" position, tempering normative demands with humanistic tolerance (or vice versa) describes the characteristic posture of most Americans. Such a posture permits a creative synthesis of the humanistic *and* normative ideologies that are equally part of our heritage.

In a democratic society, the outcomes of public policy debates depend very much on public resonance to humanistic or normative implications. Thus it is of more than passing interest to consider how ideological postures influence political decisions. We know that in times of economic hardship there is a trend toward the normative. We know that normative positions lend themselves to more simplistic presentations of issues, as nicely shown in Tetlock's (1983) content-analyses of speeches in the U. S. Senate. We know that Tomkins's ideology theory gives a richer picture of the nature of moral judgments (compared with Kohlberg's "cognitive stage" approach) from a recent study by Lieberman (1982). We know that normatives are more likely to derogate and blame victims, as shown in Williams's (1983) findings that welfare clients and victims of severe theft evoked more disgust in normatives, and more empathic distress in humanists.

Extrapolating from such empirical findings to the realm of current public policy may help to clarify a distinction between the *content* of a social issue and the ideological posture that dictates its script. For example, both "pro-choice" and "pro-life" stances on abortion appear to embody humanistic scenes; both express concern for potentialities of unborn life (and thus may attract adherents for different ideological reasons). However, at the level of policy-formation, the pro-life position (as advanced by the Reagan administration and other prominent spokesmen) is clearly normative: the thrust is to prohibit human choice without offering any appreciation or financial support for the human consequences of such a policy. The point is to assert a value, punish the deviants, and thus uphold an external norm that transcends human wishes. Similar analyses apply to two other recent controversies in the realm of public policy: the "squeal rule" that would require parental notification of contraceptive information given to teenagers, and the "Baby Jane Doe" directive that would prohibit exercises of medical/parental judgment in the treatment of defective neonates. Again, both policy directives *could* be construed as humanistic appreciation of family life or the potentialities of the handicapped. Yet the essentially punitive intent of such rules was equally apparent to the public and to the courts who overturned both rules. Proponents were insisting that sexually active youngsters must be bound by parental authority, and that human judgments must be set aside in grave medical decisions. In both cases insistence on observance of an external norm was devoid of any consideration of human anguish or any provision of support for the consequences of norm-adherence.

What implications follow from this analysis of current policy controversies? First, we need to recognize that problems facing the poor, ethnic minorities, and refugees introduce new features into the texture of policy deliberations. Concurrently, we have seen a steady decline in public confidence in our social institutions over the past 20 years (Lipset & Schneider, 1983). Distrust of the establishment, a sense of political inefficacy, has been thoroughly documented. If Elshtain's (1981) vision of an "ethical polity" is to be reflected in public policy, an unrelenting normative ideology must be tempered with the more compassionate vision of humanism in our executive offices, legislatures, and electorate. Issues need to be discussed in the cognitively complex manner they require. Above all, we need to temper the anger, excitement, and contempt/disgust (the stereotypic "masculine" affects) with the more benign ("feminine") affects of enjoyment, empathic distress, and even vicarious shame that are equally a part of our collective heritage.

The most challenging implications bring us full circle. If ideology is born in the socializaiton of affect, in those family scenes that provide the prototypic actors, actions, affects, and outcomes of our personal scripts, then the quality of affect-socialization is of utmost importance. Here developmental psychologists may hold the keys that we most desperately need: How to understand the processes and conditions of affect-socialization that may determine the future of our polity?

ON DEVELOPMENTAL PSYCHOLOGY AND PUBLIC POLICY

In our post-positivist era, we know that the psychology of the investigator is closely bound up with the substance and style of the investigation. We now embrace a "constructivist" ideology of science, whether or not we practice it. But it is worth reassessing the issues in script-theoretic terms. What does the investigator bring *to* a problem? What (collectively) emerges *from* our investigations? Among workers in psychology's far-flung vineyards, developmentalists are probably the least sterotyped, and thus least vulnerable to criticisms of our field as a whole. Yet it seems worth considering the unexamined constraints that we may bring to the study of men, women, children, and implications for social policy.

Constraints on the Investigator

Psychology, like any field of knowledge, is basically sustained by the affect of excitement. The pursuit of novelty, of discovery, and the clarification of problems must be powered by a disciplined curiosity. Often conjoined with other affects (anger at social injustice, contempt for foolish work, anxiety engendered by the publish-or-perish mystique), intellectual excitement is basic. In any era, what is worth becoming excited *about* depends on sharable interests of a scientific community. In our time, we tend to seek "hot" (fundable) problems, to wish for quick answers, and to disregard any history older than last year's journals. As Freidrich-Cofer's Chapter 3, "Body, Mind, and Morals in the Framing of Social Policy," tells us, such constraints are far from unique to our time; an impressive legacy of research on children in the early nineteenth century was "lost" to succeeding generations of investigators whose interest was directed to other facets of developmental issues.

The dominant ideology of contemporary psychology is normative. Its norms, bequeathed by our long captivity in the camps of positivism, are for methodological orthodoxy, most clearly shown in the demands for experimental manipulation of variables and for the quantification of aggregate (group) data. A consequence of this normative orientation is an extraordinary confusion of means and ends. Two illustrations of this trend may suffice.

First, pick up any recent directory of graduate programs in psychology, and you will find that the only course work universally required for graduate work in psychology consists of courses in experimental methods and statistical analysis. Mastery of a limited set of research methods is sanctified as the means to *any* intellectual inquiry in our field. Implicitly, we communicate indifference about (because we cannot measure) a candidate's breadth of knowledge, depth of insight, or engagement in substantive problems. Essentially, our academic socialization is that of providing our symbolic children with hammers; we should not be surprised when they go about hammering everything in sight.

My second illustration is an historical one. During the 1930s through the 1950s the work of Jean Piaget was alternately ignored or excoriated by all but a handful of insightful scholars. Its implications of "nativism" were held to be absurd, and its methods were ridiculously unscientific. Imagine writing a scholarly work based on mere observation of your own kids! Piaget's later attainment of respectability and near-deification owed less to the wisdom of our field than to the social problems of the 1960s. Warring-on-poverty and intervening on behalf of the cognitive development of "disadvantaged" children required attention to the ways youngsters actually cognize their worlds. Piagetian thought offered a handle on the problem, and provided a tool kit when issues of "conservation," "egocentrism," and the like could be adapted to experimental procedures. Now assimilable to norms of methodological orthodoxy (standard prodecures and group data), variations on Piagetian problems flooded our journals for two decades. Again, we see a confusion of means-ends relationships in which consideration of method preempted the choice and framing of questions.

What of scripts in developmental psychology? An idealized "scientific method" is popularly supposed to be such a script, and it is one that we tell ourselves and our students. For most of us, the pursuit of knowledge is neither a "nuclear script," powered by urgent and unsolved personal problems, nor a "commitment script" in which passionate dedication to a positive intellectual goal enables us to absorb defeats and punishments. Rather, our science is too often an "habitual" script: the exercise of highly competent skills in our chosen craft — "professional" in a slightly pejorative sense. Its affective pay- off tends to be derivative, marked by increments in professional in- fluence, rather than the intrinsically passionate quest for knowledge.

Constraints on the Investigations

Assumptions shared by investigators in any field of knowledge are bound to stamp the content of the field, as we have known since Kuhn's (1962) analysis of scientific paradigms. Psychologists, as a group, seem to share the excitement orientation that leads to interest in what is new (but not too new) at the expense of attention to enduring (and unpopular) problems, a normative ideology that values methodological purity over conceptual power, and an habitual scien- tific script that favors attainment of short-range empirical objectives over long-term commitment to complex and difficult problems. How do these shared assumptions shape the content of our field in terms of affect, ideology, and scripts?

Affects.

Since the study of emotions (affects) is now the "hottest" area of psychological inquiry, it is awkward to acknowledge how recent — and how limited — is our interest. For most of this century first "drives" and then "cognitions" provided our basic motivational principles. A compelling illustration is given in Tomkins's (1981) account of this problem. For two decades, the Schachter and Singer (1962) formulation of emotion as "arousal plus cognition" dominated the thinking of pro- fessional scholars and the lore perpetuated in our textbooks. This despite the facts that the basic experiments demonstrated no main ef- fects; were inconsistent with solid neuropsychological knowledge; and could not be replicated by any other investigators. As it turns out, few psychologists actually *read* the key studies. Rather, the field was so in- vested in the "cognitive revolution" as a corrective to the bad old behaviorism that the Schachter-Singer formulation *had* to be "right," and point out the wave of our intellectual future.

But the basic distrust of affect predates the recent era. Emotions, when considered at all, were regarded as disorganizing, disruptive in- trusions into performances of action or thought. While the rest of the world celebrated affective experience, psychologists systematically excluded it *except* as deplorable anxiety or aggression. This is nicely documented in the work of two colleagues. A content-analysis of psychology's textbooks over 85 years (Carlson, 1966) revealed the steady decline of interest in positive affects, and a limited preoccupation with negative affects. Over the same period, a frequency count of references to affects in novels, poetry, quotations, and short stories (Lindauer, 1968) established that humanistic studies maintained a steady interest in feelings, and a tilt toward exploring positive affects.

When affects were finally readmitted to scientific respectability, the usual barriers had to be hurdled. First, cultural relativism ("the Chinese have different expressions of emotion") had to give way to the demonstration of pan-cultural affective meanings (Ekman, 1971). Next affects were — and often remain — construed as merely by-products of cognition. ("Behind every emotion lies a hidden cognition.") Now that we have established laboratory procedures for encoding, decoding, and inducing affects, even the most skeptical psychologists were rushing to the field of affect.

I do not mean to disparage the belated recognition of affect, the competence and dedication of scholars newly recruited to this field, or the importance of their findings. However, little of this inquiry approaches the most important aspect of the affective domain: the understanding of affect in individual lives. As an example of the most promising work, I would point to studies of the socialization of affect through detailed mapping of mother-child interactions in the first two years of life (Tronick, 1982). More generally, we need to study the nature of the affective-cognitive complexes shown in lives governed by positive versus negative affects, and the significance of *specific* affects in personality and life histories.

Ideology.

Psychologists are no longer so naive about proclaiming a "value-free" science as was once the case. Obviously psychology is imbued with the individualistic biases of a capitalistic Western society. This need not be a fatal handicap, so long as psychological inquiry succeeds in rendering an intellectually convincing account of the conditions that lead to reasonably benign developmental outcomes in such a society, and is equally alert to the costs and failures.

But I am here concerned with ideology in Tomkins's sense. One could make a case that the ideology of current developmental psychology is normative on several grounds. The choice of research problems gives us a clue as to what's important — what is most valuable about human beings, what people *should* be like. The answer seems to be that people (especially children) should be smart. An informal content analysis of our two leading developmental journals revealed that "cognitive processes" define what most psychologists think important about human beings. Another, perhaps less obvious, trend is that psychology is normative in a more subtly ideological sense: in its very tools of inquiry whereby the *meaning* of a person's measured performance is entirely determined by his/her standing relative to other people. All of our favored psychometric and statistical methods rest on the notion that "individuality" is to be studied in terms of "individual differences." This is a highly controversial issues in personality psychology (cf. Lamiell, 1981; Carlson, 1984) but too technical to pursue in the present context.

When we turn to ideology in the more familiar political sense, it seems that psychologists are mainly reactive to events in the public sphere. Only when a social issue generates excitement in the larger society does it command serious attention from psychologists. Then it becomes an "important" matter to be studied in our conventional (normative) fashion. The issue of "gender" provides an excellent example.

Until the late 1960s, a great deal of information about sex differences in personality accumulated, uninterpreted and largely unread, in the archives of differential psychology. As recently as 1969, the influential five-volume *Handbook of Social Psychology* (Lindzey & Aronson, 1968/1969) contained only one indexed reference to "femininity"; that dealt with hypomasculinity in preadolescent boys! With the rise of the women's movement, psychologists instantly developed a new intellectual industry devoted to the study of "sex roles," "androgyny," and the like. New careers, institutes, journals, and programs were established almost overnight. Yet the entire effort was based on unexamined premises: the instrumental, agentic, masculine modes of inquiry that had impoverished our view of human nature all along (Carlson, 1971, 1972).

Perhaps this point should be clarified in terms of content, method, and impact of our response to feminist critiques. First off, inquiry immediately focused on the issue of "achievement" (a masculine speciality, valued in our society). The thrust of new work was to deny, disprove, or explain why women didn't appear to be achievers or achievement-oriented. External villains were easily identified: sexist stereotypes, social programming, and the like. Internal villains came from attribution-theory: women attributed successes to luck or chance, men claimed their successes as intrinsic. A new prescription—that of an "androgynous" ideal celebrating those who were *both* masculine/feminine on quickie personality measures—came to dominate discourse. (A permanent embarrassment is that the "masculine" component of androgyny scales continues to yield the best predictors of psychological well-being.) Methods of inquiry were firmly established in the normative (masculine) tradition: quantitative and criterion-oriented predictions of behavioral outcomes. The voluminous output of research on sex roles and androgyny has become so sheerly *boring* that few psychologists even bother to read it, while continuing to contribute studies of this genre.

Why do I "blame" our psychological establishment for this state of affairs? Apart from what we know intuitively, there is a nice study (Lykes & Stewart, 1983) demonstrating that feminists' studies are quite different when published in mainstream and other journals. In psychological journals the quantitative, hard-science prevails; in feminist journals, a looser interpretive mode is acceptable. Unhappily, neither style of inquiry is totally convincing. We have yet to consider seriously ("scientifically") the powerful messages implicit in feminist critiques—discerning the significant intellectual challenges, not put off by either angry exaggerations nor beguiled by special pleading, special constructs. As yet, I doubt that psychologists (male or female) have really *thought* about the issues in sufficient depth to consider that these require a revision of our assumptions of "normal science."

In the realm of child welfare, psychologists speak most convincingly when issues are delimited by immediate political and practical concerns. Thus, Zigler and Muenchow's (1983) call for providing infant day care and infant-care leaves rests on an analysis of cross-national data on employment and disability provisions. More "psychological," but equally tailored to current realities, is Greenberger's (1983) testimony demonstrating the costs of youth employment—a policy favored by the Reagan administration. But psychologists are unlikely to *initiate* policy questions that fall outside the sphere of their expertise. For example, the stark findings of the Department of Human Services in the State of Maine, showing a three-to-one difference in death ratios of poor versus nonpoor children, make a strong indictment of our economic system that would never have been raised by psychologists.

When larger, more diffuse questions are at issue, ideological conflict within psychology emerges more clearly. Nowhere is this more apparent than in the now-classic positions of Fraiberg and Kagan on the importance of mother-child relationships in infancy. Fraiberg's insistence on the importance of "mothering" rested on clinical experience and personal conviction. Kagan's reliance on empirical data (largely the *absence* of statistically significant findings) led to a conclusion that nonmaternal care need not have deleterious consequences. This general position was expanded in an edited volume (Brim & Kagan, 1980) presenting the "new" view that experience in early years need not constrain later development.

The issues are neither simple nor settled; that is precisely what makes them ideological. Our discipline currently offers *only* methodological directives that do not speak to value questions, and can be interpreted or discounted in various ways. Let us consider this problem later.

Scenes and scripts.

An unfortunate side-effect of contemporary modes of inquiry is that we have little knowledge of the organization of experience and behavior in terms of scenes and scripts. The essence of conventional psychological research is to isolate, measure, or manipulate sets of standardized variables, heeding only those that survive statistical analysis of aggregate data. To gain a fragmentary notion of the scenes and scripts we must piece together snippets of studies. My informal analysis of individual studies reported in our two leading developmental journals yielded pleasant scenes: infants people-watching, toddlers playing, schoolchildren learning academic skills and social roles, parents parenting — and everyone cognizing. Most of the actors were middle class; the settings were laboratories, schools, and sometimes homes; actions were of relatively short duration. But *scripts* — the construction, growth, decay, and transformations of *individuals'* rules for interpreting, responding to, creating, expanding, or defending against scenes — were entirely absent. Of course journals may not be the place to seek the information we need; books and monographs are required for the full exploration of important problems. Yet we rarely encounter reports of *any* length that take into account the complexity and texture of people's lives studied over time.

Three examples of well-known books may be useful in suggesting the kind of research we need. Block's *Lives Through Time* (1971) gave us a splendid account of development from adolescence through mid-adulthood in the cohort of the California longitudinal sample. The research revealed the coherent, but distinctively qualitative patterns of development that would have been missed by even the most sophisticated of variable-centered analyses. The findings pointed to the major importance of parental care and responsibility and to the relative *un*importance of such favorite variables as measured intelligence and socioeconomic status. Block clearly acknowledged that the findings could not be generalized to the vastly different sociocultural-historical milieu of the 1980s; but it is the *style* of the research, rather than its content, that I wish to emphasize.

Carol Gilligan's *In a Different Voice* (1982) is perhaps best known as a feminist treatment of moral development. However, I think it particularly valuable because the research is based on extended qualitative study of people making moral decisions of enormous consequence in their own lives. No standardized scale, no well-honed laboratory procedure can hope to capture the complexity of the psychological processes involved in those issues that bear upon policy-formation.

My third example, not from psychology, is Susan Sheehan's *A Welfare Mother* (1976). This disturbing and moving portrayal of family life in a Puerto Rican ghetto of New York City tells us just how complicated are the multiple problems faced by the "targets" of some of our social policies. It challenges our working assumptions at every turn. How do we define a "family"? How can we hope to study experiences of people who are so alienated from the society that we take for granted? How do we resolve the ethical dilemmas that we would encounter if we even tried to do so? And how dare we presume to recommend policy *until* we have arrived at an understanding of the psychological facts of life for those whose lives we would influence?

These three books contribute precisely the kind of information, and pose just the challenges that we need in our efforts to think through issues of social policy. But this is the kind of information that we almost never seek (and rarely heed when proffered) in our expert roles as investigators and consultants.

WHAT IS TO BE DONE?

Examining the issues posed by this conference leads me to a dispiriting conclusion about the capability of developmental psychology, as a discipline, to speak to public policy issues. Yet every one of my charges could be negated by examples of superb contributions in this domain. What can we learn from our experience, and from our best work? Here are some of my conclusions and recommendations.

1. Insofar as we hope to contribute to policy making, we need to take the issues seriously enough to discard some of our inappropriate methodological dogma. Massing evidence based on short-term, cross-sectional studies of isolated variables will be of little help in developing sound social policy, although this is not a totally useless effort. However, we need to know more about the long-term consequences of social policies as these influence individual lives. Significant questions are amenable to study by developmental psychologists, but only if we are willing

to invest more time and more thought than our academic schedules encourage or permit. In urging the personological perspective, I hope to alert my colleagues to the possibilities of truly basic research. An example of the kind of research that we could produce is Ravenna Helson's (Helson, Mitchell, & Moane, 1984) thoughtful longitudinal study of college women who did/didn't adhere to the "social clock." While hers was a special cohort, Helson's approach combined expert use of psychometric tools with profound understanding of theoretical issues that enabled a powerful analysis of how bright college seniors turned-out 20 years later in relation to the social directives of their era. No amount of tinkering with graduate programs could assure such styles of investigation. The point is that we should identify and support scholars capable of such sustained and dedicated work.

2. We need to become more sophisticated about the polity that we would influence. We have enough horror stories about ill-advised, premature intervention by psychologists in the public policy domain. (Token economies in prisons, and doubtful programs for "controlled drinking" among alcoholics come to mind.) The complexity of the issues and our vulnerability to misinterpretation of data are nicely illustrated by two contrasting accounts of social scientists' role in school desegregation. Gerard's (1983) account of social psychologists' harmful intervention has been corrected by Cook's (1984) more scholarly and historically accurate discussion of what "really" happened in 1954—and why. Elsewhere, 15 years of research on the impact of television, backed by the might of the Surgeon General's office and career-long work by developmental psychologists, has made little appreciable difference in what our youngsters see on the tube. It should be no secret that corporate America is effective in using social science data that it finds congenial, and equally effective in discounting data that threaten its business decisions. In the public sector, we find that the gruesome picture of children abused and killed by their parents (reported and updated in a recent television program) has been totally unchanged by agencies entrusted with protecting children. Official belief in the mystique of the "family" (abetted by professionals' faith in their rehabilitative work with abusing parents) leaves vulnerable children as vulnerable as ever.

3. We may need apprenticeship as citizens before we attempt to speak as professionals. The exploitation and distortion of

feminists' critiques at the hands of psychologists (noted in an earlier part of my chapter) is a case in point. When we approach grave social issues with little beyond unexamined ideology and a methodological tool kit, our researches may be fundable, but will not be very significant. Until we have thought hard, and worked hard to understand the implications of our inquiry for decisions in a complex and pluralistic society, perhaps we should remain silent. It is probably the case that most psychologists will be most effective when following the dictates of their scientific scripts in professional life, and entering the realm of public policy only as deeply concerned citizens.

4. When we *do* enter the policy realm, we need a theoretical framework capable of transcending the self-imposed constraints of our scientific ideology. How do we account for the absurd public squabbles about heredity/environment in the "IQ controversy"? Equally passionate quarrels about dichotomies of affect versus cognition, continuity versus discontinuity in development, idiographic versus nomothetic modes of inquiry? How do we place our work into larger socio-historical contexts? How can we provide our graduate students with the broader, more humane and sophisticated appreciation of human complexity than *we* were ever taught?

So I return to my original premise: that psychologists' contributions to public policy must rest on some version of a personological perspective. Social policy impacts on real lives of real persons — and we had better know about such particularities. Yet we need a theoretical vision enabling us to understand, in appropriately abstract terms, just *how* such diversity of personality structures comes from a common human heritage. Thus I am urging Tomkins's theory as worth close study for its insights into precisely the issues of our deepest interest and concern.

REFERENCES

Allport, G. W. (1937). *Personality: A psychological interpretion.* New York: Holt.

Aries, P. (1962). *Centuries of childhood.* New York: Random House.

Block, J. (1971). *Lives through time.* Berkeley, Calif.: Bancroft Books.

Block, J. H. (1973). Conceptions of sex role: Some cross-cultural and longitudinal perspectives. *American Psychologist, 28,* 512-26.

Brim, O. G., & Kagan, J. (Eds.). (1980). *Constancy and change in human development.* Cambridge, Mass: Harvard University Press.

Carlson, E. R. (1966). The affective tone of psychology. *Journal of General Psychology, 75,* 65-78.

Carlson, L., & Carlson, R. (1984). Affect and psychological magnification: Derivations from Tomkins' script theory. *Journal of Personality, 52,* 36-45.

Carlson, R. (1971) Where is the person in personality research? *Psychological Bulletin, 75,* 203-19.

_____. (1972). Understanding women: Implications for personality theory and research. *Journal of Social Issues. 28,* 17-32.

_____. (1981). Studies in script theory: I. Adult analogs of a childhood nuclear scene. *Journal of Personality and Social Psychology, 40,* 501-10.

_____. (1982). Studies in script theory: II. Altruistic nuclear scripts. *Perceptual and Motor Skills, 55,* 595-610.

_____. (1984). What's social about social psychology? Where's the person in personality research? *Journal of Personality and Social Psychology, 47, 1,* 304-10.

Carlson, R., & Levy, N. (1970). Self, values, and affects: Derivations from Tomkins' polarity theory. *Journal of Personality and Social Psychology, 16,* 338-45.

Cook, S. W. (1984). The 1954 social science statement and school desegration. *The American Psychologist, 39,* 819-32.

Ekman, P. (1971). Universal and cultural differences in facial expression of emotion. In J. R. Cole (Ed.), *Nebraska Symposium on Motivation* (Vol. 19). Lincoln: University of Nebraska Press.

Elshtain, J. B. (1981). *Public man, private woman.* Princeton N.J.: Princeton University Press.

Gerard, H. B. (1983). School desegregation: The social science role. *The American Psychologist,* 38, 869-77.

Gilligan, C. (1982). *In a different voice.* Cambridge, Mass: Harvard University Press.

Greenberger, E. (1983). A researcher in the policy arena: The case of child labor. *The American Psychologist, 38,* 104-11.

Haviland, J. (1983). Looking smart: The relationship between affect and intelligence. In M. Lewis (Ed.), *Origins of infant intelligence.* New York: Plenum.

Helson, R., Mitchell, V., & Moane, G. (1984). Personality and patterns of adherence and nonadherence to the social clock. *Journal of Personality and Social Psychology, 46,* 1,079-96.

Kuhn, T. (1962). *The structure of scientific revolutions.* Chicago: Chicago University Press.

Lamb, M. E. (Ed.). (1982). *Nontraditional families: Parenting and child development.* Hillsdale, N.J.: Erlbaum.

Lamiell, J. T. (1981). Toward an idiothetic psychology of personality. *The American Psychologist, 36,* 276-89.

Lewin, K. (1935). *Dynamic theory of personality.* New York: McGraw Hill.

Lieberman, M. (1982). *The role of affect in making humanistic choices in moral dilemmas.* Unpublished doctoral dissertation, Rutgers University.

Lindauer, M. S. (1968). Pleasant and unpleasant emotions in literature: A comparison with the affective tone of psychology. *Journal of Psychology, 70,* 55-67.

Lindzey, G., & Aronson, E. (Eds.). (1968/1969). *Handbook of social psychology* (2d. ed.), (5 vols.). Reading, Mass.: Addison-Wesley.

Lipset, S. M., & Schneider, W. (1983). *The confidence gap: Business, labor, and government in the public mind.* New York: Free Press.

Lykes, M. B., & Stewart, A. J. (1983). Evaluating the feminist challenge in psychology: 1963-1983. Paper presented at the 91st Annual Meeting of the American Psychological Association, Anaheim, CA.

Murphy, G., Murphy, L. B., & Newcomb, T. M. (1937). *Experimental social psychology.* (Rev. ed.). New York: Harper.

Murray, H. A. (1938). *Explorations in personality.* New York: Oxford University Press.

Schacter, S., & Singer, J. E. (1962). Cognitive, social, and physiological determinants of emotional state. *Psychological Review, 69,* 419-27.

Sheehan, S. (1976). *A welfare mother.* New York: Houghton Mifflin.

Stone, L. J., (1979). *The family, sex and marriage in England 1500-1800* (Abridged ed.). New York: Harper & Row.

Tetlock, P. E. (1983). Cognitive style and political ideology. *Journal of Personality and Social Psychology, 45,* 118-26.

Tomkins. S. S. (1962). *Affect, imagery, consciousness* (Vol. 1). New York: Springer.

––––––. (1963a). *Affect, imagery, consciousness* (Vol. 2). New York: Springer.

––––––. (1963b). The right and the left: A basic dimension of ideology and personality. In R. W. White (Ed.), *The study of lives.* New York: Atherton.

––––––. (1965). Affect and the psychology of knowledge. In S. S. Tomkins & C. Izard (Eds.), *Affect, cognition, and personality.* New York: Springer.

––––––. (1979). Script theory: Differential magnification of affects. In H. E. Howe & R. A. Dienstbier (Eds.), *Nebraska Symposium on Motivation* (Vol. 26). Lincoln: University of Nebraska Press.

––––––. (1981a). The quest for primary motives: Biography and autobiography of an idea. *Journal of Personality and Social Psychology, 41,* 306-29.

––––––.(1981b). The rise, fall, and resurrection of the study of personality. *Journal of Mind and Behavior, 2,* 443-52.

Tronick, E. Z. (Ed.). (1982). *Social interchange in infancy: Affect, cognition, and communication.* Baltimore, MD: University Park Press.

Vasquez, J. (1975). *The face and ideology.* Unpublished doctoral dissertation, Rutgers University.

Williams, S. (1983). *Left-right ideological differences in blaming victims.* Paper presented at Sixth Annual Scientific Meeting in the International Society of Political Psychology, Oxford University, July.

Zigler, E., & Muenchow, S. (1983). Infant day care and infant-care leaves: A policy vacuum. *The American Psychologist, 38,* 91-94.

NOTES

1. "Humanistic" and "normative" are technical terms in Tomkins's theory that should not be confused with their common sense meanings nor with traditional liberal/conservative political ideologies. See text for explication.
2. Tomkins's script theory is a comprehensive formulation applicable to socio-historical events as well as its primary target of personality. Current notions of "scripts" in cognitive-social psychology, sociology, and Transactional Analysis are assimilable as special cases in Tomkins's more general theory. Further explication, along with empirical studies testing Tomkins' theory, may be found in Carlson (1981, 1982).
3. Examples are drawn from syndicated cartoons appearing in major newspapers several years ago.

Afterwords
Jean Bethke Elshtain

There are a number of important general concerns shared by the chapter writers. The first is best summarized as a focus on *methodology*, on how we do what we do. Second, each writer explicitly or implicitly addresses the perennially vexing question of human nature: what *is* it? What might it be and how does our approach to research open up or foreclose multiple perspectives on the question? Finally, a vital theme in the chapters, sometimes as text, at other times as subtext, is that of research-policy configurations and our understandings of the family and gender differences. I shall take up each of these issues briefly.

RESEARCH AND INTERPRETATION

What approaches are available to us as laborers in the vineyards of the *Geisteswissenschaften*? A number of avenues or possible avenues are suggested by our authors — from personalism to historicism, from antifoundationalism to normativism, and so on. Every essayist agrees, however, that not just 'anything goes'. But what goes, and why, is an open question. One approach that is uniformly rejected is the old mechanistic model of hard-line positivism, a causal account along the lines of "If x, then ineluctably y...."

Several of the writers in this volume are engaging in, or flirting with, what the epistemologist calls a hermeneutical or interpretive approach to the human science. Such an approach requires that the researcher take the first person accounts of his or her subjects seriously. This means that those individuals who are the subjects of one's research should not, indeed cannot, be constituted as abstract objects by one's methods. If one is committed to an interpretive social science it bears important implications for how one does research. The interpretive method presents difficulties — most importantly in requiring long-term, in-depth explorations of human subjects and webs of social meaning. The hermeneuticist cannot grind out quickie pieces like so many sausages. That each writer, in his or her own way, is prepared to take the more difficult epistemic road is dramatic evidence of the vitality of developmental psychology.

Perhaps an example from my own field, political theory, will clarify what is at stake in this matter of epistemology. The study of meaning is central to the theoretical enterprise as I understand it. This means, for example, that when I discuss great political theorists like Thomas Hobbes or John Stuart Mill what I take up is not a pristine or purified given—the text or problem *as such*—but texts from a particular angle of vision, with certain questions or concerns in mind. The problem of theory's relationship to society's practices remains even, or most especially, after one has rejected the reductionism I noted above ("If x, then y . . . "). What can interpretation offer on this score? A few things can be stated simply though they are by no means simple. Political and social theory has as its object a society's practices. Theory can never be the simple determinant of practice but it can, argues Charles Taylor, transform its object in some ways. It can do this by providing a richer and more complex description of what is really going on; by exposing self-defeating practices; by buttressing or rescuing practices that are vital to a particular vision of the human community. Theory helps to constitute our self-understandings, to ground our social identities. I owe these insights to Taylor who observes that " . . . our society is a very theory prone one. A great deal of our political life is related to theories. The political struggle is often seen as between rival theories, the programmes of government are justified by theories, and so on. There never has been an age so theory-drenched as ours" (Taylor, 1981-1982).

To argue that actions express theory-laden beliefs, or to claim that theory is a form of action, is not to endow ideas with some "life of their own." Instead, it is to recognize that theory is, as Taylor claims, one of the major practices of our world, the one we involved in the "knowledge field" know best. To explore theories, whether classical political theory or developmental psychology, is to take part in a complex practice, one enmeshed in a world that gives rise to theorizing. Theory of the sort I am talking about evokes both individual and social determinants. It explores connections between contemplation and action, between our private fears, wishes and hopes, and our public beliefs and ideals. One word for this might be reconceptualization, turning the conceptual structures we inherit inside out in order to reveal the experience they may conceal.

There are a number of ways to talk about this enterprise. Clifford Geertz, the leading exemplar of interpretive cultural anthropology, argues in *The Interpretation of Cultures*, that the human animal is a creature "suspended in webs of significance." If culture is those webs, the analysis of culture must be "an interpretive one in search of meaning" (Geertz, 1973, p. 5). A "good interpretation," in Geertz's view, should take us "into the heart of that of which it is an interpretation" (p. 26). The theorist helps to make "thick description possible" rather than pursuing some "grand strategy" searching for "universal, empirical uniformities" that run roughshod over diversity and particularity (p. 38). Interestingly, these Geertzian imperatives make contact with a dominant motif in contemporary feminist inquiry—and I'll say more on this below—the matter of difference, most especially differences between the sexes, how they are to be understood, how they are used, how they are abused, and so on.

The plot thickens immediately. For to locate *difference* as central to one's enterprise rather than an obstacle to be overcome or a problem to be simply fixed is to embrace rather than to deny the intractibility of conflict. Differences—between men and women, political ideologies, cultures—means conflict as well as the possibility of mutually fructifying diversity or, sadly, of domination as some seek to quash the 'difference' of others either through assimilation or crude suppression. Differences are never given as such. One way we are confronted with and compelled to consider difference is textual as we traverse the terrain between one imaginative and theoretical vision and another. Another way difference gets placed on the agenda is when an individual or group—women and blacks in our own time are key exemplars—begin to question customary categories and classifications, asking why and how 'difference' got assimilated to or became the ground of 'inequality'.

Conflict—between values, persons, politics—is central to an understanding of all these issues. The aim of the authors in this volume, therefore, is not to overcome conflict nor to smooth over the rough edges of understanding but to promote what might be called "fruitful confusion"—a confusion inescapable if one listens to different voices and different theoretical languages. Premature reconciliation between and among competing points of view invites premature closure on debate. The vision of political and theoretical realities I here invoke makes life more complex: "Nothing is as simple as one thinks"—or might like to think, as the problem of human nature demonstrates.

HUMAN NATURE, POLITICS, AND DISCOURSE

Each essayist also works from, or with, an implied or explicit conception of human nature. Cofer interestingly points to shifts in the normative vision of psychology historically on this vital matter, showing that our construction of standards for assessment of what is 'human' are powerfully related to transformations in social context. The political theorist, too, observes the terms and effects of our an-thropological constructions. Both a strength and pitfall of American society, for example, is the fact that we lack a single, shared concept of human nature. For example: very definite views of human nature appear in our great civic documents — the *Federalist Papers* and the *Declaration of Independence*.

Some critics of American life have attacked the way we set things up at the start by arguing that our presumptions about human beings are specifically 'Hobbesian', drawn from the writing of the sixteenth-early seventeenth-century political philosopher, Thomas Hobbes, whose masterwork, *The Leviathan*, sets the basis for what the late Richard Hofstadter once called "the paranoid style" in political thinking. That is, Hobbes portrays a world in which each is an enemy to all and life, in the 'state of nature', is nasty, brutish, and short. But this seems to fall wide of the mark if the focal point is that 'human nature' that animated the architects of American national life. For these gentlemen of the enlightenment placed great faith in natural reason and in natural right. Their world is more in the image of John Locke's social contract than Hobbes's dreadful war of all against all.

But there was a worm in the democratic apple at the start: several in fact. Slavery has been much remarked on. But there is another. The social contract image as the basis of community features adult males springing full-blown from the head of John Locke. Where are women, children, and families? Certainly they were there all along, but their importance goes unrecognized and unacknowledged in social contract theory. We are not seen as beings having constitutive attach-ments — to others, to friends, to a community, a place, a religion, an ethnic identity, and so on. Yet most people's lives most of the time revolve around precisely these markers of social identity. It follows that one way to explore our society's values and theory of human nature is to ask: what attachments do we openly acknowledge and what connections do we seek to sever or to flee from? What might this tell us about ourselves?

Once we made "man the measure" of all things what sort of man did we have in mind? In otherwords: what kind of body is the body politic? Enter the body, then, and more conceptual headaches. Friedrich-Cofer's chapter reminds us of another interesting discovery of our epoch in the human sciences: we now concede that we have bodies. The fact that we made this 'discovery' indicates that some sort of denial was going on, at least for some of us some of the time if not all of us all of the time. We can trace this disconcern with bodies, or at-tempts to reintroduce the body as an isolable variable, or other less than compelling possibilities, to the potent dualisms that structure much of the Western mind. We have been saddled with a number of splits — mind from body; nature from culture. Women got stuck on the 'nature' side. But, as Freud reminds us, the repressed always returns and the body is making a complex reappearance. (As the ads used to say, "You can't fool Mother Nature"). We are now asking about differences in male and female bodies but from perspectives infused with, rather than at odds with, feminist concerns. We are thinking about current disorders to which young women seem peculiarly susceptible — anorexia being the most troubling — and questioning whether such disorders may not have part of their origin in the fact that the body politic, the normative standards of embodiment, have been covertly male all along.

Take ads for example. (Many of us no doubt plea silently: "please.") Advertisements for women's clothing show the 'woman' as, or *in* the body of, an adolescent male but with tiny breasts attached. The body, we are more and more told, must be not only thin but tough: above all one must not look female and soft. Feminist discourse is not exempt from disdain of, or denial of, female embodiment. One prominent radical feminist in the early 1970s insisted that men and women were identical "except for reproductive organs," as if genitals were little paste-ons we could attach and reattach and pretty much be any-*body* we chose. We also got treated to such future ideals as one in which our respective embodiments as males and females would have become as unimportant as hair color. These reductionistic approaches to the body reflect and strengthen rather than challenge much of the anti-woman aspects of dualistic thought. In raising the issue of the body, Friedrich-Cofer touches on another reductionism: the ease with which some have gone from the insistence that there is no sufficient evidence of a distinct woman's nature, to the claim that all sex differences are due to the environment, to the claim that all sex-based social differences are unjust. She implicitly criticizes the ease with which these connections have been made, just as Scarr also reminds us that children are more than the sum of their environmental parts, more than the additive totals of the "environmental stimuli" to which they have been subjected. One reason children are "more" in this sense is precisely because they are embodied beings, not little shells or free-floating ghosts.

Having found the body have we lost our conceptual thread? Not at all. For putting the body in place, rather than in its place in a trivialized manner, we come back to human nature and emotion *in context*, to the questions posed by Cofer and Carlson, and, as well, we are compelled to think about the violent ways in which young men and women use their bodies by the Cairns; on the disproportionate vulnerabilities of male and female populations at different life stages by the Baldwins; at the structure of the mother-child dyad by Scarr and, by all our writers, at the relationship between what Jane Addams called "the family claim" and "the social claim."

Let me get a bit more specific. Friedrich-Cofer offers powerful evidence of what happens when thinkers deny the body and social scientists and activists structure activities for real human beings around this denial. The Cairns remind us those vital embodied matters — hormonal change at puberty — are associated with many other kinds of changes. They challenge us to ask: What is going on when hormone change goes on? What social contexts, meanings, institutions, forces, and stereotypes structure the meaning and significance of hormonal changes for males and females respectively? One might, for example, think of a society that de-emphasizes activities that place a high stress on male physical qualities (a society unlike our own), looking at the ways in which what the Cairns call "the normal life space" is altered thereby. The Cairns also apprise us of the fact that even our definitions of what is to count as aggressive behavior are sex-bound; hence, female aggression often goes unrecognized for our normative paradigm of aggression is structured around a male model.

Scarr and the Baldwins remind us of those bodies-in-context we call mothers, fathers, and children and the ways in which society and social science either valorizes or neglects each or all. For example: the Baldwins note that the father got neglected in much of the literature for the years 1940-70 in discussions of the family. One might trace at least some of that neglect in social science literature to the influence of functionalism. The great functionalist theorist, Talcott Parsons, divided the world into male instrumental/adaptive role players (out of the house) and female nurturant/expressive role players (in the house). This theory sanctioned locating fathers out of the home and mothers very much in it. The father became a shadow in his own home: this shadowy Dad is a common butt of comedy and farce in the decades in question as well. It speaks, certainly, to a very real social reality but it also distorts and exaggerates that reality rather than simply or merely reflecting it.

In addition, Scarr's essay reminds us that the women's movement has also made some powerful assumptions about father-absent families (or fathers away more than they are home). The dominant view of the moment is that father-absent homes are bad and have specific, baneful effects on the construction of male and female identity. The argument is that matriphobia — fear and hatred of maternal power and the desire to control and dominate the mother — is more likely to flow from exclusive (or nearly so) mother rearing. Whatever the problems with this thesis—and I think there are several—the debate indicates to us how social context shifts our way of looking at things: we have moved from the Parsonian formulation in which father-absence is the way the world is structured and it is all to the best to the feminist formulation in which such father-absence is the source of many woes, for the psychological substructure of sexist attitudes is rooted, in this view, in that social fact. The interpretive social scientist, whether political theorist or psychologist, must weave his or her way between and among these contradictory formulations on the route to deeper under-standing.

FAMILIES AND THE STATE: APPEARANCES AND REALITIES

I indicated at the beginning that research-policy configurations and questions of the family and gender difference are themes explicit and implicit throughout this text. Having already assayed the embodi-ment debate as this revolves around male and female, I shall turn to the question of the family and the state with insights and formulations drawn from political theory and public policy debates and from con-temporary feminist argumentation.

Perhaps the best way to begin is to take up a case study that highlights our current ambivalence on the alliance between research and public policy from the viewpoint of participatory feminist politics. I have chosen the battered women's movement as my exemplar. We now have available several histories, indeed celebrations, of that movement and I think they are instructive. Recent histories document efforts in behalf of battered women which, since 1974, have resulted in over 300 shelters, 48 state coalitions or service providers, a national grass roots organization, and a multitude of social and legal reforms, according to the author of *Women and Male Violence: The Visions and Struggles of the Battered Women's Movement* (Schechter, 1982). What Susan Schechter aims to do is to document the effort and to "topple theories of psychopathology and the intergenerational transmission of family violence, thereby refuting the notion that profes-sionals—professional members of the service professions—know more about battered women than 'feminist activists' "(Schechter, 1982, p. 2). (Notice that Schechter does not say—"than battered women themselves." The assumption is that they may well be blind to what is going on but feminist politics provides the answer.)

Let me begin, as most commentators do, with an alarming statistic. Estimates of the number of women battered annually range from 2 to 4 million. Here, then, is a fact as well as potential target for reform, for politicization, or both. The phenomenon suggests a number of fascinating questions: How do social realities become political problems? Who identifies and names problems and to what end? The founders of the battered women's movement answered that the social reality of battering became a political problem given "raised consciousness" as a result of the women's movement. They also indicated that feminists identified the problem and their aims were at least twofold: (1) to provide a refuge for battered women, (2) to politicize battered women in order to make them critical of the lives they had been living that implicated them in abuse.

One fascinating aspect of the movement is the persistent antiprofessional, antiresearch-policy alliance suspicions of its founders and the difference they marked between a politics of participatory commitment and a politics of professional complacency and distancing. Wariness of professional social service providers was rooted from the start in the decentralizing, democratic impulses of movement activists, an ethos at odds with hierarchical, top-down structures and political models revolving around a policy-making and implementing elite and a group of passive, dependent clients. This set the stage for struggles over the hiring of professional staff and assimilation of the effort to extant welfare or service networks given the 'costs' of government funding in terms of loss of movement autonomy, and so on.

The activists of the battered women's movement viewed those they served through a very different lens from that of the welfare bureaucrat. As I noted in the Introduction, "On Reading this Text," a welfare 'client' is often seen as a consumer of services whose case is 'managed' by a professional. But a battered victim, from the standpoint of the battered women's movement, is seen as a woman who can reconstitute her identity in ways that empower her. By helping the victim to place her individual suffering within a wider social and political framework, activists set the stage for possible shifts in self-perception: the once-victim can work to transform a situation that damages her, unlike the welfare client locked into static dependency on agencies and experts.

Let me suggest the following as a way to deepen our reflections on the difference between the client-case worker connection and the activist-victim relationship. A feminist volunteer, who may be working 16 hours a day in a shelter, is needed by women who seek refuge but she also needs them. Their existence as victims points to the reasons for her own commitment and, as well, reinforces a perspective that tends, often relentlessly, to construe men and families as violent and women as more or less universally and consistently victimized. But the nuances in the relationship call to mind Jane Addams's provocative reflections on "The Subjective Necessity for the Social Settlements" in which she traced the reciprocal needs at work linking educated, middle-class female reformers with undereducated, underclass immigrants. Addams recognized that her own solution to problems of self-identity and purpose lay in the creation of a movement for social change that implicated her with others in complex ways. Although Addams's self-reflectiveness is rare, then or now, the activist-victim nexus brought into being by the battered women's movement holds forth the possibility for mutual self-revelation and change that is either absent or far less likely within a client-provider relationship given the larger structure in which, and the language through which, that relationship is constituted.

The feminist brief against the professionalization of the battered women's movement has a double-prong: condemning statist bureaucracies and the cult of expertise, on the one hand, yet simultaneously blasting the very assumption of a private, intimate sphere that should remain free from external interference by the state, on the other. The first prong goes like this. Writers on the battered women's movement are unabashed celebrants of *feminist* volunteerism, highlighting the ways in which our social life would be enormously coarser and more impoverished if volunteer efforts, old and new, were wholly subliminated into public policy. This is a major break from the early mainstream feminist line which derided all unpaid-for efforts and condemned volunteerism as exploitation of women pure and simple. The analyses of Schechter and others invites an explicit critic of problematic features of the bureaucratic welfare state from a participatory, feminist perspective — not the usual sort of conservative lament coming, as it does, from a radical not retrenchment perspective.

There is ample documentation of the negative ways in which government agencies moved in on movement terrain. There is what Schechter calls the "nightmare" of the New York City case, for example, which saw the city eroding the autonomy of shelter programs by (among other things) forcing each battered woman to be verified by the welfare bureaucracy as eligible for shelter and by giving each shelter resident a two-party welfare check which had to be turned over to the shelter to pay for food and rent, immediately transforming the shelter into a quasi-landlord, away from a supportive refuge (p. 126). These and other events justify the movement's suspicions of the state.

But the second prong of the case made by movement theoreticians exists in tension with the first. The very state that is condemned for its authoritarian and degrading policies and methods is called upon in its capacity as a coercive policeman to prevent and to punish the violence of men. Rejecting most research on the topic and all "social learning" or "psychological" theories of violence and its transmission, Schechter takes male violence as a generic given. This is the way the question gets put: "Why are men violent and what role does violence play in women's oppression?" (p. 44). This formulation dehistoricizes the problem, thus foreclosing a look at the historic particulars and the social construction of battering.

Violence is presumed to be constant and endemic so long as we have men and families not available for incessant public scrutiny and reproof. Battering is seen as a self-conscious tool of male power and an outgrowth of that power. But if one goes to the best available data, and the most detailed studies, one learns that half or more of battered women are *not* living in stable families at all. Write Evan Stark, Ann Flitcraft, and their associates: "At least half of the American women battered each year have no blood or legal ties to the men who assault them" (Stark, Flitcraft, & Frazier, 1979). This suggests that violence may be a major symptom of family disintegration and social dislocation rather than a feature of secure relationships in stable settings. Perhaps we would come closer to understanding male violence against women if we explored the unraveling of male social identity in different epochs, including our own, in line with often brutal vagaries of the political economy.

The point I wish to stress — and that the most complex, interpretive social science helps us to understand — is that violence is not a spin-off of secure authority but signifies fear, loss of identity, loss of control, and a damaging need to reaffirm it. One can agree with those critics who argue that we cannot treat the family as a simple private institution — it is a social institution, albeit an arena for privacy and intimacy. We cannot insulate the family from its social surround. But if we take this injunction seriously, it means we must underscore the privatizing tendencies of modern life, the drive toward atomism and the breaking of social connections. Star, Flitcraft, and Frazier contend that battering appears "only when persons have been forcibly isolated from potentially supportive kin and peer relations and virtually locked into isolated situations where their objectification and punishment are inevitable" (p. 479). We are not, then, looking at an intrinsic feature of family life but at a more likely outcome of the break-down of wider social supports for and constraints on families — food for thought for analysts and policy makers alike. Stripped of constitutive ties to neighborhood, place, and a wider network of kin and friends, isolated male-female relations, including those of families, become an emotional cauldron. The male-violence hypothesis is too crude to deal with these complex social determinations.

What agenda is offered by Schechter and other spokeswomen for the battered women's movement? Interestingly that agenda pushes the movement into a far more total, controlling mode with regard to the very state of which movement feminists are suspicious. We require, the argument goes, (1) new laws, (2) expansion of the discretionary arrest powers of the police, (3) deepening of the presumption that women are a special target population in need of protection—paradoxical at a time when many other feminists are challenging the whole concept of protection and what they see as the deeper purpose of protective legislation, keeping women in a subordinate economic status, (4) mandated counseling to condition the behavior of violent or potentially violent men, or a combination of court-mandated, anti-sexist counseling together with compulsory punishment for second offenses. The potential for abuse in these vast extentions of the therapeutic and punishment powers of the state are glossed over. The ultimate solution, in a total reconstructed social world, would be a "family life open to community scrutiny at all times because the family would be accountable to the community. Community institutions could hear complaints and dispense justice" (p. 239) and so on. But this injunction is at odds with another stated aim—that, in Schechter's words, "who women choose as emotional and sexual partners cannot be open for public scrutiny" (p. 271).

I have gone over this material at length because I think it highlights dramatically the internal tensions in reformist proposals, feminist in this instance, namely, an indictment of the state, its managerial elites, and its knowledge-research collaborators coupled with a call for the state to intervene to complete one's own political agenda. We fear moving the state into the family sanctuary. But we also fear abuse of family members behind closed doors. We are caught between the proverbial rock and the hard place. Part of what is at stake in the current debate, a debate to which the essays in this text make a contribution, is this: the family, having been exposed, targeted, celebrated, condemned, analyzed, scrutinized, and reorganized remains the place where our society's often contradictory imperatives collide. Our collective fears and disjunctures together with our hopes and ideals coalesce at that nodal point. As Kurt Vonnegut might say: So it goes. We live in a kaleidoscopic world and perspectives are in a continuous movement. Is there any solid ground at all?

Our authors are trying to get a foothold but they find themselves constantly in quicksand: methodological, normative, political. This is not their peculiarity; instead, it is a tribute to their critical honesty in pursuing the implications of their work. Those implications are of the policy sort—and it is social policy as it revolves around women, children, and families that serves as the nodal point for reflection in the first place. Carlson points to an enormous problem of the present moment: the delegitimization of American institutions and the decline of the social authority of institutional structures. This presents great difficulties for public policy formulation and implementation. For policy makers are not insulated from the broader structural features of American life—our troubled political economy, our rising militarism, our continuing perplexity over sexual identity and justice. Carlson suggests that it is probably not possible to articulate any coherent notion of public-social policy unless one has a normative ideal of some sort and strong notions about the quality of life. But in a period of institutional disintegration and the decline of social authority, this ideal becomes more and more difficult to 'see' and to attempt to realize. Friedrich-Cofer also points to the fact that liberals, decent to the man and woman, nonetheless often focus on the most optimistic possible outcomes of social change—hence they often evade and avoid the search for a vision of equality that respects difference and refuses to set up a single standard by which to measure human accomplishment. Cofer, as noted above, alerts us to the changes of normative standards inside psychology itself suggesting that Carlson's yardstick of judgment cannot be searched for inside psychology alone but must draw upon deeper roots of a shared civic morality—if we are to find or recapture such standards at all.

There is, finally, not so much pessimism as skepticism running through the chapters as our authors survey what role developmental psychologists have played up to now in the policy process. They take us 'back to basics', alerting us to the fact that the policy-making process, if it is seen as the preserve of a handful of experts, has specific antidemocratic implications. How can we create a process in which complicated initiatives come in from various publics with diverse needs and interests—yet hold relatively constant some notion of the common good? Questioning what one has to offer, whether one is a social scientist or a political theorist, is important for it indicates that we are acknowledging the inherent difficulties involved in forcing concrete outcomes from conceptual formulations. All our writers agree that there has been too much facile oversimplification, too much the presumption that one can or should find immediate pragmatic outcomes lurking in almost every piece of research concerning women, children, and families. I welcome the humility in the essays—the recognition that the world is often intractable, that human beings are not so much Silly Putty to be molded any way a social science or policy elite sees fit. We know, or have come to understand, that double-edge to reform I mentioned earlier. We know that contempt and compassion can get fused as we try to intervene with various groups or classes. If we presume a policy elite we restrict who is in the conversation and policy becomes something to apply to an inert mass (this may explain the passive voice some of our essayists deploy when policy is talked about, as if it is something that happens to us rather like a natural disaster). But, finally, we want to intervene in the world: we want to make a difference.

By alerting us to how difficult it is to make the difference we hope to make, yet not using a recognition of the complexities as an excuse for inaction, the authors of this volume have contributed not only to their own discipline of developmental psychology they have, as well, played a part in the continuing story of the democratic experiment and the narrative of civil society. In our parlous time we all need all the help we can get and a continuing conversation between political theorists and developmental psychologists, as we dare to 'play upon the instrument of the soul', individual and collective, is one strand of sanity in an often very mixed-up world.

REFERENCES

Geertz, C. (1973). *The interpretation of cultures*. New York: Basic Books.

Schechter, S. (1982). *Women and male violence. The visions and struggles of the Battered Women's Movement*. Boston: South End Press.

Stark, E., Flitcraft, A., and Frazier, W. (1979). Medicine and patriarchal violence: The social construction of a "private" event. *International Journal of Health Services, 9* (3), 461-93.

Taylor, C. (1981-1982). Social theory as political practice. Paper presented to the Social Science Seminar, Institute for Advanced Study, Princeton, NJ. Readily available is Taylor, C. (1971). Interpretation and the sciences of man. *Review of Metaphysics, 26*, 4-51.

Index

abortion, 302

Abzug, Bella, 141

academic excellence, priority of in education, 134

achievement, 75-77

active faculties, 52

adolescent aggression, 23-26

adolescent growth, phases of, 131

affect theory, 290-291

affiliation, 75-77

aggression, 78

aggressive behavior pattern development, role of gender in, 181-192; developmental studies, 183-187; individual studies, 187-191; relevance of development, 181-183; social ecology, 191-192; social structure, 191-192

Albert, E. M., 79

Albrecht, F. M., 52

Alger, Horatio, 118, 214

Alienation, 10

Allport, Gordon, 32, 82, 83, 288

Almighty, defined, 7

Amateur Athletic Union (AAU), 125

Amateur Sports Act (1977), 149

amenorrhea, 146

American Academy of Arts and Sciences, 137

American Alliance for Physical Education, Health, Recreation and Dance (AAPHERD), 149

American Association for the Advancement of Physical Education (AAAPE), 113, 114, 116

American Association for the Advancement of Science, 111

American Association of Physical Education, 15

American Statistical Association, 109

Anderson, N. H., 83

Anderson, William G., 115

androgyny, 204, 295, 307, 308

Angell, J. R., 60

Anglican church, 44

animal powers, 53

anorexia, increase of in U. S., 146

anthropometric measurement, 113, 114, 115

anthropometric research, 114

anti-instinct movement, 68-69

anxiety, 78-79

Apostle of Unitarianism, 39

Aries, P., 297

Aristotle, 6, 49, 57

Arnold, Thomas, 117

Articles of Confederation, 42

Association for Intercollegiate Athletics for Women (AIAW), 140

athletic competition, women educators and, 125-127

athletics: and elite virtue, 117-121; as feature of college life, 119; organized games in England, 117

Atkinson, John, 75

Bache, A. D., 108

Bacon, Francis, 44, 45

Bakan, D., 55, 56

Baldwin, Alfred, 26, 28, 193

Baldwin, B. T., 128

Baldwin, Clara, 26, 28, 193

Baldwin, James Mark, 8, 187, 191

Bales, R. F., 262, 263

Bancroft, George, 108

Barker, Roger, 24, 27, 188

About the Editor and Contributors

Alfred L. Baldwin is professor of psychology (retired) at the University of Rochester.

Dr. Baldwin has been studying parent-child relations and family interactions since 1941. He has also written on social cognition, particularly "naive psychology," as a framework for studying children's understanding of interpersonal behavior. He has authored numerous journal articles and monographs as well as a major text — *Theories of child development* (Wiley, 1980, 2d ed.). He received the G. Stanley Award from the Developmental Psychology Division of the American Psychological Association in 1978.

He is a Harvard Ph.D. and has been at Fels Research Institute, University of Kansas, Cornell University, and New York University.

Clara P. Baldwin is associate professor of psychology at the University of Rochester.

Dr. Baldwin has collaborated with her husband, Alfred L. Baldwin, on research projects on social and cognitive development of children and on studies of family interaction. They have jointly authored papers and monographs, including a 1982 Society for Research in Child Development Monograph, *Parental pathology, family interaction and the competence of the child in school.* She is currently principal investigator of a ten year follow-up study of children and families originally seen by Arnold Sameroff and his colleagues in Rochester.

Dr. Baldwin received her Ph.D. from Stanford University. She has served on the faculties of Cornell University and New York University.

Beverly D. Cairns is research associate at the University of North Carolina at Chapel Hill in the Department of Psychology.

Since 1981 she has been involved in the logitudinal investigation of violent youth in school settings, and has served as co-investigator of the National Science Foundation project, "The organization and development of aggressive behavior." Her work has appeared in *Developmental Review, Journal of Early Adolescence, Aggressive Behavior,* and in *Development of Antisocial and Prosocial Behavior* (D. Olweus, J. Block, & M. Radke-Yarrow, Eds., Academic Press, 1986). She earlier had extensive experience in classroom teaching and school administration.

She completed her training in education at Pasadena College (A.B.) and at the Graduate School of Education, Stanford University.

Robert B. Cairns is a professor at the University of North Carolina at Chapel Hill in the Department of Psychology.

His major concern is social development, and he has worked jointly with his wife Beverly on the study of the development of aggression in adolescence. He has published *Social Development: The origins and plasticity of interchanges* (Freeman, 1979) and edited *The Analysis of Social Interactions: Methods, issues, and illustrations* (Erlbaum, 1979).

He completed his training in psychology at Pasadena College (A.B.) and at Stanford University (Ph.D.). Prior to his present position, he taught at the University of Pennsylvania and Indiana University.

Rae Carlson is professor of psychology at Rutgers University.

Dr. Carlson's research has centered on issues of personality theory and research. She is currently working on a book presenting personality theory from a script-theoretic standpoint; her publications have appeared in the *Journal of Personality and Social Psychology, the Journal of Personality, Psychological Bulletin,* and the *Annual Review of Psychology.* She is a founder and president of the Society for Personology.

She received her B.A. from the University of Nebraska, an M.S. from the University of Washington, and a Ph.D. in clinical psychology from the University of Michigan.

Charles N. Cofer is research professor of psychology at the University of North Carolina, Chapel Hill, and lecturer, Duke University.

He is currently working on a book on motivation and a historical project. He has published numerous journal articles, and has authored, co-authored, edited and co-edited several books, including *Motivation: Theory and research* (Wiley, 1964) and two other books on motivation. He is a past editor of the *Psychological Review.*

Dr. Cofer holds a B.A. from Southeast Missouri State University in social science and history, an M.A. in psychology from the University of Iowa, and a Ph.D. in psychology from Brown University, where he was awarded a Distinguished Achievement Citation in 1983. Dr. Cofer has served on the psychology department faculties of George Washington University, the University of Maryland, New York University, The University of California, Berkeley, and the University of Houston. He is Professor Emeritus of Psychology, the Pennsylvania State University.

Robert E. Cole is clinical assistant professor of psychiatry at the University of Rochester.

Dr. Cole's research interests include the study of children at risk for mental illness, primarily the identification of protective factors, and the family factors associated with the course, outcome, and treatment of schizophrenia. He is currently a member of the NIMH-sponsored Family Research Consortium and the faculty of the Multisite Family Research Training Program based at the University of Virginia.

He received his Ph.D. from Cornell University.

John Demos is professor of history at Yale University.

Professor Demos is a social historian, whose research interests include the history of family life. He is author and editor of several books, including, *A little commonwealth: Family life in Plymouth Colony* (Oxford, 1972); *Turning points: Historical and sociological essays on the family* (Chicago, 1978); and *Past, present, and personal: The family and the life course in historical perspective* (Oxford, 1983).

He is an alumnus of Harvard College, and did graduate work at Oxford, Harvard, and the University of California. Prior to his recent appointment, he served on the faculty of Brandeis University.

Jean Bethke Elshtain is professor of political science, University of Massachusetts, Amherst.

Dr. Elshtain's publications include *Public man, private woman: Women in social and political thought,* selected by *Choice* as one of the top academic books of 1981-82; an edited volume on *The family in political thought;* and *Meditations on western political thought.* She has published many essays in scholarly journals and journals of civic opinion including *The New Republic, The Nation, Dissent, Commonweal, Democracy,* and *Christianity and Crisis.*

Dr. Elshtain received her Ph.D. in 1973 from Brandeis University. She has been a Visiting Professor at Oberlin College, Smith College, and Yale University.

Lynette K. Friedrich-Cofer is research associate professor of psychology at the University of North Carolina, Chapel Hill.

Dr. Friedrich-Cofer's research has focused primarily on the effects of prosocial and violent television on the social development of children and youth. Her current interests include the history of public policy affecting children, and psychobiological approaches to adolescent development. Her independent publications, and those with her long-term collaborator Alethe Stein (Huston) have appeared in a Society for Research in Child Development monograph, *Child Development, Development*

Psychology, Review of Child Development Research, and the *Minnesota Symposium on Child Psychology.*

Dr. Friedrich-Cofer received her B.A. from Stanford University, and her Ph.D. from Cornell University. She has been on the faculties of Cornell University, The Pennsylvania State University, and The University of Houston.

Sandra Scarr is commonwealth professor of psychology and chair of the Department of Psychology, University of Virginia.

Dr. Scarr's current research concerns malleability of development in the normal range of environments, and intervention programs with developmentally delayed children. A longitudinal follow-up of transracially adopted children, who are now adolescents, is underway. Her recent book *Mother Care/Other Care,* was awarded the National Psychology Book Award by the American Psychological Association. She has published several books and numerous studies on child development. She is a past editor of *Developmental Psychology,* and president of the Behavior Genetics Association.

Dr. Scarr holds an A.B. in sociology from Vassar College, and a Ph.D. in psychology from Harvard University. She has served on the faculties of the University of Maryland, the University of Pennsylvania, Bryn Mawr College, the University of Minnesota, and Yale University.

Sheldon H. White is professor of psychology in the Department of Psychology at Harvard University, where he currently serves as chairman.

A developmental psychologist, he studied the processes of learning and cognitive development in preschool and school-aged children. In the 1960s and early 1970s, he participated in the development of federal programs and policies for children, and this work led him to become interested in the social history of psychology. He has recently published several articles and chapters dealing with the history of psychology and is currently writing a book about the establishment of American psychology.

Dr. White received his Ph.D. from the State University of Iowa in 1957. He was a member of the Psychology Department of the University of Chicago and of the Laboratory of Human Development of the Harvard Graduate School of Education before moving to his present position.